Glass House Books

Dreaming of a National Socialist Australia

Barbara Winter was born in Western Australia in 1931, and graduated from the University of Western Australia with an Honours degree in modern languages. She won a scholarship that enabled her to study at the Karl-Ruprecht University in Heidelberg, 1954-1955, before returning to teaching in Western Australia and Queensland. She gave up teaching in 1977 for domesticity and a writing career.

Bruce Muirden's book on the Australia-First Movement left her wondering whether he had given a fair account of the events, and she determined to try to reach the heart of the matter through documents that became available in the National Archives of Australia. This developed into a Master of Arts thesis for the University of Queensland. The thesis has been re-worked into a book for general readers interested in Australian affairs, as well as for academics who may need to know the extensive ramifications of this strange phenomenon.

Barbara lives and works in Brisbane, Australia.

Glass House Books
Brisbane

Dreaming of a National Socialist Australia:

The Australia-First Movement and the *Publicist*, 1936–1942

Barbara Winter

Glass House Books
Brisbane

Glass ***H***ouse ***B***ooks
an imprint of Interactive Publications
Treetop Studio • 9 Kuhler Court
Carindale, Queensland, Australia 4152
sales@ipoz.biz
www.ipoz.biz/ghb/ghb.htm

First published by Glass House Books, 2005

Lightning Source edition, 2007

Printed in 18 pt Book Antiqua Bold on 11 pt Book Antiqua by Lightning Source.

National Library of Australia
Cataloguing-in-Publication data:

Winter, Barbara.
Dreaming of a national socialist Australia : the Australia-First Movement.

2nd. ed.
Bibliography.
Includes index.
ISBN 9781876819415.

1. Australia First Movement. 2. Nationalism - Australia.
3. Civil rights - Australia. I. Title.

320.540994

Books by the same author:
Atlantis is Missing
HMAS Sydney. Fact. Fantasy and Fraud
Stalag Australia
The Intrigue Master

Contents

Acknowledgments

Many people have contributed support and advice to assist with this work. Thanks are due in the first place to Dr Alan Corkhill of the Department of German and Russian Studies and Dr Tom Poole of the Department of History of the University of Queensland for supervising the thesis from which this book was developed. The Department of German and Russian Studies awarded a Research Grant to help the author with travel expenses. Professor T. Stannage, University of Western Australia, assisted with an introduction. Dr Charles Fox in Western Australia and Dr Drew Cottle of the University of Western Sydney kindly made their theses available, and Dr Craig Munro of the University of Queensland Press gave me some of his valuable time.

Reg Bartram, John Lockyer and Eric Stephensen contributed to an understanding of the psychological dimension. Daphne Pyke checked some Western Australian documents that I had missed on my trip to Perth, and Dr A. Bonnell identified an important quotation.

Most information comes from archival material, and I received generous vital support from the staff of the Fryer Library of the University of Queensland and the National Archives in Canberra, Sydney, Brisbane, Melbourne, Adelaide and Perth, especially Cheryl McNamara in Brisbane. Also greatly appreciated was the assistance of staff of the Australian War Memorial, in particular for retrieving the Hasluck papers during a difficult time of reconstruction, the Mitchell Library in Sydney for the Stephensen papers, the La Trobe Library in Melbourne and the National Library of Australia, the University of Queensland Archives, and the John Oxley Library and the Special Collections of the State Library of Queensland. Thanks are also due to the Inter-Library Loan services of the University of Queensland and the Redland Shire Council for obtaining copies of rare books, and to the Queensland Genealogical Society (Woolloongabba) and the Church of Jesus Christ of Latter Day Saints (Kangaroo Point) for access to genealogical records.

However, decisions as to the interpretation of material and the relative merits of conflicting evidence are the sole responsibility of the author. Those who furnished information and assistance do not necessarily agree with these.

Abbreviations

ADB	*Australian Dictionary of Biography*
AFM	Australia-First Movement
AIF	Australian Imperial Forces
AIPS	Australian Institute of Political Science
ALP	Australian Labor Party
AMF	Australian Military Forces
AMP	Australian Mutual Provident (Society)
ANA	Australian Natives Association
ASIO	Australian Security Intelligence Organisation
AWM	Australian War Memorial
B.A.R.B.	British-Australian Racial Body
BUF	British Union of Fascists
CIB	Commonwealth Investigation Branch
CP	Country Party
CPA	Communist Party of Australia
CPD	*Commonwealth Parliamentary Debates*
CSS	Commonwealth Security Service
DD	Deputy Director
ILF	Imperial League of Fascists
IRA	Irish Republican Army
ISGS	Intelligence Section General Staff
IWW	Industrial Workers of the World (Wobblies)
MHR	Member of the House of Representatives
MI	Military Intelligence
ML	Mitchell Library (Sydney)
MLA	Member of the Legislative Assembly
MLC	Member of the Legislative Council
MPI	Military Police Intelligence
MUP	Melbourne University Press
NLA	National Library of Australia (Canberra)
NSDAP	*Nationalsozialistische Deutsche Arbeiter-Partei*
NSR	National Security Regulations
NSW	New South Wales
OUP	Oxford University Press
PPA	Primary Producers' Association
RSWU	Relief and Sustenance Workers' Union
SA	*Sturmabteilung*
SMH	*Sydney Morning Herald*
UAP	United Australia Party
UQA	University of Queensland Archives
UQFL	University of Queensland, Fryer Library
UQP	University of Queensland Press
UWA	University of Western Australia
WA	Western Australia

Preface

On 9 March 1942, three men and one woman were arrested in Western Australia in connection with an alleged plot to contact the Japanese armed forces, surrender the Australian armed forces and assassinate leading public figures. They had formed themselves into a body called the Australia-First Group. Within a few days, sixteen persons connected with a loosely related group of a similar name, the Australia-First Movement, were arrested in New South Wales. They knew nothing of this plot, and few were acquainted with those arrested in Perth. In the House of Representatives on 26 March, the Minister for the Army, Francis Michael Forde, denounced the plot and appeared to brand all twenty as traitors and assassins.

In 1944, Justice T. S. Clyne was appointed to investigate whether the initial arrests and subsequent internments were legal and justified. He found that they were legal, but that not all were justified. The Clyne Report was tabled in House of Representatives on 12 September 1945 and debated in March 1946. The lengthy and complex inquiry satisfied few completely.

The Australia-First Movement (AFM) gathered together people who had extreme views on Australia's relationships with Britain but did not necessarily agree on much else. Although the AFM was not formed officially until November 1941, the founders had come together by July 1936, when a monthly magazine, the *Publicist*, was first issued. Members and associates considered themselves patriots promoting a strong and independent Australia with a distinctive national character, but its advocacy of an isolationist policy, with a strong but undemocratic system of 'Corporate' government, left it with few friends apart from Germany, Japan and Italy. It attracted some unbalanced extremists whose actions compromised the whole Movement, leading to disaster and grief for others who did not understand how their good intentions had been so misunderstood.

This work attempts to explain the conflict of interests, when people who loved Australia had drastically different ideas on what was best for Australia.

Several books and articles have been written about the AFM, of which the most important are *Puzzled Patriots*, by Bruce Muirden; Appendix 5 of Volume II of Paul Hasluck's work, *The Government and the People*;[1] and the later chapters of Craig Munro's *Wild Man of Letters*. Verna Coleman, in *Adela Pankhurst. The Wayward Suffragette*, devotes three Chapters to Adela Pankhurst Walsh's role in the AFM, while *Xavier Herbert*, by Frances de Groen, examines Herbert's relationships with AFM members.

Writing in 1968, Muirden had no access to official documents, except the Clyne Inquiry transcripts, which he obtained from Keith Bath. His contacts with the Australia-First internees cannot be repeated, as almost all have since died. Paul Hasluck's exposition is a useful summary, but in one sense superficial. He apparently did not read the dossiers of individuals involved or even the Clyne Inquiry transcripts. Dr Munro, who interviewed Hasluck, felt that he had access to material not available to the public.[2] However, the only secret material he seems to have used were some general reports by Military Intelligence (MI) or the Commonwealth Security Service (CSS).[3] The Appendix seems to have been compiled mainly from the Clyne Report, Commonwealth Parliamentary Debates, proceedings of the War Cabinet and Advisory War Council, letters written to him by Stephensen, Hooper and Masey, and Bath's pamphlet, *Injustice within the Law*.[4] His work contains minor inaccuracies, but it is important that he does not mention Melanie O'Loughlin, whose role was crucial. His attacks on Forde and Evatt are only partly justified and appear to be politically motivated.

Being concerned with Stephensen mainly as a literary figure, Munro barely mentions some key figures, as the Australia-First affair is not his central theme. Verna Coleman assumes correctly that the Japanese paid Tom Walsh for writing articles for the *Empire Gazette* but found no evidence of this, although dates and amounts are recorded in several files in the National Archives, Sydney.[5] Frances de Groen, in *Xavier Herbert*, recounts Herbert's relationship with Stephensen and Miles, but naturally does not cover the Australia-

First groups in Victoria and Western Australia.

Minor factual errors in Richard Hall's *The Secret State*,[6] are unimportant, but his statement that 'investigating bodies' agreed in describing the AFM as harmless is misleading and was not true of Military Police Intelligence (MPI). While none of the Sydney group knew of the plans hatched in Perth, it was untrue that there was no contact between the groups in Perth and Sydney.[7]

An Honours thesis by Richard Fotheringham dealt comprehensively with Stephensen's early life and literary career, but superficially with Australia-First. This was unavoidable, as Stephensen's life was so packed with incident.[8] Fotheringham's research material, lodged in the Fryer Library, contains much valuable unused material, including some of Muirden's research, and Eric Stephensen's analysis of Muirden's book. Documents presented to the Fryer Library by Stephensen's stepson, John Lockyer, resolve some matters that have hitherto been the subject of speculation.[9]

No thorough analysis of the AFM, using original reports and individual dossiers, has yet been published. Reports compiled by the CIB, the State Police Special Branches, Military Police Intelligence, the infant CSS, Military and Naval Intelligence reveal much that even Justice Clyne did not know. Not all information could be presented, owing to the way it had been obtained: through secret mail scrutiny, deep cover agents and phone taps of dubious legality.[10] As reports were spread over four states, and at least four organisations in each state, no individual knew everything about the case. From available documents, it can be seen that the ramifications of the AFM were wider than has been realised. This work explores some of these ramifications and puts them into context. Hasluck writes:

> The detention of some of the 21 persons concerned was the grossest infringement of individual liberty made during the war and the tardiness in rectifying it was a matter of shame to the democratic institution and to the authorities concerned.[11]

It is not valid to conclude that Hasluck intended to imply that *none* of the internments was justified. Muirden wrote that some were unjust and unnecessary, but Australia was in real danger, thus: 'Drastic measures may well have been justified.'[12] The situation in

March 1942 was so grave that, even if members of the Australia-First Movement had the best of motives, failure to restrain them in some way would have involved too great a risk to Australia's security. While MI officers can be criticised for the way they handled the situation in Sydney, they did not have two luxuries enjoyed by latter-day critics: plenty of time for reflection and relative security for their country. More stringent criticism can be made of politicians who did not correct injustices, even when it became clear these had occurred.

This book traces the ideological development of central figures in the AFM and examines how the central theme of 'Australia First' assumed different guises in different locations, thereby giving a factual basis on which evaluations may be made. Many of the AFM aims have been achieved and seem quite natural; others seem quaintly old-fashioned, and some now seem even more offensive.

Chapter 1

The Beginnings

Owing to his flamboyant character and controversial utterances, and because of the devotion and detestation he aroused, Percy Reginald Stephensen was the best known of the Australia-First Movement personalities. However, Stephensen was a latecomer to political nationalism. Perhaps the sentiments of Australia-First, if not the slogan, date back to the time when the first 'currency' (Australian-born) lads and lasses reached adulthood. *Australasia*, a poem for which William Charles Wentworth won a prize in England in 1823, expressed the rudiments of true national sentiment.[1] Henry Lawson used the phrase in 1910,[2] and Archbishop Daniel Mannix in 1916.[3] George Waite of the Sane Democracy League wrote that 'Australia First' was a 'catchcry used by conflicting groups lacking cohesion, with ideals as far apart as the poles, by local Sinn Feiners, Soviet Rationalists, chaotic-minded Laborites and highbrow eccentric individualists'.[4] From time to time, attempts are still made to appropriate the slogan.

The search for a national political identity went through several stages: from representative government to responsible government, which different states obtained at different times. The process continued through Federation in 1901, to the Statute of Westminster in 1931, which formalised limitations on the power of Britain to make laws affecting the dominions, and its adoption by the Commonwealth Parliament in 1942. It continues still in the quest for a republican Australia. This book concentrates on the segment of this process that produced the monthly magazine the *Publicist* from July 1936 to March 1942 and led to the Australia-First Movement in Sydney in November 1941.

William John Miles, not Percy Stephensen, was the key figure. Without his money, neither the *Publicist* nor the Australia-First Movement would have existed. He might have found another collaborator for his monthly magazine; Stephensen could not have found another sponsor willing to lose vast sums of money.[5] Those who followed Stephensen into the orbit of the *Publicist*, the AFM or the Yabber Club were mainly literary figures, such as Miles Franklin, Eleanor Dark, Ian Mudie, Rex Ingamells and others from the Fellowship of Australian Writers, of which Stephensen was Honorary Vice-President.[6] Their nationalism was not rabid. Those who followed Miles came from the Rationalist Association or the Victorian Socialist Party; they were hostile to mainstream Australia. The danger in rejecting the beliefs prevailing in one's own society is that one will be left with a spiritual vacuum that will be filled with something alien and detrimental to that society.

Born on 27 August 1871 in Woolloomooloo, Sydney, New South Wales, Miles was the only child of John Balfour Clement Miles and Ellen, née Munton, widow of W. J. Cordner. His father was a wealthy accountant, and both parents were said to be 'very English'. Not enough is known about his childhood to sustain an argument that his anti-British attitude was partly a revolt against his parents, but it is a plausible theory. The family lived very comfortably at Ashfield, and he spent four years at the expensive Newington College. Under Ellen's influence, Miles joined the Sydney Philharmonic Choir, sang in St Mary's Basilica, and he played the piano well. For several years he was treasurer of the Sydney Shakespeare Society.[7]

In 1882–83, Miles toured Europe with his parents, visiting Germany, Austria and Hungary as well at Britain. His biography in the *Australian Dictionary of Biography* (*ADB*) mentions five trips to Europe.[8] There is no evidence that Miles could understand any modern foreign language, and the family apparently travelled the world in a cocoon of Britishness. About 1892, he visited Europe again, including Russia, and the United States. In 1897, Miles married Maria Louisa Binnington, born in Queensland in 1876; they had six children, five of whom survived infancy.[9]

Miles was in poor health from a fairly young age, and this might have contributed to his nasty temper. A telling portrayal of his character, albeit as a caricature, is given by Xavier Herbert in *Poor Fellow My Country*, where he appears as 'The Chief'.[10] He is depicted as Albion Singer in Kate Grenville's *Lilian's Story*, another hostile fictional portrayal, based on the life of his daughter Beatrice.

One telling remark is made by 'Aunt Kitty', the fictional sister of Singer: 'Albion was always a bully.'[11] A later informant described Miles as a crabby fascist, who liked to be a little autocrat.[12] He was contemptuous of women, and life would not have been easy for his wife and daughters.[13]

Miles was a partner in his father's accountancy firm of Miles Vane & Miles until the death of his father on 11 August 1907.[14] In 1908, this firm became Yarwood Vane & Miles, and Miles set up his own firm in Martin Place in 1912. He held directorships in several firms, including Peapes and Shaw menswear store, in which he was a major shareholder.[15] He was a young man at the time of the conferences leading to Federation and the foundation of the Commonwealth. By 1914, he was well set on the course that led to the Australia-First debacle in 1942. He was allegedly co-founder in 1912 of the Rationalist Press Association, and a member of the Executive, until he quarrelled with other members and resigned in 1920.[16]

Throughout the 1914–18 war, Miles was convinced that Germany would win. By the tone of his letters, he seemed to think it would be good for Australia if Germany beat England, for Australia might then achieve total independence. Having written to Hooper on 16 October 1914 that the Germans would win on land in the East (Russia) and West (France), he added on 12 May 1915, 'I am in complete agreement with German opinion… and think that the Allies have shown themselves incapable of winning this War.' He continued to believe in and apparently to hope for a German victory, writing on 29 October 1915, 'How anybody can view the Military position today and think the Allies are going to win I cannot understand.' On 12 December 1916 he commented, 'So far as the War itself goes it was lost irretrievably long ago.'[17]

Miles campaigned against conscription, as for varying reasons did others including John Curtin, Adela Pankhurst and Archbishop Mannix. No common motive united them. The Irish saw it as the wrong war, while for others any war was wrong. In 1940, Miles said that police had taken shorthand notes when he spoke in the Domain, but they were 'never cleverer' than he was.[18] Miles set great store by his cleverness, but he was playing a dangerous game. Adela Pankhurst was also noted as one of the main speakers at a Socialist meeting at Yarra Bank on 3 December 1916.[19]

In 1916–17, Miles was connected with an Australia-First Committee. It is not clear if he was its organiser, but Miles and possibly Hooper used stationery with its letterhead.[20] On record is his attempt to found an 'Advance Australia' League with these aims:

1. To Resist any Reduction of Australian Autonomy.
2. To Maintain a 'White Australia.'
3. To Foster Australian National Sentiment.
4. To Urge Australians to Make the Most of their Country's Resources.

This League was spurred by antagonism to a proposed Imperial Federation. Miles also assisted Robert Samuel Ross with *Ross's Monthly of Protest, Personality and Progress*,[21] a contact point for several people who became involved in the AFM, among them W. D. Cookes, Adela Pankhurst and Tom Walsh. A close friend of the Ross family, Adela wrote an article for its first issue in December 1915; Miles wrote for its second issue in January 1916 that 'war is a biological necessity, like birth or death'.

Miles's wife died on 11 November 1925, at the relatively young age of 49, and Miles went overseas again in 1926 and 1929.[22] It is surprising that an intelligent and well-travelled man should have become such a narrow nationalist. A similar thought occurred to Hardy Wilson, an architect friend of Miles, who wrote to Stephensen on 30 January 1942, 'W. J. Miles was unusual. I have not known a man so intelligent and without instinct for beauty.'[23] At the Clyne Inquiry in 1944, S. B. Hooper said of Miles: 'He was the most serious as well as the most honest man I have ever met.' Miles perhaps took himself too seriously, but it can be disputed that he was honest, particularly in thrusting Stephensen forward to bear the opprobrium of the obnoxious aspects of the *Publicist*, while he wrote under pseudonyms. Hooper may have meant that Miles did not cheat his business associates, or that he could be 'honest' with people to the point of rudeness.

Official reports contain much misinformation about Miles's family. He was not linked with the communist orator 'Red' Miles, nor with Betsy Miles, a Lang Labor supporter.[24] 'Red' Miles was John Bramwell Miles, while Miles's son was John Balfour Miles, and

Betsy Miles was not Beatrice. A CIB report of November 1941 alleged that Stephensen was married to Beatrice, an error copied from one report to another.[25]

Miles retired from his accounting firm in 1935, though he retained some directorships. The devil finds mischief for idle hands, particularly the idle hands of the wealthy. With his children grown and his wife dead, and no longer engaged in business, Miles devoted his remaining years and a lot of money to the 'CAUSE' that had long inspired him.

Sydney Benjamin Hooper, one of Miles's oldest friends, was born on 12 February 1869 in St Kilda, Melbourne. Both his parents were English, his father having arrived in Australia in 1850. He began working for the Union Bank in 1890, spending twenty years in Deniliquin.[26] He became manager of the branch in George Street, Sydney, in 1917.[27] In 1909, after his first wife died, he married Ida Margherita Fiorelli, born in Naples to an Italian father and Australian mother. There were no children from either marriage.[28] By 1914, Hooper was associated with Miles through accounting and banking and the Rationalist Association. He held similar views on Australian nationalism, but was less argumentative and anti-Semitic.

Hooper and his wife made three trips to Europe. In 1911 they visited England and Italy, the latter country probably to see Fiorelli's relatives; in 1923 they visited Ida's sister in America, then went to Britain, Paris, Florence and Germany. On this trip, Hooper met in Hamburg a German businessman, Henry Joosten, who was to have a crucial influence on his fate.[29] After Hooper retired on a bank pension in 1929, he and his wife made a longer trip from about 1930 to 1933. They visited England, Holland and Germany (Hamburg and Berlin), and Florence again briefly, in an Italy that had been under Fascism for almost a decade. Hooper was an admirer of Mussolini, although he wrote later that he had always detested Nazism, fascism and communism as systems of government for Australia.[30] He met Joosten again in Hamburg, and the chaos and misery of Germany in 1932 made an impression on him. He heard Sir Oswald Mosley, leader of the British Union of Fascists, address two meetings in London, and exchanged a few words with him at a luncheon.[31] He met the racist author Morley Roberts, and he knew later that fascist leader Arnold Leese received the *Publicist* free.[32] Hooper's political affiliations in Australia are not clear; he was a long-standing friend of Jack Beasley of the Lang-Beasley-Ward Labor Party, but he had friends in other political parties.

Valentine Crowley, the third member of the original Australia-First clique, was born on 18 October 1884 in South Melbourne and educated at Mornington State School. After working as an electrical engineer in Melbourne and New Zealand, he went to the United States in about 1906. After working in Berlin for a year (1911), handling English-language enquiries for a firm there, he returned to Australia in 1912 or 1913.[33] Like Miles, he opposed conscription and was fined £10 for his activities in World War I. At that time he was not linked with Miles or Hooper, or with the Ross-Curtin-Pankhurst-Walsh set,[34] although like Hooper he was a friend of Jack Beasley.[35] Passionately and vehemently anti-English, Crowley claimed to be of Irish descent, but his father, Cornelius, who arrived in Australia as an infant, had been born in Scotland.[36] For Miles, vilification of Britain was perhaps only a means to advance Australian culture and character; for Crowley, it seemed to be an end in itself.

Crowley set himself up in Melbourne as a Consulting Electrical Engineer, and by 1920 was wealthy enough to retire and move to Sydney, intending to live on the income from property investments. During the Depression his rentals dwindled, and in 1930 he took a position with the AMP Society as an insurance agent. He first met Miles in late 1935 or early 1936 through Cecil Salier, who also worked for the AMP.[37] Crowley had no connection with the Rationalist Association, but he was a member of the Australian Institute of Political Science (AIPS), the Constitutional Association of New South Wales, the Economic Society of Australia and New Zealand, and the Royal Zoological Society. Whereas Miles rejected all established political parties and the party system itself, boasting that he always voted informal, Crowley became involved with the United Australia Party, and was on the electoral committee of Percy Spender.[38]

Cecil Walter Salier was the fourth member. Born on 24 October 1880 in Sydney, he had worked for the AMP for more than 40 years.

A close friend of Miles through the Rationalist Association before the war, he too had visited Europe. He wrote later of visiting Venice, Assisi, the Jungfrau and Rome, and of his delight at the first sight of Rottnest Island from the ship when returning to Australia. He was knowledgable about Western Australia, having lived there for several years.[39] Like Crowley, Salier was a member of several learned societies in Sydney, among them the AIPS, the Royal Australian Historical Society, and the Shakespeare Society.[40] He wrote for the AIPS magazine, *Australian Quarterly*, and Edward Masey (see below) was a director and member of the editorial staff of the magazine.

These men were the core of the early Australia-First Group. All born in Australia between 1869 and 1884, they could remember the struggle for Federation. All were comfortably situated financially and were retired or on the verge of retirement. All had travelled abroad extensively at a time when it was not common to do so. Three were Rationalists. All were committed to a narrow view of Australian nationalism, and all were ready to poke their fingers into many different pies in ways that caused public controversy and devastated individual lives.

Percy Reginald Stephensen came into the group through the only issue of the *Australian Mercury*, the remnant of his attempt to establish a monthly devoted to Australian culture and literature. Like many of Stephensen's ventures, it began in a blaze of passion, and fizzled out in the ashes of financial failure.[41] When Miles retired in 1935 and was toying with the idea of publishing a monthly magazine to further his concept of Australia-First, he came across a copy of the magazine. Political nationalism appealed to Miles, although he had little interest in culture. When Miles was willing to lose a great deal of money on a magazine, he needed somebody with publishing experience.[42] Stephensen, an experienced publisher and editor, but in desperate financial straits, was adept at losing money on financially doomed projects.

Stephensen was born on 20 November 1901 in Maryborough. His father was Christian Julius Stephensen, his mother Marie Louise Aimee Tardent. Chris's Danish father, Jens Christian Julius Stephensen, had arrived in Maryborough in 1873. Marie's father, Henri Alexis Tardent, was born in Switzerland and had taught at the

University of St Petersburg, which may account for rumours that Stephensen's grandmother was Russian. With his wife Hortense and daughter Marie, then aged five, he arrived in Queensland in 1888.[43] The well-educated Tardents were involved in political, journalistic and academic activities.

Chris Stephensen married Marie Tardent on 28 December 1900, when she was only seventeen or eighteen. Percy was born the following November. Over the next twenty-four years, they had several more children. Percy spent his early childhood mainly in the small country town of Biggenden, and at the end of his primary school years he won a scholarship to Maryborough Boys' Grammar School. Chris Stephensen was a wheelwright, but with the advent of the motorcar and pneumatic tyres the trade dwindled. He became a shopkeeper, but the family struggled financially, so educating Percy entailed sacrifice. In Maryborough, Percy was active in student affairs, but in his Senior Examination in 1918 he obtained only mediocre passes in six subjects with no merit passes.[44]

In 1919 Stephensen went to Brisbane to the University. Founded only eight years earlier, it was situated then in the city, near the Botanic Gardens and Parliament House. St John's College, where he resided, was at Kangaroo Point on the other side of the river. The University was small, with no faculty of medicine, law or education. Many of the best students still went to Sydney or even to England. As Percy had not studied physics and his results in mathematics were poor, his matriculation was virtually limited to the Faculty of Arts.[45] At the University, he acquired the nickname 'Inky', which stuck to him for life.[46] His family's financial situation meant that Percy had to work to support himself at the University. During term, he taught part-time at the Technical College, and while on vacation he drove drought-stricken cattle overland to agistment, laboured on a dairy farm, drove a cart on a cream-collecting run, and worked as a junior shop assistant.[47]

Stephensen spread his activities over a very wide area. He played football and cricket for both his college and the Arts Faculty, and was a member of the athletics teams. In 1921, his final year, he was secretary of the Debating Society, vice president of the Dramatic Society, editor of the University magazine, librarian for St John's

College and a member of the Union Committee. However, in the 1920s the University had a very small student body from which to select leaders. As Stephensen won a Rhodes Scholarship, his academic ability has been rather over-rated. Competition not nearly as great as it became later. In 1922, when Percy graduated, there were only thirty male graduates in Queensland, and females were not eligible for Rhodes Scholarships until 1976. A scientist or an engineer would gain little from two years at Oxford. In Stephensen's year, there were only seventeen male graduates in the Arts Faculty, and Stephensen did not have the best results. The Queensland Rhodes Scholarship for 1922 was won by Herbert Burton, who had a Second Class Honours degree in modern languages. The next year, it was won by Robert Hall.[48]

Stephensen, with no teacher training, began teaching at Ipswich Grammar School.[49] In 1921, his last year at university, Stephensen had joined the Communist Party, and influenced Fred Paterson to join as well.[50] Stephensen changed his mind, but Paterson stayed with the Party, becoming the only communist elected to any Australian parliament. Stephensen's activities for the Party attracted notice at the University, but notoriety in Ipswich, where there were many coal miners and railway workers.

Stephensen re-applied for the Rhodes Scholarship in 1924 and won it. Several comments in testimonials accompanying his application are worth noting. R. A. Kerr, Head of Ipswich Grammar, wrote of his originality and ability and exceptional force of character, adding that he would 'make his presence felt for good in any company'. W. H. W. Stevensen, Warden of St John's College, excused Stephensen's results, which were not of the quality usually required of Rhodes Scholars, writing that Stephensen's opinion that education should be as broad as possible prevented him from specialising with a view to taking an Honours degree. 'I have a very high opinion of his character and ideals,' he wrote. 'He has a fearless desire to do what he considers right.' Both L. D. Edwards, his tutor in Logic and Psychology, and J. T. Noble Wallace, Headmaster of Maryborough Grammar, suggested that his experience overseas would be used to advance education in Queensland. Edwards also noted that his French lesson was 'a brilliant application of the "direct" method of teaching'. Rather, as Munro notes, it was a fraud; Edwards did not understand French, and Stephensen primed his boys to answer promptly and fluently with anything that came into their minds.[51]

Stephensen left for England on 9 August 1924 aboard *Jervis Bay*, equipped with a *Daily Standard* press pass supplied by Henri Tardent, who sometimes wrote for this paper.[52] At Oxford he enrolled for the course known as P.P.E.: Philosophy, Politics and Economics (Modern Greats). His tutors sent back favourable reports on his progress, his Economics tutor noting his 'remarkable tenacity' in maintaining an unorthodox point of view. Stephensen narrowly escaped expulsion for his communist propaganda work among Indian students. He was mentioned in *The Times* of 19 January 1925, and in the *Daily Mail* and the *Brisbane Courier* two days later.[53] Ordered to leave the Communist Party or leave the University, he chose to stay at the University, although in April 1925 he was learning Russian in preparation for a planned trip to Russia in June. At this time he wrote, 'I have now an unshakable faith in the future of the Communist Party.'[54]

His plans changed when he met Winifred Sarah Venus, née Lockyer, with whom he developed an intimate relationship. Munro writes that she was born Winifred Lockyer in England in September 1886, and that in 1900 she went to Melbourne with her father when her parents separated. She returned to England in 1910, then went to the United States, where she married about 1912. The marriage did not last long; she took her son Jack to Australia about 1918, before returning to England in 1922. Dainty, pretty Winifred, by repute a classical ballerina, lived two constant deceptions. She told Percy that she was born on 23 September 1893; and, as she could not get a divorce, they did not marry until 7 November 1947, though they claimed that they had married in England.[55]

Leaving Oxford in 1927 with Second Class Honours, Stephensen joined John Thomas (Jack) Kirtley's Fanfrolico Press and tried to establish himself in London as a publisher and bookseller.[56] Kirtley and Stephensen delighted in fine printing and bookbinding. In 1928, they published Stephensen's translation of Nietzsche's *Antichrist*, a work both anti-Semitic and anti-Christian.[57] When Kirtley left for Australia, he handed the business over to Stephensen, who was joined by Jack Lindsay, whom Stephensen knew from his university days.

Fanfrolico became largely a vehicle for publishing Lindsay's writings and translations, illustrated by his father, Norman Lindsay.[58] Within the Fanfrolico environment of the ingrained anti-Semitism of Kirtley and Lindsay, Stephensen discovered the *Protocols of the Meetings of the Learned Elders of Zion*, allegedly a record of a Zionist congress held in Switzerland in 1897, describing how to enslave people and nations by encouraging vice and discouraging independence.[59] If they had been genuine, outrage over the plans they set out would be understandable; what is less understandable is how anybody with common sense would not see through the fraud.

In 1929, Stephensen founded his own publishing house, Mandrake Press, which was funded by a Jewish bookseller, Edward Goldston, with whom he formed a partnership.[60] He published both an illegal underground edition of D. H. Lawrence's banned *Lady Chatterley's Lover*, and a deluxe edition of his rather raunchy paintings.[61] By 1932, he was deeply in debt. At this time, Norman Lindsay visited Britain and made him a tentative offer of a job with a publishing venture being considered by the *Bulletin*. Leaving Robert Hall to settle his debts, Stephensen left Britain on 3 September with Winifred and her son. On reaching Fremantle on 4 October, he received a telegram offering him the position of manager of Endeavour Press.[62] Colonel Sir Vernon Kell, head of MI-5, wrote to Australia on 31 August warning of Stephensen's return.[63]

Stephensen set up Endeavour Press and began by publishing works by Miles Franklin, Henry Handel Richardson, Eleanor Dark, and Andrew Barton (Banjo) Paterson.[64] The *Bulletin* disappointed him; he wrote later that it encouraged not fine literature but crude literature and a larrikin view of Australian life, which had a dubious effect on Australian literature.[65] He lost money, quarrelled with the manager and the printer, and parted company with the *Bulletin* shortly before his year's contract expired. In a conflict between Stephensen's visions and financial reality, reality always lost out.

Then he set up his own publishing firm, P. R. Stephensen & Co. This would probably have failed in any case, but three events sealed its fate. A book he published, Vivian Crockett's *Mezzomorto*, attracted a hostile review in the *Bulletin* of 10 October 1934, written under a pseudonym by Brian Penton, with whom he had quarrelled in London. Stephensen sued the paper and Penton for damages, claiming that sales of the book had fallen so badly as a result of the review that he had been forced into liquidation. In his plaintiff's declaration of 31 July 1935, he wrote that the defendants had falsely and maliciously claimed that he had published for reward a book of unhealthy, perverted, and immoral character and had pandered to unnatural, unhealthy, and debased psychological tendencies. Stephensen's firm had been shaky for some time, but he blamed the *Bulletin* and asked for £5,000 damages. After a case heard on 14–22 October 1936, he was awarded £750, of which the lawyers allegedly took a large share. This was too little and much too late to save the firm.[66]

The case illuminates two aspects of Stephensen's character. First, he blamed others for his own failures. Second, he believed he could outsmart and befuddle lawyers. Trying to prove that Stephensen was prepared to profit from the publication of immoral books, the defence referred to *Lady Chatterley's Lover*. Stephensen managed to confuse the defence lawyer and the jury over different editions of the book. The obfuscation and perjury that succeeded in this case did not succeed so well in later legal proceedings.

The second factor in the firm's failure was Stephensen's attempt to produce a monthly literary magazine, the *Australian Mercury*. Early in 1935, Stephensen wrote to friends and acquaintances soliciting money for the venture. The nature of his approach can be seen from his begging letter to Ian Mudie, who had first contacted Stephensen in 1933 with regard to a job with Endeavour Press. Stephensen renewed contact in June 1935, inviting Mudie to invest in the *Australian Mercury*, making glowing promises of success and profits, and publication of Mudie's poetry.[67] Stephensen gave similar guarantees to other prospective investors. On 23 September, he wrote to Mudie again saying that the magazine had been a literary success, and must be made payable. This never happened.[68] The second issue of the *Australian Mercury* was typeset, but the printer would not proceed until outstanding debts were settled.[69]

The third factor in Stephensen's failure was Xavier Herbert's novel *Capricornia*. Herbert approached Stephensen with his novel in 1933. The novel's nationalism and literary merit appealed to Stephensen. Despite its length, he agreed to publish it, but professional and personal relationships deteriorated. The book could not be finished, as Herbert failed to deliver the final chapters, and he disappeared into the bush so that Stephensen could not reach him to make the final payment required by their contract.[70] Some twenty-five years later, Herbert claimed sole 'credit' for bankrupting Stephensen.[71] Munro and de Groen consider that trouble arose because Stephensen and Herbert were opposites, in particular, that Stephensen was gregarious and enjoyed company, while Herbert was solitary and something of a misanthrope. On the other hand, in some respects, they were too alike: impulsive, abrasive, arrogant, given to exaggeration and bending the facts, each sensitive in regard to his own feelings and insensitive to those of others.

Stephensen had written from England to his sister that when he had some cash 'I can go back to the country I love and the people I hate'.[72] Herbert experienced a similar emotional dichotomy; he claimed to love Australia, the land, but to hate 'the mongrel race' that inhabited it. On the other hand, there were fundamental differences in their outlooks. In 1934, while Percy and Winifred, Xavier and Sadie were still on good terms, Stephensen told Herbert that he 'regarded all other people as gnomes to do his bidding'. When Herbert repeated this to Sadie and Winifred, Stephensen rebuked him: 'You don't want to go telling women things like that. They're only lubras, you know.'[73]

Stephensen was being sued by authors for unpaid royalties and by printers for work unpaid, and his situation was hopeless. His company went into liquidation, and eventually paid creditors 6s 3d in the pound.[74] Meanwhile, Miles had noticed the *Australian Mercury* and, attracted by the Stephensen's nationalism, contacted him in July 1935. In November, Stephensen submitted to Miles a plan for an 'Australia First Party'.[75] This envisaged breaking up Australia into thirty provinces; immigration on a racial quota basis; no foreign-born members of Parliament; compulsory purchase of all overseas-owned property; abolition of appeals to the Privy Council; abolition of censorship. Citizens were to be armed, and if the party was opposed by force or declared illegal, it would 'retaliate by force and illegality'.[76] This was an echo of Stephensen's communist past, yet there were also similarities to the methods of the New Guard, which he despised. In an article in the unpublished second issue of the *Australian Mercury*, he had written of the New Guard, 'These Fascist tykes, who boast about the A.I.F. as though it belonged to *them*, are undermining all that the A.I.F. established and fought for.'[77]

Soon after this, Miles made Stephensen an attractive offer. He would pay to publish as a book Stephensen's essay, the second part already written and a third part not yet written. In return, for a reasonable though not lavish salary, Stephensen would produce a monthly magazine as a vehicle for Miles's nationalism, and he would have space in which to expound on current affairs and literature.[78] Miles already published the monthly *Independent Sydney Secularist*, a four-page newsletter that Muirden describes as combining nationalism and agnosticism.[79] Now he had wider ambitions. So Stephensen, virtually bankrupt, entered into a Faustian pact with Miles. The book was published as *Foundations of Culture in Australia: an Essay towards National Self-Respect.*[80]

Miles might have had doubts about Stephensen's suitability as a collaborator or employee, for in February 1936 this advertisement appeared in a Sydney newspaper:

> Australia First Party – Wanted a young man – not more than 35 years of age – of good personality and education – not necessarily University – willing to devote the whole or part of his time to 'Australia First' political propaganda. He would need to be Australian-born of British Aryan stock; and feel fully sympathetic with the nature of the particular propaganda. He would need to be able to write and speak clearly and forcibly and have capacity for research. He would be required to travel for propaganda purposes throughout Sydney metropolitan area, and address audiences. On request, intending applicants would be sent preliminary propaganda leaflets. Apply J.B. Box 1783 K, G.P.O., Sydney.[81]

This advertisement attracted official attention. The CIB soon found that the box was held by W. J. Miles, and he became what Intelligence agencies call 'a person of interest'.[82]

Although Stephensen was not of British stock, Miles made do with him. In March Miles gave a dinner to celebrate publication of the book and to bring together some of those who would collaborate in producing the *Publicist*. They were all men: Miles, Hooper, Salier, Crowley and Stephensen. Few women wrote for the *Publicist*. He introduced into this gathering a young accountant with Johnson & Johnson medical supplies, **Edward Cory de la Roche Masey**.[83] Born in Sydney on 6 January 1906, he lived in Killara with his mother, whom Miles had known before she married.[84] A foundation member and director of the AIPS, and a member of the Australian Institute of International Affairs, he was well known as a lecturer and radio commentator, and in 1936 he published a booklet *Is it Necessary?* in which he criticised Australian trade policy and advocated friendship with Japan.[85] At this dinner, Miles asked each of them to contribute an article for the first issue of the *Publicist*, which was due to appear in July.[86]

In retrospect, *Foundations of Culture in Australia* seems an amazing book. Many ideas were ahead of their time, but the most surprising feature is that Stephensen, who only two years later sounded like a fascist bigot and a fairly vicious anti-Semite, was in 1936 both anti-fascist and lavish in his praise of two Jews: General Sir John Monash and the recently retired Sir Isaac Isaacs, whom he described as 'the well-loved Australian-born Governor-General'.[87] A few quotes illustrate how far he was then from the politics of the *Publicist*:

> Huns like Hitler, who are intrinsically lacking in culture, mentally equipped like a school bully. It is possible to be proud of one's nationality without wishing to prove it by slaughter. (p. 25) At a time when Europe was full of alarms, in the period when Napoleon had assumed the role of military terrorist which Hitler and Mussolini would assume today, Wentworth desired that his native land should learn from Europe mainly what to avoid. (p. 50) Fascism is a greater menace to us than Bolshevism could ever be; for Fascism is a schoolboy bully, armed. It has no intellectual pretensions, aims at imposing discipline 'from above', is a Junker-idea, a Hun-idea which Australians have fought to abolish from the earth. (p. 127)

Strangely, Stephensen derided 'the sub-civilised culture of sabre-rattling Europeans such as Hitler, Mussolini and Winston Churchill' with almost equal fervour, but he did not mention Stalin. He claimed that he left the Communist Party in 1926, but he seems to have retained a lingering attachment to communist ideology for another ten years.[88] Another sign that he had not yet turned his back completely on communism was his support for the Czech communist writer, Egon Kisch, in 1934.[89] The following year, he published a book on the Kisch incident: *On the Pacific Front*, by 'Julian Smith' (Tom Fitzgerald).[90]

Soon after publication of *Foundations of Culture in Australia*, his outlook altered drastically, and Miles probably caused the change. Eric Stephensen wrote in 1970, 'I regarded Billy Miles with considerable awe. In later years, rightly or wrongly, I came to regard him as a malevolent influence on Perc... [He] influenced P.R.S. insidiously and thoroughly, steering him away from his hope of establishing an Australian book publishing industry, and pushing him on to an extreme political viewpoint.'[91]

There is an unresolved mystery concerning a 'Group of Seven'. An article in praise of Miles, found among Hooper's papers in 1942, bore the note: 'Read by S.H. to the group – all seven – at the home of V. Crowley, Clanalpine Street, Mosman on the evening of Thursday 26th August 1937.' On 22 June 1942, during his brief appearance before an Appeals Tribunal, Hooper named these as himself, Miles, Crowley, Salier, Stephensen, Masey and Les Cahill, but Cahill had not been in Sydney before June 1941, so the seventh man is a mystery.[92] It might have been simply a gathering of regular contributors to the *Publicist*, but it had echoes of Lenin's alleged Revolutionary Committee of Seven. Stephensen and the others named, even Cahill who could not have been there, were to pay a high price for submitting to the dominance of Miles, who escaped retribution by dying before the crisis came.

Chapter 2

The Publicist *in Time of Peace*

W. J. Miles set up The Publicist Publishing Company with an office and bookshop at street level in the T & G building at 209a Elizabeth Street opposite Hyde Park. A secretary-typist was in constant attendance. Miles was present much of the time, and Hooper, Crowley and Jack Lockyer sometimes. Stephensen was often away, compiling the magazine or writing articles at home.[1] For the first year, Miles paid Stephensen £20 a month, rising later to £42. Stephensen also earned about £100 a year from ghostwriting for Frank Clune.[2]

The first *Publicist* appeared in July 1936. It ran no advertising, except publicity for books sold at the shop, although Miles offered to accept advertisements from those who supported national unity.[3] He never left any doubt that he determined policy. Harley Matthews told Muirden, 'Stephensen was just an employee and several times in my presence was told so in almost insulting terms. Miles always insisted that he alone was Editor of the Publicist.'[4] Eric Stephensen wrote, '[Although] Perc liked to say he "wrote what he pleased" in "The Publicist", in actual fact he wrote what pleased Billy Miles.'[5] In dire financial straits, Stephensen had to defer to Miles, who at times employed also his brother and stepson, and jobs were scarce in 1936.

The *Publicist,* styling itself 'The Paper Loyal to Australia First', set out its policy on the first page of the first issue:

> The prime object of this 'Publicist' is to help to create and foster the spirit of nationalism in Australia... There has not yet been an Australian-born patriot, but we are confident there will be... The rock upon which the foundation of this paper's policy rests is the rock of 'Australia First.'[6]

The first item in each edition was a polemical, political article by John 'Benauster', one of the names Miles used, and which he explained combined 'good' and 'south'. There was no suggestion yet of forming an 'Australia-First' movement.[7] As 'Benauster', Miles wrote that he was a conservative who supported the Monarchy and Parliament, but opposed 'all forms of Socialism or Communism, believing them to lead to the disintegration of a community, or to military oligarchy'. The paper's tone was anti-British, and Miles seemed unaware of contradictions inherent in his position. Opposed to *all* forms of Socialism, he later supported *National* Socialism. He was against British influence in Australia, but *for* the Monarchy. He wrote that Australia might not 'cut the painter'; Britain might do so, but eventually it would *break*, so his objective was 'to encourage in Australians a distinctive national culture'. He predicted war in the near future and denounced Britain and the United States for warmongering in Asia in the 19th century.[8]

The 'Benauster' article would be followed by a section called 'The Bunyip Critic. Experiments in Australianity', by P. R. Stephensen (author of 'The Foundations of Culture in Australia')'. He explained that the Bunyip represented the primitive spirit of Australia. This section of about six pages consisted generally of short paragraphs on topics such as literature, politics or Aboriginal welfare. Stephensen also used the alias 'Rex Williams'.[9]

The first issue contained little that was highly controversial, except for the two notorious advertisements. Stephensen predicted that war would break out in Europe in 1937 or 1938, but it was none of Australia's business, and there should be no conscription for service abroad. A framed satirical advertisement appeared:

> Wanted, 500,000 young Australians, must be physically fit, perfect in wind and limb, for use in Europe as soil-fertiliser. Apply stating nitrate content of body, to No. 10 Downing Street, London, England.[10]

This bad taste was not forgiven. Stephensen had written something similar in 1935, 'as a warning to the nation never to be fooled again into participation in a war of European conquest'.[11] Another advertisement asked for he-men with 'no brains, to act as lethal-gas inhalers in Europe'.[12] There was no need to pay the *Publicist* to purvey this propaganda; it was done in the belief that it was good for Australia, but it would suit Germany well if Australia refused to support Britain in a future war. Yet Stephensen still despised fascism and Nazism, for he wrote, 'Is the posturing megalomania of military-minded Europe today in any antique sense heroic? Of course not. Hitler screams when he speaks. Have you heard him? The scream of neurosis.'[13]

Publicist support for Australian literature or Aboriginal issues is beyond the scope of this book,[14] but it might be noted that Nazi racial doctrine classed Australian Aborigines as Aryan, as they were certainly not Jewish. In the partial manuscript of a novel Stephensen was writing, one character, Dr Morpeth, expounded on theories of evolution and race, 'The Aryan race began in Australia.'[15] Stephensen synthesised an odd mixture of Aryanism and 'Australianity'. Even in *Foundations of Culture in Australia*, he rejoiced that Australia was 'the only whiteman's continent' and denounced the United States as a 'vast crucible of miscegenation'.[16] Although the first issue had been mostly moderate in tone, there had apparently been accusations of fascist tendencies, for in August Stephensen wrote:

> If any zealous Marxist imagines from the foregoing, or from anything that I might write that I am a 'Fascist', let him guess again; his first guess was wrong. Fascism, as evolved in Europe, is the old imperialist wolf, and not even in sheep's clothing.[17]

There was an exposition of the first platform of the AFM. Some points, such as conserving water and soil, were desirable; in others there were hidden dangers. Point 12, for example, referred to encouraging fertility of 'our best stock' while discouraging 'breeding by the unfit'. Point 11 was good in intention – 'To educate our Aborigines, concede them complete civil and social equality, cease exploiting them and encourage them to interbreed with the whites.' – but this could have meant cultural extinction.[18] This edition saw the first appearance of an advertisement that was repeated in five issues in 1937. This view was widely held, but in official circles it was regarded with disfavour.

DON'T GO!
Your Country Needs You
Australia will be here![19]

In September, 'Benauster' denounced 'The Humbug of Democracy', saying he always voted informal. The Bunyip Critic defined disloyalty thus: 'Any Australian person who puts the interests of any other country before Australia's interests, is disloyal to Australia.' Stephensen had raised this question in *Foundations of Culture in Australia*:

> Imperialism is international. This fact gives rise to paradoxes – as for example that an Australian *loyalist*, one who puts Australia's development first in his thoughts, might find himself termed *disloyal* to the larger entity in which Australia is assumed to hold a place of secondary importance.[20]

From October Miles wrote also as 'Alcedo Gigas', an anagram of *Dacelo gigas*, the scientific name for kookaburra; sometimes he used the initials K.S.K. – King of the Sydney Kookaburras. As 'Alcedo Gigas', he was less hectoring than as 'Benauster'.

November–December 1936 was 'Special Double Number', for Stephensen had been busy in court with his case against the *Bulletin*. He took ten pages to present his view of his case.[21] 'Benauster' provided a seven-page article on Australian foreign policy and defence, returning to the theme that war was biologically inevitable: 'Were there not life there would be no war. Were there not death there would be no life.'[22]

From 28 December 1936, Stephensen gave ten-minute talks on Monday evenings at 7.30 on Radio 2SM, a station owned by the Catholic Church, to bring the *Publicist* and the AFM to the attention of a wider audience. Miles paid for the Publicist Session, and occasionally, when Stephensen was away from Sydney, he spoke as 'John Benauster'. The sessions lasted for two and a half years and cost Miles £5 each.[23] Miles spent heavily on publicity, advertising on other radio stations, on cinema screens, in the *Sydney Morning Herald* every Saturday, and in the official German paper, *Die Brücke*.[24]

At the beginning of 1937, the *Publicist* was still not markedly pro-fascist or pro-Nazi, although Stephensen predicted that a world war would break out that year. The Bunyip Critic segment contained another tasteless piece of irony:

> If you, gentle reader, are of military age, male, and physically fit, you may proceed to console yourself with the thought that, within twelve months from now,

> the Imperial Meat Exporters' Association will have you packed up in khaki, for shipment overseas, as first-class human meat (on the hoof).[25]

By the end of 1937, the *Publicist* was available in bookstores in Melbourne, Canberra and Brisbane, and it was sold at the Yarra Bank public forum in Melbourne, but circulation was little greater than that of the Parents and Citizens circular from a major secondary school. Copies were sold on subscription as far afield as Perth and Darwin, and several copies were sent overseas, notably to Leese, leader of the Imperial League of Fascists.[26] Muirden writes that the print run was 3,000, of which never more than 2,250 were sold, while at the end there were only 258 subscribers.[27] This was fairly insignificant, but sales of *Völkischer Beobachter* when the Nazis bought it in December 1920 were only 800.[28]

The *Publicist* had other large fish to fry in early 1938, namely the Sesquicentenary Celebrations and publicity for Xavier Herbert's *Capricornia*. Financed by Miles and produced by Stephensen, it won the £250 sesquicentenary prize for an Australian novel.[29] Once it was launched, the *Publicist* lost interest in Aboriginal affairs.

In November–December 1938 and the early months of 1939, the *Publicist* tried to form discussion groups as a basis for an Australia-First Party, although Stephensen wrote that he was not political, his activities being directed towards forming a national sentiment favourable to Australian book publishing. 'I have no personal political ambition,' he wrote. 'I do not intend to take any active part in *organising* a new Australian party.' Calling on people to form small discussion groups and to report the results to the *Publicist*, he listed twelve points for discussion.[30] The December issue published extracts from the responses.[31] There had been three groups in Queensland (two in Brisbane, one in Maryborough); one in South Australia (Eden Hills); one in Western Australia (Burekup); and several in Victoria.[32] Most were in New South Wales, including one at Moorebank, this latter consisting of Harley Matthews and Martin and Dora Watts.

Matthews was one of the Anzacs who landed on 25 April 1915 at Gallipoli, where he had been badly wounded, and he had served as a model for Epstein's sculpture, 'Spirit of Anzac'.[33] Watts had been gassed in the trenches in France. They were neighbours at

Moorebank, where Matthews had a vineyard and winery, and Watts ran a small poultry farm to supplement his war pension. Matthews introduced Watts to the Publicist group.[34] Matthews had an article on military training published in July 1938.[35] Three months later, Dora Watts wrote a letter saying she was a convert to the Australia-First doctrine, for England would not stand by Australia unless it was to her advantage.[36]

Stephensen found something to cavil about in most responses from the groups. To one correspondent he responded, 'Are Jewish immigrants an assimilable element, or do they forever remain Jews first?' To another, who suggested segregating non-detribalised natives in reserves, he replied, 'Why not segregate the Jews also?'[37] Stephensen seemed to bring 'the Jews' into almost any topic under discussion.

The attempt to form discussion groups reveals some interesting relationships. Hooper had been in contact with Clement Byrne Christesen in Brisbane regarding support for a literary magazine that Christesen hoped to found; this turned into *Meanjin Papers*. Hooper must have asked him to form a discussion group, for Christesen wrote on 17 November that he appreciated information about the genesis of the Movement. He could not see his way clear to found a group but would join if one existed.[38] At the Clyne Inquiry, Hooper denied writing to Brisbane about an AF branch, then admitted asking Christesen to form a group.[39] This made Hooper look like a liar, but he possibly did not consider the 1938 discussion groups to be part of the AFM. He gave generous support to Australian national causes, subsidising both *Meanjin Papers* and *Jindyworobak*, which wished to foster Australian sentiment and literature.

The discussion groups fizzled out, but in 1939 Watts and his wife began to write for the *Publicist*. Dora, using the pseudonym 'Anna Brabant', attacked feminism and the education system.[40] Martin wrote on the inadequacy of militia training (1 January, pp. 8–10), the deterioration of military spirit and national pride (1 February, pp. 8–11, 1 March, p. 9), and the rationalisation of defence (1 April, pp. 8–10). As he knew his subject, the articles were mainly sound. They impressed Hooper, who wrote: 'Our last recruit Watts is an excellent addition; he is energy typified, mental and physical.'[41] MI could not have objected to those articles, but they would hardly have been pleased when Watts, after writing that German concentration camps might be 'uncomfortable places', denounced British and Australian military brutality, some of which he had witnessed personally.[42]

John Kirtley, as 'Merry Mathew', also wrote on defence: one article advanced the heresy that Singapore could not defend Australia, another that Australia 'should forget about the English and their powerful navy'.[43] An accurate but unappreciated comment, in a Letter to the Editor, said, 'Granted the willingness of Britain to give Australia help, such help is unlikely to be needed until Britain is so beset as to be unable to give it!'[44]

At the end of 1936, Miles began to argue for closer ties between Australia and Japan. He considered whether standing for Australia-First entailed being pro-Japanese, warning that 'a foreign power in possession of Western Australia could well nigh maroon the people in Eastern Australia'.[45] He would have remembered not only the help of the Japanese navy in the war - meagre though this was - but also that Japan had fought beside British and Australian forces during the Boxer Rebellion in China. That was not remote history to him; he had lived through it, as had Hooper, Crowley and Cookes.[46]

The *Publicist* supported Japan not for love of the Japanese but as an ally against communism. As 'Rex Williams', Stephensen denounced the boycott on export of scrap iron to Japan as an abuse of trade union power, organised not for humanitarian reasons but to embitter relations between Australia and Japan. He wrote, 'Russia's Foreign Policy may require hostility to Japan, *for Russian reasons*; but Australia's Foreign Policy requires peace and friendship with Japan, *for Australian reasons*.'[47] In this campaign, he had the tacit support of the business community, and it aligned him with Adela Walsh.

At the Yabber Club, Miles revealed another reason for his pro-Japanese stance; he sometimes mentioned a friend, a retired Indian army officer, but did not name him until March 1941.[48] This was Lieutenant-Colonel Douglas Henry Graves. Born in India in 1868, he had served in the Indian Medical Service, 1902–21; he and his wife Charlotte first visited Japan in 1903, and both were actively pro-Japanese. In 1938 they were living in Kings Cross, Sydney. Whenever the Japanese had a notable victory in China, Graves went to the Consulate-General to offer congratulations and make a substantial donation to the Japanese National Defence Funds to support the army in China.[49]

In January 1937, Masey wrote on trade with Japan.[50] Salier also began to write pro-Japanese material under the pseudonym of 'H. Bruno Thomas'. Thus the March issue contained an inoffensive article by Salier on Barrier Reef holidays, and one entitled 'Pacific Problems. The Threat to Australia. European or Asiatic?' by 'H. B. Thomas'. He scorned the idea that Japan could or would attack Australia, which he called 'the latest bogey manifested by the imperialists for Australian delectation'. He wrote that problems of supply ships and troopships over the long distance would prove insurmountable.[51] He overlooked the fact that Japan would not need to attack from the home islands if she could secure by treaty or conquest bases closer to Australia. After the League of Nations allocated the control of former German colonies in the Pacific as mandates, Japan and Australia shared a theoretical ocean frontier at the Equator. In the same issue, a spurious 'Letter to the Editor' by 'James White' (Stephensen again) approved of Thomas's article: 'Unless Britain and America attack Japan in Japan's Home Waters and Home Territory, there will be no war waged by Japan... Let the Japanese have a free hand in China!'[52] At the Clyne Inquiry, Stephensen denied writing this letter, then admitted he wrote it when Miles asked him to fill up a space.[53] Fear and anger lay behind the support for Japan. On 15 April 1937, Hooper wrote in a private letter, 'Who in the scrap is likely to be squeezed dry in money and men then left in the bloody Pacific with the first class powers whom we have affronted by high-handed trade disruptions and war activities?'[54]

In August 1937 Miles began using the name 'L. M. Veron' for his defence of Japan and attacks on China, his bitter anti-Semitic articles and his pro-Hitler articles. In support of an article by K. Kawakumi in the *Herald*, 26 June, Miles wrote that Japan had no fortified positions near Britain and had never attacked Britain, but Britain had attacked Japan.[55] He blamed Chinese weakness and official corruption for the war with Japan: 'The real causes of the present war thus lie wholly in China... There is no doubt that the Chinese became the aggressors early in July last, and soon got themselves into trouble.'[56] In October 1937, accepting the Japanese version of events at the Marco Polo Bridge, Miles wrote that on 7 July Chinese soldiers had fired on Japanese troops.[57] 'H. B. Thomas' commented satirically on the prospect of Australians being dragged into the China-Japan war, and 'Rex Williams' quoted a cable from Australian businessman Thomas Gordon, then in New York:

> We Australians find the Japanese splendid business men and commercial friends. The China War is not our affair. Japan will never worry Australia. I regard her as one of our best customers, and I shall have the pleasure of visiting her.[58]

In November 1937, after the Sydney Trades Hall Council called for a boycott of Japanese goods, 'Rex Williams' accused them of being in league with Chinese mandarins and capitalists to prevent Japan from modernising China. He denounced stories of Japanese atrocities as propaganda; Japan would bring law and order to China and put down bribery, corruption and banditry. As himself, Stephensen wrote, 'It is far better that Australia should rise with Japan in the Pacific than decline with Britain in the Atlantic.' No nation had a higher standard of politeness, cleanliness, honour and courtesy, and they did not want lands to colonise.[59] He seemed not to have heard Japanese complaints about having nowhere to settle her expanding population.

The Japanese were pleased with this issue. The Colonial Secretary's Office in Fiji reported in March 1938 that a bundle of *Publicists* had been sent to the Japanese Society in Suva. According to a CIB report, the Japanese used the prestige of a Rhodes Scholar to present *Publicist* material as an unbiased view.[60] Whenever there was a pro-Japanese article in the *Publicist*, the Consulate-General bought multiple copies for circulation. In December, 'Veron' wrote an article unaptly called 'The World at Peace', with the theme: 'Japan Marches On'.[61] Then the topic was dropped for a while. Japanese savagery in Nanking that month could not be defended; it could only be denied.

In April 1938 'Veron' quoted from a speech by Koki Hirota, the Minister for Foreign Affairs: 'Japan has no territorial ambitions in China, nor has she any intention of separating North China from the rest of the country.' There would be peace as soon as the Nationalists 'evinced a sincere desire to work together for this ideal of Japan'.[62]

An official translation of Hirota's speech was made available at the *Publicist* office.[63]

Meanwhile, Vice-Consul Kijiro Miyake had arrived in Sydney. The Consul-General, Torao Wakamatsu, appointed him to coordinate work of an 'Enlightenment Committee' set up by the Japanese Chamber of Commerce in Sydney in April 1938 to control propaganda funds.[64] They were told that they had to 'win over *those persons who have influence over the shaping of public opinion*'. (Emphasis added) Miyake, who handled Australians who might promote Japan's aims, was directed to the *Publicist.* The Japanese helped to distribute it more widely. The *Publicist* re-printed a letter that Miyake had sent to the *Sydney Morning Herald,* in which he said that 'Japan harbours no territorial designs upon Australia, and strives to keep on the best possible terms with Australia'.[65]

In June 1938, 'Veron' wrote, 'The Publicist is probably the only Australian newspaper that has not been more or less anti-Japanese since July 7, 1937 – the date when the Chinese started the ridiculous present war.' Few Australians shared the view that China started the war. (There was no Chinese army in Japan.) In the same issue, Miles condemned the ban on mining Yampi Sound iron ore and exporting it to Japan.[66]

The March 1939 issue was called the 'Japanese Number'. Four pages of the Bunyip Critic section eulogised Japan on the occasion of the alleged 2,599th anniversary of the founding of the Japanese nation, which the Sydney Japanese community celebrated on 11 February. Stephensen used it for wide-ranging attacks. He claimed that Japan was the only country in the world completely free of 'International Jew Finance'; having incurred 'the hatred of the world's capitalist democratic journalists, more particularly the yapping lap-dogs of those obese capitalist democra-imperiums, Britain and France and the U.S.A.', it had the 'distinction of being the most lied about nation'.[67] It was suspected that the Consulate-General had supplied the material. In fact, it came from Frank Clune, who had recently returned from Japan with books and pamphlets.[68] The Consul-General sent this issue to the Foreign Minister, drawing his attention to the article by Stephensen:

> in which he refers to the superiority of the Japanese national constitution, the glorious history of our race,

> Anglo-Japanese co-operation in the past, especially the aid rendered to Australia by Japan during the 1914-1918 War, and the importance of cordial relations between Japan and Australia.[69]

He reported that a local current affairs association had purchased 2,000 copies for distribution. This probably referred to a pamphlet containing the article rather than the whole *Publicist*, but it boosted Miles's finances.[70] A booklet called *Japan's Problems*, provided by the Consulate-General, was given away with the pamphlet.[71]

Reacting to communist attacks, Stephensen continued his defence of Japan in May: 'If Japan can be sufficiently weakened, then the power-crazed and blood-soaked Dreamers of the Kremlin hope to have an easy victory in China.' He also reviewed the book *The Goal of Japanese Expansion*, by Tatsuo Kawai, at that time Director of the Information Bureau of the Japanese Foreign Office, who contended that Japan was obliged 'to take proper measures to combat the menace of the Comintern's operations in the Far East'.[72]

In 1937 the *Publicist* began to champion fascism and Nazism as well. The May issue 1937 quoted from a speech by Hitler on 30 January, the fourth anniversary of his coming to power. Miles could hardly have seen a newsreel of Hitler addressing a rally in the Berlin *Sportpalast*, for he compared his speech with one by W. M. Hughes: 'Mr Hughes appears to THE PUBLICIST to endeavour to maintain his vicarious war-fame by the public practice of rhetoric, which is quite different from Hitler's way.'[73]

By August 1937, editorial policy of the *Publicist* supported Japan and Germany completely. As 'Benauster', Miles wrote a favourable review of an official propaganda book, *Germany's Colonial Problem*, by G. Kurt Johanssen and H. H. Kraft. Miles advocated the return of Germany's colonies: 'Quite literally, Germany was robbed of her colonial possessions.'[74] In September 1937, the *Publicist* published a letter from L. P. Fox of Melbourne, which quoted from a speech by Dr Robert Ley, head of the *Deutsche Arbeitsfront* (German Labour Front): 'England must return our colonies. If she doesn't, we'll take them.'[75] Miles saw nothing wrong with that threat, nor did it disturb him when Germany later forcibly seized Czechoslovakia in two stages.

Dr George Edward Payne Philpots, a retired Melbourne dentist, sent the *Publicist* a speech he had made to the Rotary Club at Mount

Gambier, South Australia. 'Herr Hitler time and again has stated publicly that Germany does not want war,' said Philpots, 'and I sincerely believe he is sincere.' Stephensen wrote that the *Publicist* endorsed this view.[76] Philpots was clearly the contributor 'G. P.' who, from September 1937, wrote vulgar anti-Jewish verse for the *Publicist*.[77] 'Dr. Philpot - retired' was on the membership list of the Melbourne Odinist Society, so A. R. Mills might have introduced him to the *Publicist*.[78]

In February 1938, 'Alcedo Gigas' began a series of articles attacking Professor Stephen Roberts' book, *The House that Hitler Built*.[79] The Bunyip Critic joined in the criticism, yet he claimed, 'I do not support Hitler, Mussolini, and the Mikado, who support themselves and have never asked for my aid.' Then he commented on the attitude of 'the jewspapers of the world'.[80] Although Roberts had spent some time in Germany under the Nazi regime and had met many prominent Nazis, the *Publicist* group, whose members had not been in Germany since 1933, thought they knew better. What Roberts wrote about Hitler as an orator is interesting, for it applied to Stephensen as well:

> [He] can say different things in successive moments and believe in each with the same degree of fervour. It is not his honesty that is in question; it is his terrific power of self-delusion that introduces such an element of uncertainty into everything he does... His emotion drags him along behind his surging words, and he can neither stop nor restrain his impetuous belief in what he is saying.[81]

Munro says that Stephensen was by nature a debater, willing to debate in support of any issue without necessarily believing in it,[82] while Muirden writes that Stephensen 'was more apt than most to be carried away in the heat of battle'.[83] This was dangerous, for he would say impulsively things that he did not necessarily mean, forget he had said them, and call other people liars when they remembered and challenged him.[84]

In October, while publicising the book *Germany Speaks*, a collection of propaganda articles by leading Nazis, 'Benauster' wrote, 'THE PUBLICIST, as a thoroughly Australian paper, stands virtually alone in its goodwill attitude towards Germany, Italy and Japan.'[85] As 'Veron',

Miles had written in March 1938 that increases in armaments led to war. 'Britain and the U.S.A. are the only preparers for a world war, although neither of them is threatened with attack.'[86] This was untrue, for few countries were less prepared for war than Britain, and Germany had recently introduced conscription. In October, 'Benauster' repeated that war was *biologically inevitable*, and pacifism was a menace to Australia. It is hard to see how he reconciled his claim that war was inevitable with his condemnation of Britain for *preparing* for war, especially as she was not doing so.[87]

Miles decided to print Hitler's major policy speeches in full, beginning in June 1938 with Part 1 of his Reichstag speech of 20 February. Heavily decorated with swastikas, page 13 bore the headline 'Hail Hitler!'[88] Only two years earlier, Stephensen had written of the '*Heil Hitler* buncombe which goes with Fascism'.[89] Stephensen told Kirtley that Hitler was 'a damned nuisance', as he took up so much room in the *Publicist*.[90] The best that could be said of the decision was that Miles lost sight of his aim, for what relevance did the speech have to Australia-First?[91] Hitler's speech of 30 January 1939 was also published, using a translation by the Anglo-German Information Service in London.[92] It was legitimate to print the speech for information, but Miles seemed to endorse it, and Stephensen wrote, 'We need here a Mahomet, a Hideyoshi, a Cromwell - or a Hitler - a man of harsh vitality and vigour, a born leader, a man of action.'[93]

The *Publicist* began as a culturally nationalist journal; it changed into a politically Nationalist one. Germans in Sydney had little contact with the *Publicist* group, for Nazi Party members were ordered to stay away from them,[94] except Arnold von Skerst, who provided material from the Consulate-General for use in the *Publicist*.[95] Thus it is surprising that there was a suggestion that the *Publicist* might be made a member of the German Chamber of Commerce, but not surprising that this was rejected.[96] A statement made later by Nellie Louise Bell, an employee of the Chamber, claimed that Skerst was 'commissioned' by Nazi leaders to cultivate a friendship with Miles and Stephensen, show them hospitality and induce them to publish articles sympathetic towards Nazism.[97] According to Bell, instructions on how to influence foreigners came from E. W. Bohle, head of the Foreign Organisation of the Nazi Party.[98]

Stephensen, for his part, insisted that he had met Skerst only once, in May 1935, for three minutes, when he inquired into the prices of Junkers aircraft used in New Guinea.[99] He was blamed falsely for writing a pro-Japanese pamphlet, but an anonymous pamphlet written for the Germans was probably his work. This pamphlet, *Trade Without Money*, by 'An Economist', advocated barter trading, which would have allowed German goods to be exchanged directly for Australian wool.[100] This bartering, promoted by Douglas Social Credit and exploited by the Nazis, was known as ASKI trading.[101] The information for the pamphlet must have come from a German source and could not have been supplied in 'three minutes'. Nevertheless, Stephensen claimed that he was not in contact with the German Consulate or any Germans.[102] 'Those people,' he said, 'did not come anywhere near the *Publicist* and we did not go near them.' This was manifestly untrue, for arrangements had to be made to pay for *Publicist* advertisements in *Die Brücke*; the *Publicist* was available in the office of *Die Brücke*, and *Die Brücke* in the Publicist bookshop.[103] Bell said that Miles visited Skerst at his office each week, and that the *Publicist* was available at the German Chamber of Commerce.[104] Her evidence at the Clyne Inquiry, as Nellie Dyer, was confused and inaccurate. A more coherent written statement of 25 January 1941 shows how the Nazi propaganda machine operated, and why the *Publicist* was a danger:

> Co-operation arranged between German newspapers in foreign countries and *susceptible newspapers* in the language of the foreign countries in question, e.g. the 'Publicist' was influenced in such a subtle manner that possibly even the Editor of the newspaper in question co-operated without actually realising that he was doing so... Mr. Von Skerst systematically and repeatedly discussed the relationship between Australia and England, with the proprietors of the 'Publicist' also the 'Bulletin', as well as his individual Australian associates.
>
> For instance, he impressed upon them the existence of English domination in Australian affairs... This was the long-range propaganda of which Von Skerst and his

> fellow Party Members availed themselves, in order to encourage an Isolationist Policy in Australia - thereby weakening Britain's stand against Nazi Germany.
>
> Thus he fostered in them i.e. in all Australians with whom he came in contact - sometimes men in high Government positions - a slight doubt as to the good intentions of England.
>
> With this 'AUSTRALIA FIRST' slogan of his theme song, von Skerst, acting under direct instructions from the Foreign Organisation of the N.S.D.A.P. Berlin - in the capacity of N.S.D.A.P. Propaganda Leader for Australia - successfully fostered disloyalty which he encouraged under cover of his 'AUSTRALIA FIRST' smoke screen, designed to hide his true purpose...
>
> I heard Mr. Von Skerst mention to Schwarz von Berk, Editor of 'Der Angriff', chief organ of the Nazi Party, during his stay here—shortly prior to the outbreak of war—that the stronger an Australian becomes in anti-Semitic feeling, the less objection he will have for a country which advocates an anti-Semitic policy.[105]

These were the points on which *Publicist* policy and Nazi interests coincided:

Break with Britain.
Foster anti-Semitism.
Attack communism.

Miles and Stephensen were never spies or paid agents, but they supported Nazi policy for what they saw as Australian reasons. They would continue to do this even if Germany and Australia were at war, for they did not understand the implications.

In mid August, the September *Publicist* went to press with the final instalment of Hitler's speech and two articles that served German interests. Watts wrote that there was a weakness in society caused by corruption, vice and high taxation, such as had existed in Germany and Italy before Hitler and Mussolini had taken over. Miles wrote, 'What is German Danzig to Australia that Australians should weep for her?'[106] Thus Miles and Stephensen must have found the Soviet-German Pact of 23 August as awkward as did the communists. Communism was no longer a defence against fascism; fascism was no longer a defence against communism; the foundations of their beliefs were shaken. There was also an article on 'The Link' in September. Miles mentioned the organisation's founder, Admiral Sir Barry Domvile, and a book by Professor A. P. Laurie.[107] A Security report said, '"THE LINK" was one of the subtle mediums for the dissemination of Nazi propaganda abroad.' It had the support of men in high places, in Australia as well as England, and Skerst was the official representative in Australia.[108] Bell wrote:

> The Publicist office frequently received letters from 'Link' members or Australians interested in beginning a correspondence with people in Germany. These letters were forwarded by the Publicist Office to the 'Brucke' office - the Party had told Mr. von Skerst to make this arrangement.[109]

Laurie was one of Mosley's fascists, and the dedication in his book read: 'It is with admiration and gratitude that I dedicate this book to the Fuehrer.'[110] His book was mentioned in a letter to the *Publicist* from the *Deutscher Fichte-Bund* (sub-titled Union for World Veracity), written on 1 August 1939. The writer thanked Miles for his letter, offered to send him 'literature' (propaganda), and commented, 'You are quite right in saying that a prosperous Germany will be to the benefit of the world.'[111] In March 1942, the letter was allegedly found in Stephensen's property. He denied having seen it; at the Clyne Inquiry, he said of the *Fichte-Bund,* 'I never heard of it until these proceedings, and I still do not know what it means.'[112] Stephensen *ought* to have heard of it. Miles knew; Hooper knew.[113] Miles discussed The Link with him. Why would he not have mentioned correspondence with the *Fichte-Bund*?

The *Publicist* had been anti-communist almost from its beginning; fairly soon it became anti-Semitic as well. It is difficult to untangle its attacks on Jews from its attacks on communists, for Nazis considered Jews and communists to be almost identical, and could quote selected examples to make their point. Karl Marx was of Jewish ancestry; so was Leon Trotsky (born Bronstein); but Stalin was not Jewish. Leading German communists Kurt Eisner and Rosa Luxemburg were Jewish, but Karl Liebknecht and Ernst Thälmann were not. As communism denies the existence of a deity, it is inimical to orthodox

Jews as well as to Christians and Moslems. Stephensen wrote in June 1939:

> Capitalism is the head, and Marxism is the back-side, of the Jew-God... Four great men now living, namely Gandhi, de Valera, Hitler, and Mussolini, and one great man now dead, Lenin, have all been called 'mad' by money-grubbing Britishers, who cannot believe that the true leaders of humanity could act just for an idea... Why need Australians bemoan the absorption of Czechoslovakia by Germany, when Australia is already 'absorbed' by British and American Jew-Capitalists?[114]

Muirden writes of 'a mild but persistent anti-Semitism' in the *Publicist*, remarking that Stephensen's habitual response to people who annoyed him was that they were or might be Jewish.[115] If they were not Jews, they were 'Jew-duped'. Far from being mild, its anti-Semitism was at times almost rabid. The Jews were constant targets of *Publicist* abuse. In his second article attacking Roberts' book, in March 1938, Miles dealt with the chapter on the situation of the Jews in Germany:

> In fact it is because the Jews are of the Semitic Races that anti-semitism exists against them – if there were no semitism there would be no anti-semitism... Everywhere that Jews exist there exists more or less anti-semitism.[116]

As 'Veron', he wrote in August 1938, 'There could be no anti-Semitism, were there no Semitism... The Jewish religion is a racial religion, and the Jews do not proselytise.'[117] In September, he attacked Dr Shein, who was visiting Australia from Jerusalem:

> What does Jew Shein want Australians to do? Subscribe money for Jewish benefit, traduce Gentile Hitler for Jewish benefit, wage war against Gentile Germans for Jewish benefit, wage war against Gentile Arabs for Jewish benefit?[118]

In November, Dora Watts introduced the anti-Semitic works of Houston Stewart Chamberlain into the *Publicist*–Yabber group.[119]

Another main target of the *Publicist* was the Communist Party of Australia, with its links with the Soviet Union. Stephensen had not been a financial member of the Party since 1926, although he did not reject communism totally until perhaps as late as 1936. He wrote in 1939 that he did not regret leaving the Communist Party, nor did he regret having belonged to it, for 'you do not know what a disease is like until you have had it'.[120] Stephensen and Miles increased their attacks from December 1937.[121] At the same time, Stephensen was feuding with the press, in particular the former *Labor Daily*, which had become the *Daily News*.[122] In reference to an article of 9 December 1938, he labelled it a paper conducted by:

> Smart-Alecs, Yids, Hooey-Merchants, Leftists... the snarling irresponsibles who lurk anonymously in modern newspaper offices, defaming whom they choose, lying as they please, suppressing truth, exaggerating rumours, and inciting the public to hatred, hysteria and disorder. [123]

Stephensen also attacked Eric Baume, editor of the *Sunday Sun*, saying he had forgotten a 'Primary Rule of Sound Journalism in Sydney', which was: *'Never attack P. R. Stephensen or "The Publicist"; these animals are awful creatures; when you attack them, they defend themselves.'*[124] He referred to a talk by Baume, reprinted 'in the insane London-New-York moron-catching smart-alec jewspaper style', in which Baume had said sarcastically of 'Stephenson', 'I want to thank him for making a god out of Hitler, the most loathsome swine that ever lived.' 'Benauster' too attacked the *Daily News* and 2KY, writing that they wanted 'the liberty to lie freely in their own money-making interests... The journalists of Australia are as lying and hypocritical a professional set of men and women as are to be found in the world.'[125] If Australia-First and the *Publicist* needed support from the press in the future, they would find little sympathy.

As a result of *Publicist* attacks on the Labor paper, the *Workers' Weekly* (sub-titled the Central Organ of the Communist Party of Australia) ran a front-page article on 7 April 1939 with the headline 'Propagandists for Nazis and Jap War Lords', with an advertising placard saying 'Sydney's Nazi Underworld'. Part of the article read:

> The countries threatened by Nazi aggression are full of spies and agents paid by the fascists. Among the tools of the Nazis are traitors to their own country, native-born traitors, who are prepared to

> sell their own people to the foreign aggressors... Are there similar sinister people in our midst?[126]

The paper implied that Stephensen was such a person, outdoing even Japanese government propagandists, adding that 'we cannot afford to have the unity and strength of Australian democracy white-anted from within'. [This from communists!] Stephensen took out writs for damages of £5,000 against the publisher, Francis Harold Devanny, and the printers, Forward Press, which had printed his own book, *Foundations of Culture*.[127] When the case was heard in April 1940, the international situation was quite different.[128]

In February 1939, Watts wrote a moderate article, in which he said that Jews succeeded through shrewdness or guile, and they would intermarry and disappear, or buy or take by force a land of their own. 'Alcedo Gigas' accused the Fellowship of Australian Writers of being pro-Semitic and pro-communist; there were Communist Party members on the committee, but others besides them objected to fascism.[129] In March, an anonymous letter said, 'No rational person opposed to the entrance of Jews into Australia has ever intimated that a Jew with wealth is any more welcome than a poor one.'[130] No ethnic group should have a unique right to be exempt from criticism or an uncontested right to everything it wants, and there should have been no embargo on discussing immigration, Jewish or otherwise. Such discussions or criticisms cannot justly be judged in the light of what happened later; wisdom in hindsight is the handmaiden of hypocrisy. The point at issue was whether the *Publicist*'s constant anti-Semitism was detrimental to Australian security, not whether the criticisms were valid or ethical. In the atmosphere of the Munich crisis over the Sudetenland in September and October, and the *Kristallnacht* attacks on Jewish persons and property in November, Miles and Stephensen returned to their original topic of Australian national identity.

Soon the war forced Miles and Stephensen to reconsider their tactics, if not their philosophy. On 26 June 1939, Miles ended the last Publicist Session: 'If you are *not* for *Australia First*, for *what* country *are* you first?'[131] This is the dilemma that fanatics present to moderate and sensible people. It was possible to support women's suffrage without chaining oneself to railings, to care about peace without joining a communist front organisation, to care about the environment without standing in front of bulldozers. It was possible to care about Australia while abhorring the pseudo-intellectual drivel with which Miles burdened the cause.

The contacts of Miles and Stephensen looked sinister to Security authorities. Besides the *Publicist* and some Australian books, the bookshop sold the *Protocols of Zion*, and allegedly *Die Brücke* and the Fascist *Italo-Australian*; it sold or gave away pamphlets published by the Japan-Pacific Association and the Japanese Chamber of Commerce. William Harold Barnwell, one of the CIB's most knowledgeable and experienced agents, reported that on 6 May 1938 he saw six issues of *Die Brücke* on Miles's desk, and he had seen the *Publicist* on the desk of Ladendorff, the leader in Australia of the Nazi Party.[132] If the bookshop had been truly international, it would have sold *Le courrier australien*; if it had been exclusively Australian, it would not have touched the German, Italian and Japanese material.

Hasluck writes that the *Publicist* contained 'disordered propaganda, more vehement in protest than clear in exposition... It was erratic, declamatory and self-contradictory. In short, it was a soap box with tatters of "literature" and "culture" hanging to it'.[133] Munro quotes a comment by Robert Hall, who wrote that some of Stephensen's plans were good, a lot were 'rotten', some 'just wrong', and others 'terrifying'.[134] Muirden writes:

> The *Publicist* gave the impression of saying things that badly needed saying but which others were either not saying at all, or not saying loudly enough. Yet, searching for detail to buttress this opinion, surprisingly little can be found...
>
> Both Miles and Stephensen lacked a sense of proportion; most successful political proselytizers do. They flogged the same tired arguments through edition after edition.[135]

At the Clyne Inquiry, Hooper said that he had challenged Miles about what Stephensen was doing, and Salier and Masey had tried to moderate 'his habit of offensive expressions', for they realised it was a 'gross blunder', but Miles paid the piper and called the tune.[136] Xavier Herbert put these words into the mouth of 'the Chief' (his fictional Miles): 'It was largely a joke... Saying the things that infuriated doctrinaire fat heads like Communists and clever people like Jews, simply amused me.'[137] Miles did appear to derive pleasure from hurting people or making them angry, but if the *Publicist* was 'largely a joke', few people saw it that way. Stephensen wrote, 'THE PUBLICIST specialises in unpalatable truths.'[138] Many of his articles were unpalatable, but they were not necessarily true.

While the *Publicist* was not the tool of the NSDAP, its policy was consistently pro-Italian, pro-German, pro-Japanese. Japanese support was limited to flattery and legitimate business transactions, e.g. financial support by purchasing multiple copies. The *Publicist* set out to make enemies and offend people; it cultivated false friends. It had sown the wind; and in time it reaped the whirlwind.

Chapter 3

The Melbourne Connections

As early as 1916, there had been contact between persons who later became connected with the *Publicist* in Sydney and those in several loosely knit groups in Melbourne. Some links were forged through the anti-conscription campaigns, the Rationalist Association and the Socialist magazine, *Ross's Monthly*. Other associates, however, had different ideological backgrounds.

Alexander Rud Mills, a Melbourne solicitor, was one of the most dangerous adherents of Australia-First. He discovered the *Publicist* while in Sydney in late 1936. At the Clyne Inquiry, he denied having met Stephensen until they were interned together,[1] but admitted meeting Miles. After buying *Foundations of Culture in Australia* from the Publicist shop, he returned several times.[2] Hooper denied knowing Mills *or his work*,[3] but admitted later that he knew of Mills's article in the *Publicist*, saying, 'It only interested me as a freak.'[4] It has been claimed that Mills should not have been interned, as he had never even attended an AFM meeting, but he was interned for other reasons.

Born on 15 July 1885 at Forth in Tasmania, Mills was 'of British stock'. Not being married, he named his mother in Burnie as next of kin when interned. He and Robert Gordon Menzies knew each other well, having studied law at the University of Melbourne together, although Mills was nine years older. He had to complete his school studies while labouring for a local council in Western Australia.[5]

Mills was admitted to the bar in Victoria in 1917.[6] He was never wealthy, but in 1922 he could afford to travel around Europe for twelve months. During 1931-33 he was abroad again, visiting not only England, Holland, Belgium and Germany, but also Russia, India and North and West Africa.[7] In England he started the Moot of the Anglekin Body, a Nordic Society, then he spent several months in Germany. Returning to England, he heard Sir Oswald Mosley speak, but attached himself to the smaller, virulent Imperial League of Fascists (ILF); Arnold Leese had founded this League and its publication, the *Fascist*, in 1929.[8] Leese had discovered the *Protocols of Zion* through a group called 'The Britons' and was violently anti-Semitic. Point 3 of the ILF programme read: 'Elimination of evil alien influences, especially that of the Jews.'[9] He took as his emblem a swastika superimposed on a Union Jack. Associated with Leese was William Joyce,[10] whom Mills knew slightly. Leese allegedly sent Mills instructions and propaganda through a stewardess aboard the liner *Oronsay*.[11]

Mills returned to Germany in order to meet Hitler, allegedly walking into the Brown House with no introduction. He wrote, 'I saw him. Talked to him. He would not discuss my theme.'[12] He said that he saw no cruelty in Germany; concentration camps were very well conducted, and he had detected 'a strong sense of deep kindness' in Hitler.[13] Mills also contacted General Erich Ludendorff and his domineering wife, Mathilde, who in 1925 had founded the *Tannenbergbund* to promote Odinism.[14] Correspondence with the Ludendorffs was found when his premises were searched in 1942.[15]

Odinism has been regarded as a Nazi initiative to destroy Christianity, but as long as Hitler wanted to harness the churches in the service of Nazism his old comrade-in-arms was an embarrassment. Helmreich writes, 'Hitler did not have a high opinion of the Nordic groups and never lent them his personal support.'[16] In 1933, the *Tannenbergbund* was dissolved. In early 1937, the Ludendorffs organised a new movement, which was permitted to hold closed meetings. After General Ludendorff died in December 1937, Mathilde continued this movement.[17] Mills was perhaps too weird even for her, for she wrote that they stood on different ground.[18]

Mills brought back an English translation of the 25-point NSDAP programme, and as early as August 1933 he received a letter in German from Goebbels' Propaganda Ministry to 'Herr Mills', and on 9 February 1937 one in English from the *Fichte-Bund*, an organisation that distributed Nazi propaganda in foreign countries. A copy of a letter he wrote to the *Fichte-Bund* in Hamburg, dated 26 February 1937, concluded, 'Yours in National Socialism, A. R. Mills'.[19]

After returning from Europe, Mills spent several years in Melbourne. Under the name Tasman Forth, he wrote *Hael Odin*, a book of poems glorifying Nordic gods and vilifying Judaeo-Christianity. He complained that 'the Jews' obtained a copy before he did and took it to the Victorian Attorney-General. The police were called and the Crown Solicitor threatened to prosecute and imprison him for blasphemy. He started the Anglekin Body in Melbourne, and claimed that up to 120 members used to practise 'the Ritual' every Thursday evening and hold Odinist ceremonies on Mills's land at Croydon.[20] In 1935 he founded the British Australian Racial Body (B.A.R.B.) to foster the 'preservation of the national character and British reputation for justice and honour and the creation of adequate military forces in this country and in the Empire'.[21] This resembled some fringe groups in Britain with a similar philosophy: for example, the English Mistery, the Paladin League and the English Array.[22]

There is no evidence that Mills was associated with these bodies, but he was certainly connected with similar groups. One was the 'Anglocyn' group of which H. H. Lockwood was secretary, whose terminology Mills used and who was mentioned during Mills's appeal against internment.[23] Another was 'The Britons', which H. H. Beamish founded in 1919. In 1922, he established the Britons Publishing Co., which issued the *Protocols of Zion*.[24] Mills claimed he had authority from Britain to found an Anglo-Saxon racial body, and its most likely source was The Britons. In March 1935, he registered 'The Angle Press' as a business name and began publishing a magazine called the *Angle* for B.A.R.B. At the Clyne Inquiry, reference was made to six copies of the *Angle*.[25]

An attempt in April 1926 to found a fascist organisation in Adelaide had lapsed for want of support. In 1936, a new attempt was made in Adelaide, when Dr W. Erich Meier, a teacher at Renmark and the son of a pastor, returned from study in Germany with his head full of Hitlerism. This too made no great progress, but among its main interstate contacts was listed A. R. Mills, Melbourne solicitor.[26]

Police kept up pressure on Mills. He was refused the use of halls for his meetings. His typists became afraid. In 1935 he visited Western Australia and held Odinist meetings fairly discreetly. He wrote, 'I met a few people and good ones.'[27] In 1936 Mills moved to Sydney, where he published two issues of a paper called the *National Socialist*. The first, of which five hundred copies were printed,[28] appeared in December 1936 with a swastika in the upper left corner of the front page. It styled itself 'A PAPER DEVOTED TO THE BRITISH RACE AND BRITISH CULTURE', identifying its Editor and Director as A. R. Mills, 76 Pitt Street, Sydney.[29] There is no evidence that British fascists subsidised him, but in applying for a Ministerial Warrant to intern or restrict Mills, an MI officer noted that Mills did little legal work, and it was 'a matter of interest' how he could afford to travel so widely and publish so much.[30]

The *National Socialist* lasted only two issues. Most articles in the first issue were virulently anti-Semitic, almost in the style of Julius Streicher. In a linguistic trick, he claimed the name Israel was derived from the names of three 'alien' gods: IS, RA and EL. The Ukrainians, he wrote, offered up the prayer, in churches and newspapers: 'God send Hitler to deliver us from the power of the Jews!'

Mills too equated communists with Jews. 'The friends of Soviet Russia, Jews and their dupes, fear Japan,' he wrote. 'They want to see Japan crushed. The Japanese have no superstitious awe toward the Jews.' Concerning the war in Spain, he asked, 'How many Jew-boys from Russia (or elsewhere) have been killed in the Spanish civil war they admittedly formented [*sic*] in Spain?' He referred to the 'Jew-boys of the Press in England…' who 'sloganised': 'Britain will march side by side with France and Russia.' Mills responded, 'Now we assure the Jew-boys this: "Oh no, we won't."' This, he indicated, was thanks to the work of Leese and Mosley.

In a long rambling article, he elaborated upon a parable of 'noble bunyips' who worshipped the 'alien dingo', aping its ways until they were exterminated. He compared the bunyip to the Aryan Anglo-Saxon, and the dingo to Judaeo-Christianity. He referred to 'our ancestor Sigge' (George), who was called the Son of Odin. He advertised that he could supply copies of Tasman Forth's book, *And Fear shall be in the Way*, published in England in 1933.

Publication of this paper drew CIB attention to Mills again, and he was under observation in two states from the end of 1936.[31] Because left-wing groups were active earlier, and caused more obvious damage, they were monitored earlier and more closely, but the CIB and Special Branch (police) maintained surveillance of right-wing groups as far as staffing allowed. Reports on Nazi Party activities were being compiled within a few months of its foundation in Sydney and Melbourne in 1934.[32]

The second number of the *National Socialist* was dated February–March 1937. The swastika had disappeared from the front cover, but the content was similar. Mills invited readers to write to the Australian Unity League in Sydney for books on the Jewish Question. The paper was a failure, and Mills returned to Melbourne. The address from which the paper was published may be significant, for located on the first floor of 76 Pitt Street (Beresford Chambers) was Campbell's Employment Agency, run by Mrs H. Campbell. Mills admitted to the Clyne Inquiry that he had discussed 'problems and philosophy' with Colonel Eric Campbell, the leader of the New Guard.[33] In addition, as Mills had not been admitted to practise in New South Wales, he worked as a clerk in a law firm,[34] and this firm may have been Campbell, Campbell & Campbell.

When the Nazi Party was distributing copies of the English translation of a speech by Goebbels in August 1934, Campbell ordered 1,200 copies for the New Guard.[35] Consul-General Dr Rudolf Asmis wrote to the Foreign Office in Berlin in September saying that the leader of the local fascist organisation (the New Guard) had requested a signed picture of the Chancellor and Führer for Campbell, who had the highest esteem and admiration for the Führer.[36]

On 5 January 1935, *Die Brücke* praised *The New Road* by Eric Campbell, the well-known leader of the New Guard, the fascist organisation in New South Wales.[37] On 24 July 1935, Campbell set out for Asmis the aims of the New Guard and the Centre Party. Asmis referred his letter to Germany as coming from *der Führer der hiesigen faschistischen Organisation, der New Guard* (the leader of the local fascist organisation, the New Guard).[38] It is amazing that Campbell should have informed Asmis of New Guard business.

Mills put his own name to his *First Guide Book to the Anglecyn Church of Odin,* which he wrote while in Sydney. Although it denounced communism, he had it printed by the Communist Forward Press.[39] Mills defined 'Anglecyn' as the kin of the Angle nation, in the ancient Anglo-Saxon spelling.[40] The first part listed 'Fest' days, from the Fest of Beowulf and the Fest of Hengist and Horsa to Canute's Day and the Defeat of the Spanish Armada. The second part was a legalistic series of paragraphs beginning with 'And whereas'. The third part contained 'Services' to be conducted by a 'priest' called the Skald; they mimicked Christian communion, baptism, marriage and burial, but used the Edda and the utterances of Francis Drake, Thomas Cromwell, Edward I, etc. as their basis. The fourth part featured 'hymns' composed by Mills. The book had pale blue covers with embossed gold lettering, for the Odinist symbol was a golden sun-wheel on a background of blue sky. *Hael Odin* flaunted a golden swastika as well.[41]

After publishing an article (12 December 1936) on the *National Socialist, Smith's Weekly* attacked two books by Mills in the issue of 2 January 1937. Anti-Christian Nazis now in Australia, said the paper, wanted to destroy Christianity and replace it with Odinism. The first was *Hael Odin*; the second was the *Ritual Book of the Moots of the Anglecyn Body*, the aim of which was to promote paganism. The Nazi salute that was to be given was described in detail. Its emblems were a winged sandal and a sword.[42] It has not been possible to obtain a copy of this second book, but at the Clyne Inquiry somebody recognised that the 'Ritual' was based on Masonic ritual and questioned Mills about its format. 'I have heard it in the Masonic ritual,' said Mills. 'Where did you hear it in the Masonic ritual?' he was asked. Mills refused to answer. Then he said he heard it 'in a room'. Asked where the room was, he said it was 'in a house'. As some of the barristers were probably Masons and did not really want Mills to answer, the question was not pressed, but a note was produced in which Mills had written, in April 1930, that he wanted a Masonic funeral.[43]

In 1939, Mills published *The Odinist Religion Overcoming Jewish Christianity*. On 23 May he wrote to the Japanese Consulate-General asking help to find a literary agent in Japan. When he received an answer suggesting a firm in Tokyo, he sent a copy of the book to be presented to the 'Mikado' as a token of his 'honour and respect'.[44] This book contained adaptations of pamphlets he had published and lectures he had given on both Odinism and 'racial purity' over the previous six or seven years.[45]

As religion is a matter of faith, Mills was entitled to reject Judaeo-Christian scripture, to maintain that the Jews were not the Chosen Race and that man was not born in original sin.[46] However, in advocating a racist, anti-Semitic society he was coming close to Nazism, while in condemning everything Christian and praising Japan for rejecting the 'lie' of Christianity, he antagonised both the Catholic hierarchy and the Anglican establishment; he would be seen as both an enemy of religion and a threat to national security. In turning against Judaism and Christianity, he also turned against Freemasonry:

> Christianity has made us a nation of Jew-worshippers … The fact, too, that we neglect the Spirit of our own race, in favour of that of the Jews is enough to ruin us, and the fact that we, in our religion and Freemasonry, revere Jews and Jewish holy places before our own, is enough to ruin us.[47]

Before an Appeals Tribunal in November 1942, Mills said that he had never written to Hitler. Then he admitted writing once; then he said he had sent a book; then he admitted sending two books. He said he had sent books to many places: England, France, Italy, America, Norway, Sweden. Later he admitted getting a letter back from Hitler, through the German Consulate in Melbourne, stating he had heard of Mills's work with interest.[48]

Mills and Dr Friedrich Wilhelm Buettner, whom he had known at University, founded an Odinist Society in Melbourne about 1938, and they held weekend ceremonies at a shack at Lockwood.[49] By repute, Buettner was one of Melbourne's earliest Nazis although, as he was an Australian citizen by birth, he could not be a member of the NSDAP.[50] Mills later denied that Buettner was a member of the Odinist Society, but admitted he had attended some meetings and had given a lecture on 'racial hygiene'.[51] Besides Mills, Buettner and Philpots, three men and one woman were recorded as being associated with the Odinist Society; another woman had infiltrated the society as an agent of one of the Security services.[52] Mills wrote to Stephensen about Odinist ceremonies held in the bush outside Melbourne. It was suspected that he attended an Odinist ceremony at the Nazi Brown House in Belgrave in 1938, but he denied this.[53]

Mills remained in contact with Leese at least until the outbreak of war, and his Odinists distributed Leese's magazine, the *Fascist*. Mills advertised the Odinist Association in the August 1939 issue of this magazine.[54] In connection with Mills, Miles and others, a comment by Griffiths is relevant:

> In the 1939-40 period, Leese, like other anti-Semitic pro-Nazis such as Domvile and Ramsay, was aggrieved to find himself considered as being hostile to his own country, when he was merely trying to save it from the Jews by producing pamphlets against the war.[55]

Security tried to link Mills with Wilhelm Heiler, a prominent Nazi. Heiler's office was at 24 Collins Street and Mills was at 20 Collins Street, but Mills claimed he barely knew Heiler, who had visited his Melbourne office once in 1935 and had spoken to him once in the street in Sydney in 1936.[56] That might have been true, for as a rule German Nazis in Australia were ordered to stay away from Australian Nazis and fascists. Heiler, who had served in the German Navy during World War I, arrived in Australia as a wireless operator aboard *Freiburg* in July 1927. He joined the Nazi Party in August 1933 and he was leader for all Australia of the *Hafendienst* (Port Service).[57] While 'Gestapo agent' has been used loosely as a term of abuse, there were grounds for applying it to Heiler, for the *Hafendienst* reported to the Gestapo on the behaviour of ship's crews. In 1936 Heiler moved to Sydney where he transcribed Morse broadcasts from Germany for Asmis and worked for the *Arbeitsfront* (Labour Front). Security could not prove a link between Mills and Heiler, but Mills was under observation from the outbreak of war.[58]

Mills probably returned to Western Australia late in 1939. Laurence Bullock told F. J. Thomas that they should 'introduce the Nordic religion of Wotan and Valhalla'.[59] Bullock might have known of Mills's Odinism only from a *Publicist* article in January 1940, but he might have attended a lecture by Mills in 1935.[60] An unidentified female undercover security agent reported in 1939 that Mills was going to Perth. He had told her that Odinism was only a *cover* for fascism, as the Australian Constitution permitted the practice of any religion.[61] In October or November, he sent her a note asking that future communications to him should be sent care of the Commercial

Travellers' Club in Perth, as he was going to *organise the movement over there*.[62] It is not clear whether he meant Odinism, fascism or Australia-First.

Unaware of his peril, Mills wrote poems for the *Publicist* as Tasman Forth and an article on Odinism using his own name.[63] He also wrote an article for Miles's paper, the *Independent Sydney Secularist*.[64] However, the Anglophile Mills was out of place in the AFM. He told the Clyne Inquiry, 'I am very pleased to say that I regard myself as English.'[65] Miles and Stephensen were trying to eradicate this outlook; Stephensen commented, 'Mr Mills thinks in terms of Britain First, as against our Australia First.' In Australia Mills's Odin was also an alien god, as Ian Mudie pointed out in his poetry.[66]

Leslie Kevin Cahill, born on 1 October 1904 in Sydney, was less literary than Mills. Like Stephensen and the Walshes, he went through stages of being devoted to different causes. Of Irish extraction, he came from a Sinn Fein background. His father was allegedly connected with the Wobblies (the Industrial Workers of the World). He claimed he joined the Communist Party at the age of seventeen, that is, in 1921 or 1922.[67]

Cahill spent some time in Port Pirie, South Australia, where he had convictions for drunkenness, indecent language and resisting arrest, the last one in June 1930. (The charges might have been police harassment for his communist activities.) He married there in 1928, but in 1931 he deserted his wife and two children to go to Melbourne.[68] He boarded with Camille Bartram and was suspected of being her lover. In Security terms, she was notorious in her own right, having been secretary of the Communist Women's Committee, Fitzroy.

A notorious rough-and-tumble Yarra Bank speaker, Cahill became a leading figure in the Fitzroy branch of the Unemployed Workers' Union and was active in resisting evictions of the unemployed during the Depression.[69] Macintyre claims that Jean Devanny and Cahill were believed to have instigated an assault on Labor speakers in May 1932, but that Cahill might have been a police spy.[70] Given Cahill's background, the latter seems unlikely. According to a 1942 report, he was expelled from the Party in December 1932, and then joined the Trotskyite Fourth International and formed a short-lived

Lenin and Trotsky Association.[71] Cahill was unemployed until 1936 when he began to work for the Victorian Railways as a shunter.

Cahill claimed that he was a communist until October 1939 and changed his mind owing to the Russo-German Pact. Leaving an organisation that demands so much commitment tends to leave a large, empty space in the soul of a true believer, and Cahill needed a new cause, but it seems odd that he broke with communism over the rapprochement between Hitler and Stalin, only to take up with Australia-First.

The Kiernan Group in Melbourne was calling itself the Australia-First Group as early as 1936. It was sponsored by Esmond Lawrence Kiernan, MLC, who took the title of Director-General. Its stated aims were nothing out of the ordinary:

(i) A strong united White Australia.
(ii) A planned economy.
(iii) An objective population of 20 million.
(iv) To preserve private property and individual initiative.
(v) To oppose Communism.
(vi) To unite in one movement.

It appears to have been little more than an undergraduate talkfest, most participants being under thirty and of Irish Catholic background; some were university students simply dropping in out of curiosity. Among the alleged members was Niall Brennan, son of Frank Brennan, MHR.[72] This was significant only because it brought Stephensen and Brennan into contact. Major Hattam reported in 1942, 'Through lack of public support, this organisation had a very brief existence, and a further theory advanced for its failure was that Kiernan did not have the courage of his convictions.'[73]

The Cahill-Collins Group was founded after Kiernan's organisation folded. Cahill contacted Stephensen about founding an AF group in Melbourne. Stephensen replied on 3 October 1939 that he intended to visit Melbourne to deliver public addresses, and that Australia-First supporters in Melbourne included David Pitt and Niall Brennan of Newman College and John Gartner of Hawthorn Press,[74] but Stephensen did not make this trip. In the same letter he wrote that he expected the war to be a short one; that did not happen either.

Cahill started his group early in 1940 and became its Organising Secretary.[75] Its social and political orientation differed from that in Sydney. It was anti-English but not anti-Christian, for it had a strong Irish Catholic influence. Cahill claimed he had the support of Archbishop Mannix, but this is not substantiated.[76] Associated with Cahill was Richard Daniel Collins, who became president of the AFM in Melbourne. They operated together as Yarra Bank orators, selling the *Publicist* and collecting money for expenses. Collins hired halls and arranged for banners and pamphlets.[77] He had to restrict his work, for his employer, Ansett Airways, objected to provocative public activities by staff. Collins was never seriously under suspicion, and Security reported later that he was 'a particularly good type'.[78] Following communist methodology, Cahill organised speakers' training classes. He advertised the group meetings first on a loose sheet slipped into copies of the *Publicist* sold in Melbourne. A similar notice appeared in the *Publicist* in July 1940, and for several months Cahill submitted regular reports.[79]

Little is known about other members of the group in Melbourne, apart from some names: Bicknell, Dan Bourke, Mercia and Monica Hyde, H. Judd, Max Knight, McNamara, Bernard Rees, Janet B. Stewart-Murray, L. Wiggett.[80] Bicknell's name is on a bound set of the *Publicist* in the Queensland State Library, while Janet Stewart-Murray signed as a witness at the wedding of Percy Stephensen and Winifred Venus (Lockyer) in 1947.[81] Mercia and Monica Hyde, aged in their early twenties, and Collins, born 1911, were of Irish extraction, and several other names sound Irish.

Cahill addressed meetings in the Temperance Hall in Russell Street, but these were so poorly attended that they were soon discontinued. To keep the Movement alive, small group meetings were held, usually in the house in Richmond where Collins lived. In March 1940, there were about twelve members, but attendance seldom exceeded six.[82] With his labouring-class Irish-Communist background and passionate nature, Cahill was the only AFM member involved in violence, except in self-defence. On 27 February 1940, a Melbourne Court fined him one pound by for assaulting a communist interjector.[83]

In April 1941, Collins disbanded the group lest it hinder the war effort. Left without any political activity, Cahill went to Sydney in June to assess the situation. Agent 222 reported his presence at the Yabber Club on 21 June.[84] Returning to Melbourne, he resigned from the railways on 5 July. By then Mills had made himself known to Cahill, who asked for help to find employment, which Mills found for him with City Mutual Life Assurance.[85] Cahill attended the Bread and Cheese Club several times as Mills's guest.[86] This club, founded in June 1938, encouraged social gatherings of literary and cultural figures; in some ways, it was similar to the Yabber Club, but it eschewed politics. Having no controversial figure such as Miles or Stephensen, it did not attract CIB attention. Some harmless people who were to be connected with Australia-First attended meetings; Frank Clune, Rex Ingamells, Patrick Ignatius O'Leary, John Gartner and Niall Brennan were members, and Maurice Blackburn was a guest.[87]

When an Australia-First Movement was planned in Sydney, Cahill was invited to return as organiser. Valentine Crowley sent him the money for his fare, and he left for Sydney on 16 October 1941.[88] When the inaugural meeting was held on 20 October, Cahill was there and ready for a new task.

The *Advocate*, sub-titled 'A Catholic Review of the Week', had been founded in Melbourne in 1868; it closed in 1967. Muirden contends that there was a connection between Stephensen and O'Leary, editor of the *Advocate*, but he does not enlarge on it.[89] O'Leary and Gartner were editor and publisher of *Design: An Australian Review of Critical Thought*. Both publications reported favourably on the *Publicist*. O'Leary allegedly had links with the Irish Republican Army (IRA), and both he and Gartner were anti-English.[90] O'Leary invited Stephensen to write an article for the first issue of *Design* in January 1940.[91] It began with an alleged quotation from a Nazi source: 'When I hear a Jew talking about Culture, I reach for my revolver!'[92] This was sometimes taken to represent Stephensen's own reaction. The theme of his article was that wars were caused not by economics but by the passion of culture and politics, an arguable case. Then he attacked the 'delusion' of democracy, predicting that before 1950 it would be replaced by the 'Corporate State'.[93] He also wrote that if it was right for Australia to expel Chinese and Kanakas, it was right for Germany to expel Jews.

Gartner corresponded with Miles, probably initially about advertising for the *Publicist*, and it was possibly Miles who induced Cahill to contact Gartner. On 29 August 1940, Gartner wrote to Cahill, apologising for not replying sooner, and adding that he had been too busy to attend Cahill's meetings.[94] Gartner was also in contact with Ian Mudie, to whom he wrote that *Design* was being run at a loss.[95]

A hostile and insightful but not always accurate analysis of the *Advocate*'s connections was written by Ivy Fawcett of Camberwell to Frank Forde, Minister for the Army, on 31 March 1942. Brigadier Neil McArthur of the Sane Democracy League had employed her for two years as a propaganda analyst reporting on subversion, mainly on communists, but she made the AFM her chief objective, 'because I was convinced of its menace'. She wrote that the AFM in Melbourne received money and support from Kiernan, who had tried to draw her too into this association.[96] She was amazed to read in the press that the AFM was limited to Sydney and Western Australia, for there was a strong centre in Melbourne, organised by a Nazi, Alexander Rudolph Mills, who had been supported by the *Publicist* when he stood for Fawkner in the Federal elections. She was wrong about Mills's role in the AFM and about his middle name, but much of her information was sound. O'Leary, she wrote, had a great following in Melbourne among Catholic journalists, many of whom put out propaganda for Australia-First. Then she dealt with the connection between the *Advocate* and Australia-First:

> Stephensen has a great supporter here in P. I. O'Leary the sub-editor of the R.C. paper 'The Advocate' who is intensely anti-British and intensely Australia First... He gave, early in the war, the address of an I.R.A. cadre in Coburg, Melbourne—asking people to contact there a man called Fitzgerald.[97]

The Irish AF groups in Melbourne did nothing particularly noxious, but the Security services were concerned about what some clique within these groups *might* do. As Muirden points out, seven members of the Irish Republican Brotherhood were interned in World War I, and Mr Justice Harvey had said, '[The] view of these men was that any means were justified to injure Britain whom they saw as the enemy and oppressor of Ireland.'[98]

Security might have been even more concerned if O'Leary's

contacts with the Japanese Consulate-General in Sydney had been known. The *Advocate* of 27 November 1941 had carried a fairly innocent article, 'Some Thoughts on Peace with Japan'.[99] O'Leary sent a copy to the Consulate-General. On 29 November, Consul Tsuneo Hattori replied that it was a 'source of encouragement for us, who are, as you are no doubt aware, striving to maintain peaceful relations with our neighbouring countries'.[100] O'Leary's approach was ill timed, as Japanese aircraft carriers were already heading for Pearl Harbor.

Walter David Cookes, the third significant figure in Melbourne, was not interned, so information on him is comparatively sparse. Little has been published on his connection with Australia-First except that he sent Stephensen £250 to help save the *Publicist* in 1942. Although the Clyne Inquiry recorded (p. 2028) that Cookes came from Western Australia, he was in fact born in Bombala, New South Wales, on 12 July 1878. His father died when Walter was about a year old, leaving a pregnant widow with three children under five.[101] Beginning work in the shoe retailing business in Perth in 1895, Cookes set up his own store in Fremantle. By 1913, he was managing director of a factory in Melbourne and owned retail stores in Melbourne and Adelaide, the foundation of the Ezywalkin chain that grew to over sixty stores. Even wealthier than Miles, Cookes gave large sums of money to the Rationalist Association in Victoria and used its mailing list to send out the *Publicist* and other propaganda, some of it from the *Fichte-Bund*, although he denied corresponding with this organisation. He also distributed pro-Japanese propaganda at a directors' meeting of the Rationalist Association.[102] There is no record of his having visited Europe, but a statement dated 17 July 1942 claimed that Cookes had made a business trip to Japan and told people that he had been treated courteously.[103]

Coleman describes Cookes as 'a wealthy patron of Robert Ross', so he probably helped fund *Ross's Monthly*. He probably met Miles through the Rationalist Association. Cookes sheltered Adela Pankhurst when she was hiding from the police in 1917, and Adela married Tom Walsh at his house.[104] Socialists such as Ross and the Walshes were strange contacts for a reputed millionaire; indeed, the disparity of interests and ideologies in the group around the Ross family is surprising.

In a letter of 29 July 1938, Miles introduced Hooper's friend, Henry Joosten, to Cookes. Joosten also met Mills, but it is not known through what means.[105] Joosten was touring the British Commonwealth displaying samples of manufactured goods, advocating barter trade and lauding the improvement that Hitler had made to business conditions in Germany. After Joosten returned to Germany, Cookes sent him money for propaganda material to be distributed in Australia.[106] Cookes reported to both *Deutsche Welle* and a Japanese broadcasting technician on reception of broadcast services, and he distributed broadcasting schedules. In a letter to Japan on 26 August 1940, Cookes said he had sent out 'the 1,000 pamphlets' he had received.[107] According to MI, he held large sums in Japanese Government bonds. Although he denied this, MI was probably correct, as it could gain access to most financial records except taxation.[108]

In July 1940, Cookes was summoned to Victoria Barracks and questioned about a letter he had written to Miles.[109] MI began to build up a profile of his activities. A man who had known Cookes for twenty-five years and had been on the executive of the Rationalist Association made a comprehensive statement on 25 July. He said that Cookes had sent money to both Japan and Germany for propaganda that he distributed among Rationalists; that he was anti-British, had fascist tendencies, and blamed the Jews for 'the present trouble'; that he often listened to German radio stations and said he heard a lot of useful material; that he said Australia would not be badly off under Japanese influence, rather like Paris under the Nazis. The informant also said that Cookes had offered to pay him to write leaflets supporting these views.[110]

Cookes was lucky. He escaped internment perhaps on account of his age and poor health, possibly because he had powerful friends, but probably because he never caused a *public* scandal. In addition, he had so much to lose that threats to ruin him if he did not behave would be highly effective.

Chapter 4

The Yabber Club

From the early days of the *Publicist*, a group would gather for coffee and a chat in the Shalimar Cafe in the basement of the building in which the Publicist bookshop was located. These meetings came to be called the Yabber Club.[1] The group, consisting at first of Miles, Stephensen, Salier, Hooper, Masey and Valentine Crowley, was founded formally on 25 March 1937.[2] The 'permanent invitees' were mainly literary figures; it was not a fascist group: indeed Bartlett Adamson, Literary Editor of *Smith's Weekly*, was known to be a member of the Communist Party.

Among the invitees were authors Xavier Herbert, Eleanor Dark, Miles Franklin and Frank Dalby Davison, artist Lionel Lindsay, and American historian Hartley Grattan. Others, including Ian Mudie, were added to the list. Frank Clune attended when he was in Sydney, and he brought along Peter Russo.[3] Muirden writes that more than 200 meetings were held. He writes also that the Yabber Club was watched by Intelligence agents, including George Caiger, who reported in 1940 that they were 'harmless individuals sharpening their wits on each other'.[4] Stephensen's literary friends ensured lively cultural discussions, but Miles's contacts aroused suspicion.

Over-estimating his perspicacity, Stephensen claimed that they could always recognise Security agents, because these were too ill informed to take an intelligent part in discussions. One such agent was Alan Clement Panton (Agent 222), who joined the *Sydney Morning Herald* in 1931. Enlisting in the army in December 1939, he was taken over by Military Police Intelligence (MPI) and was a Warrant Officer by 1943. However, he stayed with the paper, working under cover. Senior men at the newspaper knew of this arrangement.[5] Panton said he started reporting on the Yabber Club early in 1941, but a report of 6 December 1940 is attributed to him.[6] His reports ceased late in 1941.

At the Clyne Inquiry, Stephensen said that Miles had invited Panton to the Yabber Club, but he showed no knowledge of politics.[7] However, Martin Watts clearly did not know of Panton's role when he called on him at the *Sydney Morning Herald* premises after being released from internment in August 1942, so it is unlikely that anyone at the Yabber Club did. Stephensen said that Panton, unlike Caiger, was not an *agent provocateur*. According to Hall, the CIB had an agent in the Yabber Club from 1937.[8] He cites no authority, but they would certainly have tried to place somebody there.

Stephensen testified before the Clyne Inquiry that no Japanese, German or Italian nationals attended the Yabber Club, but that was not strictly true. Joosten attended a Yabber meeting, introduced by Miles, and Stephensen knew that, for he denied at the Clyne Inquiry that Joosten 'used to' go to the Yabber Club, as he had been only once.[9] On 2 June 1938, after dinner, Joosten discussed the situation in Germany with Hooper, Miles and an unidentified third person. He explained how Commercial Councils promoted trade, and he supported the closing of private schools and the restrictions on churches and Jews, which seemed very reasonable to the Rationalist Hooper.[10] On 27 April 1939, while returning home aboard the tanker *Ulysses*, he wrote to ask Hooper to convey his regards to 'all my friends at the Yabber Club'.[11]

The Japanese avoided giving the appearance of a close association with Stephensen. Thus, when the British-Oriental Association was founded in August 1939, the Japanese Consulate told Hugh Millington to make membership subject to acceptance by a committee, and to ensure that neither Percy Stephensen nor Tom Walsh was accepted.[12]

Apart from permanent invitees, who attended the Yabber Club, and what, according to Agent 222, did they discuss? Obviously, discussions of cultural activities were not the subject of his reports.[13] He usually gave an attendance list, though he did not always know everybody present. The attendance list for 11 July 1940 was fairly typical. It listed Miles, Hooper, Stephensen, Crowley, Elldridge, Cook, Kenny, Lang, Ludowici, and Timmerly. The first four have already been mentioned.

John C. Eldridge was an ex-serviceman living in Mosman. On

18 February 1941 he wrote a rather unwise letter to Consul-General Akiyama congratulating him on his views as published in the *Sydney Morning Herald* that day.[14] It is not known if he was the Eldridge who associated with Mills in the Odinist Society in Melbourne.[15] L. Kenny was a retired jockey, about whom nothing further is known. 'Timmerly' was probably James Francis Timmony of Cremorne, AFM Member No. 21.

'Cook' was undoubtedly Kenneth Easton Cook, an undercover agent reporting mainly to Naval Intelligence. It would have been interesting to see if his reports tallied with Panton's, but they are not available. His main targets were Japanese businessmen and consular staff, but he also watched the Yabber Club, Stephensen and other *Publicist* people.[16] His activities were unknown to the CIB, which reported that the reputation of 'Eastern-Cook' was 'most unsavory' from a Security aspect.[17] In early 1941, Miles's friend, Colonel Graves, told Isabel Wilkins, secretary to the Domei representative in Sydney, that Cook had been followed and questioned about his activities.[18]

'Lang' was Prosper Cologne Lang, a young accountant colleague of Miles. He was Member No. 15 of the AFM and later helped run a speakers' class. A prominent member of the Australian Natives Association (ANA) and chairman of the ANA Luncheon Club formed in Sydney in January 1941, he was the link between it and the AFM. There was some overlap of members between the two groups; Hooper, Crowley, Ludowici and Watts attended the Luncheon Club and might have been ANA members. Although the groups had some things in common, the ANA did not support fascism, but there was a danger that Yabber Club members could have too much influence on its policy. Sensing the incompatibility of the groups, Hooper wrote to Salier that six of them had joined the ANA luncheon group and 'we may have some fun before being kicked out'.[19]

'Ludowici' was Richard Egon Ludowici, AFM Member No. 34. He worked from premises in the Grace Building, 77 York Street, Sydney, the building that housed the Japanese Consulate-General. It is not known how he was connected with Charles Ludowici, who was on the Committee of the Sane Democracy League. This League was anti-communist and had a reputation for being pro-Japanese and pro-fascist.[20]

Most of what Agent 222 reported was just talk, uninhibited expressions of opinion sometimes unwise in wartime. Spread over years, most were fairly insignificant. Strung together in a file that would be read in an hour, and taken as an indication of a person's true feelings, they looked quite damning. At the Clyne Inquiry, various excuses were offered: remarks had been taken out of context; they were merely meant to provoke discussion; they had not been said at all. Despite denials, most statements probably were made. People may sincerely deny having said things, even when confronted with transcripts or tape recordings only days later.

On 13 June 1940, Stephensen allegedly said that Japan would soon bring to a head the position regarding the ban on exports of iron ore from Yampi Sound, and would open up the ore deposits, 'Jews or no Jews'. As something similar had appeared in the *Publicist,* he probably did say this.[21] Crowley said that the sooner England was bombed, the better. Masey allegedly recommended that members read *Mein Kampf,* as it was the only worthwhile political philosophy, and declared that 'a defeatist feeling was whipping up in his office and he was adding fuel to it where it was safe'.[22] A fortnight later, Crowley claimed that he had been engaging in subversive activities, but Miss Kelly of the *Bulletin* had threatened to report him, while Lang said that he had been getting favourable comments on the AFM and the *Publicist,* until he mentioned that National Socialism was part of the platform. Crowley often left copies of the *Publicist* lying around the city for people to pick up.[23]

Miles said in November that nearly everyone interested in an AF Party was of Irish descent, but as so many Australians have some Irish ancestry, it is debatable whether, except in Melbourne, Irish representation in the AFM was significant. After listening to Hitler's speech on short-wave radio, Stephensen claimed on 12 December that he had understood most of it and agreed with Hitler's denunciation of capitalists and business profiteers. Miles predicted there would be a revolt in England, and he would not be surprised if Churchill were assassinated.[24] Early in January 1941, Stephensen said, 'The Japanese desire to create a new order in East Asia and that means they only want each country to have what areas actually belong to them.' (What, then, were they doing in Korea, Manchuria, China and Indo-

China?) On 16 January, Miles mentioned sending press cuttings to a Tokyo newspaper.

A report from a different source confirmed in a general way what Agent 222 reported. Victor Le Roy Alldis, a registered surveyor living in Young, had written articles on soil conservation for the *Publicist*, and while in Sydney for Christmas 1940 he visited the Yabber Club. Learning of his visit, a representative of MI sought him out on 20 January and obtained a statement that included the following:

> The general tone of conversation was a prevailing subversive and defeatist one.
>
> Stephenson [*sic*] appears pronouncedly pro-Japanese... Miles continually asserts that England is certain to be defeated and offered to bet 10:1 that it would be so...
>
> Stephenson, in re the Japanese, said that they were forming a New Order and appeared to imply that they should be allowed to form it... Anti-British separatist talk was much in evidence, especially from Miles and Crowley. Stephenson also supported same.[25]

MI commented that a 'sound contact' substantiated what Alldis reported, but he could not be used as a prosecution witness, as his future value would be lost. This shows that prosecutions were being considered.[26] MI recommended that the *Publicist* should not be allowed to continue, and that simultaneous searches be made on the premises of those involved, *in Southern and Western Command*, as well as Eastern Command. On the other hand, Detective Sergeant John William Swasbrick of MPI reported that Miles was eccentric rather than dangerous, and political rather than subversive.[27]

Crowley remarked on 13 February, 'Wherever the British flag has flown it has brought poverty, corrugated iron and dirt... Churchill is the greatest calamity that has ever fallen on Britain. I am not a Britisher.' Stephensen added that the British race was decadent because of Jewish influence. On 20 February, Stephensen produced a letter from the Australia-American Cooperation Movement and ridiculed the movement. Next week, Miles applauded Matsuoka's 'brilliant piece of diplomacy' that was too clever for British and American diplomats. He said that he sent *Publicist* articles to Akiyama, adding, 'Of course the Publicist is well known to all Japanese here.'

On 1 May, he praised the Japanese Minister to Australia, Tatsuo Kawai, as an astute diplomat, who had manoeuvred Sir Frederick Stewart into saying things that left him 'wide open'.[28]

On 3 April, Crowley said that Ireland had secured its independence through courage and determination, implying that Australia might have to fight Britain. Other Yabber Club members urged him to use more tact, but he revelled in boasting that people threatened to report him. MI officers reading Panton's reports were appalled. It was felt that Miles, Stephensen and Crowley accepted that the defeat of Britain would be the best chance for Australia to gain 'independence' as they saw it.

Agent 222 reported on 14 April that Watts had a heated argument with Miles and Stephensen. Watts abhorred the virulence of some *Publicist* articles; he joined, left and re-joined the group several times. Accusing Stephensen of being 'pedantic and yellow', and simply living off the *Publicist* and Miles's money, Watts virtually severed his connection with the AFM and the *Publicist*.[29] After an article in March, he wrote no more until September. He allegedly agreed to report to MI anything he heard that was disloyal or subversive.[30] This was probably true, as Dora Watts testified that Captain Blood had visited them in 1940 or 1941, and Martin had made a statement to him.[31] Salier too fell out with Stephensen, writing him a hostile letter on 23 January.[32]

When Lang commented on 1 May that people were turning off the BBC news because it told lies, and listening to German stations to hear 'the truth', Stephensen added that Germany could tell the truth, because she was winning. Hooper read out a letter from Morley Roberts on 29 May; they lamented that his book *Bio-Politics*, often quoted in the *Publicist*, had not sold well. That is not surprising, for a possibly tenable argument was lost amid rambling verbiage, with so many rare words that Stephensen compiled a glossary. Its central theme was that life is a constant process of dying and rebirth, whether of a single cell, an individual or a nation, and war is a natural part of this process: 'To call war unreasonable is just about as justifiable as to call insanity, crime, disease, surgery, and cure unreasonable.'[33] Roberts writes that the Jews are 'foreign bodies' in other nations, and have to be encapsulated in ghettos, immured or ejected.[34]

Agent 222 reported on 2 June that Clive Evatt, Minister for Education in the New South Wales Government and younger brother of Dr H. V. Evatt (soon to be Minister for External Affairs and Attorney-General), had spoken at the Yabber Club on educational reforms he hoped to introduce, saying:

> This community is a low-class community. The overwhelming majority of Australians have no responsibility to this land and everyone believed that something should be done about it. The reason we have such a bad educational system is that it was designed by Englishmen around about 1886 to make good cannon fodder for colonial wars.[35]

Cahill arrived in Sydney on 16 June and at the meeting of 19 June he explained the situation in Melbourne. Later he told a 'reliable person' that the aim was to establish an Australia-First Movement for the general public, then they would *establish an Inner Group*.[36] Cahill apparently intended to be a key figure in this inner group that, in keeping with his communist background, he called a Council of Seven.[37] At the meeting of 9 July, J. H. Rhodes, also from Melbourne and a former member of the old Socialist Club, advocated the 'gentle feeding of the public *with the mild stuff* to secure interest and support', for the *Publicist* was antagonising the very people it wanted to attract. Crowley said that it was no use to suggest this to Miles.

To return to Agent 222 and other undercover agents: Hall suggests that a CIB agent was interned with the Sydney group.[38] Only sixteen men were arrested in Sydney in connection with the AFM, and nobody seems to fit the bill. Stephensen, Val Crowley and Hooper must be rejected, because they had for years been convinced of their cause. Edwin Arnold was too erratic and unreliable. Most others were either not involved early enough or did not attend often enough, and the only theoretical possibilities seem to be Masey and Salier, who have already been mentioned, and Walter Frederick Tinker-Giles. None seems likely, but none can be ruled out totally. If, however, the agent was *not* interned but merely visited internees, then Malcolm Smith is a possibility and Lang can also not be ruled out.

In March 1940, **Walter Frederick Tinker-Giles**, born at Camperdown, New South Wales, on 24 March 1906, had left school at fourteen. A self-made small businessman, he owned three shoe stores in the St Peters-Newtown district by 1941. Married, with four children, he was not an agitator or polemicist. The fact that he used the name 'Giles' in business dealings and 'Tinker' within the AFM seemed suspicious, but there was a simple reason. At birth he had been registered as the son of William and Caroline Jane Giles. His parents divorced, and his mother married Alfred Tinker. At the time of his marriage, he obtained his birth certificate, and found that his Christian names were entered as 'Walter Frederick Tinker'. He did not draw the conclusion that, if his mother gave him the Christian name 'Tinker' while she was still married to Giles, and later married Tinker, then Tinker was his father. His staff did not open mail addressed to 'Tinker', for that was private correspondence.[39] MI drew sinister conclusions in a purely personal matter.

Seeing advertisements for *Capricornia* and *Foundations of Culture in Australia* in a *Publicist* he had bought from a news agency, Tinker went into the Publicist shop to buy them.[40] Miles accosted him, asked if he was interested in Australian culture, and invited him to the Yabber Club. Tinker said later he attended about eight times in eighteen months.[41] Miles or Hooper or Crowley often used a customer's interest in *Capricornia* to entice him into the Yabber Club. He would seem an unlikely informant, except for two oversights in documents. The first was that he was never mentioned in Agent 222's reports as being present although, according to Security, he attended about one in three meetings – about one in nine according to Tinker. The second was that someone wrote in ink in small, neat script at the top of a report, 'Tinker-Giles presence never mentioned.' Somebody else had crossed out the note with a thick blue censor's pencil, but it could still be read. It looked as though this person knew why Tinker was not mentioned. If he was not an undercover agent, this is a little puzzling.

There is evidence that there were in the AFM other agents who were not interned. Justice Clyne asked about someone whose name was passed around in writing. He had allegedly spoken from the platform at an AFM meeting in Sydney, but he still cannot be identified. It cannot have been Ken Cook, for he neither spoke at a meeting nor joined the AFM.[42] Undercover agents were not meant to be identified. Sometimes their cover was broken when they appeared in court; sometimes they talked too much to the wrong people; but it is usually only when a mistake is made that identification is possible.

Then there was Frank Clune. In June 1938, Lieutenant-Colonel W. J. R. Scott of MI had 'an amazing talk' with Clune. He told Brigadier Bertrand Combes that he thought Clune could be 'made use of', and Clune had asked to be put in touch with MI. Recently returned from Singapore, he had travelled widely in China, Japan and Manchuria where, as an author, he had been able to ask questions. Scott wrote, 'I think he will be a most useful fellow.' There is no record as to whether Clune in fact became useful.[43]

An unknown informant reported that the Yabber Club was 'of no assistance either to the enemy or Australia, but is a futile group of old men whose theories were not to be taken seriously'.[44] Mere attendance at the Yabber Club was not considered grounds for internment, but what people had allegedly said there was used as supporting evidence when making out a case for internment.

Chapter 5

The Walshes

Adela Walsh was not a natural ally of Miles or Stephensen. Miles told Masey that she was a woman 'with the utmost contempt for the truth'.[1] Perhaps she did not intend to lie, but whatever she said became the truth for her, irrespective of the gap between that and the facts.[2] Miles and Stephensen rejected Imperial ties with Britain in favour of narrow Australian nationalism, but Adela was strongly Imperialist. Miles viewed war as biologically inevitable, while Adela was a pacifist. Their main common cause was an abhorrence of communism, and they viewed Germany, Italy, Spain and Japan as the world's strongest bulwarks against communism.

Adela Constantia Mary Pankhurst Walsh was born in Manchester, England, on 19 June 1885, daughter of suffragette Emmeline Pankhurst. After falling out with her mother and sister, she was sent to Australia, arriving in Melbourne on 27 March 1914. Through Vida Goldstein, she became associated with the Victorian Socialist Party.[3] Suffragette aims had already been achieved in Australia, but at the outbreak of war in August 1914 Adela found a new cause: pacifism. She joined the socialists, including John Curtin, preaching peace at Yarra Bank meetings, and during the anti-conscription campaign she travelled around Australia addressing meetings.[4] When Curtin went to Western Australia to become editor of the *Westralian Worker*, Adela sailed in the same ship, arriving in Fremantle in February 1917. Curtin chaired Adela's meeting on 19 February, when she called for workers to reduce production to force an end to the war.[5] She claimed later that Curtin's views were 'entirely in accord' with hers.[6]

She had little success in Perth, for censorship prevented publicity for her.[7] Returning to Melbourne, she met up again with Tom Walsh, a prominent member of the Seamen's Union. Born in County Cork, Ireland, in January 1871, Walsh was a few months older than Miles. He had little formal education, having gone to sea as a cabin boy at the age of eight. When Adela met him, he had recently been widowed, and he had three small daughters. At various times, he was General President and General Secretary of the Seamen's Union. Tom and Adela married on 30 September 1917.[8]

For her activities in Victoria, which included property damage, she was forced into hiding. Prosecuted several times, she was imprisoned from November 1917 to 10 January 1918.[9] Colonel Jones, head of the CIB, wrote later that Mrs Walsh had deliberately tried to provoke prosecution in order to obtain added notoriety.[10] Adela was sufficiently well acquainted with Miles for him to write in January 1919 to congratulate her on the birth of her son. With the war over, and having a baby to mind, Adela became less active publicly, simply supporting Tom in his union activities and writing for the Seamen's Union magazine.[11]

Adela's next cause was communism. Both she and Tom were present at the meeting on 30 October 1920 when the Communist Party of Australia was founded.[12] They were not as closely involved with the Party as is sometimes thought; Tom claimed that he attended only two party meetings in his life.[13] Adela wrote some articles for the *Australian Communist*, the last being published in January 1922. She enthused, 'Only in Russia are all fed, only in Russia have strikes ceased, only in Russia are children and mothers liberated from labour, only in Russia does production increase.'[14] Oblivious to civil war in Russia, to mass starvation, murder and torture, Adela lost herself in fantasy. Then she drifted away from the party; Tom resigned formally early in 1923.[15]

In May 1923, Tom Walsh obtained a copy of secret instructions to communist cadres, issued in July 1920. He claimed he found then 'that the Communist Party was far more interested in helping the international business of Soviet Russia than in the welfare of the workers of Australia'.[16] Tom became totally disillusioned with communism; he alleged that in July 1924 an agent sent by Bukharin tried to persuade him to undertake secret work to further communist aims:

> I told the messenger I would not agree and, further, unless he was out of Australia within fourteen days I would acquaint the authorities of his presence in the country—he was sensible enough to take my advice.[17]

Walsh gave the agent's name as 'Hercovitski'.[18] He was in fact Rubin Herscovici, a Jew with a Rumanian passport, who arrived in Sydney on 14 September 1923 and travelled around Australia under the pretext of collecting money for the Workers' International Economic Russian Relief. An undercover agent in Brisbane reported that Herscovici told a party meeting that he was in Australia on behalf of the Soviet Government to report on the Communist Party of Australia and *instruct them as to the wishes of Moscow in regard to underground work*. He also collected military information. The CIB reported he was 'dressing his wolf in sheep's clothing to enable him to better hoodwink the Australian worker'. He left for America in July 1924.[19]

Walsh was still classed as a communist, and after the maritime strike of 1925 an attempt was made to deport him. Dr H. V. Evatt defended him, and the Walshes and Evatts became friends. After vicious bickering within the union, Tom was deprived of his union position, then left the union altogether.[20] Tom's conclusion that communism was cynically using Australian workers for the benefit of Soviet Russia left him open to suggestions from Havelock Wilson, President of the British Seamen's Union, regarding the formation of an Industrial Peace Movement. To avoid interception of his letters by authorities, Tom sent letters to Wilson by the 'safe hand' of Seamen's Union members; this was futile, for Wilson handed them over to authorities in Britain. It was known that Wilson sent Walsh substantial sums of money.[21]

Something useful might have emerged from this movement, but the death of Wilson in April 1929 put an end to their plans. Half a century later, Xavier Herbert said that Walsh was a 'bastard of a man', who had been bought off by a shipping company and took money from big companies to destroy a smaller company.[22] Herbert's outburst was not necessarily factual, but he was not alone in this opinion of Walsh.

The Guild of Empire and the *Empire Gazette* provided Adela with a new cause when Tom's union career was destroyed. It was not simply a political organisation, for it did social and charitable work, and it attracted what might now be called 'the blue-rinse set': middle-aged to elderly, financially secure, and inspired do-gooders.

It was founded about July 1929.[23] The published aims of the Guild of Empire were these:

1. To advance the welfare of Australia as a part of the British Empire.
2. To establish industrial co-operation and peace.
3. To combat the doctrines of Communism and all other anti-God movements.
4. To deepen the realisation of the value of British citizenship.
5. To uphold the Christian ideals of life and safeguard the family.[24]

Three of these aims (1, 4 and 5) would have been anathema to Miles. The core of the *Publicist* clique regarded the British Empire as the greatest impediment to the growth of an Australian identity, and Christianity as a plot by Jews to enslave Gentiles. An alliance between them seemed unlikely, but within a few years, the fates of Stephensen and Adela Walsh became intertwined.

Although the Guild was not entirely Adela's creation, she quickly became its salaried campaign director, with control of the Guild's monthly magazine, the *Empire Gazette*, issued from June 1930. It was well printed on quality paper, usually four pages, but its contents appeared mostly trite, didactic and uninspired. From July 1931, Adela also broadcast weekly over station 2GB.[25]

At its peak, the Guild claimed about 8,000 members. Among the office-bearers, only two others are relevant to the AFM: the Patroness, Victoria, Lady Gordon (wife of Sir Thomas Gordon), and the 'Welfare Organizer', Vera Dorothea Parkinson, but several others had important connections. Mrs W. Fairfax and Mrs H. Fairfax were connected with the *Sydney Morning Herald*. Merle Christie, who was Acting President briefly, was the wife of solicitor George Christie, later leader of the Australian Democratic Front, which was sponsored by the CIB and financed from secret funds by the Attorney-General, W. M. Hughes.[26] They were women whose husbands were likely to be associated with either the Old Guard or the New Guard, while Tom Walsh was a member of the New Guard from September 1931 to April 1933.[27] Eric Campbell wrote later of Walsh, '[His] knowledge of the communist set-up in New South Wales, and its affiliations overseas, was both accurate and profound, and a great help to us.'[28]

In 1937 Miles fell out with Adela Walsh. The editorial in the March *Empire Gazette* criticised the *Publicist* for wanting to sever

Empire connections. In July, Miles launched a two-page attack on 'The Amazons of the British Garrison in Australia'. He agreed that America posed a greater threat to Australia than did Japan, but disagreed with the Guild's reliance on Britain, for 'at the moment Australia would need her, Britain *could not* come!'[29] As 'Benauster', he wrote that both the 'British Garrison' and the communists were subversive, and to rely on British aid was stupid and cowardly.[30]

In seeking allies against communism, Adela dragged the Guild into the propaganda orbit of Germany and Japan. She frequently expressed anti-Semitic and anti-communist views and approved of Nazi treatment of Jews and communists, claiming proudly that communists regarded her as their most dangerous opponent.[31] As well as speaking in the Domain, Adela sometimes spoke from a chair in Macquarie Place at lunchtime.[32] The offices of leading Japanese firms overlooked the Place: Mitsubishi and Yamashita (shipping) in Kyle House and Mitsui in Sirius House. Adela was performing under the noses of the managers of Mitsui and Mitsubishi, and they knew how to manipulate her.

The Guild held luncheon meetings at which there were guest speakers. With her wide range of political contacts, Adela attracted interesting speakers. Menzies spoke in June 1939, a few weeks after becoming Prime Minister.[33] She invited German or Japanese speakers only occasionally, but these attracted CIB attention. Arnold von Skerst, editor of *Die Brücke* and an official of the German Chamber of Commerce, spoke at a Guild luncheon early in 1938.[34] Their contact might have begun with a talk that Adela gave over 2UE on 5 December 1937 on Professor Roberts' book, *The House that Hitler Built*. She was not entirely wrong in claiming that the eagerness of German youth to serve their country was admirable, or that the Nazis had 'a wide vision regarding health and welfare of the masses', but she also defended restrictions on Jews.[35] On 8 December, Tom gave Vice-Consul Baron von Stechow a transcript of the lecture and a copy of a 'periodical' (probably the *Empire Gazette*) that contained material on Roberts' book. In return, Stechow gave Tom propaganda literature.[36] Stechow referred the matter to the Consul-General, who ordered that the lecture be printed in *Die Brücke*, if Mrs Walsh was willing, with a short denunciation of the book from the German standpoint as an introduction. As Adela agreed, Stechow sent the material to Skerst, requesting that it be printed 'if possible unabbreviated'.[37]

There was no formal 'cease fire' between Adela and Miles, but she was not attacked again in the *Publicist*. It was soon after *Die Brücke* published Adela's lecture that Skerst addressed the Guild, and it was probably then that he made a donation of £25.[38] This led to an allegation in September 1939 that Adela was a member of the Nazi Party, which had paid her £25. MPI reported that there was no evidence to support this charge.[39]

From the Austrian *Anschluss*, through the Sudetenland crisis and past the invasion of Czechoslovakia, Adela presented the German point of view in the *Empire Gazette* and in talks over 2UE. She was in close contact with the German Consulate-General, which sent copies of the *Gazette* to Berlin.[40] Most of her activities on behalf of Germany were not clandestine, thus the communist *Workers' Weekly* of 7 April could say that the notorious Adela Pankhurst Walsh had 'come out flat-footed for the Berlin-Rome-Tokio war axis', supporting Hitler's claim that unoccupied territories in South Africa, Australia and the Soviet Union, together with Latin America, would give Germany 'living space'.

While many of those associated with the AFM at least tolerated the fascism and anti-Semitism of the *Publicist*, few approved the pro-Japanese stance of the Walshes. There has been speculation as to whether the Walshes, apart from their trip to Japan in 1939-1940, received money secretly from the Japanese. They did. From 17 March 1938, Tom was paid £10 for every pro-Japanese article he wrote for the *Empire Gazette*; he also received £400 in 1941.[41] Adela denied knowing about financial arrangements between Tom and the Japanese, but an investigating officer wrote, 'We find ourselves unable to accept this profession of ignorance, particularly owing to their close association in carrying out the work and to the fact that the money received was used for household expenses.'[42]

Kuramatsu Murai, who had been Consul-General in Shanghai during the incidents in January 1932, lectured at a Guild luncheon on 'My Country' in June 1935.[43] Adela was passed from one Consul-General to the next. Her daughters went skating with the daughters of Torao Wakamatsu, who took office in Sydney on 15 February

1937 after holding a position in the Foreign Office in Tokyo. When he left on 21 May 1939, she was passed on to Masatoshi Akiyama. She told an appeals tribunal in May 1942 that she had often visited the Akiyamas at home.[44] Akiyama had been Secretary to the Foreign Minister, Koki Hirota, in 1935, and Chief of the Intelligence Section of the Foreign Office, 1935–37. Then he had been First Secretary to the Japanese Embassy in Peking, 1937–39, a post said to be a cover for Intelligence activities.[45] The Walshes were being manipulated by skilful operators.

In 1938, Tom submitted a manuscript to Angus & Robertson. Walter G. Cousins of this firm sent it to Wakamatsu on 17 September, saying that it was not a commercial venture, but they would publish it if the Consulate would buy a large number of copies at a reduced price, as in the case of F. Morley Cutlack's book, *Manchurian Arena*. Having probably already seen and approved the manuscript, Wakamatsu agreed, but haggled over the discount price. This book, *The Sino-Japanese Conflict*, was published in 1939.[46] Tom wrote that a new day was dawning for Asia, and Japan would rescue China from misery and ignorance, bringing them well-being and power. A member of the ISGS commented that the book could have been written inside the Japanese Consulate, as it quoted documents and authorities that had obviously been procured from Japan.[47]

Adela also meddled in the *Dalfram* dispute, which began when waterside workers refused to load pig iron for Japan on 15 November 1938. On 16 December, she harangued Port Kembla workers about playing into the hands of the communists, who wanted to embitter relations between Australia and Japan to benefit the Soviet Union. This could have been part of her anti-communist crusade, but she wrote a report on her activities for Masao Shibusawa, president of a Japanese iron and steel firm.[48]

The *Empire Gazette* of May 1939 contained an article advocating friendship with Japan as 'the surest – indeed, the only defence of our White Australia'.[49] Stephensen also claimed that the Japanese would help maintain the White Australia Policy, even though they said repeatedly that the main points of contention between Australia and Japan were the White Australia policy and preferential trade barriers. Even when told this personally, Stephensen and Adela closed their minds to what they did not want to know.

On 6 June 1939, Mitsui gave a private dinner party so that some pro-Japanese Australians could meet Ichiro Oka, Osaka Editor of *Asahi Shimbun*, who had just arrived from Java. These included Stephensen, the Walshes, Hugh Millington (editor of the *Far Eastern Trade Bulletin* of the Japanese Chamber of Commerce) and Major Jack Scott.[50] The Japanese asked that the meeting be kept confidential. They did not know that Scott was in charge of counter-espionage against Japanese in Australia, so a report of what was said at the meeting was in MI hands the next day. Most of what was said is irrelevant to this topic, but Tom Walsh expressed the hope that Japan would interpret International Law 'by force', and Stephensen made a 'passionate speech' supporting Japan in China and denouncing any contrary opinion as coming from Moscow. Oka confirmed that there were two matters on which Japan was adamant, and it was *only if these matters could be satisfactorily arranged that Australia could be said to be free of any thought of Japanese invasion.*

1. Cancellation of White Australia policy, allowing Japanese immigration into Australia.
2. Much more equal trading than in the past.

Despite this, Stephensen continued to assert that Japan would help Australia maintain the White Australia policy. Neither he nor the Walshes seemed to notice the mention of a 'Japanese invasion', for they continued to ridicule the possibility.

Apart from recording what had been said at the meeting, Major Scott reported that Tom Walsh had recently published a booklet giving the Japanese side of the war in China, and it was believed the Japanese had paid him for this.[51] Unfortunately, he also claimed that Stephensen wrote pamphlets for the Japanese under an assumed Japanese name. This was unlikely; Scott might have had in mind works published under the name Miles Cheguin, although this is not a Japanese name.[52] 'Cheguin' was journalist John Harvey Crothers Sleeman. He had been imprisoned for trying to bribe a Queensland politician, and later he had run the gambling rackets (fruit machines and greyhound racing) that kept the Lang Labor Party afloat financially. For three years the Japanese paid him a monthly retainer of sixteen guineas, plus bonuses for secret information.[53] What Stephensen had said and written became interwoven with things for which he was not responsible.

By mid 1939 political and financial support for the Guild was declining, and Adela's support for Hitler in Czechoslovakia and for Japan in China was becoming embarrassing.[54] However, she still had good political contacts. She represented the Guild at a reception after Menzies became Prime Minister in April 1939 and claimed in an interview that in July he had told her to go ahead with her attempts to secure peaceful relations with Japan.[55]

When war broke out in September 1939, the Guild was in financial difficulties, and there was mounting opposition to Adela. In October, the executive asked for her resignation because of a speech she had made in the Domain.[56] At first she refused, but on 13 October police were called to a rowdy meeting where the President, at that time Merle Christie, was in tears and asking for protection. Adela resigned from the Guild, which went into recess and was dissolved on 24 October.[57]

The Walshes were already committed to a trip to Japan, sponsored by the Japanese Government allegedly to promote goodwill. Jisuke Toyoda, Sydney representative of Domei news, might have selected the Walshes for the trip, but the invitation came from the Japanese Chamber of Commerce.[58] They left for Japan on 29 October aboard *Atsuta Maru*. Adela's hectoring ways made enemies for them, and British passengers demanded unsuccessfully that the Walshes be put off the ship at Hong Kong.

In Japan they met the head of the Information Bureau of the Foreign Office, Yokichiro Suma, a suave character who spoke excellent English. This bureau collated espionage material and, perhaps without realising it, the Walshes were recruited as agents, for on their return to Australia they were reporting to Suma. To evade censorship, the Consulate-General sent the reports to Japan with consular mail or by the masters of Japanese ships.[59]

The Walshes returned to Australia in *Kitano Maru* on 15 February 1940. Australian papers, they said, were full of lies. Reporters resent being told they are ignorant and untruthful, and the Walshes were reviled for telling some unpalatable truths. They wrote a report for the Japanese Government on their impressions of Japan and on methods of improving trade with Australia. It was published by the Japan Foreign Trade Federation as a bilingual booklet, *Japan as viewed by Foreigners*, 18 November 1940. The CIB commented that they saw and reported correctly things that were good about Japan, but were totally blind to things that were bad.[60] Thus they could write:

> People who glibly say Japan could conquer the Philippine Islands and then come and conquer Australia can only be speaking of some remote possibility a thousand years hence, but not of present day politics or possibilities.[61]

As the Guild and the *Empire Gazette* had collapsed, the Japanese were getting less value from the Walshes than they expected. Adela claimed later that on returning from Japan she did not have much to do with the Japanese.[62] To some extent this was true, for in May Akiyama reported, 'Since his return he [Tom] has avoided me and has not even observed ordinary politeness.'[63] However, the Walshes attended the Consul-General's reception for Sir John Latham before he took up a diplomatic appointment in Japan.[64] Adela and a friend, Charlotte Graves, were also entertained at the expense of the secret propaganda budget of the Japanese Chamber of Commerce after they distributed official propaganda pamphlets.[65]

The People's Guild and the *Voice of the People* provided Adela with a new power base when she lost her previous support group. In March, she produced a two-page manifesto for a new political party to combat communism. It proposed barring communists from public office and banning the CPA as an agent of a foreign power, and called on Britain to lead a coalition of nations to suppress communism. Germany, she wrote, should be offered membership of this body.[66] What she founded in May 1940, however, was the People's Guild, comprised largely of a few supporters from the Guild of Empire, including Vera Parkinson and Elaine Elizabeth Pope. The Guild's stated aims were:

> (1) To build a united Australian commonwealth within the British Empire.
> (2) To strengthen the Christian ideals of life and safeguard the family.
> (3) Peaceful co-operation of all classes to this end.[67]

Printed on her own duplicator, Adela produced the *Voice of the People*, a small pamphlet that was handed out free at the Domain.[68] It contained praise of Japan, constant tirades against America, and advertisements for Tom's books, including a further booklet, *The New*

Order in Asia, in which he attributed the rising tide of feeling against Japan to Communist Russia. Even such an insignificant publication would receive censorship orders specifying what the Australian Government and the military authorities did not want the enemy to know. These went automatically to the irresponsible Adela. They were still being sent to the non-existent *Voice of the People* after she was interned.[69]

The paper immediately attracted public complaints and Security attention, for its content had little to do with the Guild's aims, and much to do with defending Australia's adversaries and attacking her friends. One article was denounced as 'the most insidious piece of Fifth Column work I have read'. An informant mentioned that Mrs Walsh was poor, and suggested the paper was financed by a foreign power. In October 1940, Adela reminded readers that Prime Minister Lyons had said the country was in danger of invasion: 'We now know from what quarter – from the United States of America.'[70]

Adela wrote that Australia would be incorporated into the United States defence system, although Australia's interests were not threatened in Indo-China or the Dutch East Indies, for 'we have none there, except to trade in wool, wheat and other products with a good customer and a reliable friend, with whom we have had friendly connections for 150 years'.[71] A police report said that every issue contained 'something pernicious'.[72] Copies were sent to the Consulate-General to be forwarded to Japan.[73]

Adela Walsh stood for the Senate in New South Wales in the Federal election of 21 September 1940, receiving only about 1,700 primary votes. The UAP placed her fourth on their voting ticket, after the three UAP candidates.[74] This was a technical device to deny a flow-on of preferences to the ALP rather than an endorsement of Adela.

On 24 September, Adela gave a lecture to the Geography Teachers' Association of New South Wales; issued as a pamphlet called *Conditions in Japan*, this brought her into conflict with censorship authorities. Mindful of the importance of Australia's relationship with the United States, they demanded that one paragraph be deleted:

> Except when the United States took part in the bombardment of Tientsin, she calmly watched the

> Chinese slaughter each other, but immediately Japan attempts to introduce order and protect the lives and property of her own nationals in China, she is instantly singled out by the United States as the 'menace', to overcome which America now calls on Australia for help.[75]

Adela defiantly duplicated it and handed it out on a separate sheet. This confirmed what was known about her from her conduct during World War I: Adela did not hesitate to defy the law flagrantly, and in a crisis she would be a menace.

During 1940–41, Tom wrote long letters to public figures and took copies of his letters and of the replies to the manager of Mitsui.[76] Copies were found among material seized from Mitsui in December 1941. On 24 October, Adela wrote to Menzies and Jack Beasley (Non-Communist Labor Party) to complain about censorship of the *Voice of the People*.[77] An extract of a letter of 22 April to Sir Henry Gullett, Acting Minister for Information, indicates the tenor of Tom's letters. Newspapers, he said:

> assume a license [*sic*] to deliberately incite the animosity of our own people against a neighbour who, for 150 years, has treated us with respect and courtesy and on whose help we had to rely for some measure of protection during the war of 1914-1918…
>
> I assure you that the Communist International, with its headquarters in Moscow, is much more concerned in bringing Britain and Japan into conflict than with the coal strike in Australia.[78]

Some of Tom's letters ran to eleven closely typed pages, and the recipients, if they read them at all, probably did so very cursorily. In an attempt to put an end to a series of harangues, the staff of Jack McEwen, leader of the Country Party, were instructed:

> The Minister will be glad if you will kindly prepare a courteous reply and one that will not provoke another reply or even any discussion. The Minister suggests the reply should be as brief as practicable.[79]

The People's Guild held its final meeting in March 1941.[80] Adela claimed she kept writing circulars until June, then gave up because they were futile.[81] As a result of literature that she handed out in the Sydney Domain on 29 June, a week after Germany invaded the Soviet Union, police searched the Walsh home on 9 July, confiscating some letters and a large quantity of Japanese propaganda. A move was made to prosecute her under National Security Regulations, but this was not followed through.[82] With the failure of the People's Guild, Adela again sought a new cause and source of finance. This time she turned to the AFM. It may not have been entirely her own idea, for several other things happened at about the same time.

Monitored telephone conversations showed that on 1 September Kinji Miwa, manager of Mitsui, took Tom Walsh to meet the Consul-General Itsuo Goto, who had arrived in Sydney in August. Tom called again on 22 September.[83] What they discussed was not known, but several things happened in the next few weeks. Usually Tom Walsh delivered material to Mitsui, but he visited the Consulate-General three times in September–October. There had just been two changes of Government in Australia: from the United Australia Party (Menzies) to the Country Party (Fadden) on 29 August, and to the ALP (Curtin) on 7 October, and the Japanese were suspicious of links between the ALP and Comintern and nervous about its intentions, although the sanctions that wrecked Japanese trade with Australia were imposed by the UAP.

Although the Walshes were allegedly so poor that neither had a bank account, Adela now bought a suburban weekly paper, the *Waverley–Woollahra Standard*, for £50 allegedly borrowed from a lady whom she refused to name.[84] While Victoria Gordon or Charlotte Graves might have lent her money, it must be remembered that the Japanese had paid Tom £400 in 1941. Tom's visits to the Consulate-General and the purchase of the paper fell within a short time span. Coincidence is no proof of causality, but a possible connection cannot be dismissed. The Japanese could quote the paper, however small, as Australian opinion, and it ensured that Adela would continue to receive censorship instructions.[85]

Adela also told Stephensen that she was going to found an Australia-First Movement, with or without him. She had once made the leap from communism to fascism; now she switched from the Guild of Empire, which promoted close ties with Britain, to the AFM, which wanted to break these ties, and her motives are suspect.

The Walshes depended partly on Japanese money, and one might suspect that the Japanese gave Adela the idea that an AFM, with her in a prominent position, would be advantageous.

There is no definite proof that the Japanese funded Adela's purchase of the paper, or that they instigated her move to hasten the establishment of the Australia-First Movement, but it is likely, especially as Adela, through Miwa, kept the Consulate informed about the progress of the AFM. One of the Walshes visited the Consulate-General almost weekly until a few weeks before Pearl Harbor, and Tom was certainly being paid, cash in hand.

On 17 October, Vice-Consul Kenichi Otabe telephoned Walsh and asked him to call at the Consulate-General on Monday (20 October) to meet Shintaro Fukushima, Second Secretary to the Legation in Melbourne.[86] By this time, the preliminary meeting of the AFM had been held, and the Walshes were headed for disaster, dragging the Australia-First Movement with them.

Chapter 6

The Publicist *in Wartime*

The *Publicist* of August 1939 announced that the October issue would contain Hitler's answer to President Roosevelt's requests for guarantees as to Hitler's intentions.[1] With the outbreak of war, not even Miles was brazen enough to be so provocative. On the day war was declared, the words 'NAZI HQ' were painted on the shop window of the Publicist Bookshop.[2] The *Publicist* ceased printing articles in direct support of Hitler and Germany, but still supported many fascist and Nazi policies. Despite returning partly to its 'Australianity', it now attracted more official notice and public hostility.

The October *Publicist* carried a 'Benauster' article on 'This New War of Ours', dated 9 September. On the whole, the group did not support the war; heedless of where previous negotiations with Hitler had led, Hooper declared later, 'My view is that the Polish trouble should have been settled by negotiation.'[3] In a longer article, a mixture of vision and unconscious irony, Stephensen referred to 'the true Australian, he who carries in his head a vision of *Australia in the Year Two Thousand*', a barely imaginable future. 'The War will end before Christmas,' he wrote. 'I do not know of what year... If we are to fight against Germany, let us at least fight for an Australian reason, not a Jewish reason.'[4] He stated his position at greater length in December:

> For Australians to take advantage of Britain's difficulty and attempt during war-time to 'bargain' with Britain for concessions (as the Indians are doing) would be despicable... Australians must be prepared, *without expecting much British help*, to defend Australia against any possible attack... We hope that Britain will triumph over Germany; but we do not hope that Jews and Communists will triumph over Germany, for that would amount to the use of British Armed Forces for a non-British purpose. *Jews and Communists are not only*

> *anti-German, they are also anti-British.*[5]

Stephensen commented on the Defence (National Security) Regulations that had been gazetted on 25 August. He said that they had in principle his absolute support:

> During war-time, it stands to reason, any opposition to the Government is likely to be construed as treasonable, inasmuch as any opposition to the Government must, to some extent, be prejudicial to the Government's conduct of the war…
>
> At one stroke, nine days before Australia was at war, all the props of so-called Democracy in our Commonwealth were removed, and the structure fell to the ground. Excuse me, I warned you…
>
> While this war lasts, I advise all loyal subjects of the King in Australia to remain loyal, to obey the laws patiently, and to do everything possible to strengthen Australia, defend Australia, develop Australia, and make Australia safe, secure, prosperous, and victorious.[6]

It is not always easy to know whether Stephensen was being serious or sarcastic. Was he advising people to be loyal for Australia's sake, or to emphasise the draconian nature of some of the regulations? Heedless of his own advice, he wrote that Menzies was 'an egotistical weakling', 'calamitous and dangerous', and 'intellectually and politically unfitted' to be Prime Minister.[7]

The October issue reprinted the Commonwealth White Paper on the causes of the war, fourteen documents setting out letters, notes and verbal exchanges from 22 August to 1 September, and the overt clauses of the Russo-German Pact of 23 August.[8] A few weeks later, Stephensen wrote privately, 'The campaign is not against the King, but against the English politicians and others who are trying to use Australia as a pawn in their game… Republicanism is only a red-herring.'[9] Miles was opposed to a republic for Australia, and the AFM was not a republican movement.

Stephensen often claimed that 'Australia-First' was a *Movement*, not a *Party*, but from October 1939 to April 1940 the *Publicist* ran this advertisement on its back page:

MEN WANTED!

> Australian men, with public spirit and Parliamentary ambition, between 28 and 49 years of age, are invited to communicate personally with 'The Publicist', with a view to the formation of an Australia-First Political Party after the War.

At about this time, Miles and Stephensen drew up a Fifty-Point Policy that appeared in the *Publicist* of May 1940. Stephensen sometimes called it his 'Fifty-Point Porcupine'.[10] It was meant to make people think, and also to annoy them. Many points were harmless or vague; some were desirable; but attention focussed on Point 6: 'For national socialism; against international communism.' Stephensen tried to explain that he did not mean Nazism, for Hitler had no copyright on the words 'national' and 'socialism'. On 13 July, Stephensen wrote to Mudie, 'Like Petain, I will be called in at the death-bed, after the collapse of the British Garrison, not before.' Munro comments, 'The implication was that Stephensen would likewise make an accommodation with an invading enemy.'[11] Special Branch investigated the *Publicist* in July, and compiled a report condemning it as 'a medium of dangerous anti-British propaganda'.[12]

Miles, Stephensen and Walsh did not recognise that in time of war some simple rights must to be forgone temporarily: the right to go for a car drive when you felt like it, the right to take photographs at certain places, the right to turn on outdoor lights, the right to consume whatever goods you could afford, to travel where you wanted, to live in peace at the place of your choice. The right to say and to write whatever you thought, regardless of consequences, also had to be limited.

Stephensen encouraged the AFM in Melbourne to campaign against Menzies in his electorate of Kooyong, holding a 'Monster Public Meeting' with the slogan 'One Flag! One People! One Parliament!' They hoped to win Kooyong 'to the banner of Australia First'. The meeting was not as large as hoped, and the slogan sounded like *Ein Volk! Ein Reich! Ein Führer!*[13] Miles supported A. Rud Mills, who opposed Harold Holt in Fawkner, as Mills 'gives public support to some of the most basic contentions of The Publicist'. He added, 'This Federal Election will probably be the last fought on party lines.'[14] In the same issue, Stephensen called Evatt:

> a man out-standing in intellectual ability, scholarship, and public spirit—qualities which are becoming sadly conspicuous by their absence, not only in the Labour [*sic*] Party, but in all other parliamentary parties in these days of the Australian Democratic Deadend.[15]

However, in the same edition Watts lamented that the ALP, once 'rich in vigour, and full of hope and young promise', had become senile. 'The A.L.P. is now the exact replica of the weak, cowardly, lickspittle, whining Labour Party of England.'[16] Miles wrote that the sectional principle of Labor Parties was dangerous.[17] In March, Stephensen began writing about a New Order of Australia-First replacing the Old Order.[18] In May he returned to the theme:

> The men who have actually changed history, and instituted New Orders, have been rough, crude, unlettered fellows, such as Attila, Genghis Khan, Cromwell, Napoleon, and (whether we like it or not), Corporal Hitler, the 'House-painter', a self-taught man.[19]

This is fallacious, for it overlooks Buddha, Christ, Mahomet, Confucius, Columbus, Martin Luther, Karl Marx, none of whom was crude or unlettered, and whose influence outlasted that of the warlords. A thousand copies of the 'Fifty Points' were printed as a booklet, but they remained empty words with no practical plans for implementation. Stephensen wrote again in November on Unity and Independence as Natural National Aims, saying that democracy was a farce. 'The time has arrived for the inauguration of a New Era, a New Order.'[20] The term 'New Order' was not original; Hitler was developing a New Order, Japan was spreading its New Order through Asia, and the Social Credit Movement had adopted the term 'New Era'. It was not easy to find a stirring slogan that was not already in use.

In April, the domestic political orientation of the *Publicist* changed. Miles attacked Jack Beasley and said that Menzies had 'done well' in setting up the Advisory War Council, while Cahill attacked the factional strife in the ALP.[21] In July, Stephensen wrote that the *Publicist* was trying to form a nucleus for an Australia-First Political Party after the war, adding that the end might not be far off, for Britain was hard pressed on all fronts.[22] The February edition noted that the phrase 'Australia First' was being used by politicians as diverse as Jack Lang and Arthur Fadden.[23]

Anti-Semitism and Anti-Communism went hand in hand for the fascists. In November 1939, Stephensen pointed out the 'farcical situation' in which communists found themselves, but his own situation was farcical enough. The Russo-German Pact made fools of fanatics on both sides of the political fence.[24] He was probably not in earnest when in December he told Matthews he was going to give up the *Publicist* and go into politics.[25] The November issue contained extracts from a book by Miles's friend, the architect Hardy Wilson. Blaming Jews for causing the Victorian Government to veto his appointment as Director of the National Art Gallery in Melbourne in 1936, he attacked them so savagely that the book could not be published while censorship lasted.

'The Jew is the drone of humanity,' wrote Wilson. The drone did no creative work, but its occasional presence was necessary to breed new life and fertilise new creativeness:

> Jews refuse to become tillers of the soil, because their parasitical instinct cannot be overcome... Jews were responsible for the crisis of 1938 in Czechoslovakia, as they were for that in Australia.[26]

Wilson complained that a Jew had led Australia to war in 1914–18, and a Jew was head of Australia when the financial crisis began. This contrasted with Stephensen's praise of Monash and Isaacs in *Foundations of Culture in Australia*, and it is hard to see how Monash could be blamed for the assassination of the Archduke Franz Ferdinand, or Isaacs for the Wall Street collapse. Near the end of the chapter he wrote, '[All] the fuss about the Jews being persecuted is rubbish. But the Jews control Australia.'[27]

In February 1940, commenting on *Australia and the Jews*, a booklet by L. P. Fox,[28] Miles dealt with the 'Jewish question', using the section headings in the booklet. To Sections 3, 4 and 5, where Fox asked whether Jews controlled Australia, the Press and World Finance, Miles replied, 'No, but their influence is disproportionate to their number.' He set out other headings, with a brief comment, for example:

(9) Is the Nazi Race Theory Scientific?

Yes, fundamentally.

(10) Is there an Australian Aryan theory?
Yes, the Australian Aborigines class as Aryans.

(11) What are the Protocols of the Elders of Zion?
A brilliant exposition of Jewish aims and ways.

(21) What Disabilities do Refugees Suffer?
Their just deserts as sinners.

(22) What should be our Attitude to Refugees?
Uncompromising hostility – the Germans are right in this.

(26) What is the Solution to the Jewish Problem?
There can be none while a Jew lives.[29]

This response became deservedly notorious. How could it not be taken that the *Publicist* did not advocate the physical extermination of the Jews? Watts also wrote that he had no personal grudge against the Jews, for he had met Jews he liked and respected, but he disliked the race as a whole.[30] Miles closed the *Independent Sydney Secularist* after April 1940, its 59th number. Its main purpose was to attack Jews, and the censor would no longer permit this. The April issue contained a circular to subscribers saying that its viewpoint would be expressed in the *Publicist*.[31]

The *Publicist* took over Miles's anti-Semitism from April, when he wrote that Jews formed foreign groups by voluntarily practising virtual segregation.[32] He mentioned an article by Stephensen, 'The Reasoned Case Against Semitism', in the *Australian Quarterly*, the magazine of the Australian Institute of Political Science.[33] Stephensen contended that the Jews created the 'Jewish problem', and only they could remedy it. They should intermarry and cease to be Jews: 'the Jewish Race should abolish itself, by becoming absorbed in the common stream of mankind'.[34] As with Point 11 of the Fourteen Points, with regard to Aborigines, this entailed cultural ethnocide. In any case, Hitler decreed that Jewishness was a matter of race, and race could not be renounced.

Stephensen continued to attack Jews: 'The fact that the Jews encourage decadence among Gentile Nations does not mean that Jews are themselves decadent.'[35] The tenor of these attacks had repercussions. In the House of Representatives on 17 April, Eric Harrison asked if the Acting Minister for Information had seen the seditious and disloyal articles in the *Publicist*, and what action he would take. Sir Henry Gullett replied that such articles would not appear again.[36]

As a result, the *Publicist* was ordered to submit all copy in duplicate for censorship.[37] Munro writes that only four other papers were so restricted, two of them communist, and that the censor deleted a number of anti-Semitic articles.[38] Kirtley's article on the weakness of the Maginot Line was also banned.[39] Censorship in fact protected the *Publicist.* Although there were calls to prosecute Stephensen for objectionable material, no prosecution would have succeeded in connection with material that the censor had passed. Miles wrote that he did not know if the *Protocols of Zion* were authentic or not, but they revealed 'the methods by which the Jews exercise an influence among Gentiles far in excess of *what could be expected from their numbers*'.[40] Stephensen naively believed they were authentic, and even in private wrote accordingly.

Much of the May edition covered Stephensen's suit against the *Workers' Weekly* for the article of April 1939. G. J. O'Sullivan, who had attended the Mitsui private reception in July 1939, appeared for Stephensen, who admitted he had been a communist during 1921–26 and said, 'As I view it now, after fourteen years, I think I was a silly fool to be a Communist.' O'Sullivan summed up: 'It was for a Russian reason, not for an Australian reason, that Defendants had attacked the Plaintiff.' The jury found against both the publisher and printer, awarding Stephensen one farthing on each count.[41]

When Cahill began submitting reports on the Melbourne AFM, Stephensen wrote back to 'Dear Fellow-Worker Cahill'. He said that he had never written before, but in fact he had sent Cahill a letter on 3 October 1939. Stephensen argued that 'democracy' brought nothing but chaos, bloodshed and hypocrisy, and a Jewish Secret Society had been fostered in 18th Century France in order to destroy European civilisation. [42]

The communists, most of whose newspapers were already banned, called for the suppression of the *Publicist,* but it was the Communist Party that was declared illegal on 15 June 1940. Stephensen approved, writing to Mudie that in an emergency the Government had a duty to suppress agents of a foreign power. He did not imagine that these powers would later be used against him.[43]

In January 1941, Stephensen attacked Max Harris,[44] and he

asked Mudie to get Rex Ingamells and others to declare themselves as Australians supporting Mudie, or as 'Jew-dupes' supporting Harris:

> Of course the Jews *hate* Nationalism! Unfortunately, the censor won't let us have a go at them in 'The Publicist', as this is a Jew-war; so I'm biding my time at present on the Jewish question. Our turn will come.[45]

Stephensen prepared an annotated list of the '53 public topics' covered by the magazine. This included the 'Jewish Problem', which he said was created by the Jews in their desire to preserve their racial purity.[46] In the same issue he attacked the Australian Broadcasting Commission for sponsoring a series of lectures on 'Conflict', alleging that about half the books prescribed for study were written by Jews, some lecturers had Jewish names, and it looked like part of the 'Secret Plan' of Zionist fanatics to dominate Gentile Nations.[47] From reading the *Publicist* during the war, it might be thought that Stephensen and Miles had relented a little about anti-Semitism, but Stephensen's letter to Mudie and a letter by Miles made it clear that their attacks on the Jews moderated only because the censor would not pass them.[48]

Support for the Japanese continued in the *Publicist* after war broke out, still cordial but less effusive. The issue of February 1940 contained a congratulatory message on Japan's 2,600th Anniversary, short in comparison with the article the previous year.[49] In May Stephensen wrote to Vice-Consul Kenichi Otabe asking for a job for Jack Lockyer with the Japanese Commercial Service. Otabe sent the letter to Kinichi Sohno of Kanematsu, but the outcome was not favourable.[50] Threats of boycotts of Japanese goods meant that trade with Japan was uncertain. The letter was mentioned at the Clyne Inquiry;[51] Stephensen's recollections of Otabe and Sohno seemed vague. There was no need for Stephensen to ask the Japanese for help. Jobs were no longer scarce, and he had friends able to help Lockyer. They had little difficulty finding a job for Cahill when he moved to Sydney. MI knew what Stephensen did not know: Otabe's task was to handle agents of influence or any other potentially useful Australians,[52] so anybody in contact with him was suspect.

The *Publicist* welcomed the arrival of the Japanese Minister Tatsuo Kawai in Australia.[53] No other diplomat had been welcomed, but perhaps no *Publicist* representative had been invited to other official receptions. Stephensen complained that Australia had sent a representative to the government of Chiang Kai-shek in Chungking, but none to the (Japanese-backed) government of Wang Ching-wei in Nanking.[54] After August 1941, little more comment on Japan appeared in the *Publicist*.

In February 1942, Xavier Herbert returned to Sydney. He was clearly no longer reading the *Publicist*, for he did not know the office had been moved. On meeting Val Crowley in the street he asked what had happened. Some of what passed between them is recorded in a report made by Helen Mabel Humphries, a National Emergency Service Warden, who was rostered to the post in Crowley's house.[55] Crowley allegedly told her:

> A friend of mine is setting out for the north of Australia and is going to live amongst the aboriginal tribes, so as he can study how the Japanese treat Australia when they land, and if the Japs treat Australia better than the mongrel breed living here at present, he will join them and help them.[56]

At the Clyne Inquiry, Crowley denounced this story as 'Pure nonsense… Pure fabrication',[57] but independent evidence shows it was true in essence. Humphries did not know that Crowley's friend was Herbert, so she could not have invented a phrase that he often applied to Australians: 'mongrel breed'. She could not have known that Herbert had close connections with the Japanese, that he had been the only non-Japanese member of the Darwin Japanese Society, that its president had in 1938 commended him to the Consul-General in Sydney as being pro-Japanese and anti-British, or that Herbert would write later of the intention of his *alter ego*, Alfie Candlemas, to join the Japanese in Timor.[58]

As she did not know enough to invent this conversation, it must have happened. Crowley's denial is not plausible; if one gives him the benefit of the doubt and accepts that he had forgotten, then it must be allowed that he might have been wrong when he denied saying things reported by Agent 222. MI was concentrating so much on Crowley that nobody asked, 'Who was this friend?'

Publicist support for Japan during 1940–1941 was not conspicuously injudicious, but in public speeches and private letters some AFM members gave greater support, which was taken to reflect on all those involved.

Support for Fascist and Nazi Policies continued during the war, for one of Skerst's aims was to have Australians accept at least some Nazi policies as justified, so that they would continue to support them of their own accord. The extent to which these were acceptable is a moral and philosophical question; that support for them, at that time, was construed as sympathy with the enemy is historical fact.

In November 1939, Stephensen wrote to his brother Eric (whom he often addressed as 'Rik') two significant letters. It is unlikely that Stephensen's mail was being intercepted then, so they were probably found among Eric Stephensen's property.[59] In one letter he wrote, no doubt in continuation of a discussion on eugenics:

> The Christian sentimentality, which opposes the judicial slaughter of imbeciles, is responsible for much suffering and expense to the people who have to look after such monstrosities. We must get rid of Christian sentimentality![60]

By the end of the 20th Century, ultra-sound scans of the foetus *in utero* to allow termination of pregnancy in cases of obvious malformations had become commonplace. In the 1930s and 1940s, it smacked too much of Nazism, although other countries, tacitly at least, allowed doctors to kill infants with serious defects.

Not all mail to and from Australia was censored, but in Britain and Australia certain individuals were singled out for attention. Thus a copy of a letter from Miles to the Arnold Leese, picked up in England, was sent to the CIB on 27 August 1940: 'Although we are restricted in 'The Publicist' *we are continuing our anti-Jew propaganda otherwise* and will again use our 'Publicist' to attack as soon as we can.'[61]

In December 1940, having imported a hundred copies of Roberts' book, *Bio-Politics,* for sale, Miles gave it wide publicity.[62] Sir Frederic Eggleston reviewed the book,[63] saying that Roberts was 'a perfect Hitlerite, and his followers in Australia... should acknowledge that they are preaching a Nazi philosophy'. 'Benauster' savaged him, saying he was 'showing his utter incompetency for such a biological-philosophic job'.[64] However, German rights to *Bio-Politics* had been sold for a substantial sum, so the Nazis must have thought it useful.[65]

Reviewing the steps taken to form an AF Party, Stephensen lamented the lack of a hereditary ruling class in Australia. He wrote to Cahill on 4 August that they were not attacking the monarchy 'for a start', as it would antagonise too many people, and there was a great deal to be said for Monarchism. 'Surely you do not hold up President Roosevelt as a superior product to the Emperor of Japan!'[66] He advocated the Rule of the Best: '[The] Best must select themselves, not wait to be selected… The Best are the hardest, the strongest, the bravest: the far-sighted.'[67] This too was a Hitlerian precept. Self-selection, however, produces a Hitler, a Stalin, an Idi Amin, a Pol Pot or a Saddam Hussein more often than a Mahatma Gandhi or a Nelson Mandela.

THE PACIFIC WAR

The first issue of 1942 was the first under the Stephensen's control and the first after Japan's attack on Pearl Harbor. He wrote that the USA and Japan were so far apart that it was difficult to see how either could decisively damage the other, so the Pacific war would be largely a matter of 'skirmishes between outposts'.[68] The distance from Yokohama to Sydney, he pointed out, was 4,200 miles by the shortest sea-route, but in fact this was not as important as the distance from the Caroline Islands to New Guinea. Stephensen conceded that there was 'nothing for honorable Australians to do except to stand loyally by their Government, to help their Government in all things relating to the conduct of the war'.[69] That did not deter him from making savage and at least partly unjust attacks on the Government during the following weeks.

Miles died on 10 January 1942. On hearing the news, Cookes wrote to Stephensen, 'Mr Miles foresaw what was coming to Australia. How he would have liked to be here now that we have reached the critical stage.'[70] The February edition contained a lengthy obituary on 'John Benauster', but did not name him as Miles, 'in accordance with his wishes'.[71] This was futile, as the previous edition, mentioning the change of ownership and the need for finance, named Miles as former sole proprietor and editor, while Kirtley wrote a 'Sonnet in

Memory of William John Miles'.[72]

There were changes of format in February. In the upper left corner of the first page, there now appeared a statement of *Publicist* policy: 'An independent, non-sectional, organ of Australian public opinion, advocating Australian National Unity and Self-reliance, and the greatest possible measure of Australian Independence and Self-defence'. On the back cover was a 'Manager's Page' written by either Hooper or Crowley, while Hooper looked after finance and kept the cash book.[73]

The last issue, March 1942, was called the 'Strategy Number'. On 4 February, Forde repeated what Casey had said two years earlier: 'If England goes down, Australia will go down.' Stephensen objected: 'The Casey-Forde metaphor is not only pessimistic but fallacious.' He wrote that it would have been more appropriate if Forde had said, 'Even if England goes down, Australia will NOT go down' or 'If England goes down, Australia will go down *fighting*.'[74] Forde might also have said, 'If Rabaul goes down, Australia goes down', for that at least made sense. Stephensen attacked Forde for the state of Rabaul's defences, writing that he should 'quit moaning' and 'get out'.[75]

This attack was unjust, for the situation was not Forde's fault. He had been Minister only since 9 October 1941; it would have been impossible, in that time, to recruit and train enough soldiers, or to manufacture or buy and transport heavy guns, and to build foundations and install them. It was even unfair to blame previous governments, as New Britain was mandated territory, and the terms of the mandate forbade all but the most basic defensive measures. If Rabaul had been heavily defended, it would have been by-passed and other places attacked. Forde's resignation would have solved nothing. Nobody in the Labor Cabinet and few in the parliamentary ALP had worthwhile military experience, while the inquiry Stephensen advocated would have given the Japanese useful material for disruptive propaganda.

The criticism smacked of hypocrisy, as Stephensen had insisted that Japan's intentions were peaceful, and no other country was likely to attack New Guinea. In addition, defence preparations are costly, and Miles had complained in 1939, 'Why should the seven-million Australians need to spend enormous sums on defence preparations?'[76]

A letter on the next page attacked Forde's statement of 7 February: 'Many great movements of which I cannot speak are even now under way. Many great decisions secretly made, are being just as secretly carried out.'[77] The letter said that the Australian people were entitled to this information.[78] Australian troops were already returning from the Middle East, and the troops at sea were entitled to secrecy. It was an appalling thought that Stephensen might goad some politician into announcing the transfer prematurely, thus inviting Japanese submarines to sink the troopships.[79]

With little knowledge of current strategic planning and political consultations, writers for the *Publicist* and speakers for the AFM seemed confident that they could run the country and the war better than could the Chiefs of Staff or any politician.

THE SALE OF THE *PUBLICIST*

By 1941 Miles's strength was failing; his finances were not unlimited, and he did not expect the censor to let him write what he wanted. On 24 January 1941, he wrote to Hooper that he intended to suspend the *Publicist* after the June issue.[80] As early as January 1939, Miles had been considering closing the magazine.[81] Each time, he decided to keep going a little longer, but he made no provision to finance it after his death.

In June 1941, Stephensen reviewed the five years of publication. There had been fifty-five different writers for the *Publicist*, of whom thirty-nine wrote under authentic names. Thus sixteen never used their own names.[82] As sixty-three pennames were used, some writers used more than one. He had written ninety-two items under his own name, and fifty-four under aliases, including Rex Williams. At the Clyne Inquiry, he was forced to admit that he had also written as James White and Mary Mulga.[83] The edition contained an alphabetical list of contributors and a list of articles sorted by topic.[84] It sounded like a farewell, but it was not.

Miles, who had been ill for many years, took to his bed on 13 June 1941.[85] Stephensen visited him every day. Miles attended to finance and handled correspondence until about October,[86] but he wrote little more for the *Publicist*. Articles by 'Louis M. Veron' and 'Alcedo Gigas' in the July edition were the last under these names. He might have written the 'Benauster' articles for a little longer. Stephensen, chafing at the way Miles dominated the *Publicist* and bullied him, looked forward to having editorial control, if he could secure finance. In August he wrote to Kirtley that if Miles were to die and leave him penniless, he would still be better off than he had been six years earlier:

> At least now I am free of debt, and I have gained experience and prestige, and I have preserved myself against compromising with the Plutoc-rats and Democ-rats, and their Plutocrotten, Democrotten view of public life and behaviour... As long as he is on deck, I'll play second fiddle. My turn will come, and I have infinite patience.[87]

Although Stephensen told the Clyne Inquiry that Miles expected to recover, by August he had apparently accepted that he was dying. On 25 August, he wrote to Hooper:

> Because the doctor and I agree in thinking that the effects of my attack of dropsy will end my life more or less soon, I think it will be best to give you notice now that I intend the coming December number of 'The Publicist' to be its last.[88]

He asked Hooper, Crowley and Stephensen to confer with him to discuss possibilities, such as selling the *Publicist* to them. If they agreed, he would ask Cookes to help them.[89] Hooper told Justice Clyne that Miles wanted the *Publicist* to continue.[90] In September, Stephensen announced that the editor of the *Publicist* had been taken ill, and there might be changes in the outward form of the magazine, but not in political principles.[91] This issue contained the only article written by Stephensen's brother Eric, a harmless piece on diversification and self-sufficiency in agriculture.[92] The October edition was largely a literary number with little political content.

Miles now decided to sell the *Publicist*. Early in 1940, when Cookes visited Sydney, he offered Miles £100 to help cover losses, but Miles rejected it as unnecessary. Cookes said, 'Well, if it ever does become necessary, let me know.'[93] However, he did not want his name to be known. With the end of Miles's financial support in view, finance from Cookes became necessary. On 27 October, Stephensen wrote to him that they had promises of support to a total of £500, but needed £250 more to keep the paper going for another year.[94] On 29 October, Cookes promised £250 and suggested he might be given shares in the company; if that was not possible, it should be treated as an anonymous donation. Stephensen had scraped together almost enough money to carry on. [95]

Miles apparently did not trust Stephensen with the *Publicist* and wanted somebody more levelheaded to supervise it. Hooper said later that it was Miles's dying request that he help take over the *Publicist.*[96] Miles apparently made a similar request to Salier and Masey, for on 28 October Stephensen wrote indignantly to Crowley asking what right they had to share control. In the end, control went to Stephensen, Hooper and Crowley alone, when on 25 November Miles sold them the *Publicist* for £5.[97] Miles left a substantial estate, but nothing to help keep the *Publicist* going.[98] Cookes had given large sums of money to various causes, including at least £1,000 to the Rationalists to fight 'supernaturalism and hypocrisy'.[99] On 6 January 1942, he authorised Stephensen to collect money from the Union Bank. This letter was intercepted and copied and a note made: 'Letter seen, 8 January; MI/X'.[100]

In December, Stephensen announced that there would be a change of ownership, management and editorship of the *Publicist* from 1 January; on 1 February, the office would move to 5 Hunter Street.[101] On 31 January, a Security Service agent noted that furniture and stock were being moved from 209a Elizabeth Street to 5 Hunter Street in a truck belonging to Gordon Rice, and that Stephensen, Hooper and Crowley were helping in the removal.[102] At the same time, Yabber Club meetings moved to Ann's Pantry.[103]

Opposition to the Publicist policies was not lacking. Almost from its beginning, the CIB had the *Publicist* group under observation, but took little action until the outbreak of war. In October 1939, banks were ordered, in accordance with Regulation 17, to disclose the financial affairs of the *Publicist* and of Miles and Stephensen personally,[104] but there was nothing incriminating to be disclosed.

The CIB and the communists were unlikely allies, but they had common cause in opposing the *Publicist*. Soon after Stephensen's libel suit against the *Workers' Weekly*, Miles and Stephensen granted an interview to a reporter from the *Daily News* (formerly the *Labor Daily*). They should have known better, and they were lucky that the report did not turn out worse, for connected with both the *Daily News* and the *Workers' Weekly* (by then the *Tribune*) was Rupert Lockwood. He arranged for reporter Alan Fraser to interview them, and obviously the report would not be a flattering.[105] Miles apparently did most of the talking. Fraser asked why women were excluded from the party that was being formed. Miles replied, 'We can't be bothered with women. They are no good to us.' Fraser queried whether Miles would accept money from Hitler if he offered it. Miles replied unwisely that he would think Hitler was mad, but he would accept.[106]

Miles and Stephensen knew that their activities were of interest to the CIB, the police and Military Intelligence. An irate Mrs Leah Margaret Veron, whom police had interviewed concerning the 'L. M. Veron' articles, demanded that a statement be printed in the *Publicist* and the *Sydney Morning Herald* that she was not the person writing under that name. Miles explained that Louis Marie Veron, who had died about fifty years earlier, was an English-born French *émigré* who had married into his family, and henceforth he wrote as 'Louis M. Veron'.[107]

The *Sunday Telegraph* of 21 September 1941 commented that Attorney-General Hughes had banned the Australian National Guard twenty-four hours after he heard of its existence.[108] 'Mr Hughes did well to nip this little Fascist seedling in the bud,' it reported. 'But if he looks around he'll find a few similar plants, fed from the same anti-democratic sources, that demand just as drastic treatment.' The *Telegraph*, without naming the *Publicist*, went on to describe it as 'a stale mixture of rabid, anti-British nationalism, Nazi-inspired anti-Semitism, and windy Fascist pseudo-philosophy'. Stephensen responded in the *Publicist* in November, labelling the *Sunday Telegraph* 'a typical fungoid growth on Australian decadence', adding that its Editor, if not a Jew, had 'a Gentile's respect for the advertising potential of the very considerable financial interests wielded by Jews in the Australian community'.[109]

On 7 October, there was a change of Government, with John

Curtin becoming Prime Minister. The response within the Yabber Club was ambivalent. Curtin, Chifley and Evatt, though more Australia-orientated than Menzies and his Ministers, were less likely to put up with fascist nonsense. The *Publicist* attacked governments, and now it attacked Labor. An unsourced report on the AFM and the *Publicist*, dated 6 November 1941, stated, 'The future of the movement depends on the oratory of L. K. Cahill, the pen of P. R. Stephenson [*sic*] and the financial backing of W. J. Miles.'[110] Possibly it was hoped that finance would cease when Miles died, and the paper would fold. Stephensen's success in raising money ensured that the *Publicist* would continue.

Without taking into consideration the events in Western Australia, changing circumstances had by March 1942 made the situation of the AFM–*Publicist* group precarious. It was clear that the *Publicist* would not fold after Miles died. To prevent public disorder at AFM meetings would entail a drain on police manpower or the emergence of a private army. Stephensen had attacked, savagely and unjustly, the person who at that time had the ultimate power to intern him: Forde (not Evatt).

Singapore had fallen. Darwin, Broome and Wyndham had been bombed. To the north-west the Japanese were advancing through the Netherlands East Indies and Timor. To the north-east, they had taken Rabaul and were advancing through New Guinea and the Solomon Islands. They were no longer 4,200 miles away.

Later debate as to whether or not the Japanese seriously intended to invade Australia is irrelevant; at that time it was believed they probably would, and anybody who might constitute the slightest threat to Australia's defence had to be rendered harmless.

Chapter 7

The Australia-First Movement

All sorts of people used the slogan 'Australia First'. Lieutenant R. E. Finzel reported an attempt in 1936 by Ernst Dieckmann to establish an Australasian Free Economy League along Social Credit lines in New South Wales. Its aim was to 'free the world of Jewish capitalist high finance', and it subscribed to most of the tenets of Nazism.[1] Finzel suggested a connection between Dieckmann, the *Publicist* and The Link.[2] Dieckmann had written to Miles in 1939, ending his letter with: 'Jude verrecke, ehe wir verrecken.'[3] Miles replied: 'Hitler must be a blessing for Germany; we hold him in high regard.' However, Social Credit was anathema to Miles and Stephensen.[4]

The Australia-First Movement was confined mainly to Sydney, with few members in country areas or interstate, and it lasted only four months. Stephensen wrote in a private letter in October 1940, 'Propaganda must precede organization… [The] aim of organization should be nothing less than the conquest of power.'[5] However, he took no steps to found an AFM until Adela Walsh forced his hand when she said that she would found an Australia-First Movement, with or without him.

For twenty-five years Miles had been writing about an 'Australia-First' Movement, but had done nothing more than that. If he had been fit, he would probably have sent Adela packing, for he was opposed to women in politics and despised her personally. Miles had been adamant that it was futile to found a new party during the war, but the July issue of the *Publicist* foreshadowed an attempt to form a *nucleus* to be expanded into an AF Party *after* the war.[6] By October, it seemed that Germany would soon defeat the Soviet Union; then Britain would be alone and obliged to sue for peace. Stephensen and Adela refused to consider that Japan might exploit the situation and attack American and British territory.[7] The war would end soon, and preparations for the new party should begin. Although he too had doubts about Adela, Stephensen decided to found the Movement at once, for if there was to be an Australia-First Movement, he meant to lead it, and he thought he could use her and the two hundred supporters she claimed she still had.[8]

A preliminary meeting was held on Wednesday, 15 October, in Marjorie Corby's flat in Cremorne. The widow of a returned soldier, she had two sons in the army and a son-in-law in the navy. A follower of Adela, she had been a fund-raiser for the Guild of Empire.[9] According to Mrs Corby, those present were 'the Australia First men', Evelyn Pope (wife of H. N. Pope, Managing Director of Farmer & Co.) and her daughter Elaine, Mrs Anita Davis of the Housewives' Association, Mary Elizabeth Collingridge, and W. J. Dovey.[10] Among those known to have been there were Stephensen, Hooper, Crowley, Tinker-Giles, Jack Lockyer and John Phillips.[11] Mrs Collingridge joined the AFM but played no active role. Anita Davis, who had stood for the Mosman Council, was an energetic woman with a ferocious temper and a habit of lashing out with an umbrella; it was claimed she had been expelled from the Housewives' Association.[12] At this meeting, a draft constitution, rules and a ten-point manifesto were distributed, and a date set for a meeting to form the AFM and adopt the constitution.

Consideration might have been given to founding the AFM before October, for Ian Mudie arrived in Sydney in September,[13] and on 21 September, at Stephensen's suggestion, Crowley invited Cahill to move to Sydney.[14] Cahill accepted the proposal, and he left Melbourne by train on 16 October, after Crowley sent him the money for his fare and arranged a job for him with Ludowici & Co.[15]

The inaugural AFM meeting was held on Monday, 20 October, in the Shalimar Cafe. The Constitution was adopted and a committee appointed. Stephensen was elected president, Tinker-Giles treasurer, and Sheila Rice secretary. The executive committee consisted of Ian Mudie, Gordon Rice, Vera Parkinson, Marjorie Corby and Elaine Pope. Les Cahill and Adela Walsh were appointed organisers at £5 a week,[16] but they were unlikely to work harmoniously together; Cahill considered returning to Melbourne when he learnt that Adela was involved.[17] Members of the executive signed a promise not to initiate any action without the knowledge of the others.[18] An office was rented at 26 O'Connell Street, and a printing sub-committee including Stephensen and Mudie was set up.[19] Mrs Corby tried to raise funds to defray the cost of hiring halls for public meetings, for which she would receive 20% commission. Adela hoped for business donations, but those who had supported the Guild would not support the AFM.[20]

The Rices have barely been mentioned previously. Gordon Rice had been a printer and letterpress machinist for seven years,[21] but in 1941 he was owner-driver of a truck. Rice's father had deserted his wife and ten children, and Rice had to leave school to help provide for the family. In 1938, he married Catherine Sheila Rahaley, adding another Irish connection to the AF group. He had subscribed to the *Publicist* since 1940.[22] Owing to his poor formal education, Rice was reluctant to write for publication, but he took the chair at two meetings. When his premises were searched, a note was found among his papers: 'Britain and America live on other people's blood, sweat and tears. Japan's victory will remove this. Japan will make the world safe from democracy.' MI noted that the phrase 'safe from democracy' was used often in Japanese broadcasts.[23]

At the request of Tinker-Giles, Walter Leonard Currey of Undercliffe donated an Australian flag.[24] Tinker-Giles promised £100 in four instalments, allegedly from a friend. It was meant to cover the cost of taking city boys out to show them the Australian bush, and only Cahill and the Rices knew it was from him.[25] Tinker-Giles said before the Clyne Inquiry that he had not wanted Stephensen and Adela to know he was behind the offer. 'We wanted to keep the money out of the hands of Stephensen,' he said. When it was suggested that he did not trust Stephensen, he replied, 'Not with money.'[26]

Expressing misgivings about the AFM in Sydney, Cahill wrote to Camille Bartram that Mudie and Crowley wanted him to assume leadership, as Miles was not the right type to launch a new political party, owing to his lack of 'human feeling', while Stephensen was 'too irresponsible in the *small things* that really count'.[27]

After the initial enrolments of those connected with the *Publicist*, membership grew with disappointing slowness. Adela Walsh and

Cahill as paid organisers and Sheila Rice as secretary wrote to *Publicist* subscribers outside Sydney soliciting membership. On hearing from Cahill, Mills paid 10s 6d for a subscription. Sending his membership card on 10 November, Cahill wrote, 'Your application form is the first we have received from Victoria, so the honour of "Number" One in Victoria goes to you and there is no one more worthy of that honour than yourself.'[28]

This reference to being Number One in Victoria was misunderstood. Cahill meant that Mills was the first person in Victoria to join; Security interpreted it to mean that Mills was the leader in Victoria. Mills told an Appeals Tribunal in November 1942 that he subscribed only because Cahill asked him, and that he had never met other members or attended meetings.[29] However, he was in written contact; in the letter accompanying his subscription, he told Stephensen:

> I believe Hughes is half semite... Freemasonry is percolating throughout China. Freemasonry is Jew worship. Chiang Kai Shek is probably one of the higher orders of Freemasonry. Freemasonry is the hand maiden of Jewish Christianity. Jewish Christianity is going ahead fast in China.[30]

The ludicrous suggestion that W. M. Hughes, former Prime Minister and until recently Attorney-General, was of Jewish origin can be traced to an article written by Miles after Hughes had disparaged the *Publicist*.[31] The reference to Chinese Jews traces back to another *Publicist* article.[32] The letter belies Mills's tale of joining the AFM simply through sympathy with Cahill and casts doubt on his logical faculties, while indicating his chain of reasoning: China equals Jewish, which is bad, therefore Japan is good.

Attempts to gain members by mail were not markedly successful, though it brought in members from as far away as Cooma, Bendigo and Tennant Creek, and contact with Western Australia was renewed. Cahill had a list of practically every organisation with the name 'Australia(n)' in its title. Organisations he intended to contact included the Australian Natives Association, the United Electors of Australia (an offshoot of Social Credit), the Fellowship of Australian Writers and even the Australian Football Association.[33]

Rex Ingamells, founder of the Jindyworobak Movement, to which Hooper contributed funding, joined the AFM, persuaded by fellow South Australian, Ian Mudie. He wrote to Stephensen on 27 December that he had 'torturing doubts' about joining: 'Political propaganda and culture *may only in a limited way* be telescoped.' He criticised Stephensen's attacks on people, instead of their arguments, especially his attacks on Christesen, for *Meanjin* could do much to promote the aims of the AFM. 'Don't be a bloody fool and kill it,' wrote Ingamells.[34] On 3 January, Stephensen sent Ingamells a copy of the *Protocols of Zion* and a tirade about the 'Brit-Usa-Com-Jew' as the 'real invaders and opponents of Australia'.[35] Mudie's mail had been intercepted for some months, and now that of Ingamells was also monitored.[36]

By the beginning of 1942, the AFM was losing members by resignation rather than attracting new ones. A circular dated 14 February made a plea for new members, under the heading: 'NOW OR NEVER'. The first public meeting was held in the Australian Hall, 148 Elizabeth Street, on Wednesday, 5 November, speakers being Percy Stephensen and Adela Walsh.[37] By a door count, 212 people attended, including police shorthand writers. Stephensen complained about the reports of the meeting by the *Daily Mirror* and *Daily Telegraph*.[38] Two days before this meeting, Adela had sent Miwa a supplementary sheet of the *Voice of the People* and promised, 'Our inaugural meeting is on Wednesday night, after which I will tell you how we got on.'[39] Afterwards she sent him a copy of the AFM constitution and assured him, 'The Australia First Movement, which is now being organised will certainly be most friendly to Japan.'[40]

The AFM made great demands on the committee's time, with a public meeting every Wednesday, an executive meeting every Thursday from 30 October to 18 December, and every Monday a speakers' class run by Masey and Lang.[41] Stephensen coped with writing for the *Publicist*, arranging its publication, printing leaflets, and preparing and delivering speeches, while Winifred was confined to bed with tuberculosis.

As internments were decided partly on what people said in public, the identity of speakers at meetings is significant. The second meeting, at which the speakers were Stephensen (as chairman), Adela Walsh, Masey and Cahill, was held on 12 November; it was the first time Masey had met Adela.[42] The MPI report of the meeting was qualified with such terms as 'it appears that', 'as far as can be ascertained', and 'is alleged', but its personal information on members of the executive was fairly accurate.[43]

The third meeting was held on 19 November, the main speakers being Stephensen and Cahill, while Vera Parkinson appealed for funds in a speech written by Cahill. On 21 November, MPI reported that the AFM was 'the genesis of a Fifth Column of a most virulent kind'.[44] Another meeting was held in King's Hall, Mosman, on 25 November. Speakers were Cahill, Crowley, Adela Walsh and Anita Davis. It was reported that the fifty-five people present showed little enthusiasm. This meeting was too much for Tinker-Giles; he said later that he joined the AFM because he thought it was cultural and educational. After hearing Adela announce that she intended to appeal for a separate negotiated peace with the Axis, he tendered his resignation.[45] Stephensen refused to accept it and wrote asking him to change his mind; Tinker did not reply. However, he maintained that he had never heard any subversive talk at the Yabber Club.[46]

The next evening in the Australian Hall, Adela addressed an audience of about 200.[47] On 3 December, the last meeting before the outbreak of the Pacific War, the audience numbered about one hundred, and the only speaker was Cahill.[48] Rice took the chair on 10 December, the speakers being Stephensen and Masey, who asserted that trade rivalry had caused the war with Japan, and the defeat of Japan would not solve the problem. At the last public meeting for 1941, 17 December, Stephensen and Masey addressed an audience of sixty to seventy persons.[49]

There was already serious tension in the organisation, for Cahill wrote later about disagreements in the week before the outbreak of the Pacific War, with Stephensen being convinced that Japan would not move south, but would attack Vladivostok.[50] Cahill claimed that he had won over Mudie, Tinker-Giles, Kirkwood Downe, Lang and A. McDonnell to his way of thinking about the danger from Japan, but Stephensen, Gordon and Sheila Rice, and two of the 'Pankhurstite' women refused to accept the idea.

During November, a strange character named Edwin John Arnold joined the AFM as Member No. 43. An only child, he was born in Richmond, NSW, on 10 December 1904.[51] He began work with the NSW Railways in 1922, and in 1939 was a porter at the Town Hall station in Sydney. He had been in contact with the German Consulate-General since 1933, when he wrote suggesting ways to improve Germany's image, ending with assurances of his 'unfaltering attachment to German ideals and aspirations'.[52] On 5 April 1938, he commended the *Publicist* to Asmis and asked him to suggest a teacher of German: 'Naturally in view of the views held by me I wish to be instructed by someone whose views are those of the German Government.'[53]

Arnold first attracted official attention in September 1939, when a letter he had written in February in answer to an advertisement in the *Daily Telegraph* was found among the effects of Gerda Edith Haase, secretary to H. E. Hardt, whose firm acted as agents for The Link and the *Anglo-German Review*.[54] He had written that he was 'pro-German through and through', and 'To see and tread the sacred soil of the Fatherland is the greatest wish of my life.'[55] Arnold told the officers who questioned him that he was exaggerating to impress a prospective girlfriend, but he was dismissed from the railways on 23 October 1939 as a security danger. Three weeks later, through an oversight, he was given a National Security pass that allowed him to work at Cockatoo Island dockyard.[56]

About two years later, MI discovered the letters he had written to Dr Asmis. Arnold probably never knew that MI obtained copies, for they were in the Consulate-General archives, to which Security Service obtained secret access about late in 1941. They were mentioned in reports only as 'G.C.' or 'X.G.' documents.[57] Arnold was unknown to most AFM members, although he was in contact with Stephensen and Cahill; on 13 December, he wrote to Cahill (whose mail was being intercepted), 'I am strong for Aryanism, and I cannot possibly believe that Germany would be so unspeakably base as to allow us to become a Japanese Sphere of Influence, still less an outright Japanese possession.'[58]

AF activities resumed with a Speakers' Class attended by ten members on 6 January.[59] Next evening, Rice took the chair for a meeting in Adyar Hall; Stephensen was the only speaker, the topic being 'The Meaning of Australia First'. His theme was that Britain and America might sacrifice Australia, intending to recapture it later. 'If the Americans and Britain decide to let us go and recapture us later, we will have to stand up for our principles, stand up for Australian nationalism.'[60]

A manifesto with three AFM demands was presented to the executive meeting of 29 January:

> AUSTRALIA FIRST!
>
> The Australia-First Movement, a non-Party, non sectional organisation of Australian patriots, supports the Australian Government in all actions taken for the defence of Australia, and urges the following Three Points of Australian National Defence:
>
> 1. RECALL TO AUSTRALIA OF ALL AUSTRALIAN ARMED FORCES:
>
> 2. NATIONAL INDEPENDENCE FOR AUSTRALIA.
>
> 3. AUSTRALIA'S RIGHT TO MAKE PEACE.

They could not agree on the third point, and authorised the printing of a manifesto consisting of only the first two points. According to Munro, it was Masey who forced Stephensen to drop the demand for a separate peace with Japan.[61] However, the third point was still on record from an agent's report made two days before this meeting. The manifesto, printed on yellow paper, was placed on the seats in the hall at meetings.

At the public meeting of 5 February, Masey took the chair, and Stephensen spoke on 'Australia's Place in the World'. He criticised Curtin, who had been a pacifist in World War I, but had now declared war on Japan, and claimed that the Government exploited the Japanese threat to stay in office. He attacked both the British and Australian governments over the inadequate defence of Singapore and Rabaul, complaining that there should have been 20,000 men at Rabaul instead of in Palestine.[62]

Affairs came to a head in Adyar Hall on 19 February, when Crowley was chairman and the speakers were to be Stephensen and Masey. Some of the audience arrived with improvised weapons and the intention of starting a brawl. Next day, newspapers reported gleefully on the fracas. Eric Stephensen wrote to Fotheringham in 1970 that it was not as bad as had been reported.[63] The trouble started when Rice tapped an interjector on the shoulder and asked him to sit down and be quiet. Men sitting nearby turned on Rice to beat him up, and brawls began in several places, the main attack being directed at Stephensen, who sustained bruises, cuts and two black eyes. Plaster was knocked off the wall, and Anita Davis used her umbrella to good effect, hitting a union official on the head.[64] After the rioters left, taking with them a list of AFM members,[65] Stephensen gave a passionate speech demanding the recall of the AIF to defend Australia not just against an external enemy but against 'an alien minority element in Australia, sufficiently wealthy, and sufficiently unscrupulous, to organise the forces of disorder for the purpose of overthrowing traditional political rights and establishing a Reign of Terror', an 'Internationalist' gang that hoped to take advantage of the absence of the AIF.[66] As 'Rex Williams', he wrote, 'Communists remain Russia-firsters... Like all zealots, they believe what they wish to believe, and argument with them is a waste of time.'[67]

That evening, Josephine Ryan wrote Stephensen a passionate and damaging letter:

> Hail Inky,
>
> Let me say I am with you to the end... [When] Australia First reigns supreme, you will be our hero, and I hope there will be tune dedicated to 'close up the ranks', to stir the Australians as does the Horst Wessell [*sic*] stir up 70,000,000 people in another State, the dedication of which will be to you.[68] [Extract]

Several things may be deduced from the letter. One is that Ryan was no stranger to Stephensen; she addressed him as 'Inky'. Another is that she knew the words of the *Horst Wessel Lied*, as she quoted the phrase 'close up the ranks'. A third point is that the form of address ('Hail Inky') and the comparison between Stephensen and Horst Wessel were alarming. Stephensen was not responsible for what others wrote, but the case against him rested not just on what he had done or might do, but on the effect he had on others.

In the NSW Parliament, Abram Landa (ALP, Bondi) called for suppression of the AFM. On 2 March, Stephensen sent a circular to members of the Commonwealth and New South Wales parliaments. The *Sydney Morning Herald*, he wrote, had the previous day claimed that the Government intended to ban the AFM, a properly constituted and law-abiding political organisation entitled to the protection of the law, and that this was instigated by 'a minority group of communists and Jews'.[69] He listed some of the attacks:

> (1) False charges made under privilege in Parliament by Messrs. S. M. Falstein, M.H.R., and Abraham [*sic*] Landa, M.L.A.
>
> (2) Sensational headlines, distorted news, false suggestions in a section of the Sydney Press to convey the outrageous and lying imputation that this Movement is 'Fascist', 'Nazi', or 'Pro-Japanese'.
>
> (3) A physical attack made by hired ruffians on a peaceful Public Meeting convened by this Movement in the Adyar Hall, Sydney, on 19th February.
>
> (4) Circulation of a petition among the Armed Forces purporting to request the Minister for the Army to suppress this Movement.
>
> (5) Suggestions printed yesterday that the Government in fact intends to suppress this Movement.

Stephensen concluded, '[I] ask for the protection of the Law and of Parliament.' He seemed not to realise that the war imposed on people a number of restraints, including restrictions on public debate. The meeting due on 26 February was abandoned, and plans were made for one on 5 March, but the Adyar Hall management had had enough of the AFM. Sir Thomas Gordon donated £25 towards hiring a hall,[70] and Keith Bath, inspired by Stephensen's courage and his speech on 19 February, tried to obtain Sydney Town Hall. When they were turned down, he hired the Arcadia Theatre in Manly and circulated dodgers advertising the meeting.[71] Justifying his activities, Bath wrote later:

> What happened there was an outrage upon the right of lawful public assembly and free speech. The action of an organised gang of hoodlums was so repugnant to me that, in order to uphold the community right of freedom of public discussion, I agreed to take the chair at a protest meeting at Manly (where I had lived for twenty years) on 5th March, 1942.[72]

Bath was the most unfortunate of those associated with the AFM. Bath was born in Walcha, NSW, in 1900; both he and his wife were fourth-generation Australian-born of British stock. Elected to the Manly Council in 1925, Bath was an active member of the UAP and, like Crowley, he had been on Spender's electoral committee. A prominent real estate agent, he was a member of the Royal Empire Society, the Constitutional Association and Tattersall's Club.[73] Late in January 1941, he went to the bookshop to buy some books advertised in the *Publicist*. As often happened in the shop, Bath was waylaid, this time by Hooper and Clarence Crowley, who questioned him on his views on Australia-First and invited him to hear Stephensen speak. As he had read *Foundations of Culture in Australia*, he went to the meeting of 12 February. Stephensen made what Bath considered was 'a loyal speech for a strong Australia within the Empire'. Bath met him, applied for membership and paid a subscription on 17 February. This would have been accepted at the executive meeting due on 20 February, but the turbulent public meeting on 19 February upset the routine. Within seven weeks of entering the shop, Bath was interned, and soon his business had been destroyed, and his house and reputation lost.[74]

It was intended, at the meeting, to continue the attack on Forde over the lack of defences at Rabaul and call for his resignation. The meeting and the policy Stephensen intended to put forward were advertised in the *Sydney Morning Herald* on 4 March.

> 1. National Non-Party Government and no Party Legislation during the war-emergency.
>
> 2. Active Defence against Air-Raids by Fighter Planes rather than Passive Defence by 'Blackout'.
>
> 3. Fighting Spirit instead of 'Deep Shelters', 'Scorched Earth', 'Evacuation', 'Maginot Mentality' and Retreatism.
>
> 4. Courageous and Positive War Leadership instead of 'Scare Advertising'.
>
> 5. Public Enquiry into Ministerial Responsibility for the Insufficient Defence of Rabaul.
>
> 6. No formation of irregular 'People's' Army.

> 7. Recall when practicable of the A.I.F. and the R.A.A.F. for Australia's Defence.
>
> 8. Aid for Australia First (i.e. before Russia).
>
> 9. Independent Voice for Australia in Pacific War Councils.
>
> 10. Immediate Transfer of all Commonwealth Government Departments to Canberra.

Some comments on the points in this programme are necessary.

Point 1: Labor had rejected the Non-Party Government proposed by Menzies.

Point 2: The Government was doing its best to obtain fighters; they would not materialise out of thin air, and Britain needed all her aircraft.

Points 3 and 4: were mere posturing.

Point 5: A public inquiry during wartime into a defence matter was hardly desirable.

Point 7: This was already being done, but it would have been dangerous to advertise the fact that the troops were at sea.

Point 10: This would have required an intensive construction programme that would have diverted resources from defence projects.

At 5.30 p.m. on the day of the meeting, Stephensen was taken to see the Commissioner of Police, William J. MacKay, who had an order signed by Evatt forbidding the meeting under Regulation 44, Sub-Regulation 2 of National Security (General) Regulations. MacKay had been instructed not to produce the order unless absolutely necessary. First he asked Stephensen not to hold the meeting; then he ordered that the meeting not be held. Stephensen called off the meeting, and went to Manly to see Bath and put a cancellation notice on the hall door. On 7 March MacKay reported to Sir George Knowles that he had not needed to use the order, and he recommended banning the AFM.[75]

Stephensen was already considering winding up the AFM for the duration of the war, as the treasurer and both organisers had resigned. Cahill claimed that the Speakers' Class would not provide speakers without his approval.[76] Financial records were in a mess, and late in February, at Stephensen's request, Tinker-Giles straightened out accounts and located the discrepancy.[77] A few days after the

Manly meeting was cancelled, Stephensen rang him again, saying he was disbanding the AFM and asking help to wind up finances. Tinker-Giles went to the office for the last time on 9 March to sign outstanding cheques.[78]

Soon after Pearl Harbor, Cahill contacted Stephensen to suggest that the most important members confer about the changed situation, but Stephensen refused. Cahill thought he was afraid the Yabber Club would 'chaff' him for being naive, but there might have been more to Stephensen's reaction than this. Instead of following Menzies' lead when he declared that Australia was automatically at war with Germany because Britain was, Curtin had made an independent declaration of war against Japan, affirming that Australia had the right to make war *and peace*. Cahill wrote:

> I was amazed at the attitude taken by Stephensen... His reactions were like a man robbed of his life work, he acted like a petulant child. I then realised that Evatt has 'stolen P.R's thunder'.[79]

Hardly anyone would still tolerate Adela Walsh. Her continued advocacy of a separate peace with Japan caused a quarrel with Cahill, who was about to enlist in the army.[80] At the executive meeting on 11 December, Rice moved that she be asked to resign; Mudie seconded the motion.[81] Her resignation was accepted on 18 December. Tinker-Giles and Cahill had the lock on the office door changed so that she could not gain access to the premises.[82] Cahill wrote later that the AFM could have gone into recess in a blaze of glory and the stigma of pro-Japanese statements by Stephensen and Mrs Walsh would have been forgotten, but the opportunity was lost.[83]

A circular dated 30 December notified members that Adela and Cahill had resigned, and Phyllis Walton and M. F. Watts had replaced them on the committee.[84] This was repeated in the *Publicist* on 1 February. Few regretted the loss of Adela. Hooper had said he would attend no more meetings unless both she and Cahill disappeared from the platform.[85] Matthews wrote to Hooper that he could not work enthusiastically for the AFM while she had a voice in affairs.[86] Kirtley wrote to Stephensen, 'I am glad Adela has gone, never liked her from the start, and Cahill was perhaps too effervescent.'[87]

Many AFM members were unfit or too old for active service, but some joined the militia or a civil defence unit. Mills became an Air Raid Warden.[88] Val Crowley had an Air Raid Warden Post in his home.[89] Tinker-Giles lent one of his shops rent-free to the National Emergency Service (NES).[90] Clarence Crowley was an NES warden.[91] Kirtley was a Police Reservist at Woy Woy,[92] and Watts a Peace Officer (guard) at a munitions factory, where he had prevented a fire.[93] Hooper, who was in his seventies, gave £25 to the fund to replace the cruiser *Sydney* and took up £150 in a War Loan.[94] Rejected by the RAAF in May 1940 on account of his eyesight, Clive Kirkwood Downe was accepted by the army in December 1941.[95] When Cahill tried to enlist in the AIF on 5 January, he was rejected owing to an old football injury; the next day the AMF accepted him.[96]

The CIB and Military Intelligence had been watching the *Publicist* group almost since its formation. With the founding of an AFM calling for members, scrutiny became more intense. MI used its emergency powers to intercept mail such as this letter that Cahill wrote to Mills shortly after arriving in Sydney:

> Doing what I can to impress P.R.S. with some Odinist Philosophy. Remembered you to W.J.M. He has a great liking and respect for you and hoped that you felt kindly towards him. I fear he has not long to go before he passes on to Valhalla.[97]

In Report No. 25 for the week ended 30 October 1941, the Security Service, Victoria, commented: 'Apparently the cult of ODIN is being used as a cloak for the more secret operations of this pro-Fascist, pro-Nazi, anti-Semitic organisation.'[98] The mention of Odinism twitched a nerve in Security circles, for *Die Brücke* had described an Odinist ceremony conducted by Nazis near Melbourne on 25 June 1939. It was reported that Stephensen, through Cahill ('a converted communist and friend of MILLS'), was trying to unite Odinists and AFM followers.[99] Although there was some basis for this conclusion in view of Mills's article in the *Publicist*,[100] Stephensen had little interest in Odinism. For most AFM followers, Odinism was either unknown or regarded as a crank belief.

Official concern at AFM activities continued to escalate. On 25 November, Sydney Max Falstein (ALP, Watson, NSW) asked in the House of Representatives:

> I ask the Attorney-General whether it is a fact that an anti-war, anti-democratic, and pro-fascist organization masquerading under the name or style of 'The Australia-First Party' recently held three meetings at the Australia Hall, Sydney? Will he call for a report on the activities of that organization and inform the House of the result as soon as possible?[101]

Dr Evatt replied briefly, 'Yes.' As Falstein was a member of Evatt's party, this was apparently a pre-arranged question. It was perhaps regrettable that it was one of the few Jews in Parliament who posed the question, as it gave Stephensen an excuse to blame 'the Jews' for attacks on the *Publicist* and the AFM.[102]

The NSW Premier, William John McKell, wrote to Curtin on 26 November asking that AFM activities be restricted.[103] At the same time, Captain Tyrrell, head of the NSW branch of the Security Service, reported that at the meeting of 19 November anti-conscription propaganda and support for the Japanese system of government had been put forward, and it was 'distressing to see unfavourable references to America when that country is doing so much to assist the British Commonwealth of Nations'.[104] He included the impressions of a member of the Censorship Staff who attended 'of his own volition and not acting on instructions', and wrote that Cahill was 'shifty, untrustworthy' and Stephensen was 'untrustworthy', adding:

> This man looks what he reveals himself as being, a shameless twister with plenty of cunning and effrontery… Under the guise of emphasising the national importance of Australia, the speaker Stephenson [*sic*] was definitely seeking to sow ill-feeling between Australia and Britain and Australia and the U.S.A… He asserted that Australia could well copy the Japanese form of Government and that we had much to learn from Japan…
>
> Rightly or wrongly should chance place authority in my hands I would not for a moment debate the disposal of such a man, I should intern him.[105]

Reporting to Canberra on 28 November, Tyrrell added, 'There is growing evidence that this Movement is causing public unrest and your attention is invited to the request for authority to search, as set out in submission to Army early this year.'[106]

Calls for the suppression of the AFM and internment of members came from a cross-section of society. The NSW State Labor Party reacted quickly to the formation of the AFM. This was not the NSW branch of the ALP, but an extreme left-wing group of quasi-communists including Rupert Lockwood. On 14 November, the executive demanded a public trial of the pro-fascist 'Australia First gang'. A meeting in the Town Hall on 18 November called for internment of the leaders.[107] In its paper, *Progress*, on 30 November, it again demanded a ban on the AFM and public trial of its leaders.[108] However, there was no clear law covering subversion or sedition, and the combined powers of National Security Regulations and peacetime legislation allowed a treason charge only in flagrant cases of overt action. On 7 December 1941, Major-General S. E. Rowell, Deputy Chief of the General Staff, reported that there were five people likely to be a menace to security in the event of war with Japan, among them Adela and Tom Walsh and John Sleeman. Stephensen was not on that list.[109]

All might have been well if the *Publicist* had closed in December 1941, and public meetings had ceased. MI and the Security Service might merely have kept a close watch or imposed restriction orders. The changed war situation meant that the question of restricting, interning or prosecuting leaders of the AFM was re-examined. The Walshes' dossier was shown to Evatt on 11 December. Referring to them and to other pro-Japanese persons, he made a note that he had discussed the case with Colonel Longfield Lloyd, then head of the CSS, to see if there was a breach of National Security Regulations. Evatt wrote, 'The submissions rather suggest old or ageing and eccentric persons with a zest for taking the unpopular side in discussion.' Longfield Lloyd suggested a reprimand and a strict bond.[110] Those who had had experience with Adela during the anti-conscription campaigns would have known that reprimands, restrictions and bonds had no effect on her. However, Evatt was not entirely unpartisan. He had defended Tom Walsh against the threat of deportation in 1925, and his wife had been a good friend of Adela,[111] although the relationship had soured by 1941.

There were differences of opinion about how to handle Stephensen and the AFM. Munro writes that Colonel Jones of the

CIB recommended to Evatt just before Christmas that it was time to curtail AFM activities,[112] but on 8 January Captain Blood reported that there was insufficient evidence to warrant restricting Stephensen.[113] Nevertheless, on 20 January, the Security Service applied for an Order to Restrict with regard to Stephensen. Adela's name had already been submitted for internment; Cahill, Masey, Ludowici and Crowley were under consideration.[114] However, Constables Walsh and Wilson reported on 30 January, 'The Australia First Movement is not subversive.'[115]

Early in January, MI applied for a Ministerial Order under National Security (General) Regulations 25 and 26, requesting that Stephensen be placed under restriction. This was signed on 9 January by Major J. M. Prentice, and on 14 January by Lieutenant-General H. D. Wynter and the Command Legal Officer.[116] The report said there was as yet not sufficient evidence to intern Stephensen but made out a case for a Ministerial Restriction, in the following terms:

> 1. Stephenson [*sic*] shall not associate directly or indirectly or communicate directly or indirectly with any alien.
>
> 2. Stephenson shall not change his address without notification to the nearest Police Station.
>
> 3. Stephenson shall submit all speeches or writings to Censorship prior to utterance or publication.
>
> 4. Stephenson shall not attend or participate in any meetings or gatherings unless all speeches to be made at the meetings or gatherings have first been submitted for Censorship approval.
>
> 5. Stephenson shall not become or remain a member of or in any way associate with any subversive organisations.
>
> 6. Upon breach of any of the above restrictions, Stephenson will submit to immediate internment.[117]

If the Restriction Order had been imposed and Stephensen had complied with it, the question of internment might not have arisen. Documentation setting out the case for restriction, however, contained errors of fact. It reported that the Yabba [*sic*] Club met each week for a luncheon at which there was a guest speaker; this was clearly the ANA luncheon club. It suggested that Stephensen and Miles were closely associated with The Link, 'which has as its policy the fostering of British and Nazi ideals'. In fact, neither knew much about The Link. One might also wonder what MI considered wrong about 'the fostering of *British*... ideals'.[118] The report, however, accurately described speeches at the AFM meetings as being to some extent anti-British, anti-American, pro-Japanese and pro-Nazi, but mainly in favour of an isolationist Australia.[119] The crux of the matter was whether at that stage of the war isolationism was *per se* a dangerous policy.

On 13 January, MacKay reported inaccurately that both Cahill and Mills were on the executive of the AFM, and that Hitler fostered Odinism. He was concerned that 'the religious philosophy of the Nazi Party' was being introduced into the AFM, and even if they were not 'intentionally subversive', the damage that might be done 'by such clever and unscrupulous propagandists, Stephensen, Cahill, Mills, Walsh and others' could not be foretold.[120] Soon after this, Tyrrell recommended that the AFM be declared an illegal organisation and that Stephensen be restricted. He added that members were 'more or less at the mercy of rather clever propagandists, whose inclinations are pro-Axis'.[121] Preparations were made to go further. This file contains an 'Information form, relating to National Security Act 1939–1940 Section 10(1); National Security (General) Regulations. Regulation 42(1)(a). New South Wales Warrant for Prosecution'. The name of the Crown Solicitor, H. F. E. Whitlam, was typed in. The complaint was listed for hearing at the Central Police Court, Sydney. It read that:

> [On] or about the fifth day of February 1942 at Sydney in the said State PERCY REGINALD STEPHENSON [*sic*] of 5 Hunter Street, Sydney aforesaid did contravene a provision of the National Security (General) Regulations made in pursuance of the National Security Act 1939-1940 in that contrary to regulation 42(1)(a) of the said Regulations he did endeavour to influence public opinion in a manner likely to be prejudicial to the efficient prosecution of the war by means of a certain speech delivered by him on the said date at Adyar Hall, Bligh Street, Sydney aforesaid.[122]

Attached was a transcript of Stephensen's speech of 5 February. The speech might have been offensive, but no specific statement was actionable. The form was never signed or dated. Just when the CIB had decided to reduce surveillance, however, MPI wanted the Movement declared unlawful and asked police to search the premises of key members, as MPI had no authority to act against civilians. MacKay replied on 17 February that it was up to the Federal Attorney-General to declare organisations illegal,[123] and he was not yet prepared to authorise searches.[124]

Meanwhile, Cahill had written to Stephensen on stationery provided to soldiers by the Salvation Army. Over the small red map of Australia printed in one top corner, Cahill had printed 'CO7'.[125] He must have done the same on other letters, for on 18 February he wrote to Camille Bartram, 'The C.O.7 means the Council of Seven – for the National Revolution – Reggie was very nearly right.'[126] This made sinister sense to MI. At the Clyne Inquiry, it was claimed that Lenin had once headed a Revolutionary Committee of Seven. Elsewhere, Cahill named his Council: himself as leader, Collins, Lang, Mudie, Masey, Tinker-Giles, Val Crowley. They had no idea that Cahill had selected them, cutting out Stephensen and Hooper.[127]

After the Adyar Hall incident, Security authorities needed little more provocation. On 23 February, Captain Newman of Intelligence Section Ib urged Tyrrell 'very strongly' that the AFM be declared illegal.[128] The March *Publicist* added weight to the case, when Stephensen announced, 'The Australia-First Movement will make proper arrangements to protect its meetings and speakers from criminal assault in future.'[129] Perhaps he meant to seek police protection, but it could be interpreted that the AFM would found a private army similar to the New Guard, Mosley's Blackshirts or Hitler's Storm Troops.

On 6 March, Senator W. P. Ashley, representing the Attorney-General, replied to a question upon notice. Naming seven members of the executive, including Stephensen, he stated that the AFM was being closely watched, and that action had been and would be taken to restrict or prohibit activities detrimental to national security.[130]

Complaining anew about Falstein and Landa, Stephensen protested against the suppression of the meeting on 5 March.[131] 'The position has thus arisen,' he wrote, 'that a lawless minority, by threat or rumour of using force, has been able to prevent the holding of a Public Meeting of law-abiding citizens.'[132] The receipt date stamp for the filed copy is 10 March, by which time Stephensen had been arrested by order of Forde, the Minister for the Army, on the recommendation of Military Intelligence.

Chapter 8

The Western Australian Connections

Some Australia-First adherents were examples of how extremist intellectuals can incite emotionally and mentally unstable people to acts of incredible lunacy. Beginning as anti-communist or anti-Jewish, they became in varying degrees anti-Christian, anti-democratic, anti-parliamentarian, against any authority but their own, and in Western Australia some allegedly planned treason, sabotage and murder.

On 9 March 1942, three men and a woman regarded as the WA branch of the AFM were arrested. They were Laurence Frederick Bullock, Charles Leonard Albert Williams, Edward Cunningham Quicke and Nancy Rachel Moss, also known by her maiden name, Krakouer.[1] After a preliminary hearing in May, they were committed for trial in the Supreme Court in June. The most sensational evidence consisted of two documents. One announced the surrender of Australia to Japanese forces and contained plans for a puppet government; the other listed targets for sabotage or assassination. These had been drawn up with encouragement from a police agent, Frederick James Thomas. Bullock's attorney, Thomas John ('Diver') Hughes said, 'No Thomas, no conspiracy.'[2] However, Thomas's main target was not a harmless innocent; the police already had a mass of evidence against Bullock. Thomas was told to find evidence admissible in court.[3] The pivotal figures were Bullock and Melanie O'Loughlin. Without them, there would indeed have been no conspiracy.

Melanie Libuse Eva O'Loughlin was born in Moravia on 15 December 1886, to Waclaw and Caroline Jancik, with a mixed ancestry not unusual in the Austro-Hungarian Empire.[4] The family lived mostly in Vienna, but also in Bohemia, Moravia, Galicia, Bosnia and Hungary.[5] Melanie's mother was born near Budapest to parents from Swabia, Germany. Her father was Austrian, born in Graz to an

Austrian mother and a Polish father. (She could speak Polish as well as German, English, French and Czech.) Melanie mentioned several army officers in her family: her father, stepfather and at least one grandfather. She said in 1942 that her stepfather had been Jewish. If so, perhaps a poor relationship with him fuelled her hatred of Jews, and caused her to migrate to Australia alone in 1908.[6] In 1942 she wrote, 'Here I found a home, a real happiness after all the sadness I left in Austria.'[7] She spent several years in New South Wales, mainly teaching in a convent, before going to Western Australia.[8]

Soon after the outbreak of war in August 1914, Melanie acquired British nationality by marrying German-born British-naturalised (1900) Wilhelm August Werner Fettbach, a telegraph linesman, later postmaster at Onslow and Carnarvon, finally an inspector in the metropolitan area. During the war, it was reported that Fettbach, who had been in Australia since 1887, had a good reputation. Although a prominent member of the German Club, he showed 'no evidence of incorrect national feeling', but there was doubt about his wife.[9]

In 1928, they visited their families in Germany and Austria. Melanie was still in touch with her married sister in Vienna in 1938. In October 1932, Fettbach died. In 1933, Melanie married Thomas O'Loughlin, whose wife had also died in 1932. He was much older than Melanie, poorly educated but in comfortable financial circumstances. Melanie dominated him and was constantly at loggerheads with his family because she had taken him away from the Catholic Church. She introduced Tom to *Mein Kampf,* which they owned not only in German, but also in English and French translations.

In *Die Brücke,* Melanie discovered The Link and the *Publicist.* She contacted Arnold von Skerst, who had been appointed Australian representative of The Link, and she became its agent in Western Australia.[10] The Link, aimed at fostering Anglo-German friendship among the middle class, was founded in Britain in July 1937 at the suggestion of C. E. Carroll, editor of the *Anglo-German Review.*[11] It was sponsored by Admiral Sir Barry Domvile, who invented the term 'Judmas' to describe an alleged plot by Jews and Freemasons to take over the world.[12] In Britain, it was an open organisation, with some prominent parliamentarians, pressmen and businessmen as members. In Australia, it was clandestine, therefore suspicious.

Misunderstandings about The Link led to serious consequences. According to an undated summary of notes found on the premises of *Die Brücke*, Skerst had been a representative of The Link since 1934. This is nonsense, because The Link did not exist then. One paper translated and quoted reads in part:

> Alliance of Friends ((Link?))
>
> To unite friends of the Hitler Movement living abroad ((in foreign countries)) who do not possess German nationality and for this reason cannot become members of the NSDAP, in order to give them the possibility of furthering in common effort the fight of the National-Socialist Movement lead [*sic*] by Adolf Hitler for the internal and external freedom of the German people – with all its might.[13]

The addition of '((Link?))' shows the confusion. Organisations committed to Nazi policy existed in Queensland, South Australia, Victoria and New South Wales; they were known as Friends of the New Germany, Friends of the Third Reich, or Friends of the Hitler Movement. The Link was not overtly Nazi, promoting ostensibly only friendship with Germany. MI made incorrect connections: the *Publicist*, The Link, the Friends of the Hitler Movement. The Link was connected with a meeting held by O'Loughlin on 15 April 1939 for people she thought sympathetic to the 'New Germany'. One was a member of the Australian Natives Association, of which Tom had been a member for fifty years.[14] Another was Elfreda Sylvia Conegrave, Vice-President of the Women's Service Guild, Fremantle. She thrust herself upon the meeting because she distrusted O'Loughlin, who had 'created a scene' at a meeting when a lecturer spoke of the suppression of women in Germany. When the Guild rejected O'Loughlin as a member, she interviewed her lawyer, wrote to members of Parliament, and went to the *Sunday Times*, which printed her complaint without checking facts.[15]

O'Loughlin's guest was Willy 'Trader' Horn from Melbourne; he said later that 'a spiritually minded old couple, Mr. and Mrs. Ashton' had taken him to meet O'Loughlin. They are not mentioned elsewhere, but as Horn later joined the Theosophy movement, they might have been Theosophists. Horn spoke for several hours, but the gist of the talk was this: Hitler had done much good in Germany; the Hitler Youth was marvellous; and the treatment of Jews was justified. He said he was for 'Australia-First', although there is no evidence of contact with the AFM. O'Loughlin asked Mrs Conegrave to become the twentieth member of an organisation that already had nineteen members in WA, including two members of parliament, while millions around the world supported it. However, her name would have to be submitted to Melbourne for approval.[16]

On 20 April 1939 (Hitler's 50th birthday), Melanie wrote to the Editor of the *Publicist*, saying she had seen an advertisement for the magazine in *Die Brücke*, but could not buy it in Western Australia. '[How] gratifying it must be for Germany to read in The Publicist,' Melanie told Miles, 'a meditator [*sic*] for peace, and the New Germany will find an Echo in the Australia First Paper The Publicist.' Miles answered on 28 April that there were only three subscribers in Western Australia: Edgar K. Crampton of Burekup, G. N. Harding of Bodallin, and Miss Emily Alexandrine Taylor of Nedlands, whose married sister he had met in Sydney.

On 19 June, Melanie told Miles she had been appointed representative of The Link for Western Australia.[17] When the press ran criticism of The Link in July, members whom Melanie had enrolled were worried. She complained to the editor of the *West Australian*, showed him the *Anglo-German Review* and *Die Brücke*, and protested that The Link was not political, but a plea for friendship at a time of crisis. After her complaint appeared on 27 July as a Letter to the Editor, she received many letters from interested people. She sent a registered letter to Skerst telling him what she had done. Receiving no answer, she sent him another letter on 10 August, enclosing it in a letter to the *Publicist*, and asking that it be passed on.[18] She wrote that it was sad to see hatred between 'these two nations' being spread by Bolshevik lies, ending her letter with the Nazi closing formula '*Mit Deutschem Gruss*', and seeing nothing incongruous in adding, 'Australia First'.[19]

When the Attorney-General, W. M. Hughes, said there was no branch of The Link in Australia, he was wrong,[20] for Melanie wrote to Miles that she had enrolled many members in Western Australia.[21] Miles replied on 16 August that he had sent her letter to German-

Australian Publications, but he knew nothing of The Link except what had been in the press. The copy of her letter to the *West Australian* arrived too late for the September *Publicist*, but he promised it would appear in October.[22] By then, not even Miles dared print material on Anglo-German friendship. The inconsistency in Melanie's position was that she protested constantly her love for Australia, but she thought that it would be better if it adopted some aspects of National Socialism, e.g.: 'If only the Government would not give Jews permits to drive cars, and buy up properties.'[23] Melanie was an inveterate writer of long letters on many topics, often on the wickedness of the Jews. Across the bottom of a letter to Miles she scrawled in block capitals:

(JEWS!) (EXPLOITERS!) (KIKES!)[24]

With the outbreak of war, Melanie was under suspicion again. Police interviewed her and searched her house on 12 September but found nothing 'definitely subversive'. She wrote to Miles on 19 September that people she had enrolled in The Link were nervous, and she had told detectives that there was no branch in Western Australia, and no meetings had been held in her house.[25] She promised Colonel Henry Doyle Moseley that she would not communicate with The Link during the war, nor lend anybody anything connected with Germany.[26] Melanie assured Miles that none of his letters had been taken, as they were in her husband's desk.[27] Police described O'Loughlin as eccentric, garrulous and verbose. Western Command reported to Intelligence Section General Staff in Melbourne on 25 September 1940 that her attempts to form a branch of The Link in Perth had been unsuccessful.[28]

Some activities of the O'Loughlins were harmless. They sold *Foundations of Culture in Australia*, although Miles wrote that Stephensen had changed his mind on some matters.[29] She commented in a letter of 11 December that the *Publicist* was 'another *Mein Kampf* – but for Australia'.[30] This was what Security feared. Melanie subscribed to two copies of the *Publicist*: one to keep and one to lend. She had lent one to Hermann Christian Ittershagen, an importer of German goods and a manufacturer.[31] He had lived in Perth for many years and had been naturalised in 1908. In September 1928, he was appointed German consular agent for WA. He went abroad for six months in 1933, visiting Germany at this early stage of Hitler's regime. As part of his job, he distributed Nazi propaganda from the Consulate-General. When he resigned in 1938, for reasons of age and health, the agency was closed pending appointment of a new consul.[32] After reading the *Publicist*, Ittershagen gave O'Loughlin's address to Laurence Bullock.

Laurence Frederick Bullock, born on 15 May 1897 in Richmond, Surrey, had served with the British army at Gallipoli. In 1924, he migrated to Western Australia, taking up a dairy farm in a group settlement scheme. These settlements were a disaster, and in 1929 Bullock was forced off the land. He went on relief work during the Depression and became active politically. Blaming 'the Jews' for the Depression, he joined the Douglas Social Credit Movement, of which he became Assistant State Secretary.[33] An attempt to link Social Credit with the ALP was thwarted in 1932 by an adverse report from John Curtin.[34]

Bullock was a leading figure in the Relief and Sustenance Workers' Union (RSWU), founded in Bunbury early in 1933. The RSWU spread through the South-West, and at a meeting in Perth in October, a state-wide union was formed with Bullock as treasurer and 'Diver' Hughes as secretary. Hughes had been the MLA for East Perth (1922–1927), but left the ALP under acrimonious circumstances, accusing its leadership of corruption. He qualified as an accountant, graduated in law and was admitted to the Bar in 1936. An attempt to have the RSWU recognised as a union, so that members could benefit from union preference policies, was rejected when it refused to pay capitation fees to the ALP. On 8 November 1933 it was ruled that anyone connected with the RSWU after 30 November would place himself outside the Labor Movement. Bullock then formed and became president of an Unemployed, Relief and Sustenance Workers' Union, while Hughes stood as an independent in the 1936 election. Bullock chaired some of his meetings, and they spoke together at workers' camps. As Hughes defeated a Labor Minister, almost toppling the Labor Government, they made enemies.[35]

In May 1939, Bullock drew up a Constitution and By-Laws for a People's Party.[36] The Constitution was an irrational mixture of Social Credit, fascism and communism, and the following clause drew police attention when a copy was found.

> The party stands for and is determined to overthrow (*by violence*) if necessary, the financial dictatorship of the Jewish and other financial monopolists, and to establish a true democracy i.e. 'ECONOMIC DEMOCRACY'.[37] [Emphasis added]

By 1939, Bullock was Secretary and Field Organiser of the Primary Producers' Association (PPA). As he travelled around talking to farmers, he tried to recruit converts to Social Credit. Then he discovered Melanie O'Loughlin, the *Publicist* and the AFM. Bullock's behaviour during the first two years of the war was not only disloyal: it was crazy. He wrote to the German Consulate-General in New York, offered his services to help Germany win the war and asked for propaganda material to distribute.[38] He seemed unaware that overseas mail addressed to a German organisation would be handed to MI, and a dossier would be opened on him. He later told Thomas that Hans Duckhoff [*sic*], the German Ambassador to Washington, had sent him propaganda material, but he could not get in touch since America entered the war.[39]

Bullock spoke to Ittershagen on 18 November about the collapse of a firm called Rural Services, of which he was liquidator. That night, and again on 20 November, Bullock drafted letters asking him for money with which to start a Farmers' Service to replace Rural Services.[40] To support his request, he wrote that he was enclosing the Constitution and By-Laws of the People's Party he proposed to form and offered to raise a revolution to assist the German cause.[41] Bullock did not post the letters but, foolishly, he kept them. On 11 December, O'Loughlin told Miles that a Mr Bullock had telephoned about two weeks earlier regarding The Link. She said that The Link no longer existed, and the application form that she sent him was endorsed 'Cancelled'.[42]

At about the same time, there were moves afoot in WA among sane and respectable people to form an AF Party. Among those allegedly involved with the AFM or The Link were the following:

Emily Taylor: Miles directed O'Loughlin to her as a subscriber to the *Publicist*.

Ittershagen, Shenton Park: Honorary Consul. It was his business to keep in touch.

Eduard Gunther Fabarius, Honorary Consul Designate for Perth.

Reverend Edward Mallon Collick, Fremantle.

Edgar Kimberley Crampton, Burekup, who had been mentioned in the *Publicist*.

Victor Courtney, journalist with the *Sunday Times*; Courtney spoke German, had lived in Germany and loved it; but when he visited Germany shortly before the war, friends there had told him what was really happening, and he wrote some bitterly anti-Nazi articles for the paper.[43]

Crampton became involved owing to a letter he wrote to the *London Morning Post* in 1937 concerning Australian nationality. Stephensen, approving of his sentiments, sent him *Foundations of Culture in Australia* and two bound volumes of the *Publicist*. He became a subscriber and contributed in 1938 to the debate about the formation of an AFM. Early in 1939, O'Loughlin invited him to call on her, saying she had heard of him from Stephensen. In December 1939, Bullock wrote that Stephensen had referred him to Crampton; he asked if he could put Crampton's name down as a member of a party he would be forming after the war. Crampton wisely did not take up either offer. When he heard of Bullock's arrest in 1942, he handed Bullock's letter to the police.[44]

At the end of 1939, intent on founding an AF Party in Western Australia, Bullock wrote to Miles for authorisation. Miles advised O'Loughlin on 15 December that any attempt to found a new political party during the war would fail; however, 'I have written to Mr Bullock, but he has no need to be in any way dependent on us: we hold no authority.'[45] Bullock did not heed him. On 18 December he declared, in a letter to O'Loughlin, 'I believe in Germany's struggle and I desire them to win the war.' She forwarded this letter to Miles on 8 January 1940, commenting that Tom had done his best to persuade Bullock to drop the idea of linking a Farmers Service to the *Publicist*.[46] They had told Bullock he should not use the *Publicist* to advertise his business and begged him not to be hasty. Melanie told Miles that Bullock was 'too well known from his former political "Odysee"'.[47] Miles warned on 12 January that Bullock was saying more than he should.[48] Miles realised, even if Stephensen did not, that the lamp they had been rubbing had produced a dangerous genie. Miles also commented, 'Stephensen & I together read your letters.'[49]

In late January or early February 1940, police searched Miles's house in Gordon, not in connection with the *Publicist*, but to find O'Loughlin's letters and trace members of The Link. Constable G. F. Marshall in Sydney reported to MPI on 10 July that there was concrete evidence of a branch of The Link in Western Australia, and its secretary was Mrs O'Loughlin, who had told Miles that branches existed in Sydney and Melbourne.[50] The search obtained incriminating information on Bullock. Miles told O'Loughlin that the police had taken their letters and wrote with respect to a recent letter of hers: 'Mr Stephensen has enjoyed it too and we have chatted about many of its items.'[51] They both knew Bullock's intentions up to that time.

When Cahill's report on the AF Group in Melbourne appeared in the *Publicist* in July 1940, O'Loughlin contacted him, 'I greet you with Australia First and congratulate you to have started the Australia First Movement in Melbourne.' She asked for advice on forming a group in Perth, adding the slogan: 'One flag, one people, one government'.[52] Cahill's reply has not been found, but O'Loughlin on 22 July thanked him for his 'very interesting and prompt reply', adding that they would be staunch supporters if the movement was established in Perth. There must have been a suggestion that Cahill go to Perth, for Tom O'Loughlin added, 'We will be delighted to meet you on your arrival in Perth.' Melanie asked Cahill to put them in touch with Melbourne members.[53] Finding her letter rather strange, Cahill checked with Miles, who replied that she was 'a woman of dynamic energy, emotional and impulsive, warm hearted and public spirited, very much in earnest and probably lacking in a sense of humour'.[54]

On 28 February 1941 Melanie told Miles, 'I have heard that there is a moving towards an Australia First Party going on quietly in Perth.' She wrote that during sleepless nights she visualised 'a crusade of men and women crying for truths' and carrying 'a banner with a dragon stabbed by a youthful figure, truth'.[55] A youth slaying the dragon of 'Jewish lies' was the logo used on *Fichte-Bund* propaganda leaflets. John Gartner became involved in this correspondence. In February 1940, O'Loughlin had sent Miles an article for O'Leary's *Design*; Miles replied that he thought it was unsuitable but would forward it to Gartner.[56] Later, Melanie and Gartner were in direct contact.[57] The 'moving' to which Melanie referred involved Bullock:

> In October 1940 a complaint was received that Bullock was spreading verbal propaganda in Perth in favour of the founding in Perth of the 'Australia First Movement.'
>
> The matter was thoroughly investigated by Special Bureau officers and statements obtained from reputable citizens, showing that in Bullock's opinion, 'The "Australia First Movement" would, within two years after the war, be strong enough to hand over Australia to the Japanese.'[58]

Enquiries were made concerning also a booklet called *The World-Government Plot Exposed* that was circulating in Perth. The booklet was attributed to Eric Dudley Butler, who edited the *New Times* in Melbourne for the Social Credit Movement, [59] and it was suspected that Bullock was circulating it in Perth. On page 7 it said:

> At the same time a stream of Australian youth is leaving to be smashed to bloody pulp in the second war to 'save democracy' which, like the first war, was fomented by Jewish International Finance.[60]

When Bullock's premises in Adelaide Street were searched on 7 November, Nazi propaganda and the People's Party documents were found.[61] Material included copies of Mosley's fascist paper, *Action*, and issue No. VI/14, 15 July 1939, of *Welt-Dienst*, in the English-language version, *World Service*.[62] This twice-monthly bulletin advertised itself as containing 'news items collected from the press of the entire world, which deal with the dangerous and subversive activities of international Jewry'.[63] Detective Sergeant George Ronald Richards considered that Bullock could not explain satisfactorily his dealings with Ittershagen, the reference to 'violence' in the Constitution of the People's Party, or his possession of Nazi propaganda. He recommended prosecuting Bullock, but on 29 April 1941 the Crown Solicitor in Canberra advised that proceedings should not be instituted, because too much time had elapsed.[64] If he had allowed the prosecution of Bullock alone to proceed, most of the events that followed would not have happened. Walsh, Stephensen and Mills would probably still have been interned, but there would have been little controversy in the press or parliament.

Such was Bullock's reputation that O'Loughlin strove to prevent him starting an AFM branch. On 25 May 1941, Miles urged that nothing should be done until after the war. Heedless of advice, Bullock contacted Cahill on 12 July about forming a WA branch. Telling Cahill he was a regular speaker on stations 6AM and 6PM, and had subscribed to the *Publicist* for years, he asked what other political material was available.[65]

Having been confronted by the police in November 1940, Bullock kept his plans secret, recruiting only among friends. In July 1941, he gave a copy of the *Publicist* to **Edward Cunningham Quicke**. Quicke, whose father had come from New Zealand, was born at Fremantle in May 1911.[66] He was running an orchard at Balingup in 1933, the year in which he married, and by 1941 he had four children. A decent chap with a keen sense of justice, he was appalled at the situation whereby 'my fruit rots on the ground while thousands of children in my own State scarcely see apples'.[67] In 1935 this led him to support Douglas Social Credit. He appears to have had a slow but thorough intellect; it took him four years to see through the fallacies of Social Credit. Liking what he read in the *Publicist*, he took out a subscription, and he did not have enough time to see through Bullock's AFM.[68]

According to Quicke, Bullock said he was the Western Australian leader of the AF Party, which was not true, and that the *Publicist* had been banned, which was also not true. Quicke applied to Bullock for membership of the AF Party; Bullock said he had been accepted. Quicke assumed this meant he was accepted as a member of the AFM as constituted in Sydney; this too was untrue.[69] Thus, long before Thomas contacted him, Bullock claimed he had formed an AF Party. Quicke asked him for explanations of some of the Fifty-Points Policy. Bullock sent him Stephensen's pamphlet and told him that the ban on the *Publicist* had been lifted.[70] Not satisfied, Quicke wrote to Stephensen on 11 December concerning some points. On 6 February he asked the Secretary for further explanations. A copy of the Manifesto was sent on 18 February.[71] Quicke wrote later that he had joined the AFM because the aims expressed appealed to him, but he realised later that others had not the same genuine motives, and he regretted joining.[72]

Bullock stayed with Quicke at Balingup twice while representing the PPA. He claimed that many prominent persons were behind the AF Party, including two members of the House of Representatives, one of whom had been Acting Prime Minister. Quicke noticed discrepancies between what Bullock said, and *Publicist* statements that there would be no AF Party until after the war. In November, however, the *Publicist* unexpectedly announced the launching of the AFM. When Bullock met Quicke at a PPA meeting at Bridgetown in January 1942, he alleged that behind the AFM there was a small inner party, of which Miles was the leader, the AFM being only for propaganda purposes among the masses. Assuring Quicke that Miles had appointed him leader of this inner party in WA (untrue), Bullock said he would hold an AF meeting at Manjimup, but wrote later that it was not a success.[73]

By then, Bullock had left his wife, although he was not yet living with Nancy Krakouer. Melanie wrote that Bullock's 'poor wife' often came to her crying and asking for help.[74] Nancy Krakouer had been born at Kojonup in June 1912. She married Reginald Norman Moss in July 1939, but left him in April 1940, saying he was a lazy drunk who expected her to support him. Police, whose sympathies were with Moss, reported that he was 'a loyal and decent person'. Nancy was employed in the Mosman Park Post Office and was said to be kind and polite and an excellent worker. However, as evidenced by her conduct with regard to Bullock, a married man with a notorious record in public life, she does not appear to have been very sensible.[75]

Those who have said that there would have been no conspiracy in Western Australia but for Thomas can hardly have taken Bullock's background into consideration.

Frederick James Thomas, using the alias Frederick Carl Hardt, was introduced into the affair in February 1942 to bring an existing situation to a crisis quickly. Thwarted in 1940–41 in his attempt to prosecute Bullock, Richards kept adding evidence to Bullock's dossier. Bullock did not curb his colourful language when Japan entered the war. Early in February 1942, a dairy farmer from Greenbushes and his married daughter in Mosman Park reported a conversation with Bullock in a Murray Street café. Their reports did not tally precisely, but they agreed in essence on what Bullock had said: The 'Old Country' had let Australia down; Western Australia was cut off from the Eastern States; the Japanese would be in Perth in weeks, and 'we will be on our knees begging for terms'.[76] (Thomas was not involved in this.) When Richards heard that the AFM in Sydney was holding public meetings, he moved against Bullock and the proposed group in Perth, by instructing Thomas to investigate. Thomas described himself later as 'an investigator with the Special Branch of the C.I.B. attached to Military Intelligence'.[77] He was to infiltrate the group through O'Loughlin, as his target was not only the AFM, but also The Link.

A New Zealander who had arrived in Australia in 1924, Thomas had worked at various unskilled jobs in all mainland states, and he joined the ALP in 1927. He had served fourteen days in gaol in Darwin for stowing away on a ship from Thursday Island. He had already, on police orders, tried with little success to infiltrate the Communist Party.[78]

Calling on the O'Loughlins, now living in Merriwa Street, Nedlands, Thomas said Adela Walsh had given him the address, and asked how he could contact members of The Link. Melanie had not seen Bullock for months, as they had fallen out when Bullock left his wife,[79] so she gave Nancy Krakouer's telephone number. Thomas had to work quickly, for O'Loughlin, Bullock and Quicke were in contact with the AFM in Sydney, and they might check on him. On 10 February, he visited Krakouer, who contacted Bullock and asked him to return to Perth, as somebody wanted to see him urgently.[80]

Thomas and Krakouer met the evening train from Bunbury on Friday, 13 February, and Krakouer introduced Thomas to Bullock. They walked down Barrack Street and sat on the grass by the river. Bullock claimed that he was the Western Australian organiser for the AFM. When Thomas produced an AFM pamphlet from Sydney, Bullock remarked:

> Of course, this is only a facade... I have been in contact with Herr Schriener, the German propaganda chief for North America, from whom I obtain the national socialist propaganda... I am an out-and-out national socialist... I do not care who knows it, but I am going to see [?] power in this country.[81]

Bullock, who knew the names of several Nazi *Gauleiter* in Germany, named Quicke as his *Gauleiter* for the South-West. Bullock later denied most of this.

On 16 February, Bullock asked Stephensen for a list of *Publicist* subscribers in Western Australia and permission to form an official AF group.[82] The letter was allegedly found in Stephensen's residence, but Stephensen denied having seen it. Bullock wrote to Cahill also, 'I am having a private meeting of supporters next Saturday night.'[83] Although Miles had told Bullock in 1939 that he needed no authority to found an AF Movement, Rule 29 of the AFM, as constituted in October 1941, stated:

> Branches of the Movement may be established in local centres throughout Australia *on approval in writing of the Executive Committee of the Movement,* but the objects and activities of such Branches must not be in conflict with the general objects and activities of the Movement as defined in these rules.[84]

Bullock did not have this approval, but by telegram he asked Quicke to attend an Australia-First meeting in Perth on Saturday, 21 February, following it up with a letter saying that a 'Mr Hart' had come from the AFM in 'the East' on important business.[85]

On Saturday morning, Bullock drove Hardt to see the O'Loughlins. (Bullock had been out of touch for so long that he had not known they had moved to Nedlands.) She refused to give Hardt the names of members of The Link, but said she would tell them about Hardt so they could contact him if they wanted to do so. Melanie warned Bullock not to trust Hardt, but he did not heed her.[86] Bullock allegedly told Hardt, 'If Ittershagen was alive, we would be set… If we coud [*sic*] only get in touch with Captain Fritz Weidmann [*sic*],[87] the German Consul-General in San Francisco, we would be home on the pig's back.' He might have said also that they should try to obtain a wireless transmitter so they could contact the Japanese.[88]

It has been said that Bullock had no means of contacting the Japanese, but there is reason to think that the Japanese might have contacted *them*. Melanie had several Japanese connections. After she inquired about 'little dwarf trees', an officer from a visiting Japanese warship visited the O'Loughlins to show her a *bonsai* specimen, and they took him for a drive to King's Park.[89] She showed Thomas a photo of herself between two Japanese officers, saying, 'They always visit me when any of them are in Australia.'[90] The contact was innocent on her part, but the Japanese would have put her on a list of sympathisers.

She had another contact with the Japanese through Veronica Margaret Connolly, daughter of a fellow Moravian.[91] Vera was secretary to Masunori Omori, agent for Japan Mining in the Yampi Sound scheme negotiations. Arriving in Broome in November 1934,[92] he was for six years constantly travelling around WA, and between Australia and Batavia or Singapore. Vera was known as Mrs Omori, and in 1939 she had applied for a Japanese passport so that she could travel to Java with her 'husband'.[93] When Melanie said that Vera Connolly was 'a secret member of the Inner Circle of the Australia First Movement', Thomas said she was the very person he wanted to see. He could not get in touch, as she had been interned on 31 January. [94]

On Saturday evening, Bullock, Thomas, Krakouer and Quicke met in the Rex Hotel, Hay Street. Bullock declared, 'Quisling is the true patriot of Norway and we are the true patriots of Australia… I will now form the Australia First party.' He admitted that much. According to Thomas, Quicke and Bullock had rifles, and Krakouer had a revolver. Allegedly, Bullock delegated Quicke to get gelignite, which a primary producer might have legitimately for land clearing, and Hardt to get small arms, which would have been very difficult.[95] According to Bullock, Quicke ended the conversation by saying nothing could be done about an AF Party and he (Bullock) agreed. Then Hardt began 'all the foolish talk about negotiating peace with the Japanese'.[96]

According to Quicke, Hardt expected that, after the bombing of Darwin on 19 February, invasion would follow within weeks; then Perth would be bombed, so there was no time to waste. Hardt also suggested blowing up bridges; Quicke said he would have nothing to do with it, but admitted he had agreed to meet the Japanese, as he was persuaded it was the only means of saving Western Australia from useless bloodshed.[97] Quicke stated later that it was *Bullock* who suggested sabotage.[98] They all allegedly agreed to try to contact the Japanese in order to negotiate peace, following which 'The Australia

First Movement' would govern Australia under Japanese direction.[99] Quicke claimed that he thought he was going to a Primary Producers Association meeting at the Rex Hotel, but Bullock's letter had mentioned Hardt and the AFM, not the PPA.[100]

On Sunday Bullock took Charles Williams, a rural insurance agent whom he had met at Manjimup, to Thomas's residence, introducing him as an explosives expert.[101] Bullock also saw Quicke again and told him it would be necessary to seek the aid of German technicians to implement their financial policy. Quicke agreed.[102]

On Friday, 27 February, Williams picked up Bullock and Krakouer at the Wentworth Hotel and drove them to Thomas's house.[103] Thomas tried to entice them inside, so that Richards and Detective Bernard James Alford, who were concealed inside, could witness their conversation, but they declined to go in. They drove along Riverside Drive and parked at the foot of Plain Street. Here they read through a draft proclamation to be made when the Japanese landed, agreed to hand communists over to the Japanese to be shot, and discussed freeing Italian prisoners of war from Harvey Internment Camp to help them. They also discussed places to sabotage, such as the Midland Junction Railway workshops, the gas works, Bayswater subway, the Causeway, Mundaring Weir, Canning Dam, the Garrett Road Bridge, Collie powerhouse, and the viaducts at Boyanup and Balingup. Williams claimed he had checked the powerhouse and there were only eight guards. Police could not get close enough to hear what was said, but the next day Thomas gave Richards a copy of the draft proclamation, which was photographed and returned.[104]

Meanwhile, Quicke asked Nancy Krakouer to write to the AFM in Sydney inviting them to send a representative to launch a proper branch in Perth.[105] On his return home, he received a letter from Sydney advising that they would start a branch in Western Australia when there was enough support.[106] When Bullock drove back to the South-West on Wednesday, 4 March, Thomas rode with him, so that he could show Quicke the draft proclamation and obtain his handwriting on it as evidence that he was involved. Quicke added a note objecting to the abolition of the White Australia policy, for AFM policy was to maintain it.[107]

That evening, at the Waroona Hotel, Bullock regaled his dining room companions with disaster stories. They discussed the bombing of Darwin, and Bullock claimed he had just heard by telephone from Perth that Geraldton had been blown to pieces. (It was Broome that had been bombed.) The reference to Geraldton upset a PMG telephone mechanic, Robert John Leggett, whose parents lived there. Bullock alleged that an American aircraft carrier that had been in Perth a few weeks ago had been bombed and sunk 200 miles off Geraldton with only eight survivors. Then he suggested that the Japanese would be in Perth in a fortnight, but Australia would not fare worse under Japan than under Britain, rather like Norway under the Nazis. None of these wild statements could be blamed on Thomas.[108] Bullock also warned that petrol ration tickets should be used at once, because postmasters had sealed orders about them.[109] This secret information must have come from Krakouer, who handled these tickets in her job. As it was an offence to spread rumours about rationing, they could have been prosecuted for this alone.

On Saturday, 7 March, in the Riverside Drive flat that Bullock now shared with Krakouer, he and Williams revised the proclamation. Bullock made suggestions, Williams wrote them down, then Bullock or Krakouer typed them. The next day, in the same flat, they showed Thomas the proclamation. They agreed that it was dangerous and should be burnt. Thomas pretended to do this, but charred only a corner. Williams suggested points for sabotage, and they drew up a list of officials and clergy for execution. They allegedly expected the Japanese to help free Australia from 'Jews and Catholics'. They agreed that, when the Japanese were close enough, they would demand immediate peace negotiations, and would shoot any soldier who refused to lay down his arms.[110] Thomas claimed that Williams said, 'I hope the Japanese invade here, so that we can take over the Commonwealth.'[111]

Krakouer, using the name N. R. Kaye and styling herself Secretary, WA Branch of the Australia-First Movement, wrote to Sydney to ask for recognition of their group as the Western Australian section of the AFM. As it was intended for insertion in the *Publicist*, the letter did not mention sabotage, executions or contacting the Japanese.[112]

That evening, Thomas gave the documents to Richards, who now considered there was enough evidence for Bullock, Quicke, Williams and Krakouer to be arrested. Police raids were made at daybreak on 9 March. Richards and two constables arrested Bullock and Krakouer in their flat; their search found notes made by Krakouer at one of the meetings and notes of a broadcast from Tokyo. In her handbag they found military and naval information in the handwriting of Williams.[113] The proclamation drawn up a few days earlier was found in a leather case. It announced that an armistice had been arranged with the Japanese, and that an 'Australia First National Socialist Government' had been established. It paid tribute to 'the valiant efforts of the Japanese who have so successfully fought for the liberation of our peoples from Jewish domination and the danger of communism', and welcomed them as 'friends and liberators'.[114] Bullock denied having seen the proclamation previously. Richards reported on 20 March, 'This document is definitely treasonable.'[115]

Williams was arrested at his home in Maylands. Nothing subversive was found there, and he denied knowing about a proclamation. He and Bullock were lodged in Roe Street lock-up under Section 13 of the National Security Act. Quicke's house at Balingup was searched; he was arrested and taken to Roe Street later that day. Nothing incriminating was found except a copy of *Mein Kampf*, which Quicke's wife allegedly said they used to read in bed, 'chapter by chapter, like the Bible'. In court, Grace Quicke denied this.[116]

Faced with evidence that the proclamation found in *his* case had been typed on *his* typewriter, on paper identical to that found in *his* flat, and had been in an envelope matching ones also found in *his* case, Bullock admitted drawing up the proclamation with Williams. He claimed he had put in only what Thomas had told him, and it was meant as a joke. Later that evening, Bullock admitted writing the liquidation list and the notes allotting duties.[117] On 11 March, after being without cigarettes for two days, Williams 'volunteered' a written statement, admitting that he and Bullock had compiled the Proclamation *at Bullock's suggestion,* and that most ideas had come from Bullock.[118] Williams stated:

> I believe Bullock sincerely thought that a successful contact (with the Japanese) at that stage would result, if accepted, in saving the rest of Australia from needless slaughter and misery.

> He was quite serious about this matter and, in fact, each one of us seriously thought that a successfully negotiated peace under these conditions – that is, under the conditions of a successful Japanese invasion – would benefit Australia.[119]

Richards commented, 'His story upset Bullock's tale of regarding the matter as a joke.' On 13 March, Krakouer admitted writing the AFM minutes found at her flat, and said she too thought that Bullock took the matter seriously. After making enquiries in South-West coastal districts, Richards reported: 'Good evidence was obtained that Bullock had been actively engaged in spreading rumour and defeatist propaganda, and also in recruiting for the Australia First Movement.'[120]

Instead of being kept separate, the men were allowed to exercise together, with the danger of collusion and contamination of evidence. Taking advantage of this, Bullock passed Quicke notes on how to present their evidence. Quicke told Bullock that if he insisted on thrusting them on him they would be handed to the police. Bullock insisted, and Quicke gave them to Detective Alford on 17 March, complaining that Bullock was trying to make him give false evidence, particularly about events on 21 and 22 February. He objected to being forced to associate with Bullock and Williams,[121] complaining bitterly:

> [Bullock] says too that he never had any connection with the A. F. over east. All his talk about being their representative; all his lies about addressing big meetings in the Town Hall, Perth - all lies! And he has the insolence to tell me so in his statement… I do not shirk my just punishment but spare me the sight and sound of these people.[122]

Quicke told Alford, 'Bullock is the greatest bloody liar I have ever met.'[123] By 28 March, Bullock had convinced Quicke there was a misunderstanding; Quicke withdrew his statement that Bullock was trying to make him give false evidence, but that did not alter his resentment over other lies Bullock had told.[124]

Melanie O'Loughlin was writing to Stephensen on 10 March; in the first part of her letter, she repeated her regret over the death of Miles, adding that the Adyar Hall incident was terrible. She expressed her misgivings about a man named Hardt, and said she had told him that the *Publicist* 'stands for real Australian Patriotism, that is against Jews and Communists, which are taking hold of our beloved Country'. She related that Hardt and Bullock were keen to start an AFM in Perth, then wrote, 'It would be fatal if these men would with their hostile attitude upset the clean and loyal reputation of the Publicist.'[125] At that point, three police arrived, told her about the arrests, and searched the house again, taking private letters and all copies of the *Publicist*, but they overlooked the letter she had been writing. Late that evening, she wrote about Bullock's arrest:

> I am not surprised. You know what I told you in my letters about him. His ideas are so different from the Publicist policy... the men uttered some remarks, which made my husband and me worried, should they in the name of Australia First start some subversive propaganda.[126]

She wrote that she regretted giving Bullock the *Publicist*.[127] The letter was sent by registered mail on 11 March, and it would have been picked up in the interception of Stephensen's mail, but he had already been arrested. Melanie was not interned. Her husband was old and ill and needed her care;[128] she could be intimidated into promising discretion and it was believed that, unlike Adela Walsh, she would keep her word.

THE TRIAL

Evidence having been obtained, Colonel Moseley, now Deputy Director of the Security Service, and Sergeant Richards considered how to use it. They suggested action under the Criminal Code, Section 37, which dealt with treason. Newspapers had called for communists, fascists or others to be tried for treason, subversion or sedition, without considering whether this was possible. Legal advice was sought from Melbourne barristers, John Vincent Barry and Thomas Weetman Smith.[129] On 2 April, they reported:

> We do not think that there is any offence in the nature of treason or any other relevant offence existing under any common law of the Commonwealth and we therefore think that some statutory warrant must be found for

> any charge intended to be laid against the persons in question in Western Australia.[130]

They considered first the suggested Section 37, Sub-section 8, of the Western Australian Criminal Code of 1913: 'This sub-section makes it an offence punishable by death for any person to assist by any means whatsoever any public enemy at war with the Sovereign.' Section 40 required that there be two witnesses to an overt act, but there had been no overt act. Under the Commonwealth Crimes Act, Section 24(1)(b), it was a capital offence to 'assist by any means whatever any public enemy', but such a charge would also be likely to fail. Under Section 7 of the Commonwealth Crimes Act, *attempting* to assist the enemy was punishable by death, and under Section 552 of the Western Australian Code, by fourteen years' imprisonment, but they had not made an attempt. It was recommended that the charge be '*conspiring* to assist a public enemy at war with the Sovereign'. The maximum penalty under Sections 37(8) and 558 of the Western Australian Code was seven years; under Section 86 of the Commonwealth Act, it was three years.[131] There was little chance that a jury would convict on a capital charge when a more appropriate response might have been some sessions with a psychiatrist, but the War Cabinet directed on 31 March that prosecutions be initiated.[132]

The preliminary hearing before Justice William John Wallwork began on 7 May with a sensation, for that morning the *West Australian* had published evidence relevant to the case.[133] As the matter was *sub judice*, this could have caused a mistrial. The prosecutor, Gordon Bede D'Arcy, denied giving information to the paper. Hughes, Bullock's attorney, admitted doing so, as he thought it would be to the advantage of the accused. Justice Wallwork allowed the hearing to proceed.[134] It can hardly have contributed to any goodwill there might have been for the accused when Hughes, on 16 April, between the arrests and the preliminary hearing, said in the Legislative Assembly:

> To hear people talking about Hitler having caused the war and singing hymns of hate, is to my mind all wrong. After all is said and done Hitler played a very small part in causing the present war.[135]

The defence put forward by Hughes was that the case was a police frame-up. He claimed that Bullock, while touring the South-West, was attending only to PPA business. In fact, Bullock had written that he would use his business activities to advocate the overthrow of 'the present system'. Hughes argued that Bullock was not a member of the AFM, but Bullock had claimed he was. Hughes protested that Bullock had no connection with foreign powers or agents; but in fact even during the war Bullock asked Germans in America for propaganda material. Hughes alleged that Bullock was only a subscriber to the *Publicist* and did not discuss the war. Actually, he had discussed it often in terms that had caused people to report him during 1940 and 1941, which was why Thomas had been assigned to gather evidence. When the accused were committed for trial, Hughes said, 'I think the press have had a feast already. This case has been manna from heaven for them.'[136]

The trial proper, which covered roughly the same ground, began on 2 June before Chief Justice Sir John Northmore. The gist of the charge was that the accused 'conspired together to assist within the Commonwealth of Australia a public enemy, to wit, the Armed forces of Japan, contrary to Section 86 of the Crimes Act'.[137] There were eight police and five civilian witnesses for the prosecution, and sworn statements from twelve others. Most gave evidence solely against Bullock.[138] Newspapers that covered the trial were at the same time reporting the Japanese midget submarine incursion into Sydney Harbour, the shelling of Newcastle, the Battle of Midway and the fall of Tobruk.

Melanie O'Loughlin was called to testify, giving Thomas an opportunity to report that she had said she could smell a Jew at a hundred yards, and for her to be questioned about The Link. People whose identity was not revealed had threatened her, telling her not to give evidence. In general, she was a truthful witness. She confirmed things that Bullock denied, including the letter saying that he wanted Germany to win the war.[139]

On 5 June Percy Stephensen asked to testify. After being referred to Canberra and Perth, his request was refused, as he knew nothing that would assist the jury to decide the charge before the court, but simply wanted to dissociate the AFM from the case.[140]

Hughes stressed the theme: 'No Thomas, no conspiracy… The defence is that Thomas set out to find an offence. He did not find an offence so he manufactured evidence to create an offence.'[141] In fact, at that stage of the war Bullock's rumour mongering at Waroona on 4 March alone could have cost him a prison term. Hughes called the conspiracy 'the ravings of a bunch of lunatics'.[142] And solicitor Hughes was a very close political associate of the 'lunatic', and probably a member of The Link.

The defence tried to limit the conspiracy to the foundation of the Australia-First group on 21 February, when Williams was not present. In fact, the more important dates were 27 February, 7 March and 8 March, when Bullock and Williams were present but Quicke was not. On these dates the proclamation was drawn up. Hughes tried to maintain that it was a question of Bullock's word against that of Thomas, although it was more often Thomas and Quicke against Bullock, or Thomas and Williams against Bullock. D'Arcy stressed that conspiracy lay not in committing illegal acts, but in agreeing to commit them. The summing up by the Chief Justice Northmore read in part:

> [It] is important that you should thoroughly grasp what the charge is not—it is not a charge that they did assist or attempt to assist the Japanese. The charge is that they agreed if the occasion arose, i.e. invasion, then they would do what they could to assist them to enable them to bring about a negotiated peace which would leave them in charge of the country...
>
> [The] agreement if it was made was entered into at this meeting at the Rex Hotel on the 21st February... Now it is on common ground that Williams was not at this meeting at the Rex Hotel. The law is that if two or more persons enter into an agreement to do an unlawful act others who join in become just as liable... It is not necessary that all should be together on each occasion...
>
> Everyone agrees that at the meeting there was an agreement to form a party, and the only question is what it was that they agreed to do.[143]

The jury retired at 12.15 p.m. on 23 June; at 3.45 they returned a guilty verdict on Bullock and Williams, and acquitted Quicke and Krakouer.[144] Bullock was sentenced to three years' hard labour,

Williams to two years. Application for leave to appeal against their sentences was refused.[145]

At the Inquiry held in 1944–45, Justice Clyne found it difficult to believe that there was no transcript of such an important case. Hughes explained that in Western Australia there was no transcript unless one party engaged a shorthand writer.[146] It is difficult to imagine how it can be seen whether justice has been done when basic information on which to found a judgment is lacking.

Hughes tried to make out a case that, as Quicke and Krakouer had not been convicted, and Williams had not been present on 21 February, there was nobody with whom Bullock could have conspired, as a conspiracy needs more than one person. However, there had been a recent precedent in Western Australia when Justus Heinrich Behn had been convicted of conspiring to defraud His Majesty's Government, and the alleged co-conspirators had been acquitted.[147] His appeal on those very grounds was dismissed.[148]

Quicke appealed against his internment, claiming that Thomas had instigated the whole case against him. As Thomas had made a special trip to Balingup in order to involve Quicke, this was reasonable, but his appeal, heard in South Australia on 6 March 1943, was rejected. He had told the Tribunal:

> When I found myself interned, and heard in more detail of the activities of the Aust. First Movement and the Party, I was not too pleased with the part I had taken in the proceedings... I now consider that the Australia First Movement were not disloyal to Australia. The Australia First Movement were nothing to do with Bullock and Williams.[149]

It is difficult to estimate the damage done by Bullock, less by his unrealistic conspiracy than by his public rumour mongering. Irrespective of whether he meant what he said in the proclamation, of whether he intended sabotage or assassinations, of whether the Japanese would have listened to him or shot him on sight: Bullock was potentially dangerous.

The self-important Western Australians with their *folie des grandeurs* were a brief and insignificant aberration with no coherent policy or lasting influence. Whether or not they were simply 'a bunch of lunatics' is not the point. Even lunatics could do real damage.

Chapter 9

Internments and Restriction Orders

News of the arrests in Western Australia was sent interstate by coded telegram, and in Sydney it was decided overnight to arrest leaders of the Australia-First Movement that morning. This action had long been considered, but it was done so hastily that serious mistakes were made. When a crime had been committed, police could arrest and charge a person; if there had been no overt act, they could detain a person for only ten days. Only 'the Minister' could intern a British subject,[1] and National Security (General) Regulations, 26 (9), specified that this meant the Minister for Defence Co-ordination or the Minister for the Army, at that time Curtin and Forde.

Dossiers concerning internment of British subjects went also to the Attorney-General, Dr Evatt, who advised against most of them. Evatt left Australia on 9 March to visit the USA and Britain to persuade Roosevelt to send more troops and to convince Churchill to send Spitfires. The trip had been planned much earlier, but self-centred Stephensen alleged that Evatt fled Australia to avoid blame for his internment.

Apologists for the AFM have claimed that the CIB thought they were harmless and only Military Intelligence wanted them interned.[2] The CIB was not necessarily correct; MI was better informed because it controlled mail scrutiny and telephone taps, but the information so obtained could not be used at a trial. Only if a police search found letters in a later official search could they be cited, but it could not be admitted that the content of telephone conversations or consular documents was known. MI controlled agents unknown to the police; because their usefulness depended on secrecy, MI did pass on what was known from these sources.[3] Having access to more information than the CIB, MI was better placed to make valid appraisals, but the judgment of individual officers was not necessarily sound.

While the police made notes from the *Publicist* and sent shorthand writers to AFM public meetings, MI sought out people who knew Stephensen in order to build up a case against him. In a statement on 11 February, Phillip Lloyd Robbins, night officer at the Heathcote railway station near Stephensen's weekend cottage, claimed that Stephensen praised the German system and the Japanese 'New Order', and he had no doubt that Stephensen, who was known locally as the 'Mad Fascist', would assist the Japanese if they invaded.[4] Stephensen denied approving of the *Japanese* New Order,[5] and could have claimed that he meant an Australian 'New Order'.

Officers were aware of the dangers of giving too much credence to denunciations. These could be the product of a spiteful neighbour or a business rival. If a communist or a Jew laid information against an alleged fascist, it might be a lie to secure the arrest of a political foe, or it might be true. As far as manpower allowed, informants were checked for veracity and emotional stability.

From mid 1941 to early in 1942, some worrying things happened in Sydney; MI knew they were connected in some way with the AFM, but the association was not as close as was suspected. In June 1941, objectionable and illegal typewritten pamphlets called *Action Post* began circulating in Sydney. They extolled the virtues of German National Socialism and the issue of 20 June claimed: 'It is issued by the National Socialist Party of Australia (Sydney) which is associated with the National Socialist Parties of Germany, England, Scotland, Ireland, Canada, South America, and South Africa.'[6] It said that a printing machine was being assembled, although this was as untrue as the claim of association with National Socialist Parties world-wide. National Socialism, it said, was 'much better, human, and satisfying than this diseased and corrupt Democracy in which we live'; it ended with HEIL HITLER!

The writer did his own typing, which gave him security but limited his output. Appeals were made in the press for anybody knowing the identity of the author of *Action Post* to contact the police or MI, but he had confided in nobody, except that during 1940–41 he wrote to the Japanese Consulate-General to try to contact secretly the German Embassy in Tokyo. He wrote that he wished 'to convey to the Japanese people themselves that there are people who realise that the present Japanese struggle for a new order is for something more decent and fair for all concerned'. He did not give his real name, calling himself Alexander Mortimer.[7]

At the beginning of October, he offered to surrender himself, if the army guaranteed that his name would not be disclosed to the press, as his family did not share his views; otherwise he would begin a campaign of sabotage.[8] The condition was accepted, but since Stephensen claimed that he met 'Mortimer' for the first time in an internment camp,[9] he must be identified by his real name, for Miles and Stephensen and others at the Yabber Club did know William Alexander McKeand, and that was the same person.[10]

Born on 6 July 1911 in Newcastle on Tyne, McKeand arrived in Australia with his mother and younger brother in September 1922.[11] He was employed in the Postmaster-General's Department in 1927 as a messenger, and as a postman from 1930 to 1934. He had a permit to enter vital points in the Posts and Telegraphs telephonic and radio transmission stations and depots; he could have done incalculable damage if he had been more resolute. The *Publicist* had not converted him to fascism or Nazism; he claimed he had been associated with German National Socialism since June 1929, and between 1932 and 1938 had written for both Australian and German papers.[12] He had subscribed to *Die Brücke* from June 1934[13] and became associated with The Link in February 1939.[14] He was also in touch with the British Union of Fascists, and he had a badge of the *Deutsche Arbeitsfront*.[15] He had no opportunity to join the AFM, as he was already in prison when it was founded, but at the back of a booklet called *Australia First*, issued by the Cahill-Collins group in Melbourne, was found a membership application filled out by 'W. A. McKeand, Norton Street, Ashfield, N.S.W.'[16]

The *Publicist* petty cash book shows that letters were sent to Alex McKeand on 14 March and 17 March 1941.[17] He apparently visited the Yabber Club in March 1941, for he wrote to Miles on 17 April that, after his first visit, he had been looking forward to further such occasions, but he had been unable to attend the weekly meetings of the Yabberoos as he had been ill. After consulting Cahill, who probably also knew McKeand, Miles wrote that he looked forward to meeting McKeand again. The postage on this letter was debited to the *Publicist* petty cash.

On 7 November, 'Mortimer' was prosecuted for two offences under NSR (Section 13), for publishing matter prejudicial to the efficient prosecution of the war. At the Police Court hearing he said, 'I hate democracy, and will not rest until I see it crushed.' Unlike many internees, he stood by his beliefs, denied nothing, and made no excuses. He was sentenced to six months on each charge, cumulative. MI hoped that would be the end of the obnoxious pamphlets, but it was not, so they suspected that other AFM members were involved. In that they were partly correct.

As early as July 1941, there were public complaints about offensive circulars called *Gentiles Awake!* These did not cease when McKeand was imprisoned. In January and February 1942, pamphlets entitled *Australians Awake!* were mailed to many people, including editors of country newspapers, or placed in letterboxes around Sydney. They denounced 'American Imperialism' and 'Jewish International Finance', warning that American troops would stay in Australia while Australians were at the front defending American-Jewish interests.[18] One of them called on Australians to lay down their arms.[19] Many were handed straight to the police, but there were few clues as to their origin.

Finding anonymous pamphleteers who acted alone was difficult, and Stephensen was suspected. On 8 February 1942, a public typist reported that she had duplicated 500 copies of these documents for a man who had foolishly given his real name and address. The house of Thomas Potts Graham was raided the next day. A massive amount of Australia-First material was found, along with one of Mills's books, multiple copies of books by the Walshes and a letter from Stephensen. Graham also had a black shirt, which he said was part of the uniform of a National Action Council, which had lapsed for lack of membership.[20] He denied being a member of the AFM until his membership card (No. 47) was found; it was discovered that Ian Mudie had introduced him to the Yabber Club,[21] and it was suggested that other members had helped him. Charged in February, he was sentenced to six months' hard labour.[22]

Edwin Arnold also became active again. He was a Theosophist, and he claimed he had a deep knowledge of the occult. This was not MI business, but his other activities were. On 18 February

1942, Arnold advertised in the *Sydney Morning Herald* for people to help form a World Aryan Federation to 'deal with the Jews'. This appears to be the meeting held on 19 February in the building where Stephensen was holding the AFM meeting. According to Arnold, three men and three women attended, while two policemen came along later. Police attention alarmed Arnold. On 22 February, he sent Major J. Prentice a long letter setting out his philosophy and his involvement in the occult and astral projection. He expected a sympathetic hearing, for Prentice was 'a fellow-theosophist and aspirant along the Pathway'.[23]

Arnold claimed he had evolved a distinctive philosophy that he called 'Aryosophy' - Aryan Wisdom.[24] It was, he said, 'the work I was brought into incarnation to do'. Among material found during a search of his premises was his 31-Point Programme for the National Socialist Party of Australia and Oceania (N.S.P.A.O.), headed 'Australians Awake!' (Graham's slogan) and 'Advance Australia First'; he described the salute of the N.S.P.A.O. as an upraised right arm, fingers extended, with the greeting 'Australia First'. There was also his 25-Point programme of an Aryan World League, otherwise called the White International. An odd mix of Pan-Aryanism and Age of Aquarius, it advocated breeding out 'inferior races' and affirmed the existence of an 'age-long Jewish Plot to ruin the Aryan Race'. Arnold's plans were unknown to most AFM members, but MI knew about them, and about his links with the AFM. McKeand, Graham and Arnold were examples of the *Publicist*'s potential to attract unbalanced extremists. At the same time, beginning with trials in January and lasting several months, publicity was given to massive spy rings in the United States and Brazil.[25] It would need very little extra trouble to incite MI to take action.

When the telegram breaking the news of the alleged plot in Perth reached Sydney during the night of 9–10 March, there were already substantial dossiers on some AFM members. For months, MI had advocated the internment of the 'ringleaders', and the war had reached a stage where invasion seemed imminent. Even without the events in Perth, Stephensen would probably have been interned soon, and Adela Walsh certainly would have been. It is true that decisions were made too hastily, but later critics of the AF internments seem not to have taken sufficient account of the situation at the time.[26]

The purpose of internment was to *prevent* actions that might harm the country. This was the fallacy of the demand that Australian citizens should not be interned, but prosecuted if they had already committed acts of treason or sabotage. By then, it was *too late*. When assessing the possible effects of people's actions, MI preferred to err on the side of caution. If good and innocent persons were interned unjustly, they paid a smaller price than did good and innocent persons who were killed. In March and April 1942, Russian Fascists in Queensland were interned. Some could have been dangerous; most were just big talkers. Some German women were interned, usually to join husbands. Many Queensland Italians were interned; some, prior to the war, had paraded their fascist allegiance; a few had traded in contraband, including rifles, with the Japanese.[27] Some boasted about making good money while their stupid neighbours' sons were fighting.

At the Clyne Inquiry, J. W. Maund asked Lieutenant-Colonel Reginald Powell, with regard to his failure to check certain matters, 'Surely this was a matter of supreme importance?' Powell replied, 'Yes, and there were many other matters of supreme importance at the time.'[28] MI officers could not determine whether justice was being done in all cases. It is hard to see any justification for some internments, but there was a certain irony about them. For example: Point 38 of the Fifty-Point Policy said, 'For discipline; against casualness.' In the explanatory booklet, Stephensen had written:

> Military rule, the imposition of authority 'from above', may yet, under harsh necessity, prove the only practicable method of eliminating Australian slackness and casualness of mind and manners.[29]

When the military, under the harsh threat of imminent invasion, imposed their authority on Stephensen, he objected. He had perhaps never understood the implications of his proposals. Similarly, Watts had discounted reports of brutality in German concentration camps, referring to them as 'uncomfortable places'.[30] When he found himself in a less uncomfortable camp in Australia, he was loud in his complaints.

The Clyne Inquiry tried to determine who had made decisions in individual cases. There was so much disagreement that it was futile.

Responsibility rested ultimately with Colonel Powell, who said he was obliged to accept his officers' recommendations. Arrests in New South Wales were made mainly on 10 March: Percy Stephensen (AFM member No. 1), Walter Tinker-Giles (2), Gordon Rice (10), Sydney Hooper (17), Clarence Crowley (18), Eric Stephensen (19), Val Crowley (26), Edward Masey (30), Edwin Arnold (43), and Keith Bath, Harley Matthews and Martin Watts, who were not officially members. Coincidentally, Bath had an appointment that day regarding joining the RAAF in 'an administrative capacity'.[31] Downe (25) was arrested at Tamworth on the evening of 10 March, and taken to Sydney on 12 March.[32] On 11 March, Cahill (3) was arrested at the army camp at Nelson's Bay, and Kirtley at Woy Woy. On 12 March, Salier (13) was arrested at Artarmon. That brought the total in New South Wales to the sixteen who were later considered to be 'the Australia-First internees'. Belatedly, on 13 March, *Progress*, the paper of the crypto-communist NSW State Labor Party, demanded that the AFM be banned and 'Stephensen and his satellites' interned.[33] Graham was transferred from imprisonment to internment on 10 July.[34]

In total, 16 of the 65 known members of the AFM were interned, Adela Walsh being the only woman. This consisted of thirteen of the sixteen mentioned above, plus Walsh (5), Mills (32) and Graham (47). That membership of the AFM was not considered, in isolation, as grounds for internment is shown by the fact that thirty-three men were not interned. These included the poet Ian Mudie (9), who had returned to South Australia before enlisting in the AMF on 12 February; Rex Ingamells (59) of *Jindyworobak;*[35] Percy Stephensen's stepson (John Lockyer – 14) and J. B. Miles (28).

There was scant justification for interning Bath. He had not written for the *Publicist*, nor was he was officially a member of the AFM. While he became associated with the AFM when its nature should have been clear, so did Sir Thomas Gordon. At the Clyne Inquiry, Maund commented, 'It is very hard to find why flesh should have been made of one and fish of another.' He said there was more evidence against Lang, who was never questioned, and against Ludowici, Mudie and Malcolm Smith.[36]

Kenneth Bockmaster (31), a 'returned soldier' who visited Japanese firms trying to sell *Publicist* subscriptions,[37] was apparently ignored. E. J. Ward wrote to Forde on 7 April that he had received a letter saying that a leading worker for the AFM was 'located in an important position' at Garden Island, and he should be picked up or at least questioned. As this was a naval matter, it was referred to Lieutenant Buchan of Naval Intelligence. He reported that Bockmaster was working there 'in a civil capacity', and no action was taken.[38] This lack of interest in Bockmaster on the part of Naval Intelligence is the only reason to suspect that he might have been an undercover agent.

Interrogated in March 1942 in connection with the Yabber Club, Ludowici signed a Restriction Order, undertaking to have nothing more to do with the AFM.[39] Jack Lockyer, who was serving in the army, was questioned but was not under serious suspicion.[40] Smith wrote to Muirden that he had 'powerful friends', who protected him.[41] Few people were powerful or brave enough to intervene in the face of a Ministerial Order. When arrested, Hooper said he would soon be out, as he had numerous friends in the right quarter.[42] He was a close friend of Jack Beasley (Minister for Supply and Development), and he knew Archie Cameron (formerly Postmaster-General and Minister for the Navy). Bath and Val Crowley were closely associated with Spender (Member of Advisory War Council, formerly Treasurer and Minister for the Army). Stephensen had been in close contact with Evatt. They found quickly that there are few real friends in politics.

It would be instructive to examine what was apparently in the minds of those who made the decisions. The method of dealing with suspect organisations was to intern the executive committee.[43] That would have accounted for Percy Stephensen as president, Tinker-Giles as treasurer, Cahill as organiser, and Rice and Watts as committee members. Although not a financial member, Watts joined the committee when Adela Walsh and Cahill resigned. It was anomalous for him to be on the committee when he was not a member, but he attended committee meetings, and his appointment was announced in the *Publicist* of February 1942. Some women were interviewed and their premises searched, but female British citizens were not interned without cogent reasons. Thus Sheila Rice (the secretary), Vera Parkinson, Marjorie Corby and Elaine Pope were left at liberty.

When the police came for Stephensen before dawn on 10 March, he did not realise he was being detained. Only five days earlier, he had been questioned and released, and he thought this would happen again. Detective-Sergeant A. L. Nye later insisted he had told Stephensen he was being detained under National Security Regulations; Stephensen denied this.[44] After his house had been searched, he was taken to the *Publicist* office, and this too was searched. Letters that had already been intercepted and copied were found, and knowledge of their content could then be used in evidence.

A search of the house of Tinker-Giles revealed items that attracted comment: *Mein Kampf* in the form of 17 booklets and the *Far Eastern Trade Bulletin* issued by the Japanese Chamber of Commerce.[45] The Red Cross sold the booklets to raise money for the Prisoners of War Comforts Fund; if it was legal to publish and sell them, it could not be illegal to buy or possess them. The *Far Eastern Trade Bulletin* was sent free to politicians, press and businessmen, and no doubt many parliamentarians had copies.

Valentine Crowley's remarks at the Yabber Club were held against him, but as Hooper was interned without having been reported for subversive comments the determining factor was perhaps their part-ownership of the *Publicist.* However, in private letters Hooper and Miles had agreed that political assassinations would be *necessary* in Australia, while Hooper's diaries over the years showed 'consistently violent anti-British feelings'.[46] Salier and Masey had helped finance the *Publicist*; their articles on taxation and economics were not objectionable, but Salier's pro-Japanese articles under the name of 'H. Bruno Thomas' were controversial, and Masey had spoken at AFM meetings.

Jack Kirtley was annoyed but not surprised at being arrested; he had destroyed his correspondence, but other people had kept letters he had written.[47] Kirtley was an emotional and difficult man. His partnership with Stephensen in the Fanfrolico Press in England had been uneasy, and his marriage had broken up. In letters to Stephensen, he had abused Australians as 'gutless swine' and Australia's leaders as 'fools and scoundrels'. He made a virtue of not having joined the AFM, but he had written to Stephensen on 8 December 1941 that he would join when he could afford it.[48]

At the time of his arrest, Kirtley was recovering from a nervous breakdown caused by the strain of nursing his invalid mother.[49] He either did not think before he wrote, or did not mean what he wrote. Thus he could write to Stephensen on 5 December 1941, 'LABOR is a repugnant disease.'[50] Yet on 13 January 1944, when he wanted help from Arthur Calwell, he claimed that he had always voted Labor.[51] He allegedly admitted he had great contempt for Australians, and admired the leaders of Germany and Japan.[52] Moreover, MI suspected that he was involved in printing obnoxious leaflets that had been circulating in Sydney. When he was arrested, police asked him if he had a printing press.[53] They were sensitive to the possibility of printing illegal dodgers, and probably they knew that in 1939 he had consulted Miles about obtaining an Albion hand press.[54]

In 1942, Harley Matthews, separated from his wife, was living on his vineyard with his mother. Reports in his dossier that he had been a barrister and a war correspondent were untrue. He had been a solicitor's clerk,[55] and he had worked at the *Sun* for two years from March 1918.[56] Apart from some foolish letters, one thing that told against him was a rumour that the Japanese had financed his house so that they would have a place to hold meetings. This was untrue, as MI could have discovered by applying for access to his bank and mortgage records.[57]

The internment of Martin Watts, according to Captain Blood, was justified by his membership of the executive of the AFM. In addition, Watts had written in the *Publicist* that Australian society was weak and corrupt, as it had been in Germany and Italy before Hitler and Mussolini took over.[58] He was no friend of the military and political hierarchy, but he seldom attended the Yabber Club, and he quarrelled with Stephensen and Miles over their pro-Japanese attitude. Dora dominated the Watts household, and her writing was controversial. It was perhaps hoped that his internment would act as a brake on his wife.

The inoffensive Clarence Crowley seems to have been interned solely because he was Val Crowley's brother. On 12 March, he wrote to his wife about the stupid government that was 'so weak as to be afraid of a few cranks who wish to put their own country first'. Censorship noted that the letter was being 'held', i.e. not forwarded.[59]

More placid than the others, he seemed unaware of the controversial implications of AFM activity.

Eric Stephensen was interned largely because he was Percy Stephensen's brother; he was thought to be too much under Percy's influence and 'ready to give his full support to anything his brother suggested'.[60] Yet once Percy seemed to be trying to restrain Eric: 'What is the use of annoying your associates by foolish gestures against "God save the King".'[61]

Eric Stephensen might have been causing annoyance to people in his immediate vicinity, but he had not spoken in public, and the article he wrote for the *Publicist* was inoffensive. It is hard to imagine he would have been interned if he had not been a Stephensen.

Clive Kirkwood Downe was very unfortunate. He had not written for the *Publicist*, and was not a regular at the Yabber Club. He worked for the firm that had employed his father for forty-eight years. Downe had tried to join the RAAF in May 1940, being rejected on account of his eyesight. In December 1941, he was accepted into the AMF. Once his belongings were searched, and it was found that he had copies of *Mein Kampf*, *Bio-Politics* and *Germany Speaks*, he was in trouble, although, as he pointed out later to Dr Evatt, one of the books confiscated as subversive was Evatt's own book, *The Rum Rebellion*.[62] Downe might have been targeted because he had written from camp to ask Stephensen for 12 AFM membership application forms and 20 copies of the Ten-Point manifesto, but he received no reply.[63] A letter that Cahill had written to Downe, but not even posted, also caused trouble. On 31 December, Cahill had drafted the letter suggesting the formation a semi-secret AF organisation within the army to 'accomplish our complete National Independence, *if necessary by force of arms*'. Here too he mentioned a Council of Seven for National Revolution.[64] Having had trouble with communist cells in the armed forces, the military did not want a fascist cell as well.

Detainees were taken to Liverpool Camp, where they were segregated from other internees. Allotted a two-roomed hut with a veranda, they called it Australia House. Muirden said that they were taken to the Anzac Rifle Range at Moorebank, two miles from Harley Matthews' vineyard.[65] Watts also lived in this area. As there is some loose usage of names, it is not always possible to be sure whether, when a location is given as Holsworthy, what is really meant is Liverpool, and vice versa.[66] Once recovered from the initial shock, the detainees expected that it would be recognised that a mistake had been made and they would be released. They did not understand the interpretations that could be put on the evidence against them. They failed to appreciate that what they had been doing could have been harmful to national security. The situation was similar to that in Britain, of which Richard Griffiths wrote, 'Like Ramsay, Arnold Leese was appalled to be considered unpatriotic, merely because he was trying to undermine the war effort.'[67]

They lodged applications for release from detention under Section 13 of the National Security Act.[68] These lapsed when, on 25 March, they were served with orders for internment under Regulation 26, dated 20 March. Then they began to take the matter very seriously, even more so after Forde on the next day made his notorious statement to the House of Representatives, apparently linking all the AFM with a conspiracy to aid the Japanese. Most applied the next day for leave to object to internment. Stephensen lodged his application on 6 April, but withdrew it two days later, as Prime Minister Curtin had stated in Parliament that he would be charged publicly.[69]

Adela Walsh was the only female AFM member to be interned, mainly because of years of disruption and defiance and her close association with the Japanese. Eastern Command reported on 11 February that since 8 December 1941 Adela Walsh was even more pro-Japanese. She had told an 'A1' informant that Australia should not have entered the war; America, England and Australia had done everything to annoy Japan, and the Japanese were justified in their actions. She allegedly declared, 'China is done, the British Empire is going… The Australian Government should ask for any possible terms as there is no hope of holding the Japanese.'[70] Another informant, who had a conversation with Adela on Sunday, 1 March, reported to Captain Caiger that she had said:

> Japan is the rightful owner of the Pacific Islands and Australia being one of the Pacific Islands, Australia should belong to Japan. It was time that Japan came and took over Australia, as Darwin for all practical purposes already belongs to Japan…

> Australia must be part of the Asiatic scheme, just as Africa, which really belongs to Germany, must be part of the European scheme...[71]

She claimed that Darwin had been wiped out and its inhabitants were in the hands of the Japanese, and said that for over 150 years the islands had belonged to Japan spiritually, and now it was an actuality. America would not help Australia, and she had no time for Americans, as they were 'a hybrid lot'. Russia and Germany, she alleged, had a pact under which Russia was to advance no further; Germany was to have the Caucasus oilfields, and the Ukraine would be an independent state. If only a fraction of this report was true, one could not help doubting her sanity.

On 16 March, Commissioner MacKay recommended that Adela Walsh should not be interned, for the following reasons:

> 1. She would cause trouble in any internment camp and would be a disturbing influence.
>
> 2. If she followed the natural family traits, she would immediately go on a hunger strike and cause the Minister for the Army all manner of trouble and complaint through the press.
>
> 3. With a sick husband under a restriction order and this woman in camp, further cause for adverse publicity would ensue...
>
> I express the definite view that their daughter, Sylvia Walsh, who was employed in the Domei News Agency under the Japanese Toyoda, is just as subversive as her mother...[72]

He recommended restriction orders on the three Walshes, limiting them to the township of Bourke. They could be quartered in a police house and provided with sustenance on the scale allowed to internees. There would be strict censorship on telephone, telegraph and mail. Not only would the seven or so police in Bourke and the blacktracker be watching them, but so would the whole township.

Examination of the Mitsui documents, however, had produced another cogent reason to intern Adela, for a secret censorship order, addressed to the *Voice of the People* and dated 13 November, was found among them. Adela denied giving it to Kenji Miwa. First she blamed Tom's grandchildren for opening her mail and mixing up her papers. Then she held her daughter Christian responsible for slipping it into a magazine that Tom had taken to Mitsui. Next she blamed Sylvia, who took papers to Mitsui when she worked there; as Sylvia had left Mitsui in June, this made Adela look foolish. Under pressure, she admitted sending the censorship notice herself.[73]

Forde signed an internment warrant on 18 March, and two days later she was arrested at the office of the *Waverley-Woollahra Standard*. Tom Walsh, seriously ill, was placed under restriction on 9 April; he was to live with his son and unmarried daughters, to report weekly to North Sydney Police Station, and not to go beyond half a mile from his home, except when given permission to visit his wife.[74] The original Restriction Order of 18 March forbade him to reside within 100 miles of the coast, but this was not enforced, owing to his poor health.[75]

Sydney communists in the Domain crowed triumphantly, 'We have got that woman Walsh behind bars and we will see she stays there.'[76] F. R. Sinclair, Secretary of the Department of the Army, wrote, a few days after her arrest, that 'such persons as Mrs. Walsh represent a distinct and serious menace at the present time'.[77]

Although virtually the same telegram from Perth had been sent to other states, the official reaction was less dramatic. There were no AFM members in Queensland or Tasmania. The Victorian AFM had taken on a different character and had, in any case, gone into recess a year earlier. No branch existed in South Australia, although two members lived in that state, as did another generous supporter of the *Publicist*.

The action in Melbourne was supervised by Major Edward Hattam, who reported on 12 March.[78] Collins, former AFM president in Melbourne, willingly turned over documents including Cash Books and Minute Books with particulars of meetings from 24 July 1940 to 19 March 1941, as they had nothing to hide.[79] Collins, who had visited Sydney about Christmas time, 1941, said that there was a difference of opinion in Sydney over their attitude to the Japanese. Hattam summed up his findings:

> As the result of this inquiry and the searches conducted, I am satisfied that this organization as constituted in Victoria was not in any way engaged in subversive activity. It has, in fact, been inactive since the date mentioned herein.[80]

Frank Brennan, Attorney-General in the Scullin Labor government, declared later that he declined to accept an *ex parte* statement even from Forde about the guilt of AFM members.[81] This was to be expected, as he was familiar only with the Melbourne group, with which his son Niall had been associated.

Mills's office at 20 Queen Street was searched, then his room in Canterbury Mansions. Cards relating to Odinism and bearing a swastika were confiscated.[82] Shortly after this, Mills applied to visit Dr Buettner at Tatura Internment Camp on the grounds that Buettner was ill.[83] As Buettner was not ill, this application looked 'sinister'. Mills thought that his ARP and Red Cross work should show that he was a loyal citizen,[84] but on 13 March Hattam recommended that he be detained, commenting, 'From this man's past history and his association with known Nazis, I definitely regard him as a danger.'[85] Mills was arrested on 7 May because of his support for National Socialism and the work he had been doing for the Imperial League of Fascists.

Cookes was interviewed at his home at Ivanhoe. He admitted that he had been interested in the old Socialist Party and had donated £4,500 to the Rationalists. He admitted sending at least £100 to help the *Publicist* carry on, when his old friend Miles was in financial difficulties. Hattam reported:

> The loyalty of this man has at no time been questioned, but the contents of his letter to Stevenson [*sic*] would call for an explanation. He was not asked to furnish this on the occasion of this interview as it was not desired that he should know that we were in possession of a copy of the letter written by him.[86]

Camille Bartram's house at Fairfield, where Cahill had lived, was also searched, and two suitcases of books and AFM material were taken away. Nothing was found suggesting that the Victorian organisation engaged in subversive activities.[87] However, Cahill had written to Mudie advising him to return to Adelaide, saying, 'This is essential if we are to work underground.'[88] This turn of phrase sounded incriminating.

Although South Australian authorities had good reason to watch for pro-German and pro-Nazi activities, there was little Japanese presence in the state. No AF group existed there, and in this connection only three people were of security interest, the most important being Ian Mudie, whose poems had appeared regularly in the *Publicist*. Intelligence noted that his mother, Gertrude Wurm, was of German descent, but of greater concern was his high regard for Stephensen.[89] Among books noted when his home was searched was an unabridged edition of *Mein Kampf*, which he had annotated carefully. Politically muddle-headed and naive, Mudie never really understood the situation. He wrote to Ingamells, 'Well, if P. R. and the rest were guilty, so was I. If they were innocent – and that I know for a fact, despite all the justices – then I was equally so.'[90] While Mudie was in Sydney, his mail had been intercepted, including letters to friends in South Australia. He wrote to an unidentified 'Vin' on 1 October 1941:

> Ain't the war just too lovely. Russia down the drain (what price the 'world's greatest experiment'), America grabbing all she can, Britain with a clown for a Prime Minister, France long since collapsed under the weight of her popular front, and Australians giving aid to everyone but poor bloody Australia.[91]

In a letter of 12 October to C. M. A. Brown, Mudie rejoiced over the plight of the Red Army and the effects on local communists, and again on 26 November he wrote:

> Manifestos are being pasted up and letter-boxed in suburbs in all directions... the Rices, Cahill, Tinker and I form a pretty solid block on the executive, and manage pretty successfully to keep Adela [Walsh] and P. R. [Stephensen] on Australian ground.[92]

Cyril Maitland Ash Brown, a close friend of Mudie, came under notice. He was friendly with most of the AFM executive, and he had sent £90 to help keep the *Publicist* going.[93] A patron of literary causes, he was one of the Jindyworobak group; although he was in contact with Stephensen, MI reported, 'He is certainly not a force to be reckoned with from a political point of view.'[94]

The third South Australian involved was Rex Ingamells, who had joined the AFM reluctantly and had tried to curb Stephensen's excesses. His literary ability was greater than Mudie's, his interests were cultural, and he had avoided being drawn into AFM politics.[95] Security commented, 'Although he abhors British and American commercial exploitation of this country I do not believe he could be accused of disloyalty.'[96]

An unsigned, undated report declared that the South Australian associates of the AFM were artistic and temperamental types, anti-Semitic and keenly interested in the Nazis, but there was little evidence of Japanese sympathies:

> I am satisfied that this organization, as constituted in South Australia, has not been engaged in subversive activity, but its members have been in close touch with Messrs P. R. STEPHENSEN (Chairman of the Movement), L. K. CAHILL (Organiser), Adela PANKHURST WALSH (Organiser) and other executive committee members and should therefore be regarded with suspicion...[97]

Attention always focused on the internees from Sydney and Perth. On 25 March, Maurice Blackburn (ALP, Bourke, NSW) asked a question in the House of Representatives regarding the Australia-First internees. In response to an interjection, he thoughtlessly named Stephensen, whom he called 'a man of great ability, energy and courage', without knowing that he was one of those interned.[98] Like Curtin, Blackburn knew the Walshes from the anti-conscription campaigns of World War I. Unintentionally, he did a lot of damage. Frank Forde responded the next day with a statement that became notorious. It should be examined closely, for taken sentence by sentence his statement was literally true. The problem lay in what he did *not* say, which gave the press opportunity to draw unwarranted conclusions and sensationalise them.

> I wish to state that twenty persons—nineteen men and one woman - who were *believed to have been* associated with the so called Australia First Movement have been arrested and interned. *[Emphasis added. He did not say whether the belief was justified or that they were from separate movements in different states.]*
>
> Documents and papers which have been seized *purport to show* that certain people in Australia intended to make contact with the Japanese army at the moment of an invasion of Australia. *[Emphasis added. He did not say that they did in fact show this, nor specify that these persons were from Western Australia.]*

> The documents set out elaborate plans for sabotage at vulnerable points in this country, and describe methods calculated to make resistance to the Japanese impossible. Plans for the assassination of prominent people are set out. *[With the above qualifications, this was also true.]*
>
> One document *purports to be* a proclamation with the heading 'Australia First Government', and 'welcomes to this country as friends and liberators the Japanese leaders and army'. *[Emphasis added. It did indeed 'purport to be' this.]*
>
> These documents indicate a fifth column activity of the worst kind by a very small band of people. The military authorities have been investigating the activities of the so-called Australia First Movement for a considerable time, and the arrests took place as a result of these inquiries. *[The first part was debatable; the second part was true. It did not endorse the worth of the investigations.]*
>
> In view of the foregoing, I wish to warn people that, before associating themselves with any movement, they should assure themselves that it is bona fide and not an organization which, under the cloak of a pleasing name, is engaged in subversive activities. We shall stand no Quislings, whether they come from the highest or the lowest. *[This reasonable warning should not have been confined to the AFM.]*[99]

The statement's vagueness allowed the press to draw incorrect inferences and apply to the Sydney internees that which referred to the Western Australians. It was debated the following day. Asked whether charges would be laid, Forde replied that this was being considered by the Solicitor-General. As Forde's announcement did the most to damage the internees, it became the focus of their bitterness. Masey wrote to Hasluck in 1946, 'The Minister was of course not responsible for the advice given him by his officers to make the statement, but he was responsible for acting upon that advice. The decision to make the statement was political, not military.'[100]

Fadden said that internment was inadequate; there had to be a treason trial.[101] Curtin spoke largely on generalities, evading the specific issue of the AFM: 'The only action which the present

Government has taken has been to give a direction that persons suspected of engaging in activities which would be of assistance to an enemy shall not be free to carry on these activities.'[102] Forde's statement has been described as an 'hysterical outburst', but the real hysteria came from a former Attorney-General, W. M. Hughes:

> The real purpose of the Australia First Movement is to prepare the way for the coming of the Japanese... They sent their spies and shock troops into Western Australia; and they were arrested. What is the Government doing with the men who started the movement in New South Wales? They still walk the streets.[103]

The AFM had sent nobody to WA. Hughes then mentioned the 'assassination list': 'If my name is on it I shall know what to do. I shall see to it that any of these gentlemen who are not interned will not need interning.'[104]

It is claimed that officers who had advised Forde knew by then, from a report by Richards, that there was no connection between Bullock and the Sydney AFM.[105] This claim is dubious for two reasons. First there is the time factor. Richards dated his report 20 March; Inspector S. H. Read in Perth signed and dated it on Saturday, 21 March.[106] Even by air courier, it could not have reached Melbourne before Monday, 23 March, Canberra a day later; but probably it was mailed on 23 March, was in the general mail on that night's train, arriving in Melbourne on 26 March and Canberra on 27 March. Once the Ministerial statement had been made, it would have been a brave officer who would have told Forde that it was misleading.

The second point is what Richards really said in his lengthy report, which gave the history of Bullock and his associates over several years. As regards any connection between the groups in Perth and Sydney, the critical paragraphs were these:

> The extent to which the 'Australia First' Movement in Sydney is involved, is doubtful, but there is no actual evidence that the Sydney section of the Movement had any knowledge of Bullock's activities.
>
> However, the exposure of these four members of the Movement indicates the type of person attracted to it by their policy and propaganda...

> In my opinion, it is a frankly Fascist organisation and, therefore, a dangerous organisation from a Security point of view.

It is important to note that the report did *not* say that there was evidence that the AFM was not involved with the AF people in Perth. It said that there was no actual evidence that they knew of their activities. There is a difference. He also did not say that the AFM in Sydney was harmless; in his opinion it was dangerous.[107]

The mainstream press sensationalised the affair, and the left-wing press went further. *Progress: The Voice of State Labor*, dated 3 April, carried the headline: 'No Mercy for Australia First Quislings!' It used the case to attack both major parties: 'Weak handling of the incident by the Curtin-Beasley Government have [*sic*] given an opportunity to the "Guilty Men" of the U.A.P. to strut and pose as the real patriots.'[108] *Progress* shared some staff with the illegal CPA paper, *Tribune*, and they cared no more about breaking the law in respect of what it published than about the fact that it was banned altogether. Its feud with Stephensen pre-dated the time when he had sued its forerunner, the *Workers' Weekly*, for libel. In order to protect internees, Consolidated Censorship Instructions forbade the mention of their names, but as Stephensen was mentioned in Parliament, newspapers could name him. The *Tribune*, 29 April, attacked Stephensen and his 'powerful friends who control at least one newspaper', saying 'THE "BULLETIN'S" GUNS SHOULD ALSO BE SPIKED.'[109] It named most AFM internees under the heading: 'These Are The Spies'.[110] It missed Kirtley, and of the ages given, only four were correct. No responsible authority had seriously believed that the AFM people, except Adela Walsh, were spies.

> P. R. Stephenson (40); Stephenson (26); Crowley (57); Cecil Sallier (63); Keith Bath (40); Edward Massey (33); Dr. Clarence Crowley (53); G. B. Hooper (73); Walter Tinker-Giles (43); Gordon Riles (32); Nat Watts (46); Horley Matthews (50); Les Cahill (32); Kirkwood Down (28); –. Arnold (42).

The internees believed that somebody in MI or the police had leaked the names to the press, but if there had been an 'official' leak, the list should have been complete and correct. Any good Sydney journalist could have compiled an approximate list. Connected with both *Progress* and *Tribune* was Rupert Lockwood, and he had good contacts. One was revealed in 'Document J', prepared about 1950 by Lockwood for the Soviet Embassy and mentioned at the Petrov Royal Commission.[111] He cited frequently Ken Cook, the Naval Intelligence agent, who should have known better than to give information to a journalist. There was, however, a more likely source. One of the police compiling reports on the AFM was Alfred Thompson Hughes, who had allegedly been a secret communist since 1932. He gave evidence at the Clyne Inquiry[112] at about the time he was recruited by Walter Sedden Clayton as a Soviet spy with the code name BEN.[113] He was responsible for the claim that Rud Mills was on the executive of the Nazi Party.[114]

It has been alleged falsely that the AFM arrests were 'illegal'. Some could be considered unreasonable, unjust, even unconscionable, but as long as the paperwork was correct, they were not *illegal*. With regard to later internments, there appeared to be some foundation for claims of technical illegality. National Security Regulation 13(2) reads:

> If a person suspected of having committed, or of being about to commit, an offence against this Act, is arrested under the provisions of this section, a report of the fact and circumstances shall forthwith be made to the Attorney-General or to a person appointed in that behalf by the Attorney-General.

On 25 March, Acting Attorney-General Beasley admitted that he had no knowledge of the matter.[115] It looked as though the regulation had not been followed. In fact that was not so. During Evatt's absence, the duties of the Attorney-General had been divided. Beasley took over most, but those relating to the Security Service and internments were specifically excluded, being transferred to the Minister for the Army, and Forde certainly knew about them, as he had signed the orders.[116]

The AFM internments were mentioned intermittently in Parliament. On 30 April Calwell asked what action was being taken to bring to trial the AFM members arrested in Sydney. Forde replied that they were interned, not arrested, while in another state, not named, some had appeared in court.[117] On 20 May, when asked whether charges had been formulated, Forde said that it was handled by the Attorney-General's Department.[118] On 27 May, in response to a question about the number of AFM members interned, Beasley declined to answer, as it was in the province of Army Intelligence.[119] The division of responsibilities for Evatt's two portfolios confused many people. Moreover, during Evatt's absence, MacKay was appointed Director-General of a reorganised CSS. He took up this post on 14 May, and he seems not to have appreciated fully the differences between police and Security work.

Amid the confusion, the main issues tended to be overlooked. In a democracy, one is theoretically entitled to hold and express almost any political opinion, even if the reality is different. In time of peace, official restriction of political expression is not justified unless it advocates that violence be used to change the system against the wishes of the majority. If it is advocated in time of war that the nation's enemies should be assisted to enforce such a change, restriction is not only justified, but vital.

A decision is more contentious when people are simply causing disruption within a community; determining the point at which they damage morale sufficiently to impair defence capabilities is a subjective judgment. In wartime, it was possible to maintain that a recommendation for detention was justified, *even if the suspicions that led to this were not justified*. Skidelsky wrote of Mosley, 'The case against him rested, therefore, not on anything he had done, but on what he might do under different circumstances.'[120]

The internees failed to see that the impressions they had been giving were responsible for their plight, or that their activities might have done real damage. It is perhaps precisely for this reason - that they meant well by Australia and had no insight into the harm they could be doing - that some were dangerous. Security could not foretell the possible danger resulting from what some of those associated with the AFM *might do*, and they did not intend to take risks.

Chapter 10

The Appeals

The AFM membership list, stolen on 19 February, contained 65 names. Thus Justice Clyne commented that, if what had been said in camera during the Appeal Tribunals became public knowledge, 'this disclosure would probably cause a split in what is left of the Australia First Movement into 65 fragmentary parts'.[1] Thrown into close contact under stressful circumstances, the internees found that they held divergent views and they neither liked nor respected some of their fellow internees. On 8 August, Valentine Crowley was caught trying to smuggle out of Liverpool Camp some sheets of paper hidden under false bottoms of brown paper bags containing soiled linen that he wanted his wife to launder. This brief diary gives an insight into the relationships between individual internees from 28 June to 29 July.[2]

Months passed before the appeals came before a tribunal. The men complained of victimisation, as some people arrested after them had been before a tribunal and had been released before any AFM appeals were heard. However, these were simple cases involving one person. The AFM case was complex, and all cases were interconnected. Major General A. C. Fewtrell, Base Commandant, Eastern Command, reported:

> A reliable person who is keeping in touch with the Australia First Movement internees on behalf of Intelligence Section, Eastern Command, reports that the internees are insisting on a trial before a Civil court and are very confident that if this occurs they will be released.[3]

This would not necessarily follow, for Quicke and Krakouer were acquitted in court, but kept in internment. Fewtrell added several more paragraphs, of which these are relevant:

> 2. It is apparent that the internees and their sympathisers realise by demanding a trial in a Civil Court, the burden of proof will automatically be placed on the Army, and in order to establish its case it would be necessary for Army to reveal its inner methods, contacts and informants.
>
> 3. The internees also no doubt realise that in the interests of National Security this could not be done and as a result they are insisting on the action being taken in a Civil Court.[4]

For the Army to fail to establish its case, he wrote, 'would do the very thing that is part of the Fifth Columnist's work, namely, the undermining of public morale'.

On 21 May, Sinclair prepared for Sir George Knowles, the Solicitor-General, a Minute Paper on the nature of internment and the tribunals. It contained a well-constructed assessment of the situation, which many people failed to realise:

> It is necessary to show the fact that internment is a precautionary and not a punitive measure. There may be persons whose activities and spoken words indicate that their sympathies and outlook are such that if left at liberty they would be in a position to assist the enemy or otherwise wilfully imperil the safety of the country.
>
> At the same time it is realised that it might not be possible for a criminal charge to be brought against them. The judicial process is such that it can only punish wrongful acts. It cannot punish a man for wishing to assist the enemy. This is the principal reason why so few interned persons are tried in Courts of Law. Many of them have never done anything at all. *It is to prevent them from doing things that they are interned.*[5]

Sinclair pointed out that the Chairman of a tribunal had to be a person who was or had been a Judge of a Federal or State court, or was eligible for such an appointment. As tribunals were administrative, not judicial, they could consider hearsay and other evidence not admissible in court.[6] Concerning the delay in hearing appeals, Knowles wrote:

> As to the date of the hearing, there is such a lot of typing to be done that the Military Police Intelligence Branch state that another week will elapse before the material is ready to put before the Committee. There are three thousand pages of typing to be done and five typists are working on these night and day.[7]

The army claimed there were 2,000 pages to be typed in connection with the case.[8] Forde said that 16 typists were working at it constantly.[9]

Knowles reported to Forde on 21 May that some internees did not recognise the jurisdiction of the Advisory Committee. Most objected to secret hearings, but the secrecy was intended to protect the internees themselves, as at some hearings matters were raised that they would not have wanted aired in public. On 2 June, Forde admitted that it had been decided not to take court action against the NSW group.[10]

That left an appeal to an Advisory Committee practically the only option, but both Adela Walsh and Stephensen tried the *habeas corpus* approach, which gave the papers a further opportunity to publish their names. The cases failed in Australia as similar cases had failed in Britain. Their lawyers should have known this, but even Hughes, Attorney-General when the NS Regulations were formulated, seemed not to know that they took away the protection of *habeas corpus*.[11] Walsh was given leave to object on 29 April; the *habeas corpus* application was heard on 12 May and refused on 18 May. On 25 June, the Full Court of the High Court unanimously rejected an application for leave to appeal.[12] Stephensen applied to the Supreme Court of New South Wales for a writ of *habeas corpus* in July 1942, and likewise failed.[13] The Full Court refused to allow writs from Hooper and Crowley as well.[14]

In Liverpool Camp, relationships among AFM internees deteriorated. According to Crowley, they split into two groups: Val and Clarrie Crowley, Hooper, Salier, Masey, Tinker, Rice and Bath in one, Matthews, Kirtley, Arnold and Watts in the other, but the groupings were flexible. Cahill seemed to move between the groups.[15] Crowley wrote in his diary, 'Further evidence of P.R.S. deterioration; Eric is his only adherent now.'[16]

Tension was exacerbated by the arrival of outsiders, such as Jack Sleeman, who joined the Matthews-Kirtley group. Eric Stephensen wrote later, 'After a couple of weeks Sleeman was taken away and then some weeks later re-appeared again. He then told us, that he had been sent to spy on us (everyone knew this) but he said he reported to his bosses that we were harmless!'[17] In fact, Sleeman was a real danger; the Japanese had paid him to write the Cheguin pamphlet blamed on Stephensen; the only thing MI did not yet know was *how much* they paid him. Calwell said later in parliament, 'There is no more dubious character, alien or British, in this country than the same Mr. J. H. Sleeman.'[18] Strangely, Stephensen and Sleeman seem barely to have known each other, although Sleeman, as editor of the notorious weekly, *Beckett's Budget*, had published on 28 September 1928 'An Open Letter to Every Voter Who Loves Australia First'.

Tom Graham arrived about 10 July, having been interned as soon as he left prison. Stephensen welcomed him, but Graham was so abrasive and offensive that within days eight of the men had signed a petition asking for his removal. This was refused, as the other eight, including the Stephensens, did not support the request.[19]

The internees tried to make use of influential contacts. Archbishop Gilroy promised Cahill he would press for an inquiry. Hooper contacted Jack Beasley, Maurice Blackburn and Archie Cameron.[20] Several wrote to Eric Harrison and Frank Brennan. Crowley wrote to Clive Evatt on 3 July 1942, 'I believe that their view is that I am subversive if I love Australia more than I love England.'[21] Unfortunately, Crowley thought it would be good for Australia if Germany defeated England. H. Kenneth Prior, editor of the *Bulletin,* tried to honour his promise of support. Malcolm Smith (AFM member No. 11) visited Liverpool on Saturday 4 July with a promise that Prior, who had been in the same artillery battalion as Smith in France, would take up their case.[22]

Winifred Stephensen, still very ill, had to move to a small rented room. On 19 August she wrote passionately to Menzies that the men had been interned for reasons of politics, not national security, that Forde did not dare bring them to trial, and it was a disgrace to Australia that a Minister could make such a vicious and unwarranted attack on the good names of 16 Australians.[23]

By June, the war situation had worsened further, for on the night of 31 May – 1 June three Japanese midget submarines entered Sydney Harbour and torpedoed a depot ship, and on 8 June submarines shelled Newcastle and Sydney. The atmosphere did not favour the release of internees. Appeal hearings lasted from 22 June to 20 July, taking two or three days each.[24] Matthews, Arnold and Kirtley did not appeal. Cahill, Val Crowley, Downe and the Stephensens did not proceed with their appeals, while Hooper withdrew after appearing before a tribunal for a day. He was particularly upset when asked why he had married an Italian.[25] He wrote on 23 June, 'I have always detested Nazism, Fascism and Communism as systems of Government for this country.'[26] Although Crowley withdrew his appeal, he gave copious advice to others. He told Bath to 'Wave the Flag' and say that he got his ideas from books written by Hughes in 1935.[27] He gave Watts notes on legal developments in Australia and advised him to claim that the Appeals Tribunal was harming Britain's 'gift to human endeavour', the Magna Carta.[28]

Objections heard in full were from Bath, Clarence Crowley, Masey, Rice, Salier, Tinker-Giles and Watts. Because the cases were closely intertwined, the Advisory Committee headed by G. Herbert Pike submitted a unified report dated 30 July, then appended individual recommendations.[29] It recognised that there was no connection between the AFM in Western Australia and the AFM in New South Wales, although there had been correspondence between individual members. The report concluded that Miles (who was dead), Stephensen and Crowley (who did not appeal) seemed to believe that 'no better opportunity could be availed of than the defeat of Britain in the present war'.

The Committee recommended that Salier be released, as he appeared not to have recognised the significance of some AFM policies, and they accepted as genuine his undertaking to break with the AFM. They had no hesitation in recommending that Bath be released, as he had been simply 'a victim of his misplaced enthusiasm', and did not realise the real objects of the AFM until he was interned.[30] On his release, Bath vowed he would not get mixed up in 'that sort of thing' again.

Watts was ill and subject to fits of coughing. Prior to appearing before the Advisory Committee he said, 'I will tell the tribunal anything they like, whether it is true or not; I will sign any paper and agree to anything whatever – as long as I get out of here. If I stay here I will soon be dead!'[31] The Tribunal reported that he answered questions freely and without hesitation, and they did not think he had said or written anything intentionally subversive. 'At no time had we any reason to doubt his loyalty except for his association with the "Australia First Movement", nor had we, at any time, any reason to doubt his honesty or truthfulness.' According to Muirden, Watts had to promise that neither he *nor his wife* would write for publication.[32]

The Committee referred to the peculiarity of the dual names of Tinker-Giles, but rejected any sinister aspect. 'The Committee is quite satisfied that his offer to remain dissociated from the Movement and its members is genuine and on the condition that he does so, the Committee has decided to recommend his release from internment.' They found that Clarence Crowley had not said or written anything objectionable, and the only reason for his internment was that he was Val Crowley's brother. Thus it was recommended that five of the seven objectors be released. The other two, Masey and Rice, might have expected the same recommendation, but they were disappointed.

The Committee noted that Masey had never taken advantage of his membership of other associations to advocate anything subversive, nor did he agree fully with Miles and Stephensen, but at public meetings Adela Walsh had supported him. There does not seem to be any other reason why they decided, 'In the opinion of the committee, the Objector has not succeeded in discharging the onus that lay upon him of satisfying the Committee that he is entitled to released.' That was the problem; the tribunals did not have to prove that the objectors should have been interned; the objectors had to convince them that their internment was not necessary. As for Rice, he complained that he was kept interned because the tribunal objected to his 'sardonic sense of humour', but that was only part of their assessment. They reported that he had made 'many untrue statements' and they would be unable to accept any guarantee he gave concerning his future conduct.

At the end of June, Dr Evatt returned from his overseas trip, and the fate of a few internees was not his first priority. However, within weeks responsibility for internments was taken away from the Department of the Army (Forde) and placed under the jurisdiction of the Attorney-General (Evatt), as assessment of cases needed legal training. This could have been a discreet way saying that Evatt objected to Forde's handling of internments. Files and dossiers were transferred, and MI then disclaimed responsibility, as it no longer had access to files.[33] After the five men cleared had been released on 22 August, Evatt set up an inquiry into the other cases.

The topic of the AFM was canvassed in the House of Representatives on 2 September. Calwell argued that there was no foundation for linking the Sydney people with planned assassinations, and an *agent provocateur* had caused the trouble in Western Australia. Cameron interjected that the agent was a communist. Calwell explained that the agent joined the communists to foment trouble, and that Evatt had recently stated in the press that there was no association between the groups in Western Australia and New South Wales.[34] Harrison added, 'I cannot see any reason why the grounds for the internment of these people should not be revealed in open Parliament.' Then he commented on Calwell's call to release the men or bring them to trial:

> They cannot be brought to trial in open court, because, if that were done, the whole ramifications of national security and military intelligence would be disclosed to those people who wanted to know our under-cover men and our espionage system.[35]

Brennan defended a 'fellow practitioner' (of law – Mills), who had been arrested on suspicion, calling it 'absurd and preposterous', but he added, 'I admit that my view is based on quite insufficient evidence – [but] I am sufficiently well acquainted with him to know in a general way what his outlook on international affairs is.'[36] Brennan knew nothing of the clandestine activities of Mills, whom he did not mention by name, but his son Niall, like Mills, was a member of the Bread and Cheese Club. If he was really 'well acquainted', how could he have been unaware of the Mills's vile *National Socialist* paper or his crazy Odinist books?

Blackburn defended Harley Matthews as a 'distinguished man of letters, not connected in any way with the Australia First Movement'.[37] Matthews had written for newspapers, published a small volume of poetry, and had a few other poems published, but hardly deserved the title Blackburn gave him; he had signified he would join the AFM later, and he was closely connected with the *Publicist*.

To put the matter in perspective, Evatt pointed out that 'internees in this country do not consist exclusively of the Australia First Movement'.[38] Ignoring Harrison's point, Cameron asked why there could not be a trial in Sydney as there had been in Perth, and he referred to his long-standing correspondence with an unnamed member of the group.[39] Bernard Corser, member for the Wide Bay electorate, which included Maryborough, recalled that he had known Stephensen long before he went away as a Rhodes Scholar.[40] George Rankin of Bendigo put the MI viewpoint: 'Why should the rights of these twenty cranks be considered against the security of seven million persons?'[41]

At a conference of senior representatives of Intelligence and Security sections on Saturday, 5 September, dissatisfaction with the performance of the CSS was expressed, and changes were made, including the replacement of MacKay by Brigadier William Ballantyne Simpson as Director-General, and it was now *and only now* that there was a requirement that a recommendation for internment should reach the Minister within 48 hours. The fact that this was apparently not done in March 1942 has been brought forward to support claims that the AFM internments were illegal, but this provision did not apply in March 1942.[42] In the House of Representatives on 10 September, Evatt emphasised what had been overlooked: during his absence, the Security Service had been administered by the Minister for the Army (i.e. Forde, not Beasley). He stressed that the aim of restrictions on individual liberty was to prevent injury to the war effort, and guilt of a specific offence was not the test to be applied. 'The difficulty,' he explained, 'lies in the application of these general principles to the infinite variety of circumstances in the individual case.'[43]

With regard to the AFM, Evatt said, 'It is reasonably clear that there was no guilty association between the Western Australian conspirators and the sixteen New South Wales internees. This does not mean that there was no association at all because there was.' He mentioned a letter in which Quicke told Krakouer he had had a letter from the AFM in Sydney saying that the formation of a branch in Western Australia would be considered.[44] After consulting with the Director-General of Security, the Deputy Director for New South Wales and Military Intelligence in New South Wales, Evatt decided that four internments should continue, and five should be commuted to restriction orders.[45]

On 12 September, Arnold, Downe, Hooper, Matthews and Eric Stephensen were released. Downe was restricted to Moss Vale, Matthews to Katoomba and Hooper to Picton. Efforts to enforce these restrictions was sometimes farcical, for Downe re-enlisted in the army, Matthews wanted to get back to his vineyard, while Hooper had to go to hospital.[46] The situation with Arnold was even more ludicrous. He was allowed seven days in Sydney before going to Katoomba, but he protested that he had no money, no job and no accommodation, and that he did not want to be released under those conditions. The day after his release, he told his story to the *Sydney Morning Herald*; when they did not use it, he went to the *Bulletin*. Threatening him with imprisonment in Long Bay, the police ordered him to Katoomba. As he refused to go, they drove him there and found him a boarding house, and two officers gave him money out of their own pockets. Next morning, Arnold was back in Sydney; he called again on the newspapers, visited Spender's office, then went to Liverpool and asked to be interned again. After the army handed him over to the police, Arnold demanded to be released unconditionally or re-interned. The police were obliged to return him to Liverpool.[47]

The situation of those still interned was considered again. On 19 October Masey, Rice and Val Crowley were released, and Arnold was told to get out and stay out. This time he was restricted to Sydney, but now he badgered the Security Service for permission to go to Brisbane to seek guidance from his *guru* on the 'Order of Equilibrium'.[48] Of the Sydney AFM, only Stephensen, Cahill and Kirtley remained interned in Liverpool. Stephensen insisted not only that he should be compensated and publicly exonerated, but that those who interned him should be punished, even though National Security (General) Regulation 13 (3) specifically ruled this out.

While the release of the Sydney AFM internees was being considered, MI looked again at the case of Cookes. On 17 July, a fellow-member of the Rationalist Association reported that Cookes had used the association's mailing list to send out the *Publicist* and the *Independent Sydney Secularist,* which were not Rationalist, but fascist and objectionable. His premises were searched on 22 July, and a recommendation for internment was signed by Colonel S. T. Whittington on 25 July.[49]

On 28 August, MacKay wrote to Cookes that the Attorney-General wanted to see him in Canberra. Cookes replied on 5 September that he was in poor health and should not travel alone. Owing to changes in the Security Service, it was Simpson who interviewed Cookes on 23 September. Despite his long legal career, the effrontery of Cookes surprised even him. Mostly, Cookes 'did not remember' or 'did not know'. He claimed he had had nothing to do with AF and the *Publicist.* He knew a few members, but only slightly. He denied writing letters of which Simpson had copies in front of him. He denied sending money, when Simpson had copies of the bank drafts.

Evatt had proposed a severe 'talking-to'; Simpson reported on 16 October that Cookes had been very untruthful, but agreed that it would be sufficient to impose a Restriction Order binding him not to take part in or subscribe to or correspond with a society whose objects were political, economic or international.[50] Cookes had not attracted *public* notoriety; his factory handled a lot of defence contracts; he had wealthy and powerful friends; and he had so much to lose that he could be intimidated into acquiescence. To the disgust of those who knew of his involvement, Cookes appeared to go scot-free.

The appeal of A. Rud Mills, who was not considered one of the AFM internees, was heard on 22 November, and he was released on 17 December on an order from Evatt dated 10 December.[51] He was undeservedly lucky. There remained then only the most difficult cases.

In September 1942, Stephensen, Cahill, Kirtley and 'Mortimer'[52] were sent to Camp 14D at Loveday, South Australia. Little is recorded about how Cahill and Kirtley conducted themselves there, but there is plenty on Stephensen. Within days of arriving, he suggested at a camp meeting that they complain to the Swiss Consul about conditions in the camp, and ask him to bring pressure to bear through threats of reprisals against Australians in German and Japanese hands. Camp Leader Alex Graf refused to be a party to this. Concerning this incident, Muirden comments, 'Stephensen saw this as a move by Graf to ingratiate himself by pretending to be anti-Nazi.'[53] However, the military had some 30 informants in the camp, and the story came from many of them. Once again, Stephensen possibly did not remember what he had said, but others did. Young Peter Klemperer (Edler von Klemenau)[54] held that 'as white men they did not want protection from the Japanese'.[55] Some men complained to the camp authorities about Stephensen's contemptible behaviour. Others told the story in letters to their families. One wrote:

> Some of the Australia first movement fellows arrived here the other day... They hadn't been here more than a day when one of them at our general meeting advocated a policy of black mail. I won't go into detail, but believe me, they're pretty rotten.[56]

Another related how 'one full blood Australian' had moved that the Axis representative should be asked to put pressure on prisoners held by them, so that conditions in Loveday would be improved, and other Australians had supported him.[57] 'It was a most disgusting affair,' commented another.[58] This affair was mentioned during the Clyne Inquiry, and a verbatim quote shows Stephensen's attitude.

> Shand: *You addressed the meeting?*
> Stephensen: *Yes, I think I did…*
> Shand: *You suggested that the Japanese had a lot of Australian troops as prisoners, and that they could be communicated with so that pressure would be brought to bear?*
> Stephensen: *A fantastic allegation, absolutely – a lunatic allegation; no truth in it whatsoever…*
> Shand: *Did you mention the Japanese?*
> Stephensen: *No.*

After more rigorous questioning, Stephensen replied lamely that he had spoken for only three minutes and 'I mentioned Australian prisoners in Germany, too.'[59] The important word is 'too'. It was an admission that he had indeed said something about Australian prisoners in Japanese hands, and he knew he had said it.

Stephensen also tried to organise a strike over fatigue duties. One person reported that Stephensen had said that he 'hoped the Japanese would soon invade Australia', and had been supported by the Thiele brothers.[60] Another claimed that Stephensen had urged that Graf be deposed and a Nazi leader appointed, 'who would support the Japanese in their certain and successful invasion of Australia'.[61] He aroused more hostility when, on 6 December, he gave a talk on 'Gold digging in Australia', in which he said that Australia was being robbed by England and America, and that her future existence depended on whether her deliverers, Hitler and Mussolini, succeeded.[62]

Stephensen complained about being interned with Jews and communists, who abused him and were likely to attack him although he had given them no provocation.[63] He did not see that years of abusive articles in the *Publicist* and his support for Nazi policies were provocation enough. He asked to be shifted to a Nazi camp or a family camp in Victoria where he could teach the children. The problem was that, wherever he was interned, there would be men of principle who despised him, some for his anti-Semitism, others because he was seen as disloyal to his own country. 'Mortimer' too protested about being held in a camp with communists and Jews; he applied for a transfer to Tatura, claiming there were better educational opportunities there.[64] In February 1943, they were both were sent to Tatura.

Cahill and Kirtley refused to sign restriction orders, but were released on 6 February 1944 anyway. Stephensen was now the only Sydney AFM man still interned. Some of those at liberty lobbied parliamentarians to help them clear their names and gain compensation. Cahill wrote to Collins that he had seen Calwell personally, and Kirtley had written to him as well.[65] Calwell would be Evatt's future rival for leadership of the ALP and was happy to embarrass him. Cahill wrote a few weeks later that he had seen Gartner, Mills, and Stephensen's solicitor (Downing), and hoped they would get money and political influence out of the affair: 'I seem to be the only one who realises that we are at the moment holding the joker in the present situation.'[66] In fact, only the lawyers benefited, and Cahill gained only bitter experience.

Meanwhile, the Walshes were a problem, owing to Tom's illness and Adela's recalcitrance. After her *habeas corpus* application failed, Adela went through the normal appeal process. She asked that either Tom be interned with her, or she be released to nurse him. The authorities felt that Tom should be interned, but he was too ill, so on 28 August Adela was released temporarily to care for him. Her appeal was heard over five days, 7–11 September. Although it was suggested she might be released under restriction on compassionate grounds, she was interned again in Liverpool.[67]

Adela's request to have Tom interned with her was rejected. 'If this request is not granted,' she threatened on 6 October, 'I can only assure you that I will end my internment by a hunger strike and that nothing can alter my determination to do this.'[68] Authorities had taken no notice of other hunger strike threats, but a Pankhurst was different; Adela would carry out her threat and would get publicity. She began her hunger strike on 10 October. Dr Evatt kept close watch on her case, but instructed that she was not to know this. He wrote that her life should not be endangered, as this would be disastrous from a public point of view; it would be better if both the Walshes were put under a Restriction Order at a place where they could do no harm.[69] The Security Service was informed next morning. By 13 October, she was becoming weak, so she was sent to a military hospital, where she was segregated from other patients. Taking a hard line, the Deputy Director of Security for New South Wales (S. G. Taylor) wrote to the Director General in Canberra the same day, stating that it was essential that Mrs Walsh not be released. He added:

> I am of the opinion that our experience of Mrs. Walsh is such as to show that no matter what restriction is placed on her and her husband, she will use her best endeavours to bring about a condition either in herself, or in her husband, which will avoid compliance with the order.[70]

The letter reached Canberra too late. Evatt had ordered that she be sent home by ambulance as soon as she could safely be moved. She arrived home that evening.[71] Part of the Restriction Order read that she should not, without prior approval, publish or assist in publishing any article or interview in which her authorship was mentioned and should communicate only with her own family. She took little notice, and within a few days the Sydney *Sun* submitted for censorship an article based on an interview. It was not passed. A Mail Scrutiny Order was issued against her on 21 October and continued for at least two months.[72] When Tom died on 5 April 1943, some of the fight went out of Adela. On 22 August 1945, all restrictions were removed. She left the public arena and devoted herself to being a grandmother.

Watch was still kept on some AFM people who were not interned, and some internees after their release. They were subject to Mail Scrutiny (XRD) Orders or intermittent personal surveillance. On 21 April 1943, Collins wrote to Curtin, introducing himself as the son-in-law of a close friend of Curtin's sister. He wrote on behalf of friends who were still interned, for he could see nothing in AFM policy to justify this. He complained that late in 1942 an attempt had been made to 'frame' him, and 'the sinister and infamous methods of the Nazi Gestapo have got nothing on the Gestapo of Sunny Australia'.[73]

Collins boasted that he had seen through the 'vicious trick' and had given Calwell a statutory declaration to be tabled in parliament if he was arrested. Curtin passed the letter to the Attorney-General's Department, and the Secretary of this department passed it to the CSS in Canberra with the comment: 'I do not think that these allegations should be permitted to pass unchallenged... he should be called upon to substantiate or withdraw the objectionable statements referred to.'[74]

The matter was passed to the Deputy Director of Security in Melbourne, who replied on 26 May. In order to check on the AFM in Melbourne, two members of the Field Security Section had pretended to Collins that they were interested in the AFM. It was not the cleverness of Collins but the treachery of an army NCO that exposed them. They had been working with a corporal who had been discharged after he got drunk and talked in public about an operation. The corporal told Collins that the prospective sympathisers were MI personnel, and asked for a reward and a job with Ansett. Collins denounced him, but there was not enough evidence to prosecute him.[75]

The damage suffered by internees, financial and psychological, was disproportionate to any offence. Financial effects can be assessed. The military pay of Downe and Cahill continued until the day they were released. Crowley's rents and Hooper's dividends also continued, but Stephensen's income ceased. Matthews' vineyard and winery and Bath's real estate business were ruined, and Tinker-Giles's shoe business suffered from his absence. As a matter of routine, driving licences of ex-internees were cancelled. For some, this was an insult and an inconvenience; for Rice, it meant the loss of his livelihood.[76] All incurred legal expenses, some of them heavy.

The psychological damage is harder to determine. Sir Earle Page commented, 'For the rest of their lives they will suffer as a result of this.'[77] Most suffered some personal trauma. During his internment, Kirtley's mother, diabetic and almost blind, died in poverty on 8 August 1942.[78] Matthews' mother also died. Bath lost a business opportunity and had to sell his house at a loss. Comparatively placid Tinker-Giles and Clarence Crowley seemed to accept that, although they had been done an injustice, worse things happen in war, but probably none of them totally overcame the psychological effects of their internment.

Chapter 11

The Clyne Inquiry and Parliament

At the end of March 1944, R. G. Menzies, Leader of the Opposition, accused Evatt of having falsely claimed that incriminating letters read in the House on 10 September 1942 had been from internees. Evatt replied that every one of them had been.[1] Both were wrong; some were by internees, while some had probably been written years earlier by W. J. Miles. Then Menzies cited the case of 'a solicitor' whom he knew well:

> His association, so I am informed, with the Australia First Movement amounted to this: Some man who had secured appointment with the movement wrote to him and asked him to subscribe, and he forwarded 10s. 6d. as a subscription.[2]

Menzies called on Evatt to set up an inquiry to determine whether there had ever been 'real reasons for their internment' and to assess compensation.[3] Menzies meant Mills, and the reasons for his internment have been examined.

During the debate, Harrison (Liberal, Wentworth, NSW) claimed that in internment the men had been 'forced to perform the most menial tasks'.[4] This meant that they had had to peel vegetables, wash dishes, launder clothes, sweep floors and clean toilets: things they expected their wives to do for them. Blackburn was out of the debate, for he died on 31 March. J. P. Abbott (CP, New England, NSW) returned to the case of Keith Bath, noting that the Governor-General could award compensation.[5]

Ward (ALP, East Sydney) accused the Opposition of 'defending quislings', suggested that the AFM had grown out of the New Guard, and used this to attack Harrison. He showed how any action could be interpreted as incriminating once a person was under suspicion. If the suspect joined the army, it was to further his 'nefarious work'; if he donated to loans, it was to cover his tracks. Then Ward named

'Inky' Stephensen.[6] In fact, with his pre-war opposition to defence expenditure, and his spurious accusations in 1942 with regard to the Brisbane Line, Ward had done more harm to Australian security and morale than had the AFM internees individually or collectively.[7]

While Parliament was in recess, Evatt acted on Menzies' call. On 2 May, he announced that a Parliamentary Inquiry would be set up to investigate the internment of persons connected with the AFM. He added, 'Any person rushing in to make party political capital out of these cases will find, after the full facts are disclosed, that he is on the side of a group, the leaders of which were prepared to stab Australia in the back during the period of our greatest peril.'[8] Although Evatt was probably referring to Bullock, it was interpreted as meaning the Sydney group.

When the Inquiry was called, only Stephensen and the Western Australians were still interned. In January 1944 Brigadier Simpson had recommended that restrictions be removed from all the others except Arnold, owing to his correspondence with the German Consulate. Not knowing the reason, Arnold complained to Evatt that he was still restricted because of Simpson's spite and personal animosity. A few days later, the Deputy Director of Security, Sydney, wrote that the Attorney-General had instructed him to remove the restrictions on Arnold.[9]

Justice Thomas Stuart Clyne was selected to head the Inquiry. In one way, it was not a good choice, for he was so heavily committed to hearing bankruptcy cases that there were bound to be delays. He was to inquire into 'certain matters in relation to the public safety and defence of the Commonwealth' and to report under the following terms of reference:

> (1) Whether the detention in March, April and May, 1942, under Regulation 26 of the National Security (General) Regulations of certain persons connected with the 'Australia First Movement' Group, as recommended by the Army authorities, was justified:
>
> (2) Whether the said persons were given proper opportunity of appealing against their detention to the appropriate appeal tribunal, and whether those who did appeal had their cases fairly and justly considered:

> (3) Whether the continuance of the original detention was justified, and whether the restrictions imposed upon any of the said persons after release were just and reasonable in the circumstances:
> (4) Whether it is proper that any further action should be taken in respect of any of the said persons:
> (5) Whether in the case of any of the said persons, it is proper that they should receive any compensation from the Commonwealth and if so, what amount: and
> (6) All matters which, in the opinion of the said Commissioner, are relevant to any of the above matters, or should, in his opinion, be dealt with or reported upon by him.[10]

It was suggested that the terms of reference were too narrow but, as Point 6 authorised him to inquire into anything at all, Clyne considered them wide enough. On 3 June, Evatt declared, 'I am determined that, if any individual has suffered any wrong, not only will he be vindicated and vindicated publicly, but he will receive adequate compensation for the wrong that he has suffered.'[11] The ex-internees hoped for much from this, but Evatt's idea of 'adequate' differed from theirs.

The Inquiry, which lasted for 69 sitting days, began in Sydney on 19 June and ended in Melbourne on 17 May 1945. Justice Wilfred Robert Dovey, K.C., and J. G. Coyle assisted the Commission; Justice John Wentworth Shand, K.C., and H. J. H. Henchman (later Q.C.) represented the Security Services and the Department of the Army.[12] A planned sitting in Western Australia was cancelled, although Bullock had been kept in Fremantle Gaol for weeks waiting for it.[13] Four days in Sydney in June were taken up with initial statements and legal argument. Nine days in Melbourne in August and September were devoted to presentation of documents.[14]

There were early signs that neither the advisers to the Commission nor the counsel for the ex-internees had a firm grasp of details concerning the *Publicist*, the AFM or the people involved. J. W. Maund (for Clarence Crowley) claimed that *Die Brücke* advertised in the *Publicist* (p. 16), although the *Publicist* took no advertising. Dovey called the Yabber Club a 'luncheon club', confusing it with the ANA luncheon club (p. 20), and stated that Adela Walsh was interned on 3 November 1941 (p. 26). Both Coyle (p. 57) and Henchman (p. 147) repeated that Stephensen had written as Miles Cheguin. Henchman (p. 2007) referred to Mrs Dyer and 'Mrs' Bell as separate persons. There were errors and evasion by MI, Security and police personnel. Captain Blood (p. 1043) claimed that the Army had copies of Clarence Crowley's speeches, although he had never made a speech. Constable A. T. Hughes (pp. 459–60) had reported that Mills was on the executive of the Nazi Party, and still asserted that he was on the AFM executive.

Counsel for ex-internees tried to prove official incompetence and bad faith. What they found indicated rather confusion, anxiety, hasty judgment and inadequate resources. Some officers were no longer with Intelligence. Colonel Powell had left the army in May 1943. (p. 311) Colonel Moseley had left Security for Special Bureau. (p. 1790) Major Hattam had returned to the CIB. (p. 495) They no longer had access to files and had to testify from memory. Much of Powell's evidence consisted of 'I do not know' and 'I do not recollect', so that Maund asked Clyne to deal with him for contempt of court.[15]

Captain G. H. Newman mentioned some 30,000 files, (p. 1153) only a few of which related to the AFM. H. W. May (for Val Crowley) asked him whether people knew the situation at that time. Newman replied that they did not, or they would have been running around in a panic. (p. 1158) They probably had in mind the widespread feeling in 1942 that a Japanese invasion force would land somewhere in Australia within weeks.

Trying to establish the rationale behind the selection of persons for internment, Clyne asked Powell about somebody who had allegedly attended nearly every meeting of the Yabber Club. 'Assuming he was a speaker and [Clarence] Crowley did not open his mouth,' asked Clyne, 'why did you put Crowley in and leave him out?'[16] Powell had no good answer, and the name was not revealed and cannot be determined. One reason that suggests itself is that he was another undercover agent of MI. Powell accepted ultimate responsibility for the internments, even though Blood had recommended most of them.[17]

The evidence of Crown witnesses was sometimes obviously wrong, though probably mainly correct. Nellie Bell (Mrs Dyer), whose name was suppressed, asserted that Ladendorff became Nazi leader in the absence of Hardt, and that Ladendorff left Sydney *after* war broke out. (p. 626) Obviously, he would not have been able to leave once the war started, nor did he take over from Hardt, who flew out of Sydney on 25 June 1939.[18] Ladendorff left Sydney by train three days later to join the vessel *Alster* in Melbourne.[19] Nevertheless, it was true that Miles passed to Skerst a letter from Melanie O'Loughlin, true that *Die Brücke* gave Trade Bulletins to Miles, and probably true that Miles visited the office of *Die Brücke* weekly.[20]

The name of Agent 222 was also suppressed. His reports were challenged, particularly by V. Crowley. He disowned a June 1940 report attributed to him, as he had not yet gone to the Yabber Club.[21] Crowley not only denied having said anything attributed to him, but tried to confuse the issue by saying, 'I could not imagine that the Tribunal could be so divorced from reality that they would keep a man interned in 1942 for a letter he had written in 1936.' (p. 1635) There was much more behind his internment: a history of anti-British activity going back to 1916. Stephensen himself had written, 'But to be anti-English is not in itself enough to make one a good Australian.'[22] Other ex-internees evaded the issues or had convenient lapses of memory. The arch evader was Cookes; a doctor said that he was too ill to appear, owing to pulmonary fibrosis. (p. 843) While it was true that he was ill, Cookes outlived most of the others involved.

Perhaps unintentionally, Hooper dodged the issue of the AF discussion group in Brisbane, (p. 1355), but otherwise his evidence appeared straightforward. Even though a dossier described him as 'an eloquent and persuasive speaker', it could be verified that he had not addressed any AFM meeting, but had just sat in the audience and asked some questions, as though he were a stranger. (pp. 44, 1312, 1322)

Bullock denied knowing that O'Loughlin was a member of The Link, although he asked her for a membership form, and he did not remember that Ittershagen had given him her address. (p. 1889) He claimed that the People's Party platform had been adapted from the Communist Constitution, Rules and Regulations, and he had composed it for typing practice; this differed from his 1942 court evidence. (p. 1892)

Those already cleared kept close to the truth, as did Dora Watts on behalf of her husband. The main object of their appearance was to determine compensation. Masey denied having recommended reading *Mein Kampf,* saying he had not read it and would not recommend something he had not read. (p. 274)[23] As for Arnold, he had not sought the inquiry and testified reluctantly. He refused at first to give his address, saying, 'I do not want to be murdered or bashed up by communist thugs.' Then he wrote it down for Clyne.[24] This was not paranoia, for Bath had been waylaid and assaulted, while Cahill appeared at a hearing 'showing evidence of maltreatment', and two counsel had been warned to keep out of the case if they valued their safety.[25]

Although it is not stated in the transcripts that evidence was given under oath, it was noted that A. Rud Mills made an affirmation instead of taking an oath. (p. 356) It may thus be assumed that other witnesses took an oath, and that those who told deliberate untruths committed perjury. In his testimony, Mills denied having heard of Julius Streicher, whose picture he had. (p. 411) He said he did not know a single Nazi, then admitted he knew and corresponded with a few Nazis in Sydney, including the 'leader'. (pp. 359, 457) He denied corresponding with the Minister for Propaganda and Enlightenment (Goebbels), then said he could not remember, then admitted receiving a letter from the Ministry, signed by 'Wiedmann'. (p. 413)[26] He denied having heard of the AFM in Western Australia. (p. 361) He claimed he did not know that a letter from England, found in his possession, contained a code. (pp. 394–95)

Cahill hoped for nothing from the Inquiry and did not take it very seriously. Little new came out in his testimony, except that he was challenged about some coded material. He admitted using alphabetical and three-figure codes while in the Communist Party, and said he had been trying to develop a code of his own, but he had not finished working on it and nobody else knew it. (pp. 1233–34)

Stephensen, as the main witness, was before the Inquiry for part or all of six days in October 1944 and one in March 1945. He was asked about letters he claimed he had not received – although they were allegedly found on his premises; about books he claimed he had not read – although they were found in the *Publicist* office, and he ought to have read them; about people whose names he claimed he had never heard - but should have. Anyone who disagreed with him was accused of lying. Stephensen claimed he had never received a letter from Bullock, although Rice testified that Bullock's request for the rights to sell the *Publicist* in Western Australia had been discussed at a meeting. (p. 1583) In literal terms: this letter had been to Miles. In addition, Stephensen denied receiving a letter Bullock wrote to him on 16 October, although it was allegedly found at his home, saying, 'Anyone who said it was found there would be telling a lie.' (p. 780)

Stephensen denied talking with any Japanese except at functions where hundreds of people had been present. (p. 551) Had he really forgotten the 1939 Mitsui meeting that was supposed to be kept secret? He admitted lunching with Toyoda; there was no reason why they should not have dined together. (p. 762) He claimed he had never in his life seen Ladendorff, which was possible, and had not heard the name before that day, which was unlikely. (p. 653) He had only vague memories of Sohno, to whom Otabe had referred him regarding a job for his stepson. (pp. 763–65) Moreover, he denied reading pamphlets called the *Fascist*, or Laurie's book, *The Case for Germany*. (pp. 758–59)

Much of Stephensen's testimony was informative, but the overall impression is that, at critical points, he was splitting linguistic straws, making mental reservations, giving automatic denials without thinking, and at times trying to befuddle Justice Clyne as he had befuddled solicitors and jurors in his libel case against the *Bulletin*, but this time it did not work. Justice Clyne ended the final sitting day by saying, 'Gentlemen, I will do the best I can as promptly as I can. It is a very onerous task ahead of me.'[27]

Parliamentary Inquiries and Commissions often take years to complete, but naturally the ex-internees were impatient. The Inquiry had not sat during July, as Clyne had to hear some bankruptcy cases, and there was an urgent protest from the Crown Solicitor in South Australia regarding mail censorship. When the delay was mentioned in Parliament, Evatt explained that, apart from delays caused by Clyne's commitments, the men had themselves wanted a postponement.[28]

Once again, Harrison spoke in their defence, citing the examples of Matthews, Watts, Downe and Bath. He mentioned that Hooper's wife had died three weeks before he was interned, which was wrong, and that Salier could not attend the Inquiry, as he was an old man in a state of nervous breakdown.[29] He compared Evatt's attitude to the AFM internments with his response to the cases of Ratliff and Thomas, 'convicted seditionists'.[30]

In response to a question from Harold Holt (Liberal, Fawkner, Vic.), Evatt said, 'First, I was not in any way responsible for the original internments.'[31] Stephensen had persuaded his associates to accept his claim that Evatt was to blame; they passed this to Evatt's enemies, who used it to attack him. As NS Regulations had charged the Minister for the Army with this responsibility, it was Forde who signed the internment orders. When the onus was transferred to Evatt in August, he ordered a review of the cases of those still interned, and most were freed by October. For this he received no credit.[32]

In reply to a question in May 1945 by a member of his own party, who suggested appointing an acting judge in bankruptcy so that Clyne could finish the Inquiry, Acting Attorney-General Beasley (Evatt being overseas again) stated that counsel for the ex-internees had asked for the Inquiry to be adjourned for a month so they could prepare their addresses.[33] In July, he added, 'The evidence in this matter has been completed and Mr. Justice Clyne is now preparing his report, which I expect will be submitted in about a fortnight.' The following week Evatt, having returned, gave a similar reply.[34]

Having assessed the complex and sometimes contradictory testimony, Justice Clyne made some good points in his report, and some that could be disputed in the light of evidence that might not have been presented. He pointed out that members of the AFM had different views as to its aims, and some disapproved of the extreme views of others. (p. 5) He wrote that the public speeches and the activities of some members were likely 'to have caused distrust of Australia on the part of her allies, and to have created such ill will and hostility in the community as to have impaired Australia's war effort'. (p. 6)

Clyne declared that the WA internees were 'very unsatisfactory witnesses', and, 'It is difficult to imagine what moved these puny conspirators to such ambitious and dangerous designs.' While Thomas was not 'a passive investigator', Clyne considered 'that their designs, however fantastic and extravagant, were seriously intended and that there was every reason for their detention'. (pp. 7, 9) While the Ten-Point Manifesto of October 1941 might be regarded with disfavour, it was unlikely to prejudice the war effort, therefore mere membership of the AFM did not warrant detention. (p. 8) However, while the initial arrests were justified, continued detention was not justified in all cases, although Forde had been entitled to act on the army's recommendations, and he could see 'no sufficient reason' for him not to accept them. (pp. 8, 19)[35]

Referring to those he considered justly interned, he cited Cahill's reference to a semi-secret organisation within the army, and to using force of arms to gain national independence. (p. 10) However, the army had not been justified in recommending the detention of Bath, Clarence Crowley, Hooper, Masey, Matthews, Salier, Tinker-Giles and Watts. Of Val Crowley, Clyne wrote that he was ready, at a critical time, 'to cause hostility between Britain and Australia and, by stirring up strife, to impair the war effort of Australia'. (p. 11) Clyne did not refer to Crowley's activities in World War I; that would have invited comment about some current Labor leaders.

To those already cleared by Advisory Committee, Clyne added Matthews, who had not appealed; Hooper, who had withdrawn his appeal; and Masey, whose appeal had been rejected. It was evident that it had been necessary to restrain Percy Stephensen, Val Crowley, Cahill, Arnold and Kirtley in some way. Outspoken, combative and headstrong, they would probably not have consented to nor abided by Restriction Orders. In fact, Cahill and Kirtley later refused to agree to one, and Arnold broke its conditions. It is difficult to see why Justice Clyne did not clear Downe, Rice and Eric Stephensen.

In accordance with Item 5 of the Terms of Reference, Justice Clyne named those he considered to have been detained without good cause, and assessed damages. Awards of £500 were made to Bath, C. Crowley and Salier; £350 to Masey; £750 to Matthews; £400 to the widow of Watts; and legal and medical expenses only to Hooper and Tinker-Giles.[36] Matthews was awarded the largest amount, not because he was more innocent than the others, but because he had an itemised account of verifiable financial losses from his neglected vineyard, spoiled wine and damaged equipment.[37] Nor were Hooper and Tinker-Giles less deserving; they had asked only for expenses. Clyne summed up:

> I think, however, that it must not be forgotten that the persons who were wrongly detained, were largely to blame for the misfortune which overtook them. They were associated with certain persons who were using the Australia First Movement to cause dissension in the community and to foster opinions prejudicial to Australia's part in the war.
>
> In my opinion, they did not fully recognize their obligation to aid the community at a critical time in its history and failed to appreciate the danger which might have been caused to Australia's war effort by agitation and the stirring up of strife.[38]

It was 12 September before Beasley (Evatt being away again) tabled the report (dated 5 September 1945) and moved that it be printed.[39] By then, the war was over and even Stephensen had been released. On 5 October, Forde announced that the report had been considered in Cabinet and the recommendations were being implemented.[40] He added:

> War imposes dreadful necessities, and in a state of national peril the necessity for immediate action may well preclude the careful investigation which in normal times would precede arrest; and it is to be regretted that in the exercise of emergency powers, the necessity for which could not be questioned by any reasonable citizen, innocent persons were occasionally confounded with guilty. It cannot reasonably be expected that powers of this kind can always be exercised with perfect justice and with Christian charity. The original ministerial statements made on this matter were based upon material vouched for and recommendations submitted by Military Intelligence. Failure to act on those recommendations would at that time, have been inexcusable.[41]

Before Parliament went into recess until March 1946, Forde made the statement that Clyne considered was due to some internees under the terms of reference:

> On behalf of the Government, I now publicly declare that Messrs K. P. Bath, Clarence Crowley, S. B. Hooper, E. C. de la Roche Masey, Harley Matthews, C. W. Salier, W. F. Tinker-Giles and Martin F. Watts were in fact wrongly detained and were not disloyal.[42]

Commenting on Clyne's report, Muirden wonders whether there was evidence not made public at the Inquiry.[43] Obviously there was: for example, the files entered as 'privileged documents'.[44] Justice Clyne would have known the contents of these, but there was material even he probably did not see, and witnesses who could not be called. Muirden points out, 'New material uncovered by the commission came largely from the Intelligence officers… What was novel was how Army Intelligence worked.'[45] This was what the Intelligence and Security services had feared would happen if there was a public trial. They had still avoided mention of telephone taps and interception of domestic mail, but this was 'new' only to amateurs.

The AFM people would have liked to call Evatt and Forde, but they could claim privilege; on the other hand, there were people whom MI or the CSS would have liked to summon. However, they could not call Major Scott, who had reported on the secret meeting that Stephensen and the Walshes had had with the Japanese at Mitsui's dinner party in June 1939, for he was a prisoner on Ambon. Major Caiger had a vital job with the US Army Central Bureau in Brisbane translating decrypted intercepts of Japanese wireless traffic. Cook did not want his undercover work exposed. They did not call Skerst, who had deserted the Nazi cause and, passionately Russian again, had told almost all he knew about Nazi intrigues.[46]

Prosecution witnesses from Western Australia, apart from police, did not appear, and there were other undercover agents in Sydney and Melbourne who were not called. MI could not admit they knew the contents of letters that some internees had written to the German and Japanese Consulates-General. In addition, Thomas was not questioned about a statement he made in May 1944; the only sign that this might have been known to the Inquiry was that Justice Shand asked Nancy Krakouer whether she remembered the name of Alan Raymond being mentioned. When she denied this, the matter was not pursued, and it should have been, for Raymond's activities showed what MI feared could happen in Australia if the Japanese invaded.[47]

Immediately he heard of the proposed Inquiry, Thomas wrote to Prime Minister Curtin that he had information linking the AFM in Western Australia with the Eastern States, and he wanted to discuss this with a member of the Commonwealth Government *without reference to the Western Australian authorities.*[48] The Prime Minister's Department passed the letter to Brigadier Simpson. Ignoring Thomas's request, he asked Moseley to make inquiries. Moseley gave the task to Richards, which was exactly what Thomas had asked should *not* happen. Richards saw Thomas (then a private in the AMF) on 8 May, and certain statements were taken. Making a hasty judgment, Richards dismissed the statement totally on account of a few errors. On 9 May, Moseley forwarded Richards' report, saying there was nothing new to add.[49] The statements were not typed up until two weeks later, and Thomas signed the nine pages on 30 May.

Interpreted properly, Thomas's statement linked Raymond to O'Loughlin, Bullock and Mills. According to Thomas, Bullock told him, 'You know Alan Raymond we talk about, he stove a Jew's head in at Singapore… Raymond was the founder of the Breakaway from Britain Movement.' Krakouer added, 'If Alan Raymond was here he would be the man you should see but he has gone to Japan.' O'Loughlin had confirmed that Raymond was a Japanese agent.[50]

According to his 1931 passport, Alan Willoughby Raymond was born in Melbourne on 27 February 1909, son of Henry Raymond and Irene, née Johnson, but there was no such birth registration.[51] In February 1931, Raymond left Sydney for China, where he quickly attracted official notice in Shanghai and Hong Kong. The police were interested in his financial dealings and his association with 'low type' Chinese women, Security in his contacts with Japanese and Germans. He travelled widely in Asia, and in 1936 he was stranded in Japan for three months when a business venture failed.[52] At this time he may have become financially obligated to the Japanese. When the war in China resumed in July 1937, Raymond owed a lot of money, and at the Shanghai Race Club he was 'posted' for debt. Going inland, he made his way to Hong Kong, where he worked for a time as a clerk in a stock-broking firm. He was soon in trouble, and he was warned off racecourses in both Macao and Hong Kong. Vehemently anti-British and anti-Semitic, he tried to found there a movement aimed at breaking the links between Australia and Britain. British authorities quickly banned his Break Away from Britain Movement.[53]

On 15 August 1939, Raymond wrote from China to a journalist in Sydney that he was now sub-editor on a local paper. Shortly afterwards, he settled his debts and left Hong Kong.[54] He arrived in Fremantle from Singapore aboard *Centaur* on 6 December 1939. This date is significant, as Thomas told Richards that Bullock had spoken of a meeting in O'Loughlins' house in *1937*; Bullock, Miles, Ittershagen, O'Muri, Connolly and Vail attended, and plans were made to take over Australia 'when the time arrived'.[55]

As Richards realised, some things in this statement were clearly amiss. O'Loughlin first contacted Miles in April 1939; Bullock did not meet O'Loughlin until late 1939;[56] Miles had last been in Perth in August 1929.[57] Raymond was in China in 1937; Omori (not O'Muri) had not arrived in Australia until February 1939, and Vera Connolly had not met him before then. Thomas also mentioned that they 'had a good laugh' about the Munich agreement (concerning the Sudetenland), but that was not signed until September 1938. Therefore Richards rejected Thomas's statement totally, without considering that the items most likely to be wrong in statements are dates.[58]

If it is taken that the date of the meeting was in December 1939, while Raymond was in Perth, it appears feasible. Richards was wrong in claiming that Omori was not in Western Australia before 1939; he arrived in Broome on 22 November 1934.[59] From then until 1940, he travelled constantly around WA in connection with mining projects, and he had a close relationship with the Premier, John Collings Willcock.[60] Vera Connolly certainly knew Omori by then, for in August 1939 she applied for a Japanese passport so that she could travel to Java as his wife.[61]

That disposes of Richards' objections except the one concerning Miles, who had never met O'Loughlin, but Thomas also reported Bullock's comment: '(We) should introduce the Nordic religion of Wotan and Valhalla... Miles is a follower of Ludendorff's religious beliefs of Viking Worship.'[62] In fact, Miles was a Rationalist and he scorned Odinism. The Odinist was Mills; therefore it is also irrelevant that *Miles* was not in Perth for, as noted in Chapter 3, *Mills* planned to visit Perth late in 1939. Despite this, there could not have been a single meeting exactly as Thomas claimed Bullock had described it, for during the only time when Raymond was in Perth, Omori and Connolly were in Java.[63] As the conversations reported by Thomas had taken place more than two years earlier, and Bullock tended to be careless about facts, it seems probable that there had been no such single meeting, but that the persons involved had met at different times.[64]

Raymond arrived in Melbourne on 11 December, and by 8 January 1940 he was living in Potts Point, Sydney, a few blocks from the Stephensens. He applied for the post of Australian Trade Commissioner at Singapore, with references from the staff of the *Sun News Pictorial*, and for a post with a stock-broking firm using references from Hong Kong.[65] He obtained a position with the firm but could not hold it; unemployed and in debt again, he left Sydney by *Kitano Maru* early in June, arriving in Shanghai aboard *Husimi Maru* in July.[66] Not much is recorded about his stay in Sydney. He had an article published in the *Bulletin*; MI thought he had written also for the *Publicist*, but could find no evidence of this, or of contact with Miles or Stephensen. Later he denied having any contact with the AFM, but he must have been aware of the *Publicist*. Since he was so much in accord with its policy, it would have been natural to make contact.[67] Security tried in vain to find a connection between Raymond and Stephensen, but he was not reported at the Yabber Club nor mentioned in any AF correspondence.

Raymond's activities in Shanghai are not relevant until March 1942. On 15 March, a telegram from Britain informed MI of an announcement by Berlin Radio on 11 March:

> Recently an Australian independence movement was founded in Shanghai under the leadership of Alan Raymond. Raymond stated that Australia will demand complete independence, in so far as she is able to determine her own destiny at the conclusion of the present conflict. Raymond made the announcement that he would appeal to his fellow countrymen in Australia over the radio.[68]

At the first meeting, on 7 March, the Movement had resolved to approach the Japanese Government to secure leniency for

Australians, who had been tricked into the war by Britain. According to Domei's Shanghai correspondent, Raymond had said, 'Since the Japanese Government has intimated its desire to save Australia from the horrors of war the Commonwealth should negotiate for an honourable peace.'[69] That was AFM policy. It was printed in the *Publicist*, discussed at the Yabber Club and mooted at public meetings that Britain and America had involved Australia in their war, and Australia should make a separate peace. In return for his services, Raymond was allowed to trade as a broker on the Chinese stock exchange, so that he could support himself and rescue his mother from internment.[70] Raymond's activities could not have influenced the initial decision to make the AFM arrests, as they were not known on 10 March, but they were well known by the time of the trial in Perth and the appeals in Sydney.[71]

The Break Away from Britain Movement was also known as the Independent Australia League, in imitation of the Japanese-sponsored Independent India League, which they hoped to use as a Fifth Column and secret army in India.[72] The Japanese allowed it to hold meetings in the Astor Park Hotel. The committee consisted of Raymond, Wynette Cecilia ('Gwen') McDonald and her partner, a Swedish merchant captain named Olaf Linquist. Raymond began broadcasting for the Japanese station XMHA on or about 9 March, promoting the Japanese aim of creating enmity between Australia and Britain, and appealing to Australians to throw off the British yoke and make peace with Japan, under whom they would find a freedom not enjoyed under Britain.

McDonald began to broadcast a month later. Born in Melbourne in October 1912, she had arrived in China from Darwin in 1940. She spoke Japanese, and she and Linquist were the only foreigners invited to attend a Japanese celebration after Singapore fell on 15 February.[73] In one broadcast she said that Curtin was an evil, corrupting influence, and had murdered Lyons by poisoning him.[74]

A third Australian who broadcast from Shanghai was John Joseph Holland, born in 1907 in Kanowna, WA. He had been imprisoned for fraud in 1932 and he too had a dubious business reputation. Arriving in China in August 1937, he ran up debts he could not pay; late in 1938 he went from Hong Kong to Shanghai. After undertaking a dangerous and well-paid job for the Chinese, he began to work for the Japanese as well; they used him as a front man when they bought the radio station belonging to the *Shanghai Times*. He travelled widely in Japan, Indo-China, Thailand, Malaya and the Netherlands East Indies, and he spoke several Chinese dialects. By December 1941 he was in Shanghai again.[75] Using the pseudonym David Lester, he broadcast for both the Japanese XMHA and the German station XGRS until September 1942, then he was sent to Tokyo, where he broadcast for a few more months. In July 1942, Holland informed his father, 'I belong to an Australian Political Party here which is interested in endeavouring to promote a separate peace with Japan.'[76] This was the AFM line. While the AFM people in Sydney had no connection with Raymond and Holland, the *Publicist* had led the Japanese to believe that there was in Australia wider support for Japan than there was in fact.

Through the Chungking Embassy, External Affairs arranged for the Chinese Secret Service to report on Australian collaborators and supply copies of their articles in English-language Japanese papers.[77] In addition to a regular column ('An Aussie's Point of View') in the *Shanghai Times*, Raymond wrote for the *Shanghai Evening Post* and the periodical *Freedom*. Raymond was denounced bitterly when diplomatic personnel, 'protected persons' and certain internees reached British territory after an exchange of prisoners late in 1942.

McDonald's broadcasts continued until April 1943; Raymond made his last broadcast on 20 July 1945.[78] While it is likely that Military Intelligence, noting similarities in their propaganda, had Raymond in mind when Stephensen's case was being considered, Justice Clyne probably knew little about the situation in Shanghai.

The Clyne Report was debated when Parliament resumed in March 1946. Bath had begun an action against the Commonwealth for damages, but withdrew it pending this debate. When he resumed his action, the Commonwealth pleaded the Statute of Limitations Act of 1623, which applied from 10 March 1946. Bath believed that Evatt and Forde had postponed the debate simply to block his action. Parliamentary records show that this was not the case. After the summer break, Parliament resumed as usual in the first week in March. The first day was taken up with mentions of deaths and results of by-elections; then the Opposition brought forward a 'Want of Confidence' motion. Menzies did this, not Evatt or Forde, and it is unlikely he had Bath in mind. The debate lasted until the weekend adjournment. Parliament did not sit on Monday; when it resumed on 13 March, the time during which Bath could have appealed had expired. Bath condemned this as a mean trick, but the court case could not have succeeded. Regulation 13(3) of the National Security Act ruled this out:

> No action shall be against the Commonwealth, any Commonwealth officer, any constable or any other person acting in pursuance of this section in respect of any arrest or detention in pursuance of this section, but if the Governor-General is satisfied that any arrest was made without reasonable cause, he may award such compensation in respect thereof as he considers reasonable.

Bath's only reasonable course of action was to apply to the Governor-General for an *ex gratia* award, but there was little chance that Prince Henry, Duke of Gloucester, would have made such an award unless the Government recommended it.

The debate on the Clyne Report began on 13 March. The previous day, Bath, Masey and Clarence Crowley had driven to Canberra to confer with Opposition members, in particular Harrison, the Deputy Leader of the Liberal Party.[79] They later placed great value on his attack on Forde, so some of what he said needs to be examined closely, as do his motives. First he referred to Forde's 'hysterical outburst which rocked Australia to its foundations'. Although Forde's statement of 26 March 1942 was misleading, the press provided the hysteria. Harrison called the Government actions 'heinous' and 'sinister', when 'misguided and hasty' would have been more apt. He stated that under NSR (Section 13) the Attorney-General or a person appointed by him had to be notified 'forthwith' of the arrest of a person, and if no charge was laid he had to be released after ten days. However, 'forthwith' is an imprecise concept. On 13 March 1942, Captain Blood had asked 'the Minister', to approve internment of the detainees under Regulation 26. The Minister was presumably Forde, who was responsible for internments. An internment order, dated 20 March, was not served on the men until five days later.[80]

At worst, this made the detention illegal for only a few days. Of the Western Australians Harrison said:

> Indeed, it is clear from Mr. Justice Clyne's report that the utterances attributed to the Western Australian members of the movement were the gabblings of three or four imbecile windbags who had not the means even to stop a tram or kill a rabbit.[81]

Harrison clearly had no idea of the political background of Bullock, who might have resented being called an 'imbecile windbag'. Harrison incorrectly called him a former communist, and enlarged on this: 'Bullock was typical of the Communists - he would join anything and shout for anything.' He also referred to the 'unsupported evidence of this £5 a week pimp'.[82] He then canvassed three specific cases (Matthews, Bath, Watts), saying, 'I take these cases as typical of all.'[83] In fact, he should have known that he could hardly have chosen cases that were *less* typical. His motives as well as his accuracy are suspect. First he attacked Eddie Ward, linking him by implication with Thomas's approach to Bullock, then he said, 'It is a matter for comment that the Communist party knows what goes on in the Attorney-General's Department, and honorable members can draw their own conclusions from that.'[84]

He claimed that there had to be contact between communists and either the Attorney-General's Department or the Department of the Army, as a communist paper had published a full list of names of internees. In connection with leakage of information, he mentioned a letter by 'Blain',[85] a reference that made little sense until Leslie Haylen (ALP, Parkes, NSW) linked it with Allan Dalziel, Evatt's secretary.[86] It then became apparent that the opportunistic Harrison was not speaking solely in the interests of the ex-internees, but was using their case for other purposes. With an election only a few months away, he was trying to undermine Evatt by linking him to the Communist Party. Dalziel had nothing to do with the AFM case. The Liberal Party was preparing to ban the Communist Party if it won the coming election, and the practice of using the AFM case to link Evatt with communism through Dalziel continued. During the Budget Estimates Debate in October 1947, the Clyne Report was mentioned again, and Blain repeated and distorted an accusation that the indictment of the AFM members had been prepared by the Attorney-General's secretary (Dalziel), 'copying Trotsky'.[87]

Forde replied that Harrison had read 'certain extracts which suited his case', and Clyne had said that 'there was not sufficient reason to justify me as Minister in not accepting the recommendations of Military Intelligence'.[88] The debate was adjourned until the following day, when Menzies spoke in generalities, emphasising that after an arrest on some reasonable suspicion, full investigation should always be prompt.[89]

Ward matched Harrison epithet for epithet, linking the AFM with the New Guard and fascism, and referring to Harrison's 'black shirt'. He selected some unpleasant quotes from the *Publicist,* and stated that if the Opposition quoted Clyne to exculpate some internees, it was valid for him to quote the report to inculpate others. He ended by attacking the Liberal Party: 'They are a Nazi Party. They are Fascists at heart.'[90]

In response, Sir Earle Page (CP, Cowper, NSW) attacked Ward's record, calling him 'rather a unique specimen. He seems to have the shortest and most convenient memory we have ever experienced in Parliament'. A Labor Government, he said, had acted on evidence manufactured by a government pimp sent to WA as part of a communist plot. Adding that Ward had been at a communist meeting that had inspired the campaign against the AFM, he called for a Royal Commission to investigate communist infiltration of government departments. Ward interjected, 'That is a deliberate lie!'[91]

Returning to the debate, Haylen condemned Harrison for his 'impassioned and poignant plea, which he can turn on and off like a prima donna', and stigmatised his attack on a civil servant (Dalziel) as cowardly.[92] The facts of the AFM case became almost irrelevant in attempts to paint the Labor Party as crypto-communist and the Liberal Party as crypto-fascist.

In his contribution, Archie Cameron (Liberal, Wooroora, SA) referred to a section of the Crimes Act, which said that 'to excite disaffection against the Sovereign or the Government or Constitution of the United Kingdom or against either Houses of the Parliament of the United Kingdom' was a seditious intention, and the penalty was death.[93] It is questionable whether, in Australia, it should have been an offence to incite disaffection against the Government of the United Kingdom, but it was on the Statute Books, and Miles, Stephensen and Crowley had done that. So had the communists. Nobody had been prosecuted, much less imprisoned or executed for this.[94]

In comparison, Evatt's speech was restrained. He declared that Harrison's comments were grotesque and unfair. He then drew attention to the fact that the administration of internments had been transferred from the Army to the Attorney-General's Department after he returned from Washington and London, 'simply because it was considered that many legal matters were involved'.[95]

Whatever the ex-internees had hoped from the Clyne Inquiry and their lobbying of politicians, most were disappointed. In only two cases (Bath and Downe) was there any improvement on the decisions or awards made by Justice Clyne.

Chapter 12

After the War

After the war, many of Stephensen's aims for Australia were achieved by others, but it gave him little satisfaction. Soured by his internment, he turned against Evatt, whom he blamed unjustly. Whereas once he had regarded Evatt as his friend and lauded him as 'out-standing in intellectual ability, scholarship, and public spirit',[1] he now abused him as 'only a lout with a veneer of higher education'.[2] Pursuing his feud with Evatt, he supported Calwell's bid for leadership of the ALP, but not publicly, for he realised that this could be counter-productive. He wrote to Calwell on 9 December 1959 that he was the only person to lead Labor, and Calwell wrote back to him as 'Dear Percy'.

Stephensen accused Evatt of manipulating AFM internments to appease 'Communists and fanatical Jews', calling him 'the perpetrator of the outrage' and 'a whining stooge of Communism'. Despite that, he wrote, 'Having no persecution-complex, I ask for no sympathy. Nor would I raise a howl for financial compensation.'[3] In Munro's view, his 'political thinking had petrified around his paranoia', and he quotes Manning Clark who described Stephensen as a 'tragic and anachronistic figure'.[4] Munro writes also, 'He could swing wildly from one extreme to another, from elaborate and irrational optimism to sullen despair at times.'[5] Although this, combined with his reluctance to face financial facts, is a classic description of manic-depression, Stephensen was not clinically manic-depressive, for he was never suicidal. Nor was he paranoid in a clinical sense; although his delusion of being persecuted by Evatt hardened into an obsession.

After the war, Stephensen took up farming in Victoria before returning to Sydney eleven years later.[6] He still worked on behalf of Australian writers, being co-founder of the Australian Society of Authors. He earned a reasonable livelihood as author, editor and literary agent,[7] and won or regained the respect of those who felt that his services to Australian literature outweighed his political indiscretions. He continued to ghostwrite for Frank Clune, although their relationship was not always harmonious. Clune wrote to Stephensen in 1954, 'Your communist God failed you. Then you got a new God, a greater one than Christ, Buddha or Mohamet. His name was Fascism.'[8]

For at least a decade after the war, Stephensen stayed in contact with Mills, who wrote him rambling racist letters, including some from London. Mills planned to compile a book on internments worldwide and asked Stephensen to write *and dramatise* the Australian part. Stephensen replied that Australia had 'the world's blackest record of arbitrary imprisonments' (an exaggeration) and the story would take a whole book. He apparently planned to write one, for he said he would wait until Volume II of Hasluck's work appeared. Writing to Mills in 1954, he endorsed Odinism as 'perfectly normal and natural'. He still regarded the *Protocols of Zion* as authentic, and he confided to Mills his 'personal beliefs', among them: 'National Socialism will come again, with some combination of the political genius of a Hitler with the ethical intensity of a Gandhi.'[9]

Paul Hasluck had been commissioned to write part of the history of the civilian aspects of the war, to be entitled *The Government and the People*. The first volume appeared in 1952. The Australia-First story was due to appear in Volume II, and Hasluck was in contact with some of those who had been interned. In June 1946, Masey had composed a statement that referred mainly to himself, Clarence Crowley, Hooper, Matthews, Salier, Tinker-Giles and Watts. He sent Hasluck a copy in May 1949, while somebody provided a copy of Bath's pamphlet, *Injustice within the Law*.[10] Hooper too was in contact with Hasluck, and with Sir George Knowles.[11]

Stephensen wrote at least one letter to Hasluck, full of emotion but shaky on facts. He referred to Ratcliffe (*sic*) and Hall (*sic*), who had been released from internment in October 1941 'after they had actually been convicted of sabotage [*sic*]'.[12] He pointed out that Rupert Lockwood was editor of the *Tribune* when the internees' names were published, and Evatt's secretaries, Allan Dalziel and Dr John Burton, were communist sympathisers. He continued:

> My narrative would put the last nail in the coffin of Dr Evatt's political career. The Labor Party does not really trust him, but if they knew the facts of the Australia-First case, they would depose him as leader. He is the most arrant humbug who ever strutted in the guise of a defender of Civil Liberties.
>
> If your Second Volume upholds the Evatt Doctrine, making me a scapegoat for the Labor Govt's panic in 1942, I would have to publish a rejoinder to it, I suppose, or sue for libel, or do something effective to remove the filthy stigma placed on me by the Communists, with Evatt's full connivance.[13]

Stephensen invited Hasluck to send him the galley proofs for comment.[14] He might have been reluctant to sue Hasluck, but he threatened to sue the Melbourne *Herald* over an article that appeared on 24 May 1961 after Adela Walsh died. It had described an AFM scheme for 'murdering the national leaders and taking over Australia'. An out-of-court settlement for £1,000 was reached, and the *Herald* published a lengthy apology.[15]

After the war, those connected with the AFM and the *Publicist* went their separate ways. Stephensen abandoned political activities but was sought as a speaker on literary topics. On 28 May 1965, he collapsed and died at the Savage Club, just after delivering a speech on the Australian publication of *The Trial of Lady Chatterley*.[16] He had been intending to return to Queensland to write his autobiography. Heartbroken Winifred wrote, 'My life is empty and finished without the man I loved.'[17]

After Tom Walsh died in 1943, Adela withdrew from public life. She had abandoned almost every cause she had worked for, and few would still have followed her. However, she still had some aggression left. On 22 March 1946, she wrote a confronting letter to the Deputy Director of Security, Sydney, demanding immediate return of her confiscated books and threatening to complain to Evatt, his Ministerial superior and her friend.[18] However, Security feared that if they handed evidence back to Adela she would destroy it and then sue for wrongful detention. She died on 23 May 1961, having embraced Roman Catholicism as her last cause. Coleman sums up her political activism: 'Like many a reformer Adela was driven by egotism as well as by altruism.'[19]

Coleman is wrong in suggesting that Adela might have been the model for Aelfrida Candlemas in Xavier Herbert's *Poor Fellow My Country*.[20] Herbert loathed the Walshes and could not have written about them sympathetically. 'Alfie' was a composite, based mainly on Herbert himself. He was registered at birth as *Alfred* Jackson, and it is not surprising that he should depict one of his *alter egos* as a woman, as he had written that he was 'trying to overcome the Poofter' in himself.[21] Like Alfie, he had worked with Aborigines in Darwin; like Alfie, he had written a prize-winning novel.[22] Adela had done neither. The female author with whom Herbert had a passionate love affair was Dymphna Cusack.[23] The female author on the platform during the fracas of 19 February was Miles Franklin. However, Herbert's depictions of Stephensen as 'The Bloke', Miles as 'The Chief', and Hooper as 'The Banker', though distorted, are enlightening.[24]

In 1942 Bath had to sell his home to help pay his debts. He worked for a time in a factory, then for the American Army from late 1943.[25] Bath wrote that Evatt had 'shuffled and wriggled' and broken his pledge to vindicate and compensate, but he won a concession not extended to others: the Taxation Department remitted his tax arrears of £2,371.[26] Bath returned to real estate in January 1946.[27] At first the Attorney-General's Department refused to pay the compensation unless he renounced his 'rights' against the Commonwealth, but eventually paid him unconditionally in February 1946.[28] During the debate on the Clyne Report, Fadden's motion that a Commission be appointed to assess compensation was defeated on party lines, as Fadden probably foresaw.[29]

On 7 May 1947, Bath issued a writ for damages of £25,000.[30] Nearly four months later, the Commonwealth entered a defence that he had been 'duly and lawfully arrested'. After a preliminary hearing on 24 November, the case was listed for 15 December, whereupon the Commonwealth invoked the Statute of Limitations Act. Withdrawing his writ on 5 April 1948, Bath began to circularise politicians with his case. He had no success, and sometimes received no answer. Undeterred he wrote:

> But Mr. Chifley and Dr. Evatt must not imagine that ... they have heard the last of the matter... Perspective of history will reveal Dr. Evatt not as a champion of law and liberty but as one who – on the

> instigation of revolutionary communists – attempted to destroy the heritage of British Justice in Australia.[31]

On 19 December 1949, there was a change of Government. Menzies as Prime Minister, Fadden as Treasurer, and Harrison in various Ministries were no longer eager to redress the perceived wrong. It was the Menzies Government that declared in 1951 that 'the Commonwealth does not and will not admit that Mr Bath was illegally arrested'. However, they too had not heard the last of Bath, and in 1954 he was finally awarded £2,500 in settlement.[32]

Les Cahill was earning his living as a grocer in 1944.[33] He diverted his energies from politics to the safer field of football administration until he died in 1955.[34] Valentine Crowley died in August 1954 and Clarence in February 1972, without having attracted further public attention.

Clive Downe rejoined the army a few weeks after his release. After writing to Colonel Prentice to ask for an opportunity to prove his loyalty, he was posted to a cipher unit.[35] As his work was secret, he did not mention it at the Clyne Inquiry, and Justice Clyne did not exonerate him. This caused problems after the war. On 22 July 1948, Evatt wrote to Downe's employer that he had 'served well as a soldier' and 'his loyalty and discretion were beyond question'. Public exoneration was provided when the letter was read in Parliament, but it received little publicity and did not convince people who had already made up their minds.[36] In information he supplied to the Soviet Embassy, Rupert Lockwood accused Prentice of giving Downe a job not because he believed him innocent, but because he believed him guilty.[37]

Hooper kept up his correspondence with parliamentarians. He wrote that he expected 'unreserved retraction of the monstrous Ministerial allegations against us'.[38] In the Clyne Report and in Parliament, it had been declared that he had never been disloyal, but this attracted little attention. He died in August 1959. Masey had been promised his former job when he was released, but the managing director died before then, and his successor did not honour the promise.[39] Salier died in December 1949. In his funeral notice there was no mention of surviving relatives.

With the help of John Kinmont Moir, leader of the Bread and Cheese Club, Jack Kirtley established Mountainside Press at Ferntree

Gully near Melbourne, producing luxury limited editions. He died in August 1966.[40] Eric Stephensen enlisted in the army and served in the Ambulance Corps. Harley Matthews became a close friend of Cahill, one of the few AFM associations that survived the trauma of internment. His compensation payment enabled him to buy a new vineyard at Ingleburn (NSW). He died in August 1968.[41] A. Rud Mills paid another visit to England and kept talking about writing another book, but had not done so when he died on 8 April 1964.[42]

Walter Cookes died in Melbourne on 2 September 1976 at 98, a remarkable age for somebody who was too ill to attend hearings thirty years earlier. He had fifteen great-grandchildren by then. His staff took out a full column for his obituary in the *Age*.[43] Ian Mudie continued writing and was loosely associated with the Jindyworobak movement; he died in Britain on 23 October 1976. Gordon Rice had business difficulties through losing his driving licence, but his trail is lost. After his second release, Edwin Arnold told the police: 'Candidly, I do not think there is any future for me in this country; the only thing I can do is, after the war, get out and go somewhere else.'[44] It is not known if he did, for his trail too is lost.

Dora Watts continued her anti-Semitism crusade, but no longer had an outlet such as the *Publicist*. In 1962, her racist booklet, *The Dangerous Myth of Racial Equality: Genocide for the White Races?*, was distributed by the League of Rights. Although it has no cultural agenda, in political terms the League of Rights is the natural heir to the AFM and the *Publicist*.

Laurence Bullock was attacked and brutally kicked while in prison, and he was denied medical attention for a hernia.[45] He might have been baptised a Jehovah's Witness while in prison. The description of a Bullock so baptised fits him, though a letter reporting this is filed under William Bullock.[46] He was sent to Loveday briefly in January 1945, then to Tatura, whence it was reported that he 'denied any evidence against him and showed no repentance for any of his actions'.[47] Released on 17 August 1945, he flitted from cause to cause, and allegedly joined the South Australian Humanist Society. His wife was willing to take him back, and he faded from public view.[48] Tatura reports described Charles Williams as mentally unstable, irresponsible, wild, unrepentant and proud of his association with

Bullock.[49] He was released with Bullock on 17 August and no further report on him has been found. Nancy Krakouer Moss was released on 25 November 1944 but restricted to Victoria.[50] It was a long time before she returned to Perth. Edward Quicke had had a complete change of heart and refused to associate with Bullock and Williams.[51] Released on 4 August 1945, he presumably returned to his wife, children and orchard, grateful to be out of the limelight.

Mortimer also apparently had a change of heart. He appeared before an Appeals Tribunal in January 1944 and was released under restriction on 18 September 1944. In a letter of 25 June 1945, he claimed, 'I am not a Fascist – nor have I ever been one.' Police kept an eye on him and reported that he had rehabilitated himself.[52] The other pamphleteer, Graham, underwent no such conversion. He tried to smuggle out of Tatura circulars urging workers to strike, do away with the Jews and welcome the Japanese. In 1946, he lived in Mosman (Sydney), where the locals called him 'Mad Tom'. He took employment as a seaman, and Security services around the world kept track, reporting him in New Zealand, Southampton, New York and Canada. In Vancouver in January 1948, he was imprisoned for seditious libel in a leaflet, *Down with Jewmocracy*. In January 1952, the Darwin paper, *Northern Standard*, printed an anti-Semitic article by Tom Graham, and he was linked with a pamphlet distributed in South Australia by the Thiele brothers.[53] Late in 1953, he wrote to Stephensen from London.[54] David Harcourt mentions him in connection with the postwar Australian National Socialist Party.[55] Extremists such as Mills and Graham still turned to Stephensen for support.

The Shanghai group escaped retribution. John Holland was put on trial in London, but only reprimanded and released on bond. Wynette McDonald visited Australia briefly, then returned to China to work for a wool-buying firm and the Kuomintang. Alan Raymond studied at St John's University in Shanghai, married a Chinese fellow student, and resisted efforts to force him to return to Australia. When last mentioned in 1953, he was in Hong Kong. Trying Raymond for treason, successfully or not, might have solved the mystery of any connection between him, Mills and Bullock, but it was not to be.

Raymond claimed that everything he had broadcast was meant for

Australia's benefit. The AFM also sincerely believed that they were true patriots. They might have had no intention of aiding the Japanese if Australia had been invaded, but the Japanese had collected details of those who they thought would collaborate. It has been argued that more illustrious people - businessmen and politicians - had been of greater use to the Japanese before the war. While leading figures in commerce and politics, such as Sir Thomas Gordon, Sir Arthur Rickard and Percy Spender, were on friendly terms with the Japanese and tried to foster trade with Japan, despite the conflict in China,[56] they did so because it was their job to foster trade with all countries. The core of the AFM cum Yabber cum *Publicist* clique supported Japan, Germany and Italy alone, while abusing Britain and the United States as much as they abused the communists who were ostensibly their targets. This led to their downfall.

There was a great deal of similarity between *Publicist* ideology and that of fascist bodies overseas, including Britain, though there were differences in methods. Few AFM people had contact with such organisations. Hooper had met Mosley of the British Union of Fascists; Miles and Mills were in contact with Leese of the Imperial League of Fascists and National Socialists. Stephensen seems to have had no contact with either; apparently he did not even hear them speak while in England. Yet it is interesting that there were similarities in the appearance, character and family background of Mosley and Stephensen, as well as critical differences.

Like Mosley, Stephensen was the eldest child; he lorded it over younger siblings and was doted upon by his mother. Both were physically big men with loud voices (both being rather deaf), energetic, impatient, flamboyant, impetuous, easily offended but insensitive to the feelings of others. Both were litigious and sued several times for defamation; each had once received a favourable judgment with an award of only a farthing or two. However, Stephensen never followed Mosley's lead of adopting a theatrical Blackshirt uniform and would have found this laughable.

There was even a parallel between the *Bierkeller* riots in Germany in 1920s, the *mêlée* at the Olympia Stadium during one of Mosley's meetings, and the fracas at Adyar Hall in Sydney, although that was a comparatively puny affair. Fascist meetings were often broken up violently by communist heavies. Not all the assailants were altruists inspired by a shining ideal; some were simply psychotic thugs looking for an excuse to bash someone. In Germany, the Nazi Party formed the SA and in Britain the BUF developed a fighting wing. In Australia, neither the Old Guard, which had the money, nor the New Guard, which had the muscle, supported the AFM.

Mosley wanted a fascist system in Britain, but he did not want Hitler in Britain. Stephensen convinced himself that the Japanese would break alleged Jewish money-power in Australia and loosen British control, then go back home, after helping to set up a 'national socialist' system in Australia. He believed that the Japanese would help Australia maintain the White Australia policy, even though he had been told time and again that this was one of the things that most offended them. Neither seemed capable of understanding the nature of the beast he was patting.

However, Mosley understood the power that finance wielded over government, and he made concrete plans to overcome this. Stephensen regarded financial problems as a Jewish plot, imagining they would disappear if the Jews lost their power.[57] The Corporate State he advocated might be efficient, but it is wrong to assume that a one-party state will allow the most competent to govern. It more often leads to government by the most ambitious, aggressive and cruel. History furnishes plenty of examples.

Some core aims of the AFM have been achieved. Most formal ties with Britain have been broken, with the adoption of the Statute of Westminster, the abolition of appeals to the Privy Council, an independent foreign policy. As Miles predicted, it was Britain who 'cut the painter' when she joined the European Common Market. However, they were not prophets in all respects. Women have not retreated to the kitchen and the nursery; the White Australia policy has gone; privatisation of Government concerns has pushed their Corporate State even further away. The name 'Australia First' has been recycled but has been attached to different policies.

Many intelligent, compassionate people see that there is something seriously unfair in the current political and commercial systems, but fail to see that the utopian systems they espouse might be worse. The slogan 'Australia First' appealed to people's emotions, both noble and base, and people adopt and cling to their ideologies primarily for emotional reasons. That is why demagogues who work on the emotions are so successful. The presentation of facts and appeals to logic and common sense have little effect on fanatics. Neither then nor now, neither in Europe nor Australia, Asia nor Africa nor America - and certainly not in the Middle East - does logic come into an ideological equation.

And 'Inky' Stephensen? His personal tragedy was that Miles dragged him far from his earlier aims for Australian literature and publishing, so that he squandered his energies and abilities on tainted causes instead of sticking to his aim of fostering Australian literature. Many uncomplimentary adjectives can be applied to him, but his positive qualities attracted respect from people of intelligence and integrity. He had that dangerous and elusive quality: charisma. Although his own publishing ventures failed, he did a lot to further the interests of Australian authors. One of his lasting legacies was this work for the Australian Society of Authors. Contemporary Australian authors could do with someone like Stephensen to represent them - but not too much like him.

Notes

Preface

[1] Hasluck wrote in the Preface to Volume II (p. ix) that Chapters 1 to 5 and the appendices connected with them were not touched after 1951; if so, he did not take Muirden's book into consideration.
[2] Interview, Dr Craig Munro, 15 October 1998.
[3] On pp. 724-25, Hasluck cited Attorney-General's Department, File W4888, Australia First Movement; this number no longer applies, and it is not known how this file has been renumbered.
[4] This expresses Bath's justified resentment at his treatment, but he is wrong in some factual matters, and very wrong in some interpretations. Hasluck's research notes are in AWM68: 3DRL 3670/3: [Records of Paul Hasluck] Australia First Movement 1939-62. (Henceforth Hasluck Collection); AWM27: 490/3: Correspondence between Sir George Knowles and S. B. Hooper, Sydney, 1945-1946.
[5] These are mainly in the C320 (Security Service) and C443 (Japanese Consular Documents) series of records.
[6] Hall, *Secret State*, pp. 32-35.
[7] Fotheringham, Richard: THE5426, Fryer Library, University of Queensland. 'A biographical study of Percy Reginald Stephensen'.
[8] Fotheringham Papers: Fryer Library, UQ: UQFL MSS 46: Box 1.
[9] Lockyer papers: UQFL MSS 247.
[10] Authority to intercept domestic mail was given under a system known as an XRD order.
[11] Hasluck, *Government and the People,* Vol. II, p. 742. Hasluck and Menzies made no attempt to correct this 'injustice' when they won government in 1949.
[12] Muirden, *Puzzled Patriots*, pp. 180-182.

Chapter 1

[1] Stephensen analysed the poem in his book *Foundations of Culture in Australia*. It was later published in full in the *Publicist*, 1 March 1938, pp. 8-11.
[2] 'The Wattle', in *A Fantasy Of Man: Complete Works: 1901-1922 (*Sydney: Lansdowne, 1984) p. 464.
[3] W. Ebsworth, *Archbishop Mannix*, pp. 193-95; N. Brennan, *Dr Mannix*, p. 157.
[4] *Publicist*, 1 July 1939, 'What's Wrong with "The Publicist"?' p. 14.
[5] A figure of up to £2,000 per annum has been cited, which Miles wrote off as a tax deduction. Muirden, *Puzzled Patriots,* p. 30; Hasluck, *The Government and the People,* Vol. II, p. 719.
[6] Stephensen was also chairman of the Cultural Defence Committee of the FAW. Clyne Inquiry transcripts, pp. 526-27.
[7] Muirden, *Puzzled Patriots*, pp. 5-6; *Publicist,* 1 February 1942, 'The Death of "John Benauster"', pp. 2-4.
[8] *Australian Dictionary of Biography (ADB)*, Vol. 10, pp. 501-02; A8911: 17: The Link.

[9] Helen 1898, Constance 1899, John Balfour 1901, Beatrice 1902, Arthur 1905 and Louise 1907. In the *ADB* (Vol. 10, pp. 499-500, 501-02) the entry for W. J. Miles says he had six children; the entry for Beatrice Miles says he had five.
[10] Xavier Herbert, *Poor Fellow My Country*, Chapter 20, esp. parts 2 and 3 (pp.1027-1087). Stephensen appears as 'the Bloke', Hooper as 'the Banker', and Masey as 'the young Economist'. 'The Colt' is not clearly identifiable.
[11] Kate Grenville, *Lilian's Story*, p. 156. Miles had no sister.
[12] C421: 30: Valentine Crowley and Australia First Movement Group. (Henceforth: Valentine Crowley and AFM).
[13] Grenville, *Lilian's Story*. There is no public evidence that Miles's other daughters were mentally unstable, and Beatrice might have been as much to blame as her father for their quarrels.
[14] NSW Pioneer Index, Federation Series, 1889-1918; *Sydney Morning Herald*, 12 August 1907, funeral notice. *ADB*, Vol. 10, p. 501, gives the date of his death as 1908.
[15] Muirden, *Puzzled Patriots*, pp. 5-6; *ADB*, Vol. 10, p. 502.
[16] Muirden, *Puzzled Patriots*, pp. 7-10. Muirden, p. 143, dates the Rationalist Press Association from the 1890s.
[17] Copies of these letters are in C420: NN: Exhibit 75; Sydney / Sidney Benjamin Hooper. (Miles to Hooper, 16 October 1914, 12 May 1915, 12 December 1916)
[18] C421: 27: The Yabba / Yabber Club—reports by 222. (Report by Agent 222 for 25 July 1940) (Henceforth: The Yabba Club)
[19] B741: V/262: IWW [Industrial Workers of the World]—Victoria—Meetings.
[20] Clyne Inquiry transcripts, pp. 15, 1628.
[21] Muirden, *Puzzled Patriots*, pp. 8-9; *ADB*, Vol. 10, pp. 501-02, Vol. 11, pp. 457-59. As John Benauster, Miles wrote about this peculiar plan in the *Publicist*, April 1937, pp. 1-2, 5-6.
[22] *Publicist*, 1 April 1941, Louis M. Veron, p. 15; October 1936, Alcedo Gigas, p. 16.
[23] C421: 55: Dossiers of Hooper, Kirtley, Tinker-Giles, Stephenson, and Miles, Australia First Movement. (Henceforth: Dossiers, Australia First Movement); Lockyer Papers, UQFL 247/B/Folder 1.
[24] C420: NN: Sydney / Sidney Benjamin Hooper.
[25] A8911: 129: Australia First Movement, 1918-1942.
[26] C421: 55: Dossiers, Australia First Movement.
[27] The main source for information on Hooper is C420: NN: Sydney / Sidney Benjamin Hooper. Most is duplicated in C421: 30: Valentine Crowley and AFM.
[28] NSW Pioneer Index, Federation Series, 1889-1918. Her father was Inigo Fiorelli. (Between the Wars Series, 1919-1945: death of I. M. Hooper.)
[29] C420: NN: Hooper. Joosten went to New Zealand at the age of fourteen and was Honorary Consul there. Interned during World War I, he returned to Germany about 1921.Clyne Inquiry transcripts, p. 1318, describe him as a highly cultured gentleman with a good scientific mind, and note that he had been a British subject.
[30] Letter, 23 June 1942, to Appeals Tribunal. Mentioned at the Clyne Inquiry, transcript page 1325.
[31] C420: NN: Hooper.
[32] Clyne Inquiry transcripts, p. 1340, p. 14-15. Roberts, born 1857, had spent several years in Australia, ca 1876-79. He died in June 1942. For Arnold Leese and the

Imperial League of Fascists, see Chapter 3.
[33] Clyne Inquiry, pp. 1607-08; C421: 30: Valentine Crowley and AFM.
[34] Clyne Inquiry, pp. 1608, 1611.
[35] Clyne Inquiry, p. 1641; C421: 30: Valentine Crowley and AFM.
[36]A8911: 130: Australia First Movement - (ISGS Report, January 1941); C421: 30: Valentine Crowley and AFM; Victorian Births, Deaths and Marriages: Pioneer Index: 1837-1888.
[37] Clyne Inquiry transcripts, p. 1611; C421: 30: Valentine Crowley and AFM.
[38] Clyne transcripts, p. 791; C421: 30: Valentine Crowley and AFM.
[39] *Publicist*, July 1936, 'Home Coming', p. 16.
[40] A373: 4121: "Australia First" Internee: Gordon Thomas Rice; C421: 50: Summary of cases of various members of the AFM: Masey, Matthews, Tinker-Giles, Salier, P. R. Stephensen, E. D. Stephensen, Watts]. (Henceforth: Summary of cases: AFM.)
[41] Miles had a remote connection with Stephensen as early as 10 September 1918, when he wrote to the *Daily Standard* in Brisbane concerning the victimisation of Gordon Childe. (A8911: 130: Australia First Movement) Stephensen's grandfather, Henri Tardent, was connected with this paper.
[42] Muirden, *Puzzled Patriots*, p. 12, wrote of Miles: 'He was ready to finance anything that attacked either Jesus Christ or the British Empire.'
[43] For the genealogy of P. R. Stephensen, see Appendix III.
[44] UQA S154: Senior Public Examination Results Registers, 1910-1972, 1918. For Stephensen's childhood and early student life, see Craig Munro's *Wild Man of Letters*, early chapters.
[45] UQA S154: Senior Public Examination Results Registers, 1910-1972, 1918. Munro, *Wild Man of Letters*, p. 8, wrote that Stephensen 'regularly failed mathematics'.
[46] Eric Stephensen wrote to Fotheringham that Muirden was wrong in claiming (p. 15) that 'Inky' was a family name, but when asked at the Clyne Inquiry whether 'Inky' was a family name for P. R. Stephensen, Eric had answered: 'Yes.' (Clyne Inquiry transcripts, p. 811).
[47] UQA S130: Subject files, Awards—Rhodes Scholarship—Stephensen, P. R., 1924.
[48] *The University of Queensland. 1910-1922* (Brisbane: Senate of the University, 1923). J. L. Michie: *An Account of the University of Queensland during its First Twenty-five Years.* Appendix D: Biographical Register of Students.
[49] The main form of training for teachers in state schools at that time was the monitor system, with departmental examinations.
[50] *Australian Encyclopaedia*, Sixth Edition, Vol. 6, pp. 2377-78.
[51] Munro, *Wild Man of Letters*, p. 24.
[52] Stephensen Papers: Mitchell Library, MSS1284: Box 1.
[53] According to Richard Hall, *The Secret State*, p. 31, the British wrote to the Australian Prime Minister in 1925 to obtain information on Stephensen's background, which was supplied by the Investigation Branch.
[54] Stephensen Papers: ML MSS1284: Box 1: (Letter, 15 April 1925)
[55] Lockyer Papers, UQFL247/D/Personal. Winifred's lie about her age deprived Stephensen of the child he wanted, for her two pregnancies ended in miscarriages. See Munro, *Wild Man of Letters*, pp. 96, 105.
[56] Stephensen's work as a publisher is covered comprehensively in Munro's *Wild*

Man of Letters, Chapters 4 to 7.
[57] Munro, *Wild Man of Letters*, p. 66. Another person influenced by Nietzsche's anti-Semitism was the artist Norman Lindsay, whom Stephensen met in January 1932. Munro, *Wild Man of Letters*, pp. 54, 106.
[58] Jack Lindsay, who had worked on the UQ magazine with Stephensen, had an outstanding academic record with First Class Honours in Classics.
[59] Fotheringham Papers, UQFL46/6: Box 1 ('Notes about P. R. Stephensen, 1918-1932', by Robert Hall, undated) Hall gives the date as 1927 or 1928. For a brief résumé of the *Protocols of Zion*, and the analysis given by *The Times*, see Appendix IV.
[60] Registration of the name Mandrake as a trademark, in the joint names of Stephensen and Goldston, is in the Fotheringham Papers, UQFL46/3.
[61] In *Foundations of Culture in Australia*, p. 55, Stephensen cited the eroticism of D. H. Lawrence in *Lady Chatterley's Lover* as an example of decadence, 'not in a simple moral sense, but of a culture in decline'.
[62] Munro, *Wild Man of Letters*, pp. 111-15. Lindsay advanced Stephensen the money for the fares.
[63] Hall, *Secret State*, p. 32. This information would probably have gone to Lieutenant-Colonel H. E. Jones of the CIB.
[64] Winifred knew Miles Franklin in America in World War I. Lockyer Papers, UQFL47/B/Envelope 9.
[65] *Foundations of Culture*, p. 66. It is strange to read Stephensen condemning crudity in literature.
[66] This case, which had little to do with Australia-First, is covered exhaustively in the double issue of the *Publicist*, November-December 1936, pp. 15-24.
[67] According to A8911: 136: Australia First Movement, WA, Vol. 1, p. 8, Mudie had gone to England and remained there two years, so he had apparently only recently returned. In a letter to Dr F. W. Robinson, University of Queensland, Stephensen promised to repay within twelve months 24 shillings for every pound invested. P. R. Stephensen Papers, UQFL55/8/4.
[68] Mudie Papers, PRG 27/1/1930-39, Mortlock Library.
[69] Munro, *Wild Man of Letters*, p. 160. A proof copy of the planned second edition of the *Australian Mercury* is in the Lockyer Papers in the Fryer Library, UQFL247, Box 1.
[70] For dealings between Stephensen and Herbert in connection with *Capricornia*, see Munro, *Wild Man of Letters*, Chapter 9: 'Xavier Herbert, P. R. Stephensen & Co.', and Frances de Groen, *Xavier Herbert*, Chapter 9: 'Convergence of the Twain'.
[71] Sadie Herbert Collection, UQFL 83, Box 27 (Herbert to Clem Christesen, 21 December 1961).
[72] Munro, *Wild Man of Letters*, p. 51.
[73] Xavier Herbert Papers: NLA MS758: Box 1. Series 4. Several anti-feminist articles appeared in the *Publicist* during 1939. ' "Feminism" as a Symptom of Decadence', by Alcedo Gigas, 1 March 1939, p. 13; 'Our Step-Sisters—the Feminists', by Anna Brabant (Dora Watts), 1 May 1939, pp. 4-6; 'Dear Female!', by Anna Brabant, 1 August 1939, pp. 12-13.
[74] Munro, *Wild Man of Letters* p. 176.
[75] Munro, *Wild Man of Letters*, pp. 162-64; Chapter 10, note 59. Stephensen Papers, ML MSS Boxes Y2117 and Y2122 (old system).

[76] Munro, *Wild Man of Letters*, p. 16.
[77] Stephensen, *Foundations of Culture in Australia*, p. 132.
[78] Muirden, *Puzzled Patriots*, p. 12; Munro, *Wild Man of Letters*, p. 164.
[79] Muirden, *Puzzled Patriots*, p. 12. The only known copy of the *Secularist* (No. 12, June 1936) is in the Stephensen Papers, UQFL55/24/16. It announced the forthcoming launch of the *Publicist*, and used the words 'Australia First' above the title.
[80] Although Miles was vehemently anti-communist, this was printed by the communist-owned Forward Press, probably for financial reasons.
[81] A8911: 130: Australia First Movement (Report, 6 November 1941) J.B. was John Benauster, a pseudonym used by Miles.
[82] A8911: 130: Australia First Movement. The date of the advertisement is given as 4 February 1936, but it has not been located.
[83] C421: 50: Summary of cases: Australia First Movement.
[84] Clyne Inquiry transcripts, pp. 1258-9.
[85] A373: 4123: Edward Masey; C421: 50: Summary of cases: Australia First Movement. Adela Walsh participated in some Summer Schools run by the AIPS, and would have been acquainted with Salier, Masey and V. Crowley. Coleman, *Adela Pankhurst*, pp. 123, 135 and 140, mentions her attendance at these Summer Schools in 1934 and 1938.
[86] Clyne Inquiry transcripts, pp. 1258-9. Miles and the Security Service knew that Masey had been convicted in the North Sydney Police Court on 1 February 1935, in that he did 'expose his person'; a prison sentence was suspended on condition that he submitted himself to medical treatment. A467: BUNDLE 97/SF43/2: Australia First Movement. Part 2. Probably few members of the group knew this.
[87] Stephensen, *Foundations of Culture in Australia*, pp. 129, 191.
[88] Muirden, *Puzzled Patriots*, p. 178, wrote that, according to Jack Lindsay, Stephensen was 'an ardent admirer of Trotsky'.
[89] Muirden, *Puzzled Patriots*, p. 28.
[90] Munro, *Wild Man of Letters*, p. 164. Munro cites a letter from Stephensen to Jack Lindsay, 1962, in which he said that it broke his heart when Old Bolsheviks such as Bukharin and Zinoviev were executed after 'show trials'. Zinoviev was shot in August 1936, Bukharin in March 1938. Stephensen made marginal notes against an article by Nicolas Bukharin. 'The Theory of Permanent Revolution' in *The Communist Review*, February 1935. (Stephensen Papers, UQFL55/24/11)
[91] Fotheringham Papers, UQFLS 46, Box 1. (E. D. Stephensen to Fotheringham, 4 January 1970).
[92] C420: NN: Hooper. Clarence Crowley is a possibility.

Chapter 2

[1] Letter, J. W. V. Lockyer, 5 November 1998. Miles's sons, John and Arthur, were also there sometimes. The *Labor Daily*, 30 July 1936, reported that they 'bundled [Beatrice] out of the office' after a scuffle with her father.
[2] Clyne transcripts, pp. 524-25.
[3] *Publicist*, 1 June 1939, p. 1. There were apparently no offers to advertise.

[4] Fotheringham Papers, UQFL46, Box 1 (Matthews to Muirden, 11 April 1966).
[5] Fotheringham Papers, UQFL46, Box 1 (E. D. Stephensen to Fotheringham, 4 January 1970).
[6] *Publicist*, July 1936, 'John Benauster', 'This "Publicist"', p. 1.
[7] Miles used the name 'John Benauster' in the *Secularist* also. Apparently, Stephensen wrote some of the articles attributed to 'John Benauster'. C421: 27: The Yabba Club. (Report by Agent 222, 11 February 1941)
[8] *Publicist*, July 1936, 'Benauster', 'This "Publicist"', p. 1.
[9] This was an adaptation of 'King Billy'. *Publicist*, July 1936, pp. 9-12; p. 16 and pp. 14-15.
[10] *Publicist*, July 1936, Bunyip Critic, p. 4.
[11] P. R. Stephensen, *Foundations of Culture in Australia*, p. 131.
[12] *Publicist*, July 1936, Bunyip Critic, p. 6. The first issue contained a learned article by Masey and an inoffensive column by Salier.
[13] *Publicist*, July 1936, Bunyip Critic, p. 7.
[14] *Publicist*, 1 November 1937, p. 5; 1 July 1938, p. 16; 1 October 1938, pp. 15-16; Bruce Muirden, *Puzzled Patriots*, pp.47-48; Munro, *Wild Man of Letters*, pp. 181, 185.
[15] Stephensen Papers, ML MSS1284, Box Y2135, Typescript pp. 115-16; quoted in Munro, p. 123. This has been re-numbered MSS1284, Box 13.
[16] Stephensen, *Foundations of Culture in Australia*, p. 89.
[17] *Publicist*, August 1936, Bunyip Critic, p. 5.
[18] *Publicist*, August 1936, p. 6. This platform contained fourteen points. Point 8 read: 'To exterminate rabbits, foxes, starlings and other European pests here, including all Europe-minded idealists.'
[19] *Publicist*, August 1936, p. 4. This was an adaptation of a wartime song that said that 'England, Home and Beauty' had no cause to fear, for 'Australia will be there'.
[20] Stephensen, *Foundations of Culture in Australia*, p. 27.
[21] *Publicist*, November-December 1936, pp. 15-24.
[22] *Publicist*, November-December 1936, 'Benauster', 'Australia's Oceans and Her Foreign Policy', p. 1.
[23] Clyne transcripts, pp. 524, 539.
[24] Muirden, *Puzzled Patriots*, p. 40; Clyne transcripts, p. 359.
[25] *Publicist*, 1 January 1937, Bunyip Critic, p. 4.
[26] The Japanese Club in Darwin took two copies through Yasukichi Murakami: Stephensen Papers, ML MSS1284, Box 45; *Publicist* Petty Cash book, 1941.
[27] Bruce Muirden, *Puzzled Patriots*, p. 29.
[28] Z. A. B. Zeman, *Nazi Propaganda*, p. 73.
[29] When the novel was becoming a landmark in Australian literature, Angus & Robertson took it over.
[30] *Publicist*, 1 November 1938, Bunyip Critic, 'Australian Action. A Twelve Point Policy', pp. 7-9. These Twelve Points were also printed as a separate pamphlet. They are set out in full in the Appendix.
[31] *Publicist*, 1 December 1938, 'Australian Action. Towards the formation of an Australia-First Party', pp. 2-7.
[32] Miles's friend Hardy Wilson lived in Kew, and E. K. Crampton of Burekup had been mentioned in the *Publicist*, 1 November 1937, p. 1, and 1 December 1937, p. 18.

[33] Clyne transcripts, p. 220.
[34] Clyne transcripts, p. 532.
[35] *Publicist*, 1 July 1938, H. Matthews, 'My Army, O, my Army!', p. 9.
[36] *Publicist*, 1 October 1938, letter from Dora Watts, p. 16.
[37] *Publicist*, 1 January 1939, p. 14; 'Australian Action: Towards a New Party', *Publicist*, 1 February 1939, pp. 13-14; 1 March 1939: pp. 14-15. Letters from the public, comments by Stephensen.
[38] C421: 50: Summary of cases: Australia First Movement.
[39] Clyne transcripts, p. 1355.
[40] Martin Watts married Dora Levido in 1930; she was born in Adelaide on 23 August 1898, the Levido family having settled in South Australia by 1862. It is not known why she chose 'Brabant' as a pen name.
[41] A8911: 17: "The Link" Organisation to promote Anglo-German Friendship - Mrs Melanie O'Loughlin. (Hooper to Joosten, 6 March 1939).
[42] *Publicist*, 1 June 1939, M. F. Watts, 'Concentration Camps and Some Brutalities', pp. 15-16.
[43] *Publicist*, 1 May 1939, Merry Mathew, 'Singapore—Why?', pp. 13-14; 1 September 1939, Merry Mathew, 'Australia and the Invasion Myth', p. 3.
[44] *Publicist*, 1 June 1939, p. 16.
[45] *Publicist*, November-December 1936, 'Benauster', 'Australia's Oceans and Her Foreign Policy', p. 1-7.
[46] The atrocities committed by the Boxers might well have given Miles a permanent anti-Chinese bias. For Cookes see Chapter 3.
[47] *Publicist*, 1 February 1939, 'Rex Williams', 'Port Kembla and Japan', p. 16.
[48] C421: 27: The Yabba/Yabber Club - reports by 222.
[49] C443: J2: Japanese Consulate Material. The Security Service file on 'Douglas Henry Graves and wife', C77495, identified from the card index in A368, has allegedly been destroyed.
[50] *Publicist*, 1 January 1937, Masey, 'Australian Trade Policy', pp. 8-11.
[51] *Publicist*, 1 March 1937, Salier, 'Pacific Problems', pp.12-16. Quote is from p. 15.
[52] *Publicist*, 1 May 1937, J. White (Stephensen), p. 17.
[53] Clyne transcripts, p. 690. As Stephensen was giving evidence under oath, this was perjury.
[54] C421: 50: Summary of cases: Australia First Movement. In the same letter he had written concerning Hitler: 'What grievance can you or any Australian, legitimately have against him? He has been a God send to his own country.' (Hooper to unknown 'C. J.', 15 April 1937).
[55] *Publicist*, 1 August 1937, 'L. M. Veron', 'Winston Churchill and K. K. Kawakumi', pp. 11-12. In February 1831, *Lady Rowena*, a whaler from Sydney, had destroyed the fishing village of Hamanaka when refused provisions and water. (H. Frei, *Japan's Southward Advance*, p. 26) In 1863, British warships bombarded Kagoshima in reprisal for the murder of an Englishman.
[56] *Publicist*, 1 September 1937, 'L. M. Veron', 'China versus Japan', p. 13.
[57] *Publicist*, 1 October 1937, 'L. M. Veron', 'China versus Japan', p. 5.
[58]*Publicist*, 1 October 1937, 'Rex Williams', 'O, What a Happy Land', p. 16.
[59] *Publicist*, 1 November 1937, Bunyip Critic, pp. 6-7.
[60] A8911: 129: Australia First Movement, 1918-1942. This unattributed report, dated

November 1941, is inaccurate in detail.
[61] *Publicist*, 1 December 1937, 'L. M. Veron', 'The World at Peace', p. 15.
[62] *Publicist*, 1 April 1938, 'L. M. Veron', 'Japan, Still Going Strong', p. 8.
[63] The *Publicist* petty cash book for 1941 mentions fares to the Japanese Consulate several times. P. R. Stephensen papers: ML MSS1284, Box 45.
[64] A373: 10298: [Examination of Japanese Material ex Thursday Island].
[65] *Publicist*, 1 June 1938, Letter by Kijiro Miyake, p. 2.
[66] *Publicist*, 1 June 1938, The Editor, 'Yampi Unsound', p. 12.
[67] *Publicist*, 1 March 1939, Bunyip Critic, pp. 5-8. This article sat ill with the subtitle of the Bunyip section: 'Experiments in Australianity'.
[68] Clyne transcripts, p. 550; Mudie papers, PRG 27/10/5.
[69] C447 PART 1: 7: Extracted Documents and Miscellaneous Papers from Japanese Consular Files.
[70] Quoted in Munro, *Wild Man of Letters*, p. 197.
[71] A8911: 130: Australia First Movement (Report, 6 November 1941).
[72] *Publicist*, 1 May 1939, Bunyip Critic, 'Japan's Plans', pp. 10, 12. 'Information Bureau' was a euphemism for a department that disseminated propaganda and collated espionage material.
[73] *Publicist*, 1 May 1937, 'Benauster', 'The Coronation', p. 1.
[74] *Publicist*, 1 August 1937, 'Benauster', 'Germany's Colonial Problem', pp. 1-3.
[75] *Publicist*, 1 September 1937, 'Alcedo Gigas', 'The Movement against War and Fascism', p. 15. Fox was later a member of the Editorial Board of *Progress*, the official organ of the N.S.W. State Labor Party. (Introduction to 1943 edition of *Australia and the Jews*) For Fox, see Chapter 6.
[76] *Publicist*, 1 August 1937, p. 13. From 1 January 1938, members of the NSDAP and government officials were forbidden to belong to the Rotary Club, on the grounds that, in other countries, it had members who were Jews or Freemasons.
[77] For one particularly offensive poem by G. P., 'The Jew-Bossed British', with its reference to 'the race of Ikey-Mo', see the *Publicist*, 1 October 1938, p. 10.
[78] D1901: M81: MILLS, Alexander Rudd. For Mills and the Odinist Society, see Chapter 3.
[79] *Publicist*, 1 March 1938, pp. 12-14; 1 April 1938, p. 14; 1 May 1938, pp. 9-10.
[80] *Publicist*, 1 May 1938, Bunyip Critic, p. 6.
[81] Stephen Henry Roberts, *The House the Hitler Built* (London: Methuen, 1937), pp. 12-13. Roberts gives the impression that he spent about a year in Germany; after examining Roberts' documents, Bonnell concludes that he spent only a few weeks there in several visits. Andrew Bonnell, 'Stephen Roberts' "The House that Hitler Built" as a Source on Nazi Germany', pp. 207-226.
[82] Dr C. Munro, interview, 15 October 1998.
[83] Muirden, *Puzzled Patriots*, p. 188.
[84] Example: At a public meeting on 3 December 1941, Stephensen said: 'I am for National Socialism against International Communism.' On 17 December, he said that H. Alexander, Secretary of the Actors' Union, was a liar if he said Stephensen was a Nazi. A case can be made to distinguish between 'National Socialism' and 'Nazism', but it was a difficult one to argue at that time. (C421: 6: [Miscellaneous papers re the Australia First Movement, includes copies of letters to and from P.R.

Stephensen])
[85] *Publicist*, 1 October 1938, 'Benauster', 'Germany Speaks', pp. 1-2.
[86] *Publicist*, 1 March 1938, 'L. M. Veron', 'British American Co-Operation for World War', p. 2.
[87] *Publicist*, 1 October 1937, 'Benauster', 'A National Danger—Pacifists as Decadent', pp. 1-3.
[88] *Publicist*, 1 June 1938, pp. 13-16.
[89] Stephensen, *Foundations of Culture in Australia*, p. 132.
[90] Clyne transcripts, p. 1475.
[91] The speech was continued in the *Publicist* issues of 1 July 1938, pp. 11-14; 1 August, pp. 12-15; and 1 September, pp. 12-14.
[92] *Publicist*, 1 May 1939, 'Hitler's Speech, 30th January 1939', p. 1. The speech appeared in May, pp. 2-3; June, pp. 11-15; July, pp. 15-16; August, pp. 14-16; September, pp. 14-17.
[93] *Publicist*, 1 July 1939, Bunyip Critic, p. 10.
[94] A373: 3921: Walter David Cookes; D1915: SA20496: "The Link".
[95] A translation of a speech Hitler made on 28 April 1939 was endorsed: 'With Mr Schmelitschek's compliments', so Miles had other sources for such material. Clyne transcripts, p. 1354.
[96] Clyne transcripts, p. 627.
[97] A6126: 48: HARDT, Herbert Engelbert; C419: NN: General Summary—Australia First. The latter copy contains handwritten annotations. Nellie Bell worked for G. Hardt & Co. from 16 August 1937 to 1 February 1938, then for Skerst in his dual role as editor of *Die Brücke* and secretary of the German Chamber of Commerce. In 1940-41, she was employed by Military Intelligence as a translator.
[98] Clyne transcripts, p. 627. Ernst Wilhelm Bohle was head of the *Auslands-Organisation* of the Nazi Party.
[99] Clyne transcripts, pp. 535, 540, 542. This would have been in connection with some writing he was doing for Trans-Continental Airways; see Munro, *Wild Man of Letters*, pp. 160-61.
[100] Munro, *Wild Man of Letters*, p. 161.
[101] ASKI was the acronym for *Ausländer-Sonderkonto für Inlandszahlungen*: Special Account for Foreigners for Internal Payments. See Guenter Reimann, *The Vampire Economy: Doing business under Fascism* for a hostile analysis of the system.
[102] Clyne transcripts, p. 543.
[103] There is disagreement as to whether it was sold, or whether back numbers were given away. The *Publicist* advertisement appeared in *Die Brücke* for the first time on 13 November 1937, page 12.
[104] Clyne transcripts, pp. 625-33.
[105] A8911: 130: Australia First Movement. Emphasis is in the original. J. E. (Hans) Schwarz van Berk, who was in Sydney October-November 1938, was under the direct orders of Propaganda Minister Dr Josef Goebbels. Melanie O'Loughlin said he had visited Western Australia, and would meet AFM members in Sydney. (C421: 8: Miscellaneous papers on AFM; Thomas statement of 22 May 1944, p. 1)
[106] *Publicist*, 1 September 1939, M. F. Watts, 'Collapse is Imminent! A Premonition', pp. 4-9; 'L. M. Veron', 'Fascism', p. 18.

[107] *Publicist*, 1 September 1939, 'Alcedo Gigas', 'The Link', p. 19. Laurie's book, *A Case for Germany*, had been published in Berlin in May 1939.
[108] A8911: 130: Australia First Movement.
[109] C419: NN: General Summary—Australia First. 'Occasionally' might have been more apt than 'frequently'.
[110] A8911: 17: The Link.
[111] C421: 30: Valentine Crowley and AFM. The *Fichte-Bund*, founded in 1914 to propagate German views abroad, was taken over by the Nazis. Z. A. B. Zeman, *Nazi Propaganda*, p. 81. Miles was writing to the *Fichte-Bund* by February 1937. (Clyne transcripts, p. 118a)
[112] Clyne transcripts, p. 757.
[113] Clyne transcripts, p. 1341.
[114] *Publicist*, 1 June 1939, Bunyip Critic, 'War! What for?', pp. 6-10.
[115] Muirden, *Puzzled Patriots*, p. 4, p. 36.
[116] *Publicist*, 1 March 1938, pp. 12-14. Comment by 'Alcedo Gigas' on pp. 258-267 of *The House that Hitler built*.
[117] *Publicist*, 1 August 1938, 'L. M. Veron', 'Australia and the Jews', p. 16.
[118] *Publicist*, 1 September 1938, The Editor, 'Jewish Propaganda in Australia', p. 11. Of course, Arabs are also Semitic, not Gentiles.
[119] *Publicist*, 1 November 1938, Anna Brabant, 'Chamberlain and Civilisation', p. 16. Chamberlain, born 9 September 1855 in Hampshire, died 9 January 1927, Bayreuth. In 1907 he married Richard Wagner's only daughter, Eva, and in 1916 became a German citizen. It is claimed that his book *Rasse und Persönlichkeit*, 1925, influenced Hitler.
[120] *Publicist*, 1 May 1939, Bunyip Critic, p. 9.
[121] *Publicist*, 1 December 1937, 'Rex Williams', 'The Tactics of the Communist Party', pp. 12-13; January 1938, 'Benauster', 'Now or Never. Advance Australia!', p. 1.
[122] A981: NAZ 1 PART 2: Nazism. Nazi Activities. It deserved to be condemned, as it often ran stories that its staff knew were exaggerated or untrue.
[123] *Publicist*, 1 January 1939, Bunyip Critic, pp. 4-8.
[124] *Publicist*, 1 January 1939, Bunyip Critic, pp. 4-8..
[125] *Publicist*, 1 February 1939, 'Benauster', 'The "Free Speech" Humbug and 2KY', pp. 1-3.
[126] *Workers'* Weekly, 7 April 1939, p. 1.
[127] *Publicist*, 1 May 1939, p. 8.
[128] For the result of the case see Chapter 6.
[129] *Publicist*, 1 February 1939, M. F. Watts, 'As I see the Jews, without Rancour, without Hysteria', p. 3; 'Alcedo Gigas', 'The Fellowship of Australian Writers', pp. 11-12.
[130] *Publicist*, 1 March 1939, Letter from 'Cooee', p. 16.
[131] Stephensen Papers, ML MSS1284, Box 44, contains the scripts of some of the talks on 2SM.
[132] SP1714/1: N39593: Nazi Party membership.
[133] Paul Hasluck, *The Government and the People*, Vol. II (Canberra, AWM, 1970), Appendix 5, pp. 719-20
[134] Munro, *Wild Man of Letters*, p. 195. p. 195. (Robert Hall to Henry Burton, Burton to Stephensen, 25 March 1939: ML MSS Box K164720).

[135] Muirden, *Puzzled Patriots*, pp. 32-33.
[136] Clyne transcripts, pp. 1317, 1331-32.
[137] Xavier Herbert, *Poor Fellow my Country*, p. 1053.
[138] *Publicist*, 1 March 1939, Bunyip Critic, p. 7.

Chapter 3

[1] Clyne transcripts, p. 443.
[2] Clyne transcripts, pp. 397a, 400.
[3] Clyne transcripts, p. 1313A.
[4] Clyne transcripts, p. 1342. *Publicist*, 1 January 1940, Alexander Rud Mills, 'Religion and Politics', p. 8-9.
[5] C421: 11: [A. R. Mills—transcript of shorthand notes of proceedings before advisory committee (Appeal, 20 November 1942) [A. R. Mills Appeal]; CPD, Vol. 178: Menzies, 30 & 31 March 1944, p. 2455.
[6] Clyne transcripts, p. 357.
[7] C421: 11. A. R. Mills Appeal; D1901: M81: MILLS, Alexander Rudd (Annexure 10); Clyne transcripts, pp. 123, 437.
[8] In July 1936, Leese published allegations of Jewish ritual murder of Christians to get fresh blood for Passover bread; on 21 September that year he was sentenced to six months' imprisonment for 'conspiring to create a public mischief'. [Richard Griffiths, *Fellow Travellers of the Right*, p. 100].
[9] D1915: SA19070: British Union of Fascists. This programme bore a signature given in the Clyne transcript as 'Miles', but it should have been 'Mills'.
[10] Griffiths, *Fellow Travellers of the Right*, pp. 96, 98, 99, 279. Mills referred to him erroneously as *James* Joyce. (P. R. Stephensen Papers, UQFL55/20/22: Mills to Stephensen, 28 June 1954) Known later as Lord Haw-Haw, Joyce was hanged for treason in 1946.
[11] D1915: SA19070: British Union of Fascists.
[12] P. R. Stephensen Papers, UQFL55/20/22 (Mills to Stephensen: 28 June 1954).
[13] Clyne transcripts, pp. 367, 429-430.
[14] E. C. Helmreich, *German Churches under Hitler*, p. 79. At the Clyne Inquiry, p. 360, Mills explained: 'Odin means the part of God that man can understand.'
[15] Clyne transcripts, pp. 367, 882. Mills may well have become familiar with Odinism through Dr G. Wagner's book, *Asgard and the Gods*, first published 1880, reprinted as late as 1917. This was mentioned in an article in the *Courier-Mail*, 23 January 1999, *Weekend*, p. 7. Mills might have been attracted to *Nordic* mythology because his parents came from Norfolk, which had been part of the Danelaw region.
[16] Helmreich, *German Churches under Hitler*, p. 408.
[17] Helmreich, *German Churches under Hitler*, pp. 408-09.
[18] C421: 11: A. R. Mills - Appeal.
[19] Clyne transcripts, pp. 116, 117a, 118a.
[20] P. R. Stephensen Papers, UQFL55/20/22 (Mills to Stephensen, 28 June 1954) Mills is inconsistent in his spelling of Anglecyn / Anglekin.
[21] C421: 11: A. R. Mills—Appeal; Clyne transcripts, p. 127.
[22] See Griffiths, *Fellow Travellers of the Right*, pp. 102, 317–18, 321-22, 324.

[23] C421: 11: A. R. Mills - Appeal.
[24] Griffiths: *Fellow Travellers of the Right*, pp. 61, 96. Arthur Kitson of The Britons introduced Leese to anti-Semitism and the *Protocols*.
[25] Clyne transcripts, p. 127; D1901: M81: MILLS, Alexander Rudd: —Internment (Annexure 5)
[26] D1915: SA19070: British Union of Fascists.
[27] P. R. Stephensen Papers, UQFL55/20/22, (Mills to Stephensen, 28 June 1954).
[28] D1901: M81: MILLS, Alexander Rudd - Internment.
[29] Copies of the *National Socialist* are conserved in the Mitchell Library.
[30] D1901: M81: MILLS, Alexander Rudd. Annexure 5 says: 'Mr. Mills refused to disclose the source of his financial backing. He just smiled.' Annexure 2 alleges he approached a Presbyterian minister to leave his Ministry and take up the work Mills was doing, 'as there was a lot more money in it'.
[31] A8911: 130: Australia First Movement.
[32] Reports were compiled principally by W. H. Barnwell, D. A. Alexander and J. W. Swasbrick in Sydney, G. R. Richards and H. D. Moseley in Perth, S. F. Whittington and E. Hattam in Melbourne and R. F. B. Wake in Brisbane.
[33] Clyne transcripts, p. 438. A relationship between Eric Campbell and Mrs H. Campbell has not been traced. Both Campbell and Mills were associated with The Britons.
[34] Clyne transcripts, p. 392. He also did cleaning work in return for accommodation. P. R. Stephensen Papers, UQFL55/20/22, (Mills to Stephensen, 28 June 1954).
[35] A367: C18812: Frerck Johannes.
[36] C443: G1 PART 1: [Copy of record seized from German Consulates during WWI and WWII].
[37] *Die Brücke*, 5 January 1935, p. 2. This book was published by The Britons Publishing Co.
[38] C443: G2: German Consulate Records. Campbell stood for NSW parliament for Centre Movement in the Lane Cove electorate at the election on 11 May 1935.
[39] The preface is dated July 1936, Sydney.
[40] In the Clyne transcripts, 'Anglecyn' was usually given as 'Anglican', which made nonsense of key parts of Mills's evidence.
[41] The golden sun-wheel (*Sonnenrad*) on a blue ground was the symbol of the *Deutsche Glaubensbewegung*, a pagan movement sponsored by Baldur von Schirach and Dr Ley. Stephen Henry Roberts, *The House that Hitler Built*, p. 275.
[42] This seems to be similar but not identical to the *First Guide Book to the Anglecyn Church of Odin*.
[43] Clyne transcripts, pp. 454, 469.
[44] C443: J48: Alexander Rudd Mills (Mills to Japanese Consulate-General, 7 June 1939).
[45] C421: 11: A. R. Mills—Appeal. See Appendix VI for a critique of Mills's Odinism.
[46] Clyne transcripts, p. 360.
[47] A. R. Mills, *The Odinist Religion overcoming Jewish Christianity*, pp. 245-246.
[48] C421: 11: A. R. Mills - Appeal.
[49] D1901: M81: MILLS, Alexander Rudd: —Internment (Annexure 6).
[50] Australian-born persons could become Party members if they had acquired German nationality.
[51] C421: 11: A. R. Mills - Appeal.

[52] D1901: M81: MILLS, Alexander Rudd (Annexures 1 and 9) Mills claimed he had 'hundreds' of followers throughout Australia. (*Smith's Weekly*, 12 December 1936).
[53] Clyne transcripts, p. 448.
[54] D1901: M81: MILLS, Alexander Rudd (Annexure 13). The annexure attributes this paper incorrectly to Sir Oswald Mosley.
[55] Griffiths: *Fellow Travellers of the Right*, p. 101.
[56] Clyne transcripts, p. 359.
[57] Heiler's Party number was 3,286,028: A8911: 18: Nazi Activities - WA.
[58] Clyne transcripts, p. 495. Heiler returned to Germany in August 1937.
[59] C421: 8: Miscellaneous papers on AFM. (Statement, Thomas to Richards, 22 May, p. 5) For Bullock and Thomas, see Chapter 8.
[60] The final chapter of *The Odinist Religion Overcoming Jewish Christianity* is identified as points from a lecture given in Perth. Some reports attribute this Odinism to Billy Miles, but Mills is meant.
[61] D1901: M81: MILLS, Alexander Rudd (Annexure 8); Report of 5 July 1940.
[62] D1915: SA19070: British Union of Fascists. (Unattributed report dated 1 June 1940) At the Clyne Inquiry, p. 445, Mills claimed that he had not known of Mrs O'Loughlin's existence.
[63] *Publicist*, 1 January 1940, 'Religion and Politics', p. 8-9.
[64] C420: NN: Hooper (Letter, Hooper to 'Lottie' 7 April 1940).
[65] Clyne transcripts, p. 423.
[66] *Publicist*, 1 October 1938, Ian Mudie, 'As are the Gums', p. 14.
[67] C421: 27: The Yabba Club. When interned, Cahill gave his parents' names as Patrick Cahill and Diana Gunderson. At birth he was registered as Norman Patrick Cahill, his mother being Normandine Cahill, but no father was named. (Reg Bartram, letter, 25 February 1999)
[68] C421: 50: Summary of cases: Australia First Movement; A467: BUNDLE 97/ SF43/1: Australia First Movement.
[69] Reg Bartram, letter, 25 February 1999.
[70] Stuart Macintyre, *The Reds: the Communist Party of Australia*, p. 226.
[71] A8911: 130: Australia First Movement. (Report by Major Hattam, 12 March 1942. Reg Bartram, letter, 25 February 1999.
[72] Muirden, *Puzzled Patriots*, p. 72-74, 76. He associates this with a group called the Eureka Society. For Brennan's defence of the AFM, see Chapters 9 and 10.
[73] A8911: 136: Australia First Movement—WA, Vol. 1, pp. 53-56.
[74] C421: 30: Valentine Crowley and AFM.
[75] A8911: 136: Australia First Movement—WA, Vol. 1.
[76] Dr Mannix supported the principle of 'Australia First', but probably not any specific group. Miles told the Yabber Club that Archbishop Duhig in Brisbane took the *Publicist* 'indirectly', and approved of its policy with regard to the Jews. (C421: 27: The Yabba Club. Report dated 14 June 1940.)
[77] A367: C77862: Richard Daniel Collins.
[78] Clyne transcripts, pp. 1196-97, 1250. A8911: 136: Australia First Movement — WA, Vol. 1.
[79] *Publicist*, 1 July 1940, p. 15. These reports were stopped when people named in them were assaulted.

[80] C421: 27: The Yabba Club; A8911: 130: Australia First Movement; A8911: 136: Australia First Movement—WA, Vol. 1.
[81] Lockyer Papers, UQFL247, Box 1, Folder D/Personal.
[82] A8911: 136: Australia First Movement WA, Vol. 1; A467: BUNDLE 97/SF43/8: Australia First Movement: Miscellaneous Papers.
[83] A467: BUNDLE 97/SF43/1: Australia First Movement; A8911: 136: Australia First Movement—WA, Vol. 1, p. 7; C421: 14: Australia First Movement file.
[84] C421: 27: The Yabba Club.
[85] C421: 11: A. R. Mills—Appeal; Clyne transcripts, p. 357; A8911: 136: Australia First Movement—WA, Vol. 1.
[86] Clyne transcripts, p. 471.
[87] H. W. Malloch, *Fellows all: The Chronicles of the Bread and Cheese Club*. A potted biography of Mills, as he wished to present himself, is on page 224.
[88] Hattam Report.
[89] Muirden, *Puzzled Patriots*, p. 73.
[90] C421: 53: [Property seized from Leslie K. Cahill. Australia First Movement] (Henceforth: L. Cahill and AFM.); A373: 3750: Australia First Movement and the internment of E. C. Quicke. Gartner probably had German ancestry.
[91] 'Culture and Politics', P. R. Stephensen, *Design*, January 1940, pp. 9-15.
[92] Dr A. Bonnell identified this quotation as coming from a Nazi propaganda drama; the original did not mention Jews. (Friedrich Thiemann in *Schlageter*, by Hanns Johst, Act I, Scene I: 'Wenn ich Kultur höre … entsichere ich meinen Browning.')
[93] This was the phrase used to describe the Italian Fascist system; Italy was not yet at war.
[94] A8911: 136: Australia First Movement—WA, Vol. 1.
[95] Mudie Papers, PRG 27/1/1940. (Gartner to Mudie, 7 February 1940).
[96] A373: 3750: Australia First Movement. As Forde was a Catholic, he was not the person to approach with criticism of the *Advocate*.
[97] A373: 3750: Australia First Movement.
[98] Muirden, *Puzzled Patriots*, p. 3.
[99] *Advocate*, 27 November 1941, p. 8.
[100] C443: J363 PI O'Leary. Consular documents were not sorted and translated until 1946, and O'Leary died in 1944.
[101] *Who's Who in Australia* (1935); New South Wales Pioneer Index, 1788-1888.
[102] A373: 3921: Walter David Cookes.
[103] A373: 3921: Walter David Cookes.
[104] Coleman, *Adela Pankhurst*, p. 79-80. Miles had been friendly with Cookes for 20-30 years, Clyne transcripts, p. 682; Stephensen's evidence. Cookes would have known John Curtin through the Ross group.
[105] Clyne transcripts, pp. 2019, 1342. Muirden, p. 75, wrote that Mills had approached Cookes for a subscription to the *Angle*.
[106] Clyne transcripts, p. 2030. Produced at the Clyne Inquiry were a letter from Joosten to Cookes, dated 25 April 1939, and one from Cookes to Berlin Shortwave, 30 June 1939.
[107] Clyne transcripts, p. 854. His contact was Chuhei Anazawa.
[108] Documents re Cookes' business interests in Japan; produced at Clyne Inquiry.

(Censorship extract of letter from Cookes to Miles, 19 January 1942. Cookes was still unaware that Miles had died on 10 January) When taxation records are retained in dossiers, they almost always came from a tax accountant.
[109] A373: 3921: Walter David Cookes.
[110] A373: 3921: Walter David Cookes.

Chapter 4

[1] The club is sometimes written as 'Yabba'. The Clyne Inquiry used this form, but Stephensen wrote 'Yabber', which is more logical. *Webster's Dictionary* gives 'yabber', derived from an Aboriginal word 'yabba', meaning to talk. 'Yabber' will be used here, except in direct quotations.
[2] C420: NN: Hooper. Appeal, 22 June 1942.
[3] Russo was Professor of Modern Languages at the Tokyo University of Commerce.
[4] Bruce Muirden, *Puzzled Patriots*, pp. 44–46. No such report has been located, but not all Intelligence reports are available. Caiger had spent ten years teaching in Japan; he joined MI after returning to Australia in January 1940.
[5] Clyne transcripts, p. 1670, 1672, 1679. Panton, born 28 March 1894, Molong, NSW, was a nephew of Melbourne magistrate, William Edward Panton.
[6] Clyne transcripts, p. 1673; C421: 27: The Yabba Club. *Somebody* was reporting throughout 1940.
[7] Clyne transcripts, p. 533.
[8] Richard Hall, *Secret State*, pp. 33, 38.
[9] Clyne transcripts, p. 701.
[10] C420: NN: Hooper. Appeal, 22 June 1942.
[11] C421: 30: Valentine Crowley and AFM. In a similar letter of 25 September 1938, written from Melbourne, he mentioned Miles, Crowther (*sic*) and Stephensen by name. C420: NN: Hooper. Appeal, 22 June 1942.
[12] SP1714/1: N60622: Hugh Millington; C443: J12 HV Millington. Millington was employed as editor of the *Far Eastern Trade Bulletin* sponsored by the Japanese Chamber of Commerce.
[13] Reports by Agent 222 (and possibly by others) are in the National Archives, Sydney, Series C421: 27: The Yabba Club. They were mentioned during the Clyne Inquiry, transcript pages 260–267.
[14] C443: J19: John C. Eldridge.
[15] C421: 11: A. R. Mills - Appeal.
[16] A367: C73350: Inagaki - Mowsey Moshi (Cook to Forde, 22 February 1941).
[17] C320: J5: Japanese Activities.
[18] C443: J12: HV Millington.
[19] Clyne transcripts, pp. 23, 1347. He also gave the number as eight, p. 1315.
[20] According to Muirden, p. 112, Lieutenant-Colonel Reginald Powell was also connected with the Sane Democracy League. J. C. Ludowici had been a member of the committee of the Lutheran Church in Sydney, 1905–06. (AJCP, Reel M273, p. L265981.)
[21] *Publicist*, 1 June 1938, p. 12, 'Yampi Unsound', Editor. In the Fourteen Points (*Publicist*, August 1936, pp. 6–7, Point 5), Stephensen had written: 'iron mines at Yampi Sound: to place a complete embargo on the export of all industrial minerals from Australia'. He had not yet taken up the Japanese cause.

[22] C421: 50: Summary of cases: Australia First Movement. Masey denied having said any of this, or having read *Mein Kampf*; Clyne Inquiry transcripts, p. 1274.
[23] Clyne transcripts: p. 1352; *CPD*, Vol. 178: Haylen, 30 & 31 March 1944, p. 2471.
[24] A8911: 130: Australia First Movement - Miscellaneous.
[25] A8911: 130: Australia First Movement.
[26] A8911: 130: Australia First Movement.
[27] C421: 55: Dossiers, Australia First Movement. When this file was seen, it was heavily expunged. By January 1941, action against Bullock was obviously being considered.
[28] Yosuke Matsuoka was the aggressive Foreign Minister of Japan at that time. He died in prison while awaiting trial for war crimes. Sir Frederick Stewart was Minister for External Affairs.
[29] C421: 27: Yabba Club (A report dated between 14 April and 2 May has been expunged.) C421: 50: Summary of cases: Australia First Movement; Clyne transcripts, pp. 1429–33.
[30] A367: C65283: BUTTNER Wanda and Dr Friedrich Albert Buttner (father).
[31] Clyne transcripts, pp. 1431–32.
[32] C421: 11: A. R. Mills - Appeal.
[33] Morley Roberts, *Bio-Politics*, p. 82. This statement was repeated and paraphrased often by Miles in his role of John Benauster, especially in the *Publicist* of 1 June 1939, p. 1, where he wrote that war was 'a biological phenomenon, and therefore as inevitable as accident, disease, insanity and death'.
[34] Roberts, *Bio-Politics*, pp. 83–84 and 164–65.
[35] In C421: 49: Summary of cases, Australia First Movement, this comment is also attributed to Valentine Crowley. One or other report is misleading. In 1935, Clive Evatt was associated with Stephensen in the New South Wales branch of the Book Censorship Abolition League. Craig Munro, *Wild Man of Letters*, p. 161.
[36] C421: 27: The Yabba Club.
[37] The Clyne transcripts, p. 1201, noted that Lenin had a 'Revolutionary Committee of Seven'.
[38] Hall, *The Secret State*, p. 38.
[39] Genealogy of Tinker-Giles from A467: BUNDLE 97/SF43/13: Walter Frederick Tinker Giles also known as Walter Frederick Tinker. Objection against Detention. Australia First Movement (Henceforth: W. F. Tinker Giles, Objection.); A367: C18000/737: Giles Walter Frederick Tinker; C421: 55: Australia First Movement; NSW Pioneer Index, Federation Series, 1889–1918.
[40] Clyne transcripts, p. 1445.
[41] C421: 55: Australia First Movement; A467: BUNDLE 97/SF43/13: W. F. Tinker Giles.
[42] Other possibilities are Richard Ludowici; Malcolm Carlyle Smith; P. C. Lang.
[43] C320: J240: Pre-war activities of Japanese. According to Munro, *Wild Man of Letters*, p. 255, Clune had been a member of the New Guard.
[44] C421: 30: Valentine Crowley and AFM.

Chapter 5

[1] Bruce Muirden, *Puzzled Patriots*, p. 61.
[2] It is necessary to refer to the Walshes as 'Tom' and 'Adela' in order to avoid confusion.

[3] For the early life of Adela Pankhurst and her early years in Melbourne, see Verna Coleman, *Adela Pankhurst.*
[4] Coleman, *Adela Pankhurst,* p. 72. Adela lectured in Maryborough about August 1916.
[5] PP14/1: 1/9/58: Pankhurst Miss Adela.
[6] A367: C18000/719: Adela Constantia Mary Walsh; Coleman, *Adela Pankhurst.* p. 74.
[7] ST1233/1: N38433: Adela Pankhurst Walsh (Jones of IB, Melbourne, to Longfield Lloyd, 14 March 1927).
[8] Coleman, *Adela Pankhurst,* p. 81; *ADB,* Vol. 12, pp. 372-74; A367: C18000/719: Adela Constantia Mary Walsh; Chapter 1 of this thesis.
[9] For Adela's prosecutions and imprisonment, see Coleman, *Adela Pankhurst,* pp. 82-84.
[10] ST1233/1: N38433: Adela Pankhurst Walsh. (Jones to Lloyd, 14 March 1927).
[11] Coleman, *Adela Pankhurst,* pp. 86-87.
[12] Stuart Macintyre, *The Reds,* p. 12; Coleman, *Adela Pankhurst,* p. 89; A367: C18000/719: Adela Constantia Mary Walsh.
[13] C443: J9: Tom Walsh (Walsh to Percy Spender, then Treasurer, 16 April 1940).
[14] Coleman, *Adela Pankhurst,* p. 88.
[15] Coleman, *Adela Pankhurst,* p. 91.
[16] C443: J9: Tom Walsh (Walsh to Spender, 16 April 1940).
[17] C443: J9: Tom Walsh (Walsh to Spender, 16 April 1940).
[18] Coleman, *Adela Pankhurst,* p. 97.
[19] Italics are material underlined in a CIB report of 9 May 1924. D1915: SA1085: Herscovici, Rubin; A8911: 89: Rubin Herscovici aka Edgar T. Whitehead.
[20] For Walsh's activities in the Seamen's Union, see Coleman, *Adela Pankhurst,* esp. pp. 101-03.
[21] A1606: K26/1: Correspondence between Tom Walsh and Havelock Wilson. Wilson had been a Member of Parliament for sixteen years between 1892 and 1922.
[22] Sadie Herbert Collection UQFL83, Box 60. Transcript of interview, 15/12/1975, Tape 1 Track 2, pp. 12–13. Herbert was a member of the Seamen's Union for a time.
[23] Coleman, *Adela Pankhurst,* p. 115.
[24] C320: CIB222: Guild of Empire.
[25] Coleman, *Adela Pankhurst,* p. 115.
[26] A367: C18000/719: Adela Constantia Mary Walsh; Hasluck, *Government and the People, 1939-1941, Vol. I,* Appendix 9 on the Winkler affair.
[27] Coleman, *Adela Pankhurst,* p. 126–27.
[28] Eric Campbell, *The Rallying Point. My Story of the New Guard* , pp. 160–61. Campbell wrote that Walsh married *Sylvia* Pankhurst.
[29] *Publicist,* 1 July 1937, The Editor, 'The Amazons of the British Garrison in Australia', p. 4. Stephensen had written in 1936, 'The English Garrison here is armed not with rifles … but with *propaganda.' Foundations of Culture,* p. 181.
[30] *Publicist,* 1 July 1937, 'Benauster', 'Australian Self-Dependence', p. 1.
[31] A367: C18000/719: Adela Constantia Mary Walsh.
[32] Coleman, *Adela Pankhurst,* p. 116.
[33] Coleman, *Adela Pankhurst,* p. 148.
[34] Coleman, *Adela Pankhurst,* p. 141.

[35] ST1233/1: N38433: Mrs Adela Pankhurst Walsh.
[36] ST1233/1: N38433: Mrs Adela Pankhurst Walsh.
[37] ST1233/1: N38433: Mrs Adela Pankhurst Walsh. Adela's lecture appeared in *Die Brücke*, 25 December 1937, pp. 34–35; A981: CONS 133: Consuls—Germany at Sydney; C443: G1 PART 1: Translation of Consular records.
[38] A367: C18000/719: Adela Constantia Mary Walsh. Coleman, *Adela Pankhurst*, pp. 147–48, suggests the money might have been payment for writing the article published in *Die Brücke*; that is possible but unlikely.
[39] A8911: 136: Australia First Movement—WA, Vol. 1, p. 7; and C421: 14: Australia First Movement file.
[40] ST1233/1: N38433: Mrs Adela Pankhurst Walsh.
[41] Japanese Consulate-General records, especially C443: J9: Tom Walsh. £400 would be roughly equivalent to $40,000 at 2004 values, and it is unlikely that Walsh declared this sum to either the Taxation Department or Social Services. Owing to the limitations of the *katakana* syllabary in which foreign names are written, Thomas Walsh appears in the hand-written financial statements as 'Tomasu Worusu'.
[42] ST1233/1: N38433: Mrs Adela Pankhurst Walsh.
[43] Coleman, *Adela Pankhurst*, p. 134.
[44] A367: C18000/719: Adela Constantia Mary Walsh.
[45] A981: CONS 167 PART 2B: Consuls. Japan at Sydney. In 1941, as Minister to Panama, Akiyama coordinated espionage in Central and South America. [Tony Matthews, *Shadows Dancing*, pp. 20-21, 30].
[46] C443: J9: Tom Walsh. *The Sino-Japanese Conflict*. (Cousins to the Consulate-General, 17 September 1938; Wakamatsu to Angus & Robertson, 19 September 1938).
[47] A367: C64736: Thomas Walsh. Adela Constantia Mary Walsh nee Pankhurst.
[48] A367: C18000/719: Adela Constantia Mary Walsh.
[49] Coleman, *Adela Pankhurst*, p. 147.
[50] The Oka reception material is in SP1714/1: N60255: Donald McKenzie.
[51] See *Sino-Japanese Conflict*, above.
[52] SP1714/1: N60255: Donald McKenzie.
[53] C123: 15182: Sleeman, John Harvey Crothers; *Brisbane Courier*, various dates, September 1922 (re attempted bribery of F. Brennan); *Sydney Morning Herald*, various dates, July–September 1932 (Judge Swindell case) In 1922 Sleeman worked for John Wren's *Daily Mail* (Brisbane).
[54] ST1233/1: N38433: Mrs Adela Pankhurst Walsh.
[55] A367: C18000/719: Objection No. 118. Adela Constantia Mary Walsh.
[56] ST1233/1: N38433: Mrs Adela Pankhurst Walsh.
[57] Coleman, *Adela Pankhurst*, p. 149.
[58] The Walshes' daughter Sylvia worked for Toyoda, 10 March 1938 to 6 May 1940, and for his replacement, Masaichi Kurata, from 4 December 1940. A367: C64736: Thomas Walsh. Adela Constantia Mary Walsh nee Pankhurst.
[59] A367: C18000/719: Adela Constantia Mary Walsh. Early in the war, Suma became Ambassador to Spain, where he was head of Japanese espionage in the Iberian Peninsula. Matthews, *Shadows Dancing*, p. 32.
[60] ST1233/1: N38433: Mrs Adela Pankhurst Walsh.

[61] Tom Walsh, *Japan as viewed by Foreigners*, p. 40.
[62] A367: C18000/719: Adela Constantia Mary Walsh.
[63] C447 PART 1: 7: Japanese Consular Files. As the same report mentions lectures by Walsh, which would more likely refer to Adela than to Tom, it is possible that this is an ambiguous translation, and that 'his, he' should be 'her, she', or even 'their, they'. Japanese is not always specific as to gender and number.
[64] C447 PART 1: 7: Japanese Consular Files.
[65] C443: J9: Tom Walsh; C443: J170: Japanese Chamber of Commerce. Meetings.
[66] A472: W1141: Adela Pankhurst Walsh.
[67] A472: 2777: "The People's Guild". "The Voice of the People".
[68] Coleman, *Adela Pankhurst*, pp. 151-52; A472: 2777: "The People's Guild". "The Voice of the People".
[69] SP109/3: 316/13: Censorship. "Voice of the People". Adela Pankhurst Walsh. Presumably, censorship notices were also sent to the *Publicist*, but none has been found.
[70] *Voice of the People*, 1 October 1940, 'Australia's Peril', p. 6.
[71] Pages from the *Voice of the People* are retained in SP109/3/1/: 316/13: Voice of the People. Mention of '150 years' in respect of friendship with Japan immediately destroyed the Walshes' credibility as experts on Japan, but they kept repeating this. It was patently nonsense, because it was less than ninety years since the Americans had forced Japan to open her ports to international trade.
[72] SP109/3/1: 316/13: Voice of the People.
[73] ST1233/1: N38433: Mrs Adela Pankhurst Walsh.
[74] Muirden, *Puzzled Patriots*, p. 61.
[75] ST1233/1: N38433: Mrs Adela Pankhurst Walsh.
[76] A367: C18000/719: Adela Constantia Mary Walsh. Nobuji Okada was replaced by Kinji Miwa on 21 January 1941. Each is mentioned in documents as the channel for the Walsh material. (A367: C64736: Thomas Walsh. Adela Constantia Mary Walsh nee Pankhurst) On 6 December 1941, Mitsui moved its documents to the garage of an Australian employee, where they were found two days later.
[77] A367: C18000/719: Adela Constantia Mary Walsh. (Letters: Walsh to Spender, 16 April 1940; to Curtin and Hughes, 2 September 1940; to Menzies, 30 September 1940; to McEwen, 5 October 1940.)
[78] C443: J9: Tom Walsh. (Walsh to Gullet, 22 April 1940).
[79] A981: PERS 394: Personal: T. Walsh Reports. This file also contains a letter to Arthur Fadden (Treasurer), 4 February 1941 (11 pages), and one to Sir Frederick Stewart (Minister for External Affairs), 21 May (7 pages).
[80] Coleman, *Adela Pankhurst*, p. 153.
[81] A367: C18000/719: Adela Constantia Mary Walsh.
[82] A8911: 136: Australia First Movement—WA, Vol. 1, p. 7; C421: 14: Australia First Movement.
[83] A367: C64736: Thomas Walsh. Adela Constantia Mary Walsh nee Pankhurst.
[84] A367: C18000/719: Adela Constantia Mary Walsh.
[85] In April 1939, the Japanese tried to buy secretly the Sydney *Daily News*. (Rupert Lockwood, *War on the Waterfront*, pp. 26–27)) This is confirmed by the Australia Station Intelligence Report, May 1939 (MP1582/6: 1939). As this is a naval document, the information probably came from Kenneth Easton Cook. The

Waverley-Woollahra Standard, a small suburban paper, would have been a poor substitute.
[86] C443: J9: Tom Walsh.

Chapter 6

[1] *Publicist*, August 1939, Editor's comment, p. 16.
[2] Craig Munro, *Wild Man of Letters*, p. 196; Bruce Muirden, *Puzzled Patriots*, p. 49.
[3] Clyne transcripts, p. 1345. On 24 August 1939, Edwin Arnold wrote to the *Sun*, 'Why all this fuss about the barbarous and impossible Poles? [Most] of the Poles who formerly lived under German rule would much prefer the suzerainty of their former kindly masters to that of the arrogant Polish militarists and big landlords who now oppress and exploit them.' (C421: 1: Edwin Arnold and AFM).
[4] *Publicist*, 1 October 1939, Bunyip Critic, 'Might as Right', p. 3.
[5] *Publicist* 1 December 1939, Bunyip Critic, pp. 3-4. Emphasis is in the original.
[6] *Publicist*, 1 October 1939, Bunyip Critic, pp. 5-6. Crowley and the Irish did not support the monarchy.
[7] *Publicist*, 1 October 1939, Bunyip Critic, p. 7; written 9 September.
[8] *Publicist*, 1 October 1939, Bunyip Critic, pp. 8-16.
[9] C421: 6: Australia First Movement; C421: 30: Valentine Crowley and AFM. (P. R. Stephensen to E. D. Stephensen, 21 November 1939).
[10] Munro, *Wild Man of Letters*, p. 201; *Publicist*, 1 May 1940, p. 20; C421: 30: Valentine Crowley and AFM. (Stephensen to Cahill, 26 August 1941) These points are reproduced in Appendix I.
[11] Munro, *Wild Man of Letters*, pp. 203-04.
[12] This report has not been found, but it is mentioned in the Richards Report, March 1942, in A467: BUNDLE 97/SF43/3: Australia First Movement Part I.
[13] *Publicist*, 1 September 1940, Cahill's notes on Melbourne, p. 16.
[14] *Publicist*, 1 October 1940, 'Louis M. Veron', 'Independent Candidature', p. 2.
[15] *Publicist*, 1 October 1940, Bunyip Critic, pp. 3-7. Stephensen, who met Evatt in 1937, had reviewed two of his books in the *Publicist* (March 1937 and July 1938). In August 1940, Evatt invited Stephensen to his chambers to discuss Australian politics and his resignation from the Supreme Court. As the *Publicist* had attacked the leading UAP figures - Prime Minister Menzies, Treasurer R. G. Casey and Attorney-General W. M. Hughes - Evatt possibly sensed a kindred spirit and a political ally; Stephensen was no doubt flattered at being consulted.
[16] *Publicist*, 1 October 1940, M. F. Watts, 'The Labour Party Cannot Rule! An Indictment!', pp. 8-13. The article was reprinted as a pamphlet.
[17] *Publicist*, 1 December 1940, 'Benauster', 'After the War', p. 1.
[18] *Publicist*, 1 March 1941, Bunyip Critic, 'New Orders & Disorders', pp. 4-7.
[19] *Publicist*, 1 May 1941, Bunyip Critic, 'The Body Politic', p. 8-11, esp. p. 9.
[20] *Publicist*, 1 November 1941, Bunyip Critic, 'The Meaning of Australia-First', pp. 6-10.
[21] *Publicist*, 1 April 1941, 'Benauster', 'New Political Leadership Needed', p. 2: L. K. Cahill, p. 14.
[22] *Publicist*, 1 July 1939, p. 16.

[23] J. T. Lang (Labor) in *Century*, 16 January 1942; Fadden (Country Party) speaking on radio, 18 January, reported in the *Sydney Morning Herald*, 19 January 1942, p. 4.
[24] *Publicist*, 1 November 1939, Bunyip Critic, 'War of Words', p. 5.
[25] Clyne transcripts, p. 1330.
[26] *Publicist*, 1 November 1939, Hardy Wilson, 'The Jewish Influx into Australia', pp. 9-12.
[27] *Publicist*, 1 November 1939, Hardy Wilson, 'The Jewish Influx into Australia', pp. 9-12.
[28] Leonard Fox was associated with the State Labor Party (New South Wales), which was later avowedly communist. Maurice Blackburn, ALP member for Bourke, allegedly wrote a foreword to the first edition, but this is not in a later edition, the only copy found.
[29] *Publicist*, 1 February 1940, 'Benauster', 'Australia and the Jews', p. 1.
[30] *Publicist*, 1 February 1940, M. F. Watts, 'Foreign Influences in Australia', p. 2.
[31] A8911: 130: Australia First Movement - Miscellaneous.
[32] *Publicist*, 1 April 1940, 'Benauster', 'Australia and the Jews', p. 1.
[33] *Australian Quarterly*, Vol. XII, No. 1, March 1940, pp. 52-62. Masey was on the editorial staff.
[34] *Australian Quarterly*, March 1940, pp. 61-62.
[35] *Publicist*, 1 April 1940, Bunyip Critic, p. 5.
[36] *CPD*, Vol. 163: 17 April 1940, p. 32.
[37] Clyne transcripts, p. 559.
[38] Munro, *Wild Man of Letters*, p. 200.
[39] Muirden, *Puzzled Patriots*, p. 50. The Germans were aware of the weakness of French defences; it was the public in Allied countries who were being kept in the dark, for reasons of morale.
[40] *Publicist*, 1 May 1940, 'Benauster', 'Australia and the Jews', p. 1.
[41] *Publicist*, 1 May 1940, 'P. R. Stephensen's Action Against Communist Paper', Stephensen, pp. 3-9.
[42] C421: 55: Australia First Movement; C421: 30: Valentine Crowley and AFM. Emphasis is in the original. (Stephensen to Cahill, 13 June 1940)
[43] *Publicist*, 1 July 1940, Stephensen, p. 13.
[44] *Publicist*, 1 October 1941, Bunyip Critic, p. 13, in an attack on Max Harris, who called the AFM's Fifty Point Policy 'a series of dog-chasing contradictory cant catch-phrases'.
[45] Mudie papers, PRG 27/1/1941 (Stephensen to Mudie, 8 January 1941).
[46] *Publicist*, 1 July 1941, Bunyip Critic, 'An Alphabet of Nationalism', pp. 3-7. See p. 6.
[47] *Publicist*, 1 July 1941, 'Rex Williams', 'Conflict in the Community', pp. 13-14.
[48] A8911: 17: The Link (Miles to O'Loughlin, 1 July 1940).
[49] *Publicist*, 1 February 1940, Bunyip Critic, 'Banzai', p. 3.
[50] C421: 6: Australia First Movement (Stephensen to Otabe, 3 May 1940).
[51] Clyne transcripts, pp. 763-65.
[52] For Otabe's methods see SP1714/1: N45622: Consul-General for France; A367: C18000/614: Gulson, Leonard Ashworth.
[53] *Publicist*, 1 April 1941, 'Rex Williams', 'Welcome to Mr Kawai', p. 3.
[54] *Publicist*, 1 August 1941, 'Rex Williams', 'China: "De Jure" and "De Facto"', pp. 12-13.
[55] Crowley was a Senior Warden in the National Emergency Service. C421: 30:

Valentine Crowley and AFM. Herbert knew Crowley well: Miles, Hooper and Crowley had signed his application for a Commonwealth Literary Grant in 1939. (Herbert papers, NLA MS2106).
[56] C421: 49: Australia First Movement; C421: 32: Newspaper clippings—correspondence concerning the Australia First Inquiry. The Humphries statement to MPI, dated 27 May, cannot have been a factor in the decision to intern Crowley. She is named in the Clyne transcripts, p. 1643.
[57] Clyne transcripts, p. 1644.
[58] C443: J326. A. X. Herbert. (Murakami to Wakamatsu, 22 September 1938). P. R. Stephensen Papers, ML MSS1284, Box 45. The flight of Alfie Candlemas and Fergus Ferris: Herbert, *Poor Fellow My Country*, pp. 1388–1414. For the extent to which Herbert fictionalised the story of his life, see Frances de Groen, *Xavier Herbert*. The copy of the *Publicist* kept in the file C443: J326 bears the stamp of the Japanese Society of Port Darwin.
[59] E. D. Stephensen complained that they were 'stolen'; however, police have a right to search premises and gather evidence, as well as to destroy illegal materials such as weapons, drugs and contraband. (Letter, E. D. Stephensen, 9 March 1999).
[60] C421: 30: Valentine Crowley and AFM. (P. R. Stephensen to E. D. Stephensen, 12 November 1939).
[61] A8911: 130: Australia First Movement. Emphasis added.
[62] Stephensen Papers, ML MSS 1284, Box 43. Morley lived in Australia 1877-79. Clyne transcripts, p. 562.
[63] *Austral-Asiatic Bulletin*, June-July 1941, p. 22, cited in the *Publicist*, 1 August 1941.
[64] *Publicist*, 1 August 1941, John Benauster, 'Sir F. Eggleston and "Bio-Politics"', pp. 1-2.
[65] *Publicist*, 1 April 1941, Review of *Bio-Politics* by Harry Roberts, comments by Editor, pp. 8-9
[66] C421: 50: Australia First Movement. (Stephensen to Cahill, 4 August 1941). Richard Gardiner Casey, at that time, Australian Minister to the USA; formerly Treasurer in the Liberal Party Government, later a member of the British War Cabinet, Governor of Bengal, Governor-General of Australia, Baron of Berwick.
[67] *Publicist*, 1 January 1941, 'Towards a New Party', Bunyip, pp. 4-8. This *Publicist*, p. 8, also printed the Japanese Imperial Rescript, issued in Tokyo on 27 September 1940.
[68] *Publicist*, 1 January 1942, P. R. Stephensen '1942', p. 1.
[69] *Publicist*, 1 January 1942, P. R. Stephensen '1942', p. 1.
[70] C421: 55: Australia First Movement. (Cookes to Stephensen, 19 January 1942).
[71] *Publicist*, 1 February 1942, P. R. Stephensen, 'The Death of "John Benauster"', pp. 2-4.
[72] *Publicist*, 1 January 1942, p. 16; 1 March 1942, p. 5.
[73] Clyne transcripts, p. 1310.
[74] *Publicist*, 1 March 1942, P. R. Stephensen, 'If England Goes Down', p. 1. All the material attacking Forde over Rabaul comes from this page.
[75] *Publicist*, 1 March 1942, P. R. Stephensen, 'If England Goes Down', p. 1.
[76] *Publicist*, 1 April 1939, 'L. M. Veron', 'Following Britain's Bad Lead', p. 11.
[77] The recall of Australian troops from the Middle East had been discussed in the Advisory War Council on 31 December 1941. (A5954: 813/2: Advisory War Council. Minute No. 635.).

[78] *Publicist*, 1 March 1942, 'J. Blunt', 'Japan's Plans', p. 2. This was probably Stephensen again.
[79] A5954: 813/2. Advisory War Council. Minute No. 835.
[80] C421: 50: Summary of cases: Australia First Movement (Miles to Hooper, 21 January 1941).
[81] Lockyer Papers, UQFL 247/B/Folder 7 (Miles to Kirtley, 17 January 1939).
[82] Of those who never used their own full names, only Dr Philpots and Phyllis Walton could be identified.
[83] Clyne transcripts, pp. 694, 704. By style and content, Stephensen might have been John Bullant, Sydney Cove, J. Blunt, Bogan Villa and Mulga Bill.
[84] *Publicist*, 1 June 1941, Bunyip Critic, 'The Publicist's First Five Years', pp. 6-8. The lists are not complete, so it is not safe to claim that someone did *not* write for the *Publicist* on the basis of them.
[85] *Publicist*, 1 December 1941, P. R. Stephensen, 'Number Sixty-Six', p. 1.
[86] Clyne transcripts, p. 538; *Publicist*, 1 December 1941, p. 1.
[87] C421: 30: Valentine Crowley and AFM. (Stephensen to Kirtley, 5 August 1941).
[88] C421: 50: Australia First Movement. (Miles to Hooper, 25 August 1941).
[89] C421: 50: Australia First Movement.
[90] Clyne transcripts, p. 1309.
[91] *Publicist*, 1 September 1941, P. R. Stephensen, '"The Publicist's" Coming Changes', p. 1.
[92] *Publicist*, 1 September 1941, E. D. Stephensen, 'Self-Sufficient Agriculture', p. 11.
[93] Clyne transcripts, pp. 618B, 683, 1342.
[94] C421: 30: Valentine Crowley and AFM. (Stephensen to Cookes, 27 October 1941).
[95] C421: 6: Australia First Movement. (Letters, 10 January 1942, Stephensen to Cookes; 5 January, Cookes to Stephensen. In cash or promises, he had £156 from V. Crowley, £52 from Hooper, £90 from C. Brown in Adelaide, £26 each from C. Crowley and Mudie, £20 from Tinker, £13 each from Salier, Masey and Rice, and £10 from an unnamed 'recent adherent'. (Compiled from Clyne transcripts, p. 1651; C420: NN: Hooper; and C421: 6: Australia First Movement).
[96] C420: NN: Hooper.
[97] C421: 30: Valentine Crowley and AFM; C421: 55: Australia First Movement
[98] Clyne transcripts, p. 539.
[99] C421: 30: Valentine Crowley and AFM: A373: 3921: Walter David Cookes.
[100] C421: 55: Australia First Movement. MI/X was a code for MI mail interception.
[101] *Publicist*, 1 December 1941, P. R. Stephensen, 'Number Sixty-Six', p. 1; p. 16.
[102] C421: 15: Australia First Movement including information about R. G. Ingamells.
[103] Clyne transcripts, p. 1315.
[104] C421: 55: Australia First Movement; this gives the date as 11 October, and mentions Stephensen and the *Publicist*. In C421: 3: The Publicist, Miles and the *Publicist* are mentioned, and the date is given as 17 October.
[105] Rupert Lockwood, *War on the Waterfront* , p. 72. The *Tribune* was one of the communist papers banned soon after this.
[106] *Daily News* (Sydney), 9 May 1940.
[107] *Publicist*, 1 December 1939, 'L. M. Veron', p. 7.There were Verons in New South Wales, but no such marriage has been traced.

[108] The National Guard was the creation of Cyril Edward Hamilton Glassop, an electrical fitter born in New South Wales in 1910. He tried to set up a 'Motherland Front' in January 1937, and had a uniform made for himself. In mid 1941, he founded a National Guard, and he might have been the only member. He designed a symbol for it: a black circle with a stockwhip. When challenged about the discrepancies between his stories and known facts, he said, making a comment that applied to others: 'They were not lies, they were hallucinations and I believed in them.' Material on Glassop is in A367: C18000/828: GLASSOP Cyril Edward Hamilton, Advisory Committee.
[109] *Publicist*, 1 November 1941, P. R. Stephensen, 'The Meaning of "Australia First"', p. 1. In this edition, he began reporting on the progress of the AFM.
[110] A8911: 130: Australia First Movement.

Chapter 7

[1] SP1714/1: 39593: Nazi Party. (Report, 12 August 1940, by R. E. Finzel); A6122: 1 PART 2: Douglas Social Credit.
[2] SP1714/1: 39593: Nazi Party (Finzel Report, 12 August 1940).
[3] SP1714/1: N49071: Percy R Stephensen. The vulgarism translates roughly as 'Kark it, Jew, before we do.'
[4] See *Publicist*, 1 July 1938, 'Our Second Anniversary', John Benauster, pp. 1-2, and 1 November 1938, Bunyip Critic, pp. 6-7, and The Editor, 'Major Douglas and the Jews, p. 16.
[5] C421: 30: Valentine Crowley and AFM (Stephensen to Cahill, 30 October 1940).
[6] *Publicist*, 1 July 1941, 'Fifty Points', p. 16.
[7] As long as there was a strong Red Army in Siberia, it would have been risky to deplete the Japanese forces in China and Manchuria or the reserves in Japan itself.
[8] A367: C18000/737: W. F. Tinker-Giles.
[9] Clyne transcripts, pp. 1684-86. According to Verna Coleman, *Adela Pankhurst*, p. 159, Stephensen raised at the Yabber Club the idea of cooperating with Adela Walsh, but some members objected. Mrs Corby had raised £600 for the Guild.
[10] Clyne transcripts, p. 1686. Spelling of names has been corrected.
[11] A373: 4121: "Australia First" Internee: Gordon Thomas Rice.
[12] Anita Davis had a police record for assault.
[13] Craig Munro, *Wild Man of Letters*, p. 209.
[14] C421 50: Australia First Movement.
[15] A8911: 136: Australia First Movement—WA, Vol. 1. This job turned out to be unsuitable, and he obtained another as a storeman and packer.
[16] Clyne transcripts, p. 1201. These payments lasted only a few weeks.
[17] Clyne transcripts, p. 1246.
[18] Clyne transcripts, p. 1699.
[19] These developments were reported in the *Publicist*, 1 November 1941, p. 5, and 1 December 1941, p. 2.
[20] Clyne transcripts, pp. 1685, 1688–89, 1436.
[21] Clyne transcripts, p. 1578.
[22] A373: 4121: "Australia First" Internee: Gordon Thomas Rice.

[23] C421: 50: Australia First Movement. An editorial called 'Making Britain Safe from Democracy' had also appeared in the *Fascist*, March 1929. (Cited in Richard Griffiths, *Fellow Travellers of the Right*, p. 98.)
[24] C421: 55: Australia First Movement. Currey had no other link with the AFM.
[25] A367: C18000/737: Giles, Walter Frederick.
[26] Clyne transcripts, pp. 1436, 1440. Compare this with the comment by Muirden, p. 162: 'Stephensen's literary acquaintances could no longer reconcile his idealism with his increasingly dubious business dealings.' Bruce Muirden, *Puzzled Patriots*.
[27] C421: 30: Valentine Crowley and AFM. (Cahill to Camille Bartram, 29 October 1941).
[28] C421: 50: Australia First Movement. (Cahill to Mills, 10 November 1941)
[29] C421: 11: A. R. Mills; Clyne transcripts, pp. 357, 459.
[30] C421: 6: Australia First Movement; C421: 11: A. R. Mills (Mills to Stephensen, 5 November 1941).
[31] *Publicist*, 1 December 1939, The Editor, 'The Jews and Hughes', pp. 12–13. Miles wrote that Hughes was 'crassly stupid and humbugged by Jews'.
[32] *Publicist*, 1 November 1939, Hardy Wilson, 'The Jewish Influx into Australia', pp. 9–12.
[33] C421: 53: These documents were seized from Leslie K. Cahill, Australia First Movement. (Henceforth L. Cahill and AFM). Cahill was a keen football player.
[34] C421: 15: Australia First Movement including information about R.G. (Rex) Ingamells 1941-1942. (Ingamells to Stephensen, 27 December 1941). Stephensen had just savagely attacked *Meanjin* and Christesen: *Publicist,* 1 December 1941, 'A Mopoke Attacks Ian Mudie', p. 7.
[35] Ingamells papers, La Trobe Library, cited in Munro, *Wild Man of Letters*, p. 215.
[36] D1919: SS999: Secret Scrutiny of Internal Correspondence. Only a few relevant documents are retained in this file; scrutiny of both probably finished in January 1943, but the dates when it began are not certain.
[37] A467: BUNDLE 97/SF43/1 PART 1: "Australia First Movement" Meeting held at 150a Elizabeth St., Sydney on 12.11.1941. (Henceforth Australia First Meeting)
[38] *Publicist*, 1 December 1941, P. R. Stephensen, 'Distorted "Mirror" and Dilly "Telegraph"', pp. 14-15.
[39] ST1233/1: N38453: Mrs Adela Pankhurst Walsh. There are three slightly different versions of Adela's letter of 3 November.
[40] A367: C64736: Thomas Walsh. Adela Constantia Mary Walsh nee Pankhurst. If the Japanese had not been involved in Adela's move to found the AFM, why would she have informed them of its progress?
[41] C421: 50: Australia First Movement.
[42] Clyne transcripts, p. 1280.
[43] C421: 14: Australia First Movement, pp. 312-316.
[44] A467: BUNDLE 97/SF43/1PART 1: Australia First Meeting.
[45] Clyne transcripts, p. 1441.
[46] A467: BUNDLE 97/SF43/13: W. F. Tinker Giles; A367: C18000/737: W. F. Tinker-Giles; C421: 55: Australia First Movement.
[47] A467: BUNDLE 97/SF43/1 PART 1: Australia First Meeting; C421: 53: L. Cahill and AFM.
[48] A467: BUNDLE 97/SF43/1 PART 1: Australia First Meeting.
[49] A467: BUNDLE 97/SF43/1 PART 1: Australia First Meeting. In December,

Collins visited Sydney; Cahill introduced him to Stephensen and Miles, but he had little contact with the Sydney AFM. (A8911 130: Australia First Movement)
[50] C421: 50: Australia First Movement; and 53: L. Cahill and AFM. (Cahill to Bartram, 1 January 1942) The occasion was probably the Eureka commemoration evening held on 6 December. Emphasis is in the original. The consul was using Stephensen as a channel for disinformation.
[51] Arnold is another AFM-Irish link. His father's mother and his mother's father were Irish.
[52] C421: 1: Edwin Arnold and AFM. (Arnold to Asmis, 10 December 1933).
[53] C421: 50: Australia First Movement; and 1: Edwin Arnold and AFM.
[54] A9108: ROLL 8/11: Other branches of nazi organisation in Australia (Previously A779); ST1233/1: N39052: Otto Trenckmann. Hardt was an agent of German Naval Intelligence.
[55] C421: 1: Edwin Arnold and AFM. (Arnold to Haase, 13 February 1938).
[56] Information is from A373: 4120: Australia First: Edwin Arnold, and C421: 1: Edwin Arnold and AFM.
[57] Both 'G.C.' and 'X.G.' were used to denote material taken from consular records.
[58] C421: 50: Australia First Movement. (Arnold to Cahill, 13 December 1941).
[59] A467: BUNDLE 97/SF43/1 PART 1: Australia First Meeting.
[60] Quoted in Munro, *Wild Man of Letters*, p. 216.
[61] Clyne Report, p. 6. Munro, *Wild Man of Letters*, p. 216.
[62] A467: BUNDLE 97/SF43/2: "Australia First Meeting". Part II.
[63] Fotheringham Papers, UQFL46/3/14b, Box 1.
[64] C421: 14: Australia First Movement. Under NSR 42A(d), gazetted on 27 March 1941 but disallowed in Parliament on 3 July, it had been an offence to '*make any statement in relation to the war that is likely to lead to a breach of the peace*'. (*CPD*, Vol. 167: 3 July 1941, p. 881)
[65] Muirden, *Puzzled Patriots*, pp. 67-68 cited *The Hungry Mile*, Tom Nelson (1957) as his source.
[66] *Publicist*, 1 March 1942, P. R. Stephensen, 'The Adyar Hall Incident', p. 12.
[67] *Publicist*, 1 March 1942, 'Rex Williams', 'Communism and Chaos', pp. 13-14.
[68] A467: BUNDLE 97/SF43/2: "Australia First Movement" Meeting, Part 2; C421: 55: Australia First Movement. The letter was recorded on 23 February. It has not been possible to identify Josephine Ryan.
[69] A467: BUNDLE 97/SF43/2: "Australia First Movement" Meeting, Part 2.
[70] Muirden, *Puzzled Patriots*, p. 68. Gordon's wife was a friend of Adela Walsh.
[71] A373: 4121: Gordon Thomas Rice. Duplicate in C421: 49.
[72] Keith Bath, *Injustice Within the Law* (Letter to Evatt, 10 February 1948).
[73] A373: 4121: Gordon Thomas Rice. Bath and Spender: Clyne transcripts, pp. 791, 1390.
[74] A373: 4121: Gordon Thomas Rice.
[75] Clyne transcripts, p. 591; A467: BUNDLE 97/SF43/2: "Australia First Movement" Meeting, Part 2.
[76] C421: 50: Australia First Movement.
[77] A367: C18000/737: Giles Walter Frederick Tinker.
[78] A467: BUNDLE 97/SF43/13: W. F. Tinker Giles; A367: C18000/737: Giles Walter Frederick Tinker.

[79] C421: 50: Australia First Movement; and 53: L. Cahill and AFM (Cahill to Camille Bartram, 1 January 1942).
[80] A367: C18000/737: Giles Walter Frederick Tinker. The date of this quarrel is not given, but it had to be between 10 and 18 December.
[81] A367: C18000/719:. Adela Constantia Mary Walsh.
[82] A367: C18000/737: Giles Walter Frederick Tinker.
[83] C421: 53: L. Cahill and AFM. (Cahill to Camille Bartram, 1 January 1942).
[84] C421: 15: Australia First Movement including information on Rex Ingamells. Also in P. R. Stephensen papers, UQFL 55/25/7.
[85] Clyne Report, p. 12.
[86] C421: 30: Valentine Crowley and AFM. (Matthews to Hooper, 17 January 1942).
[87] C421: 50: Australia First Movement. (Kirtley to Stephensen, 20 January 1942).
[88] H. W. Malloch, *Fellows all: The Chronicles of the Bread and Cheese Club*, p. 224.
[89] C421: 50: Australia First Movement.
[90] A367: C18000/737: Giles Walter Frederick Tinker.
[91] Clyne transcripts, p. 1307A.
[92] Clyne transcripts , p. 1459.
[93] *CPD*, Vol. 186: Page, 14 March 1946, p. 329.
[94] C420: NN: Hooper.
[95] Clyne transcripts, pp. 1165, 1168.
[96] Clyne transcripts, pp. 1165, 1168.
[97] A8911: 130: Australia First Movement. (Major Hattam's report, 12 March 1942. Cahill to Mills, 21 October 1941.) In fact, Mills had known Cahill only five or six months. According to C421: 50: Cahill intended to use the reference to try for a job with AMP.
[98] C421: 14: Australia First Movement.
[99] A8911: 129: Australia First Movement, 1918-1942.
[100] *Publicist*, 1 January 1940, Alexander Rud Mills, 'Religion and Politics', pp. 8–9.
[101] *CPD*, Vol. 169: Falstein, Evatt, 25 November 1941, p. 816.
[102] Stephensen's response is in the *Publicist*, 1 January 1942, p. 15.
[103] Munro, *Wild Man of Letters*, p. 212. McKell was Governor-General, March 1947 to May 1953.
[104] C421: 14: Australia First Movement.
[105] C421: 14: Australia First Movement.
[106] C421: 14: Australia First Movement.
[107] A8911: 136: Australia First Movement—WA, Vol. 1.
[108] Munro, *Wild Man of Letters*, p. 213; A8911: 136: Australia First Movement—WA, Vol. 1; p. 120. The NSW State Labor Party later merged with the Communist Party.
[109] A367: C64736: Thomas Walsh. Adela Constantia Mary Walsh nee Pankhurst. By Australian time, 7 December was the *day before* the attack on Pearl Harbor.
[110] A367: C64736: Thomas Walsh. Adela Constantia Mary Walsh nee Pankhurst.
[111] Coleman, *Adela Pankhurst*, pp. 102–03.
[112] Munro, *Wild Man of Letters*, p. 215.
[113] Clyne transcripts, p. 1928.
[114] A8911: 130: Australia First Movement.
[115] Clyne transcripts, p. 910.

[116] A8911: 130: Australia First Movement.
[117] A8911: 130: Australia First Movement.
[118] A8911: 130: Australia First Movement. 'British' might have been a typist's error for 'fascist'.
[119] A8911: 130: Australia First Movement.
[120] A467: BUNDLE 97/SF43/2: "Australia First Movement" Meeting, Part 2.
[121] C421: 14: Australia First Movement, pp. 322-24. (Report, February 1942, B. Tyrrell).
[122] A467: BUNDLE 97SF43/2: "Australia First Movement" Meeting, Part 2.
[123] Munro, *Wild Man of Letters*, p. 217. The date of the MPI request is not given here, but it was probably in the report of 12 February, mentioned in Hasluck, *The Government and the People*, Vol. II, p. 724.
[124] A467: BUNDLE 97/SF43/2: "Australia First Movement" Meeting, Part 2.
[125] C421: 30: Valentine Crowley and AFM. (Cahill to Stephensen, 6 February 1942).
[126] C421: 50: Australia First Movement. Reginald Bartram was Camille's son; he had a temporary exemption from military service to finish his electrical apprenticeship. (Cahill to Bartram, 18 February 1942)
[127] Clyne transcripts, p. 1236.
[128] C421: 15: Australia First Movement including information on Rex Ingamells. (Newman to Tyrrell, 23 February 1942).
[129] *Publicist*, 1 March 1942, 'Adyar Hall Incident', Stephensen, p. 12.
[130] *CPD*, Vol. 170: 6 March 1942, p. 223. Stephensen's name if given as 'F. R. Stephenson'.
[131] Clyne transcripts, pp. 593–94.
[132] A467: BUNDLE 97/SF43/2: "Australia First Movement". Part 2.

Chapter 8

[1] In 1946, Rud Mills described them as 'the yokel Quicke, the schizophrenic Bullock, his woman and the vacant Williams'. P. R. Stephensen papers, ML MSS1284, Box 1.
[2] Clyne transcripts, p. 1922.
[3] Clyne, p. 1769: Thomas was instructed to approach Mrs O'Loughlin.
[4] Muirden, *Puzzled Patriots*, p. 77, calls her Madeline Labouchère Eva O'Loughlin, which was how the name appeared in the *West Australian*, 17 June 1942, p. 7.
[5] Information on Mrs O'Loughlin comes mainly from A8911: 17: The Link, but some is repeated in other files, especially D1915: SA20476: The Link. At the time in question, it was the Austro-Hungarian army.
[6] A8911: 141: "Australia First" Movement—Court Proceedings. D1915: SA20496: The Link (O'Loughlin to Miles, 27 September, 1 and 22 November 1939).
[7] C421: 8: Miscellaneous papers relating to the Australia First Movement. (Henceforth: Miscellaneous papers on AFM.) (O'Loughlin to Stephensen, 10 March 1942).
[8] She might have been the 'M. Jakic' who arrived at Sydney in *Ophir* on 21 February 1908 with a group of Austrian immigrants; passenger lists in those days were notoriously unreliable.
[9] PP14/2: PF/688: Fettbach, Liebenow and Rutland. Fettbach worked for the PMG 1892–1925, and Hughes 1906–1922, so Hughes probably knew Melanie

O'Loughlin's first husband.

[10] A8911: 17: The Link; SP1714/1: N39593: Nazi Party Membership. The address book of Hertha Schmidt, Sydney leader of the Nazi women's group and auxiliary member of the SS, contained the address of T. O'Loughlin, Gardiner Street, Como. (A367: C68205: Friedrich Wilhelm Schmidt, folio page 127).

[11] Griffiths, *Fellow Travellers of the Right*, pp. 277, 239.

[12] Admiral Sir Barry Domvile, *From Admiral to Cabin Boy*, p. 15. In his book *By and Large*, 1936, p. 240, he wrote that Himmler had 'a charming personality', and on p. 245 that the administration of Dachau concentration camp was 'excellent'. Quoted in Griffiths, *Fellow Travellers of the Right*, pp. 181-82. Carroll and Domvile were imprisoned in 1940 under Section 18B of National Security Regulations.

[13] C421: 14: Australia First Movement file (File pages 64-67).

[14] A8911: 17: The Link (Melanie O'Loughlin to Miles, 19 June 1939).

[15] Information concerning this meeting comes mainly from affidavits taken on 27-29 January 1943 and filed in the dossier of 'Trader' Horn. (B741: V/8545: HORN, Willy Hermann Johann Friedrich)

[16] B741: V/8545S: HORN. This was probably The Link, although Skerst in Sydney was supposed to run The Link. One of these members of parliament was probably T. J. Hughes.

[17] A8911: 17: The Link. (O'Loughlin to Miles, 19 June 1939).

[18] A8911: 136: Australia First Movement—WA, Vol. 1. The cutting is at p. 127, the letter at p. 128.

[19] C421: 14: Australia First Movement file; File pages 64-67; A8911: 136: Australia First Movement—WA, Vol. 1, p. 128.

[20] *Sydney Morning Herald*, 17 August 1939, p. 13.

[21] A467: BUNDLE 97/SF43/4: Australia First Movement. Part II (O'Loughlin to Miles, 5 August 1939).

[22] A8911: 17: The Link. Stephensen denied knowing anything about The Link, but admitted later that O'Loughlin sent Miles some leaflets about it. (Miles to O'Loughlin, 16 August 1939) Clyne transcripts, p. 701.

[23] D1915: SA20496: The Link (O'Loughlin to Miles, 11 December 1939).

[24] D1915: SA20496: The Link (O'Loughlin to Miles, 1 November 1939).

[25] A8911: 17: The Link.

[26] A467: BUNDLE 97/SF43/6: Australia First Movement Criminal Court Hearing; C421: 8: Miscellaneous papers on AFM. (O'Loughlin to Miles, 10 February 1940).

[27] A8911: 17: The Link. (O'Loughlin to Miles, 29 October 1939)

[28] A8911: 17: The Link.

[29] A467: BUNDLE 97/SF43/4: Australia First Movement. Part II. (Miles to Melanie O'Loughlin, 19 December 1939).

[30] DA1915: SA20496: The Link (O'Loughlin to Miles, 11 December 1939).

[31] C421: 8: Miscellaneous papers on AFM.

[32] Ittershagen died in June 1940.

[33] A367: C69207: BULLOCK Lawrence Frederick. Also Clyne transcripts, p. 1883.

[34] Material on the connections between the RSWU, Social Credit, Bullock and Hughes is from a B.A. Hons thesis, UWA 1977, by Charles Fox: 'The Relief and Sustenance Workers' Union 1933-1934. An anti-Labor political and industrial organisation'.

[35] C. Fox thesis; *Biographical Register of Member of the Parliament of Western Australia,* Volume 1; 1870-1930. In *The Light on the Hill,* p. 194, Ross McMullin called him 'a determined maverick'. Hughes was considered a Labor 'rat', and his friends could expect no favours. For Bullock, Social Credit and Jews, see A467: BUNDLE 97/ SF43/3: Australia First Movement Part I (Interview: 10 March 1942: Bullock and Richards).
[36] A8911: 136: Australia First Movement—WA, Vol. 1, pp. 217-223: Appendix "A": (This also appears as Appendix "B" in A367: C73002: Krakouer, Nancy Rachel [KRAKAUER]: pp. 17–12 (numbered backwards). This report, 20 March 1942, will be referred to henceforth as the Richards Report. See Griffiths, *Fellow-Travellers of the Right,* pp. 328. 351-52, for a similar 'People's Party' founded in Britain by Hastings Russell (later Duke of Bedford).
[37] A467: BUNDLE 97/SF43/3: Australia First Movement Part I.
[38] Another Western Australian in contact with German diplomats in America was Thomas Hugh Gilhooley, born in WA in 1921 of Irish parents. In a letter to the German Ambassador in Washington, he discussed Irish politics, denounced 'the Jewish war of 1939' and expressed his hope for a German victory. In February 1940 he contacted the British Union of Fascists, and in March he wrote, 'I don't support Germany because I love her, but because she is the only way for Irish freedom… *Delenda est Britannia.*' ('Britain must be destroyed.' Reg Bartram identified this as being derived from the call by Marcus Cato, Roman senator: *Delenda est Carthago.*) Gilhooley began to subscribe to the *Publicist* in November 1941; his correspondence with Quicke was mentioned in the Clyne transcripts, p. 1743. He was interned in May 1942. (D1915: SA21984: Thomas Hugh Gilhooley).
[39] Dr H. H. *Dieckhoff* presented his credentials in May 1937. Pelley was tried in early 1940 in connection with forging a letter to the Dies Committee on Un-American Activities. According to Bullock, the Silver Shirts had taken a blood oath to kill ten Jews each. C421: 8: Miscellaneous papers on AFM. (F. J. Thomas statement, made on 24 May 1944, pp. 1–2)
[40] A467: BUNDLE 97/SF43/6: Australia First Movement Criminal Court Hearing. (Bullock to Ittershagen, 18 November 1939).
[41] Clyne transcripts, pp. 277, 1714. (Bullock to Ittershagen, 18 November, 20 November 1939).
[42] A8911: 17: The Link. (O'Loughlin to Miles, 11 December 1939).
[43] SP1714/1: N39593: Nazi Party Membership. As O'Loughlin was a leading figure in both AF and The Link in WA, it is difficult to separate the two groups.
[44] A8911: 136: Australia First Movement—WA, Vol. 1, p. 156. Stephensen denied being in contact with either O'Loughlin or Bullock until after Miles took seriously ill, when he wrote at the request of Miles. (Clyne transcripts, p. 585) He had obviously been in contact much earlier.
[45] D1915: SA20496: The Link (Miles to O'Loughlin, 15 December 1939).
[46] A8911: 17: The Link. (O'Loughlin to Miles, 9 January 1940) She had Bullock's consent to send the letter.
[47] A8911: 136: Australia First Movement—WA, Vol. 1, p. 192.
[48] A8911: 136: Australia First Movement—WA, Vol. 1, p. 192. According to Muirden, *The Puzzled Patriots,* p. 90, Bullock denied writing this to Miles. In a

literal sense, this was true; he wrote it to O'Loughlin, and she forwarded his letter to Miles.
[49] Other known contacts were between Emily Taylor and Sheila Rice; Bullock and Cahill; Bullock and Stephensen; the O'Loughlins and Cahill; Quicke and Stephensen; and possibly Bullock and Hooper.
[50] SP1714/1: N39593: Nazi Party Membership; D1915: SA20496: The Link.
[51] P. R. Stephensen Papers, ML MSS1284, Box 43 (Miles to O'Loughlin, 21 February 1940). Several times, as early as August 1939, Miles mentioned showing Melanie's letters to Stephensen.
[52] A8911: 136: Australia First Movement—WA, Vol. 1 (O'Loughlin to Cahill, 2 July 1940).
[53] A8911: 136: Australia First Movement—WA, Vol. 1. (O'Loughlin to Cahill, 22 July 1940).
[54] A8911: 136: Australia First Movement—WA, Vol. 1. (Miles to Cahill, 30 July 1940)
[55] A8911: 136: Australia First Movement—WA, Vol. 1. (O'Loughlin to Miles, 28 February 1941).
[56] A467: BUNDLE 97/SF43/4: Australia First Movement. Part II.
[57] A8911: 136: Australia First Movement - WA, Vol. 1 (Gartner to Cahill, 29 August 1940).
[58] The Richards Report. At that time, F. J. Thomas was in no way involved.
[59] A472: W11041: Eric Butler. A6119: 1566: Eric Dudley Butler, Vol. 1. A letter from Alex Wilson, whose change of vote had helped bring down the Fadden Government in October 1941, had appeared in the *Kyabram Free Post*, 17 September 1940; in this he praised Eric Butler for his 'magnificent work in his advocacy of banking reforms'. Was the Social Credit Party involved in this change of Government?
[60] Quoted in A6119: 1566: Eric Dudley Butler. Vol. 1.
[61] A8911: 141: "Australia First" Movement—Court Proceedings; Richards Report.
[62] A467: BUNDLE 97/SF43/4: Australia First Movement. Part II. (Exhibit II).
[63] A467: BUNDLE 97/SF43/5: AFM Western Australia, Court, p. 6; A8911: 139: Australia First Movement, Court Exhibits: Exhibit G; and A467: BUNDLE 97/SF43/4: Australia First Movement. Part II. (Exhibit HH).
[64] Richards Report. Stuart Macintyre, *The Reds*, p. 398, writes that Richards was known among the local communists as the 'Black Snake', or 'Ron the Con'. He was Deputy Director of ASIO at the time of the Petrov Royal Commission.
[65] A8911: 130: Australia First movement. (Report by Major Hattam, 12 March 1942); A8911: 136: Australia First Movement:WA, Vol. 1.
[66] D1901: Q1004: QUICKE, Edward Cunningham.
[67] C421: 6: Australia First Movement (Quicke to Stephensen, 11 December 1941).
[68] A373: 3750: Australia First Movement and the internment of E. C. Quicke. Some of this and the following material is repeated in D1901: Q1004: E. C. Quicke.
[69] A373: 3750: Australia First Movement.
[70] A373: 3750: Australia First Movement.
[71] A8911: 136: Australia First Movement: WA,Vol. 1. (Quicke to Stephensen, 11 December 1941, 6 February 1942)
[72] D1901: Q1004: E. C. Quicke.
[73] A373: 3750: Australia First Movement. The *Publicist*, 1 July 1941, mentioned forming the nucleus of a party.

[74] A467: BUNDLE 97/SF43/3: Australia First Movement Part I; in a written statement to Quicke in March 1942, Bullock called Melanie O'Loughlin 'my old landlady'; C421: 8: Miscellaneous papers on AFM. (O'Loughlin to Stephensen, 10 March 1942).
[75] A367: C73002: Krakouer, Nancy Rachel ; D1901: K1003: Nancy Krakouer.
[76] A467: BUNDLE 97/SF43/5: Australia First Movement: Police v Bullock, Krakouer, Quicke & Williams. (Henceforth: AFM Western Australia. Court) (Court transcript, pp. 106–108).
[77] The Richards Report.
[78] A467: BUNDLE 97/SF43/5: AFM Western Australia, Court. (Evidence, 8 May 1942, pp. 36–40) This fortnight in prison in Darwin was the basis for calling him 'a convicted criminal'.
[79] A467: BUNDLE 97/SF43/5: AFM Western Australia. Court.
[80] A467: BUNDLE 97/SF43/5: AFM Western Australia. Court. Transcript, p. 4).
[81] A467: BUNDLE 97/SF43/5: AFM Western Australia. Court. (pp. 5-8). Probably Schreiner. A hand-written note against 'see' reads 'seize?'.
[82] Craig Munro, *Wild Man of Letters*, p. 217, repeats Stephensen's claim that this letter never reached him. However, there is an annotation on a copy of the letter: 'Seen 20.2.1942. Letter copied and released.' C421: 55: Dossiers, Australia First Movement.
[83] A8911: 136: Australia First Movement - WA, Vol. 1. This letter was not a figment of Thomas's imagination.
[84] *Publicist*, 1 December 1941, p. 2. Emphasis added.
[85] A373: 3750: Australia First Movement.
[86] A467: BUNDLE 97/SF43/3: Australia First Movement Part I. Bullock was using Williams's car. He tried to dodge mention of The Link by claiming they had asked her for a list of subscribers to the *Publicist*; this was nonsense, as Stephensen had already sent him this information. (*Ibid.*, statement handed to Quicke.)
[87] Fritz Wiedemann, Hitler's superior officer during the war, had been his personal adjutant until January 1939, when he was appointed Consul-General in San Francisco; he was transferred to Tientsin in October 1940, after an espionage scandal in July.
[88] A467: BUNDLE 97/SF43/5: AFM Western Australia. Court. Quicke testified later that it was Thomas who suggested obtaining a transmitter. (*West Australian*, 18 June 1942, p. 3).
[89] D1915: SA20496: The Link (O'Loughlin to Miles, 17 November 1939).
[90] C421: 8: Miscellaneous papers on AFM. (Statement by Thomas to Richards, 22 May 1944, p. 1). Melanie sent this photo, on loan, to Miles; he returned it on 22 November 1939. (D1915: SA20496: The Link)
[91] Mary Olga Connolly, née Glauder, arrived in Fremantle with her family in 1906.
[92] PP302/1: WA8: Japanese activities, 1918-1941; K1171: OMORI, M. says that Omori was first *registered* (as an alien) in Western Command on 5 January 1940, which is not the same thing.
[93] K1171: 1375: Veronica Margaret Connolly.
[94] A367: C69140: ALLEN, Veronica Margaret; C421: 8: Miscellaneous papers on AFM (Statement, Thomas to Richards, 22 May 1944, p. 2).

[95] A467: BUNDLE 97/SF43/5: AFM Western Australia. Court (Court transcript, p. 10) It was almost impossible to obtain weapons legally in 1942, as they were being requisitioned to arm the Volunteer Defence Corps.
[96] A467: BUNDLE 97/SF43/3: Australia First Movement Part I.
[97] D1901: Q1004: E. C. Quicke; A373: 3750: Australia First Movement.
[98] A8911: 137: Australia First Movement, Volume 2.
[99] Richards Report; A467: BUNDLE 97/SF43/3: Australia First Movement Part I.
[100] A467: BUNDLE 97/SF43/5: AFM Western Australia. Court. (Transcript, p. 12, Alford's evidence).
[101] A467: BUNDLE 97/SF43/5: AFM Western Australia. (Court transcripts, p. 11). Williams had arrived in Australia in January 1924, aged eleven. (Clyne transcripts, p. 1909) He had worked in the mines near Broad Arrow and ought to have been able to handle explosives, although he denied this. (*West Australian*, 16 June 1942, p. 4).
[102] A467: BUNDLE 97/SF43/4: Australia First Movement. Part II (Exhibit DD).
[103] A467: BUNDLE 97/SF43/3: Australia First Movement Part I.
[104] The Richards Report; A467: BUNDLE 97/SF43/5: AFM, Western Australia. Court (pp. 11-17, 26) Bullock allegedly told Thomas that it would be 'necessary to have "Blood Purges" the same as Adolf Hitler found it necessary'. (C421: 8: Miscellaneous papers on AFM. Thomas's statement of 24 May 1944, p. 1. See Chapter 11 for an explanation.)
[105] A467: BUNDLE 97/SF43/5: AFM Western Australia. Court. (p. 19).
[106] D1901: Q1004: E. C. Quicke; A373: 3750: Australia First Movement. It is not clear whether this letter was from Stephensen or from Sheila Rice.
[107] A467: BUNDLE 97/SF43/5: AFM Western Australia. Court; A8911: 136: Australia First Movement—WA, Vol. 1. Quicke had recently resigned from the Home Guard.
[108] A467: BUNDLE 97/SF43/3: Australia First Movement Part I, pp. 108-113. With minor variations, this account was supported by Reginald Lewis Kempe, Chief Inspector, Yorkshire Fire Insurance; Charlotte Isobel Hickey, hostel proprietress, Waroona; and Edward Rawlinson Fletcher, AMP inspector of Nedlands. There was no American carrier in the Indian Ocean. On 7 January, Bullock had written to Krakouer, 'You will all be caught in a deathtrap raid on the coast at any moment. Australia and Australians must now be educated by Bombs and Bayonets.'
[109] *West Australian*, 12 June 1942, p. 3.
[110] A467: BUNDLE 97/SF43/3: Australia First Movement Part I (The Richards Report).
[111] A8911: 136: Australia First Movement - WA, Vol. 1.
[112] A4671: BUNDLE 97/SF43/3: Australia First Movement Part I. (She had mistakenly dated the letter 7 March.)
[113] A8911: 141: "Australia First" Movement—Evidence tendered at Court Proceedings. It was not illegal to listen to enemy radio stations, but making or possessing notes or communicating information concerning military matters was an offence under National Security (General) Regulation 17. .
[114] A467: BUNDLE 97/SF43/3: Australia First Movement Part I.
[115] The Richards Report. He was wrong; it did not meet the legal requirements for a treason charge.

[116] A8911: 136: Australia First Movement, Western Australia, Volume 1; *West Australian*, 19 June 1942, p. 5.
[117] Empty envelopes and blank paper are in A8911: 139. Australia First Movement, Court Exhibits.
[118] Clyne transcripts, p. 1914.
[119] The Richards Report.
[120] The Richards Report. Much of this information concerned solely the incidents at Waroona on 4 March.
[121] A8911: 136: Australia First Movement - WA,Vol. 1; A467: BUNDLE 97/SF43/3: Australia First Movement Part I.
[122] A467: BUNDLE 97/SF43/3: Australia First Movement Part I.
[123] A467: BUNDLE 97/SF43/3: Australia First Movement Part I.
[124] A467: BUNDLE 97/SF43/4: Australia First Movement. Part II.
[125] C421: 8: Miscellaneous papers on AFM. She included Bullock in her condemnation.
[126] A8911: 136: Australia First Movement—WA, Vol. 1; C421: 8: Miscellaneous papers on AFM.
[127] C421: 8: Miscellaneous papers on AFM.
[128] Tom O'Loughlin died on 12 September 1944, aged 80.
[129] Barry became a KC in 1942, Justice of the Supreme Court in 1947, and was knighted in 1960; Smith became a KC in 1946, and a Judge of the Supreme Court in 1950.
[130] A467: BUNDLE 97/SF43/3: Australia First Movement Part I.
[131] A467: BUNDLE 97/SF43/3: Australia First Movement Part I.
[132] A8911: 136: Australia First Movement—WA, Vol. 1.
[133] A467: BUNDLE 97/SF43/5: AFM Western Australia. Court.
[134] A467: BUNDLE 97/SF43/5: AFM Western Australia. Court.
[135] Quoted in Muirden, *Puzzled Patriots*, pp. 88-9. For Hughes, the Jews were to blame.
[136] These points are from A467: BUNDLE 97/SF43/6: Australia First Movement Criminal Court Hearing.
[137] A467: BUNDLE 97/SF43/6: Australia First Movement.
[138] A8911: 141: "Australia First" Movement—Evidence tendered at Court Proceedings.
[139] *West Australian*, 5 June 1942, p. 4, and 17 June, p. 7.
[140] A467: BUNDLE 97/SF43/6: Australia First Movement.
[141] A467: BUNDLE 97/SF43/6: Australia First Movement.
[142] Muirden, *Puzzled Patriots*, p. 91.
[143] A8911: 137: Australia First Movement—WA, Vol. 2.
[144] A467: BUNDLE 97/SF43/6: Australia First Movement.
[145] A8911: 136: Australia First Movement - WA, Vol. 1; A467: BUNDLE SF43/6: Australia First Movement.
[146] Clyne transcripts, p. 1792. There was a transcript of the May hearing, but Clyne apparently did not ask for this. It is in A467: BUNDLE 97/SF43/5: Australia First, Western Australia.
[147] *West Australian*, 18 February 1936, p. 18.
[148] *Behn v R*, 1936, Vol. 38, *Western Australian Law Reports*, pp. 94–97. This point

is covered further in D. Brown, *Criminal Law; Western Australia*, Chapter LVII: Conspiracy. Section 558.35. *R v Darby* (1982). Hughes should have known this.
[149] A373: 3750: Australia First Movement.

Chapter 9

[1] Clyne transcripts, p. 905.
[2] Richard Hall, *The Secret State*, p. 33, claims that agents' reports '*agreed* in describing the organisation as harmless'. That was not the case.
[3] In Victoria, an MI officer had deliberately betrayed an undercover Naval Intelligence agent to a suspect who reported him to the Japanese.
[4] C421: 55: Australia First Movement; A8911: 130: Australia First Movement; C421: 30: Valentine Crowley and AFM.
[5] Clyne transcripts, p. 522. Subsequent evidence by Robbins, then an Assistant Station Master, is in the Clyne transcripts, pp. 491–93.
[6] A6119: 1194: McKeand William Alexander aka Mortimer Alexander.
[7] The Japanese had filed Mortimer's correspondence in a file called 'Letters from Eccentric Persons'. They are mentioned in MP742/1: 255/11/69: Alexander Mortimer, and in A981: DEF 364: William Alexander McKeand (Sinclair to External Affairs, 15 October 1941) Bruce Muirden, *Puzzled Patriots* (Carlton, Vic.: MUP, 1968) p. 127, refers to him as Mortimer Alexander.
[8] MP742/1: 255/11/69: Alexander Mortimer.
[9] Clyne transcripts, p. 665.
[10] Unless otherwise stated, material on Mortimer is from A6119: 1194: McKeand William Alexander aka Mortimer Alexander. Another alias used by Mortimer on his leaflets was 'Selby Price'. MP742/1: 255/11/69: Alexander Mortimer.
[11] An arrival date of 1924 is given in MP742/1: 255/11/69: Alexander Mortimer.
[12] Mortimer-McKeand did not write for the *Publicist* unless he used an alias.
[13] D1915: SA19631: Die Bruecke.
[14] MP742/1: 255/11/69: Alexander Mortimer.
[15] MP742/1: 255/11/69: Alexander Mortimer.
[16] Clyne transcripts, p. 225.
[17] Stephensen papers, Mitchell Library, Box 45.
[18] A472: W5932: Thomas P. Graham. One pamphlet was sent to A. R. Mills in January 1942, as coming from G. A. Charles & Co. D1901: M81; MILLS, Alexander Rudd - Internment.
[19] *Sydney Morning Herald*, 10 February 1942, p. 5.
[20] Unless otherwise stated, material is from ST1233/1: N38640: T. Potts Graham. Born in 1906, Graham arrived in Australia in 1936; like Mortimer, he came from Newcastle on Tyne.
[21] Clyne transcripts, p. 1320.
[22] An elusive 'T. Brown', convicted on 26 February 1942, was mentioned at the Clyne Inquiry (p. 165) as a member of the AFM. Graham used this alias.
[23] Unless otherwise stated, material on Arnold is from C421: 1: Arnold, Edwin—correspondence concerning the Australia First Inquiry. (Henceforth: Edwin Arnold and AFM.) (Arnold to Prentice, 22 February 1942)

[24] Arnold did not invent Ariosophy. For the origin and development of Ariosophy and its links with Theosophy, the occult, the Atlantis myth and fascism, see Nicholas Goodrick-Clarke, *The Occult Roots of Nazism*.
[25] See *New York Times* Index under Un-American Activities, or War - Armaments.
[26] The Japanese landed at Rabaul on 23 January; Singapore fell on 15 February; Darwin was bombed on 19 February; the Japanese invaded Portuguese Timor on 20 February and landed in New Guinea on 7 March; Java capitulated on 8 March.
[27] BP242/1: Q34603: Styles, John Thomas.
[28] Clyne transcripts, p. 331.
[29] *Fifty Points for Australia First*, p. 19.
[30] *Publicist*, 1 June 1939, pp. 15–16.
[31] C421: 49: Australia First Movement. For accounts of the arrests and early internments, see Craig Munro, *Wild Man of Letters*, Chapter 13, Behind Barbed Wire; Muirden, *Puzzled Patriots*, Chapter 9, Round-Up.
[32] Clyne transcripts, p. 1165.
[33] A8911: 136: Australia First Movement - WA, Vol. 1.
[34] ST1233/1: N38640: T. Potts Graham. Kay Saunders, in 'A Difficult Reconciliation', p. 126, in *Alien Justice*, mentions Charles Willyan and claims he was interned because of his support for the AFM. Willyan was not connected with the AFM before his internment. He contacted Stephensen *after* the war in connection with publishing his complaints about his internment. (A367: C69182: Charles Edward Willyan) His self-published book, *We of the White Race*, is a nasty piece of racism.
[35] Hooper and V. Crowley had provided finance for *Jindyworobak*, but they did not seek editorial influence. (Bruce Muirden, *Puzzled Patriots*, p. 51) Mudie had enlisted on 12 February 1942 (S47618).
[36] Clyne transcripts, p. 2222. At the Speakers' Class on the evening of 10 March, Phyllis Walton gave news of the arrests and Lang resigned from the AFM next morning. (C421: 50: Australia First Movement; Muirden, *Puzzled Patriots*, p. 113-14). As 'Public Officer' for Dychem (Australian branch of IG Farben), Malcolm Carlyle Smith was associated with prominent Nazis. (SP822/57: Whole of series: Minutes of director's meeting of the Dychem Trading Company Pty Ltd).
[37] Clyne transcripts, p. 761. Bockmaster was AFM member No. 31. He appears in most documents as 'Buckmaster'.
[38] A373: 3750: Australia First Movement.
[39] Clyne transcripts, p. 926; Muirden, *Puzzled Patriots*, p. 98.
[40] Lockyer Papers: Papers relating to P. R. Stephensen, UQFL247/H/Folder 4.
[41] Muirden, *Puzzled Patriots*, p. 183. Was Smith an undercover agent, and were his friends his controllers?
[42] C421: 30: Valentine Crowley and AFM.
[43] Clyne transcripts, p. 1122, Major Beauchamp Tyrrell.
[44] Stephensen was very deaf and tended to claim that what he had not heard had not been said.
[45] A367: C18000/737: Giles Walter Frederick Tinker; C421: 55: Australia First Movement.
[46] A373: 3750: Australia First Movement. The time span of this correspondence is not recorded; some could have been many years earlier.

[47] C421: 30: Valentine Crowley and AFM.
[48] C421: 55: Australia First Movement. (Kirtley to Stephensen, 8 December 1941) According to V. Crowley's diary (C421: 49), Kirtley while in internment became associated with John Sleeman, who had been one of J. T. Lang's speech-writers and a close friend of Lang's colleague, Eddie Ward. Another Lang supporter, Jack Beasley, was a friend of Hooper, Crowley and Bath. Sleeman's brother was Speaker of the Legislative Assembly in Western Australia.
[49] Clyne transcripts, p. 1469.
[50] C421: 8: Miscellaneous papers on AFM; and C421: 50: Australia First Movement.
[51] D1901: K680: John Thomas Kirtley.
[52] C421: 30: Valentine Crowley and AFM.
[53] C421: 50: Australia First Movement; Clyne transcripts, p. 1471.
[54] Lockyer Papers, 247/B/Folder 7. (Miles to Kirtley, 17 January 1939)
[55] C421: 30: Valentine Crowley and AFM; C421: 50: Australia First Movement.
[56] Clyne transcripts, p. 1330.
[57] Clyne transcripts, p. 1338. This was a police claim, and they did not have the same powers as MI.
[58] *Publicist*, 1 September 1939, Watts, 'Collapse is Imminent! A Premonition', pp. 4–9.
[59] C421: 50: Australia First Movement.
[60] Clyne Report. p. 17.
[61] C421: 6: [Miscellaneous papers re the Australia First Movement] (P. R. Stephensen to E. D. Stephensen, 21 November 1939).
[62] C421: 50: Australia First Movement. (Downe to Evatt, 15 September 1942).
[63] Clyne transcripts, pp. 1165–1188, Downe's testimony; A373: 4122: Clive Kirkwood Downe.
[64] C421: 50: Australia First Movement; Clyne transcripts, p. 1236; author's emphasis. Muirden, *Puzzled Patriots*, pp. 157–59.
[65] Muirden, *Puzzled Patriots*, p. 116, 118.
[66] Holsworthy was within Liverpool Military Reserve, and both Moorebank and Holsworthy were in the Local Government area of Liverpool. It is puzzling that eminent academics, responsible journalists, Hansard and even officers who lived in Holsworthy Barracks, often write 'Holdsworthy'. Any relevant road map, street directory, telephone directory or postcode book shows the correct spelling.
[67] Richard Griffiths, *Fellow Travellers of the Right*, p. 370. In May 1939, Captain Archibald Ramsay, MP, founded the anti-Semitic Right Club, of which William Joyce (Lord Haw-Haw) and Anna Wolkoff (convicted of espionage in 1940) were members.
[68] A373: 3750: Australia First Movement. AMF Report, 25 May 1942.
[69] A373: 3750: Australia First Movement. AMF Report, 25 May 1942.
[70] A367: C64736: Thomas Walsh. Adela Constantia Mary Walsh nee Pankhurst. There is nothing to indicate the identity of this informant, not even gender.
[71] A367: C64736: Thomas Walsh. Adela Constantia Mary Walsh nee Pankhurst.
[72] A367: C64736: Thomas Walsh, Adela Constantia Mary Walsh nee Pankhurst.
[73] A367: C18000/719: Objection No. 118. Adela Constantia Mary Walsh. The admission is in ST1233/1: N38433: Mrs Adela Pankhurst Walsh.
[74] A367: C64736: Thomas Walsh. Adela Constantia Mary Walsh nee Pankhurst.

Several writers have maintained that Tom Walsh was interned, including Rupert Lockwood, *War on the Waterfront*, p. 75.
[75] ST1233/1: N38433: Mrs Adela Pankhurst Walsh.
[76] A367: C18000/719: Objection No. 118. Adela Constantia Mary Walsh. They were named as Stan Moran, John Bramwell 'Red' Miles and Lance Sharkey. In 1948, Sharkey was sentenced to three years' imprisonment for sedition. [David McKnight, *Australia's Spies and their Secrets*, p. 113].
[77] A367: C64736: Thomas Walsh. Adela Constantia Mary Walsh nee Pankhurst.
[78] A8911: 130: Australia First Movement. (Henceforth: Hattam Report).
[79] A467: BUNDLE 97/SF43/8: Australia First Movement.
[80] Hattam Report.
[81] *CPD*, Vol. 171: Brennan, 27 March 1942, p. 523.
[82] D1901: M81: MILLS, Alexander Rudd (Annexure 15).
[83] D1901: M81: MILLS, Alexander Rudd.
[84] C421: 11: A. R. Mills .
[85] Hattam Report.
[86] Hattam Report.
[87] Hattam Report.
[88] C421: 50: Australia First Movement. This must have been a copy of a letter he had written to Mudie between July and October 1941.
[89] Louis Friedrich Wurm, from Dortmund, arrived in Adelaide in 1854 in *Irene*.
[90] Muirden, *Puzzled Patriots*, p. 107. The date of this letter is not given, but it appears to have been written after the Clyne Inquiry.
[91] A373: 3750: Australia First Movement .
[92] A373: 3750: Australia First Movement. This was in Mudie's favour, for it was Adela and Stephensen who were supporting Japanese interests most strongly. He was still in Sydney at this time.
[93] Clyne transcripts, p. 1651.
[94] A373: 3750: Australia First Movement .
[95] C421: 15: [Miscellaneous papers re Australia First Movement].
[96] A373: 3750: Australia First Movement.
[97] A373: 3750: Australia First Movement.
[98] *CPD*, Vol. 171: Blackburn, 25 March 1942, p. 417-18. Forde might not have made this damaging statement if Blackburn had not asked his well-intentioned question.
[99] *CPD*, Vol. 171: Forde, 26 March 1942, p. 462. Emphasis has been added.
[100] AWM68: 3DRL 3670/3: Hasluck Collection. Eric Stephensen wrote in 1970 that he believed that General MacArthur was in the House at the time of Forde's speech, and it was made to impress him. Although he was in Canberra, MacArthur was not present during this speech. He was welcomed to the floor of the House at 8.15 p.m., but Forde made his speech between 2.30 and 3.00. (Fotheringham Papers, UQFL46/3/14b: Report, 1970, p. 19, Box 1; *CPD*, Vol. 170: pp. 462 and 490).
[101] *CPD*, Vol. 171: Fadden, 27 March 1942, pp. 515-16. He was ignorant of the law regarding treason.
[102] *CPD*, Vol. 171: Curtin, 27 March 1942, p. 520. Curtin had been a friend of the Walshes, knew Cookes and Miles, and was an enemy of Bullock and 'Diver' Hughes.

[103] *CPD*, Vol. 171: Hughes, 27 March 1942, p. 522.
[104] *CPD*, Vol. 171: Hughes, 27 March 1942, p. 522.
[105] AWM68: 3DRL 3670/3: Hasluck Collection.
[106] Richards Report.
[107] Richards Report.
[108] A8911: 136: Australia First Movement—WA, Vol. 1.
[109] *Tribune*, 29 April 1942, p. 2. Kirtley had hardly ever been at the Yabber Club.
[110] *Tribune*, 29 April 1942., p. 3.
[111] A11022: 12: Copy of CRS A2606 Exhibits H and J. 1954. (Formerly part of A6202: Royal Commission on Espionage Exhibits, 1954) Communist fellow-travellers have claimed that Document "J" was forged to incriminate Lockwood; Lockwood had abused their good faith, and he admitted before he died that he had indeed written the document and had lied about it.
[112] Clyne transcripts, pp. 459-60, 28 September 1944, in Melbourne.
[113] Desmond Ball and David Horner, *Breaking the Codes*, pp. 212, 241–44, 332–36.
[114] Clyne transcripts, p. 459.
[115] *CPD*, Vol. 171: Beasley, 25 March 1942, p. 429.
[116] A5954: The Shedden Collection: 808/1: War Cabinet Minutes. 12 March 1942: 'Minute (1990)(iii) The Minister for Supply and Development to be Acting Attorney-General. (iv) The Security Service of the Attorney-General's Department to be administered by the Minister for the Army.' This was repeated in A5954: 813/2: Advisory War Council Minutes. 18 March 1942: Minute (835).
[117] *CPD*, Vol. 171: Forde, 30 April 1942, p. 702.
[118] *CPD*, Vol. 171: Forde, 20 May 1942, p. 1395.
[119] *CPD*, Vol. 171: Beasley, 27 May 1942, p. 1565.
[120] Robert Skidelsky: *Oswald Mosley*, p. 452.

Chapter 10

[1] Clyne transcripts, p. 100.
[2] C421: 49: Australia First Movement.
[3] A373: 3750: Australia First Movement (Fewtrell to Army HQ, 11 April 1942). This rather points to Malcolm Smith as an informant.
[4] A373: 3750: Australia First Movement.
[5] MP508/1: 175/791/1591: [Australia First Movement]. Emphasis added.
[6] MP508/1: 175/791/1591: [Australia First Movement].
[7] MP508/1: 175/791/1591: [Australia First Movement].
[8] A373: 3750: Australia First Movement.
[9] *CPD*, Vol. 171: Forde, 2 June 1942, p. 1828.
[10] Bruce Muirden, *Puzzled Patriots*, p. 112; *CPD*, Vol. 171: Forde, 2 June 1942, p. 1828.
[11] *CPD*, Vol. 171: Hughes, 20 May 1942, p. 1396.
[12] ST1233/1: N38433: Mrs Adela Pankhurst Walsh.
[13] Muirden, *Puzzled Patriots*, p. 123.
[14] A8911: 129: Australia First Movement, 1918-1942.
[15] C421: 49: Australia First Movement (Entry, 9 July 1942).

[16] C421: 49: Australia First Movement, (Entry, 28 June 1942).
[17] Fotheringham Papers, UQFL46, Box 3, file 14b. Sleeman was lying again.
[18] *CPD*, Vol. 191: Calwell, 26 March 1947, p. 1184. Some of Sleeman's activities are in A367: C68800: J. H. C. Sleeman. Payments to Sleeman are in C447: 7: Documents from Japanese Consular Files. Stephensen was not in Australia in 1928.
[19] C421: 49: Australia First Movement (Entry, 13 July 1942).
[20] C421: 49: Australia First Movement. (Entries, various dates) Other references are scattered through *CPD* (Hansard), 1942- 46.
[21] C421: 49: Australia First Movement.
[22] C421: 49: Australia First Movement. (Entry, 4 July 1942).
[23] A8911: 130: Australia First Movement.
[24] A373: 4121: Gordon Thomas Rice.
[25] *CPD*, Vol. 172: Blackburn, 2 September 1942, p. 48.
[26] A8911: 130: Australia First Movement.
[27] C421: 49: Australia First Movement (Entry, 7 July 1942).
[28] C421: 49: Australia First Movement (Entry, 7 July 1942).
[29] A373: 4123: Edward Masey. Repeated in A373: 4121: Gordon Thomas Rice.
[30] C421: 49: Australia First Movement Appeal.
[31] Fotheringham Papers, UQFL46/3: Box 1: 14b. (Eric Stephensen to Fotheringham, about 1970, p. 20).
[32] Muirden, *Puzzled Patriots*, p. 120.
[33] MP508/1: 175/701/1662: Statement by the Attorney-General. Responsibility was transferred on 12 August 1942. [MP729/6: 63/401/658: PR Stephensen (Downing to Stephensen, 7 July 1943.)] A letter from MI to Security, 11 July 1942, indicates that files in WA had already been transferred. As Deputy Prime Minister, Forde was senior to Evatt in Cabinet ranking.
[34] *CPD*, Vol. 172: Calwell, Cameron, 2 September 1942, pp. 42–43. Statements by both Calwell and Cameron were not all strictly accurate.
[35] *CPD*, Vol. 172: Harrison, 2 September 1942, p. 45. In April 1940, he had called for action against the AFM; for Party political reasons, he changed his stance by 1942, and changed it again by 1946.
[36] *CPD*, Vol. 172: Brennan, 2 September 1942, p. 46.
[37] *CPD*, Vol. 172: Blackburn, 2 September 1942, p. 49. This was untrue.
[38] *CPD*, Vol. 172: Evatt, 2 September 1942, p. 51.
[39] *CPD*, Vol. 172: Cameron, 2 September 1942, p. 52. He was referring to Hooper.
[40] *CPD*, Vol. 172: Corser, 2 September 1942, p. 53.
[41] *CPD*, Vol. 172: Rankin, 2 September 1942, p. 54.
[42] MP508/1: 175/701/1662: Statement by the Attorney General.
[43] MP508/1: 175/701/1662: Statement by the Attorney General; *CPD*, Vol. 172: Evatt, 10 September 1942, pp. 154-57.
[44] *CPD*, Vol. 172: Evatt, 10 September 1942, p. 155.
[45] *CPD*, Vol. 172: Evatt, 10 September 1942, pp. 156–57. Evatt's figures; they do not match the facts.
[46] Clyne transcripts, pp. 1309, 44.
[47] A373: 4120: Edwin Arnold & Reference to others.
[48] A373: 4120: Edwin Arnold.

[49] A373: 3921: Walter David Cookes; Muirden, *Puzzled Patriots*, p. 107.
[50] A373: 3921: Walter David Cookes.
[51] D1901: M81: MILLS, Alexander Rudd. C421: 11: A. R. Mills. A367: C65283: BUTTNER Wanda and Dr Friedrich Albert.
[52] 'Mortimer' indicated that he would resume publication of his pamphlets if he was released, so he was interned as soon as he left prison on 8 August.
[53] According to Muirden, *Puzzled Patriots*, pp. 126-128, this story was publicised in the *Tribune*. Having been a follower of Gregor Strasser, murdered in June 1934, Graf loathed Hitler; see C329: 401: Alex Graf.
[54] Klemperer, part Jewish, was the grandson of the founder of the Dresdner Bank.
[55] MP529/3: Peter Ralph von Klemperer; C421: 55: Australia First Movement.
[56] A8911: 136: Australia First Movement - WA, Vol. 1. This letter appears in a file relating to Bullock, as it was sent to WA, but it could not have referred to him, as he was still in prison in Western Australia.
[57] This did not refer to Cahill and Kirtley, but to some South Australian internees.
[58] C421: 30: Valentine Crowley and AFM.
[59] Clyne transcripts, pp. 661-62.
[60] D1915: SA18976: C. M. Thiele. One arrest warrant said that the subject showed 'a degree of disloyalty which has shocked and disgusted us' and he would be 'a menace even in an Internment Camp'.
[61] C421: 55: Australia First Movement. (Report of 16 October 1942).
[62] C421: 55: Australia First Movement.
[63] Muirden: *Puzzled Patriots*, p. 127.
[64] MP742/1: 255/11/69: Alexander Mortimer; D1901: M2469: Alexander Mortimer.
[65] C421: 50: Australia First Movement. (Cahill to Collins, 24 February 1944).
[66] C421: 50: Australia First Movement. (Cahill to Collins, 7 March 1944).
[67] ST1233/1: N38433: Mrs Adela Pankhurst Walsh.
[68] ST1233/1: N38433: Mrs Adela Pankhurst Walsh.
[69] A367: C64736: Thomas Walsh. Adela Constantia Mary Walsh nee Pankhurst.
[70] ST1233/1: N38433: Mrs Adela Pankhurst Walsh.
[71] ST1233/1: N38433: Mrs Adela Pankhurst Walsh. Letters in this file show that military and Security authorities resented Evatt's actions in connection with releasing Adela Walsh.
[72] A367: C64736: Thomas Walsh. Adela Constantia Mary Walsh nee Pankhurst.
[73] A367: C77862: Richard Daniel COLLINS. A copy of the letter, but not of the associated investigation, is in A467: BUNDLE 97/SF43/8. However, Collins would not have been beheaded or hanged as a result of the investigation.
[74] A367: C77862: Richard Daniel COLLINS.
[75] A367: C77862: Richard Daniel COLLINS.
[76] Clyne transcripts, pp. 1330, 1394, 1586.
[77] *CPD*, Vol. 186: Page, 14 March 1946, p. 329.
[78] C421: 50: Australia First Movement.

Chapter 11

[1] *CPD*, Vol. 178: Evatt, 30 & 31 March 1944, pp. 2454–55.

[2] *CPD*, Vol. 178: Menzies, p. 2455. The solicitor was Mills.
[3] *CPD*, Vol. 178: Menzies, p. 2456.
[4] *CPD*, Vol. 178: Harrison, p. 2462.
[5] *CPD*, Vol. 178: Abbott, p. 2472.
[6] *CPD*, Vol. 178: Ward, pp. 2475–2477.
[7] Ward had been manipulated by John Sleeman, a paid Japanese agent.
[8] *Sydney Morning Herald*, 3 May 1944, p. 4; AWM68: 3DRL 3670/3: Hasluck Collection.
[9] A373: 4120: Edwin Arnold. (Arnold to Evatt, 30 April 1944; DD of S letter, 11 May 1944). By then, MI had obtained secret access to the records of the German Consulate-General.
[10] Clyne Report, p. 3.
[11] Keith Bath, *Injustice Within the Law*.
[12] A467: 96/SF43/1 PART 1: Transcript of an Inquiry into the "Australia First Movement" Group.
[13] A367: C69207: BULLOCK. Lawrence Frederick.
[14] C418: BOX 8: Complete transcripts of Inquiry "Australia First" Movement Group S11-S12.
[15] Clyne transcripts, p. 885. Maund was acting for Clarence Crowley.
[16] Clyne Inquiry, pp. 911–12, 915.
[17] Clyne Report, p. 7. Blood, a solicitor of the Supreme Court of New South Wales, was then with the ISGS, attached to Police HQ, Sydney; p. 922.) Blood was in charge of collecting information on the AFM, (p. 891) and he claimed he had 'a man' within the Movement; Powell spoke of 'agents' in the plural. (pp. 1031, 305)
[18] A367: 66808: Karl G. G. KRAWINKEL.
[19] D1915: SA19691: Walter Ladendorff.
[20] Clyne transcripts, p. 626. Her name was suppressed at the time.
[21] Clyne transcripts, pp. 1675, 1680. He was certainly not the only undercover agent in the picture.
[22] P. R. Stephensen, *Foundations of Culture in Australia*, p. 68.
[23] This was in a report that Agent 222 denied having written.
[24] Clyne transcripts, p. 519.
[25] *CPD*, Vol. 179: Harrison, 19 July 1944, p. 224; Vol. 186: Harrison, 13 March 1946, p. 234.
[26] This might have been Captain Fritz Wiedemann, whom Bullock mentioned to F. J. Thomas.
[27] Clyne transcripts, p. 2514.
[28] *CPD*, Vol. 179: Evatt, 18 July 1944, p. 98; Evatt, 19 July 1944, pp. 195–196.
[29] *CPD*, Vol. 186, Harrison, 13 March 1946, pp. 220–21. Salier was in poor health, but he was only 61.
[30] Horace Ratliff and Max Thomas had been convicted and imprisoned in December 1940 on a charge of attempting to 'influence public opinion in a manner likely to be prejudicial to the efficient prosecution of the war'; soon after their release from prison they were interned. This caused a wave of strikes instigated by communist-controlled unions and influenced the change of Government in October 1941. Evatt released them when he became Attorney-General. See Paul

Hasluck, *The Government and the People,* Vol. I, Appendix 8.
[31] *CPD*, Vol. 179: Evatt, 14 July 1944, p. 226.
[32] Evatt claimed that when he assumed responsibility for internments there were 6,174 internees, and by July 1944 there were only 1,186. (*CPD*, Vol. 179, p. 227) In March 1946, he said he reduced the number from 7,700 to between 600 and 700. (Vol. 186, p. 386). In April 1948, he said: from 8,000 to 800. (Vol. 197, p. 1820).
[33] *CPD*, Vol. 181: Beasley, 4 May 1945, p. 1386.
[34] *CPD*, Vol. 184: Beasley, 24 July 1945, p. 4426, and Evatt, 31 July 1945, p. 4734.
[35] It would have been physically impossible for Forde to examine hundreds of internment cases in March 1942 personally.
[36] Clyne Report, pp. 19–20.
[37] On his release, Matthews found that the bank had taken over his vineyard and many of his vines had been rooted out. *Smith's Weekly*, 22 September 1945, p. 1.
[38] Clyne Report, p. 20.
[39] *CPD*, Vol. 184: Beasley, 12 September 1945, p. 5289.
[40] *CPD*, Vol. 185: Forde, 5 October 1945, pp. 6621, 6641.
[41] *CPD*, Vol. 185: Forde, 5 October 1945, p. 6642.
[42] *CPD*, Vol. 185: Forde, 5 October 1945, p. 6642.
[43] Muirden, *Puzzled Patriots*, p. 165.
[44] Such files included Exhibit 21, relating to P. R. Stephensen; Exhibit 58, relating to the *Publicist*; and Exhibit 60, relating to the AFM as a whole.
[45] Bruce Muirden, *Puzzled Patriots*, p. 145.
[46] Skerst had been a member of the Russian Diplomatic Corps and representative in Australia of Grand Duke Kyril, Legitimist Pretender to the Russian throne after the murder of Tsar Nicholas.
[47] Clyne transcripts, p. 1846. Raymond's name is given variously as Alan, Allan and Allen.
[48] A8911: 137: Australia First Movement—WA, Vol. 2. A8911: 136: Australia First Movement —WA, Vol. 1 contains at pp. 180–81 an undated report on Raymond; it is filed between items dated 10 June and 19 June 1942.
[49] A8911: 137: Australia First Movement—WA, Vol. 2.
[50] The original statements signed by Thomas are in C421: 8: Miscellaneous papers on AFM. The remark by Bullock is in the statement dated 24 May, pp. 1–2; Krakouer's is in that of 22 May, p. 3, and O'Loughlin's in 22 May, p. 4.
[51] A1838: 1542/64: Raymond, Alan W. There is a registration, early 1911, for Allan M. Johnson, son of James G. Johnson and Irene F. Richards. A postwar passport accepted that he had been born in Sydney on 26 November 1910. Irene Johnson had taken up with Henry Raymond, whom Alan Raymond might have thought was his father. Henry died on 23 December 1914, leaving his estate to his 'friend', Mary Johnson. (NSW Supreme Court. Probate Records: 4th Series, No. 67479.) They had been living in *Willoughby* Street, Naremburn. His funeral notice gives his wife as Irene Raymond, but there is no record of any such marriage.
[52] The main source of material on Raymond is A6126: 63: RAYMOND, Alan Willoughby, Vol. 2. Some is repeated in A8911: 136: Australia First Movement—WA, Vol. 1.
[53] A989: 43/235/4/8: Break away from Britain - Raymond.

[54] The source of the money that enabled him to do this is unknown.
[55] C421: 8: Miscellaneous papers on AFM. (Statement, 22 May, p. 4) Some time between June and December 1941, the O'Loughlins moved from 2 Gardner Street, Como (South Perth, corner of Labouchere Road) to 25 Merriwa Street, Nedlands. Bullock said that Vail was a student of Japanese affairs; he might have been Herbert Eugene Vail, an American-born mining engineer associated with Omori in the Yampi Sound scheme. He also owned Fairlawn racing stud at Herne Hill, but this Vail died in 1938.
[56] O'Loughlin wrote to Miles on 11 December 1939 that 'a Mr Bullock' had rung about two weeks earlier. A8911: 17: The Link.
[57] A8911: 17: The Link (Miles to O'Loughlin, 22 November 1939).
[58] Although some of the Thomas statement is suspect, he could not have invented the material. Subject to the limitations of his memory, much of it is probably true in essence, but it is strange that there is no documentary evidence of contact between Mills, Raymond and O'Loughlin, especially in the latter's voluminous correspondence.
[59] PP302/1: WA8: Japanese activities, 1918-1941; K1171: OMORI, M. says that Omori was first *registered* (as an alien) in Western Command on 5 January 1940, which is not the same thing.
[60] K1171: 1375: Veronica Margaret Connolly.
[61] A367: C69140: Allen, Veronica Margaret. This passport was refused; the Consul-General knew she could not be married to Omori, as he had a wife and children in Japan.
[62] C421: 8: Miscellaneous papers on AFM. (Statement, 22 May, p. 5).
[63] Despite a Security report that he was travelling in the South-West about December 1939, he arrived in Fremantle on 5 January 1940 from the Netherlands East Indies, aboard *Charon.* Connolly flew back.
[64] If Raymond met Omori, it might have been in Java. The extent to which Omori was engaged in espionage is unclear.
[65] The references from the Hong Kong firm appear to have been forged; as an employee, he had access to its stationery.
[66] The Japanese may have given him a free passage.
[67] A4144: 233/1946: Collaborators: Alan Raymond. The Japanese kept contact with Stephensen to a minimum; only Ken Cook and Adela Walsh were in close contact with both the Japanese and the AFM.
[68] A8911: 136: Australia First Movement—WA, Vol. 1; A6126: 63: RAYMOND, Alan Volume 2.
[69] A4144: 233/1946. Collaborators: Alan Raymond; A6126: 63: RAYMOND, Alan, Volume 2.
[70] A6126: 63: RAYMOND, Alan, Volume 2. His mother had followed him to China in November 1941.
[71] It was not entirely coincidental that these separate events occurred in the space of about a week; the timing was determined in both cases by the course of the war.
[72] MP1587: 176F: Navy Historical Section. Historical Records Files 1944 to 1975).
[73] A6126: 63: RAYMOND, Alan, Volume 2.
[74] Raymond's broadcasts for XMHA were monitored, recorded and transcribed, as

far as the generally poor reception allowed. A6126: 62: RAYMOND, Alan, Volume 1, contains transcripts. There are only occasional references to the content of McDonald's talks.
[75] SP1714/1: N38749: John Joseph Holland.
[76] SP1714/1: N38749: Holland. Very few letters from prisoners in Japanese hands were forwarded unless they contained some propaganda favourable to Japan.
[77] A989: 43/235/4/8: Break away from Britain - Raymond.
[78] A6126: 63: RAYMOND, Alan, Volume 2.
[79] Muirden, *Puzzled Patriots*, p. 168.
[80] *CPD*, Vol. 186: Harrison, 13 March 1946, p. 226–27; Clyne Report: p. 7.
[81] *CPD*, Vol. 186: Harrison, 13 March 1946, p. 228.
[82] *CPD*, Vol. 186: Harrison, 13 March 1946, p. 232.
[83] *CPD*, Vol. 186: Harrison, 13 March 1946, p. 230.
[84] *CPD*, Vol. 186: Harrison, 13 March 1946, pp. 232–33.
[85] Adair Macalister Blain, Independent Member for the Northern Territory.
[86] *CPD*, Vol. 186: Haylen, 14 March 1946, pp. 333.
[87] *CPD*, Vol. 193: Blain, 9 October 1947, p. 604.
[88] *CPD*, Vol. 186: Forde, 13 March 1946, p. 234.
[89] *CPD*, Vol. 186: Menzies, 14 March 1946, p. 318.
[90] *CPD*, Vol. 186: Ward, 14 March 1946, p. 321–26.
[91] *CPD*, Vol. 186: Page, Ward, 14 March 1946, p. 326–31. It was ridiculous to link Sergeant Richards, a relentless pursuer of communists, with a communist plot.
[92] *CPD*, Vol. 186: Haylen, 14 March 1946, p. 331–33. For Harrison's inconsistency, compare with his parliamentary question of 17 April 1940, when he called the *Publicist* 'seditious and disloyal'. Chapter 6, Note 38.
[93] *CPD*, Vol. 186: Cameron, 14 March 1946, p. 334–36.
[94] *CPD*, Vol. 186: Cameron, 14 March 1946, p. 336. See also Abbott, p. 343.
[95] *CPD*, Vol. 186: Evatt, 14 March 1946, p. 385–86. Evatt returned from abroad about 21 June.

Chapter 12

[1] *Publicist*, 1 October 1940, Bunyip Critic, pp. 3-7.
[2] Bruce Muirden, *Puzzled Patriots*, p. 129.
[3] P. R. Stephensen Papers, UQFL55/11. (Walter Stone Donation) Calwell became leader of the Labor Party in 1960 after Evatt resigned to become Chief Justice of the NSW Supreme Court. Stephensen made a virtue of not demanding compensation only after his appeal to the Governor-General had been rejected. (Senator Spicer to Stephensen, 6 October 1953, quoted in Stephensen to Mills, 14 October 1953, in UQFL55/8/8).
[4] Craig Munro, *Wild Man of Letters*, p. 266.
[5] Munro, *Wild Man of Letters*, p. 268.
[6] For details of Stephensen's life postwar, see Munro, *Wild Man of Letters*.
[7] P. R. Stephensen Papers, UQFL55. (Various letters) After returning to Sydney, Stephensen kept writing for Frank Clune and under his own name, and he acted as a literary agent for other writers. Among the works he handled was a highly untruthful book, *I deserted Rommel*, by Gunther Bahnemann, written in prison

while he was serving a sentence for the alleged attempted murder of Terry Lewis. (Later Queensland Commissioner of Police, and imprisoned for corruption.)
[8] P. R. Stephensen Papers, ML MSS1284, Box Y2132. Clune to Stephensen, 16 December 1954, quoted in Munro, *Wild Man of Letters*, p. 255.
[9] P. R. Stephensen Papers, UQFL55/8/11 and 55/8/12. (Walter Stone donation) (Stephensen to Mills, 23 June 1954, 1 July 1954) Mills had contacted The Britons concerning publication of this book.
[10] AWM68: 3DRL 3670/3: Hasluck Collection.
[11] AWM27: 490/3: Correspondence between Sir George Knowles and Hooper, 1945-1946.
[12] Horace Ratliff and Max Thomas were communist pamphleteers, not saboteurs. The letter was written while the Petrov Royal Commission was in progress.
[13] AWM68: 3DRL 3670/3: Hasluck Collection. (Stephensen to Hasluck, 25 July 1954, p. 7).
[14] Volume II of *The Government and the People* did not appear until five years after Stephensen died.
[15] Munro, *Wild Man of Letters*, p. 265.
[16] P. R. Stephensen Papers, UQFL55/11. (Walter Stone Donation; account pasted in grey book).
[17] P. R. Stephensen Papers, UQFL55/11/79. (Winifred Stephensen to Walter and Jean Stone, 21 March 1966).
[18] ST1233/1: N38433: Mrs Adela Pankhurst Walsh.
[19] Verna Coleman, *Adela Pankhurst*, p. 169.
[20] Coleman, *Adela Pankhurst*, pp. 174-75.
[21] Sadie Herbert Collection UQFL 83, Box 33 (Herbert to Laurel Hall, 2 November 1972). For Herbert's ambiguous sexuality, see F. de Groen, *Xavier Herbert*, Index.
[22] For Herbert's time in the Northern Territory, 1927, see de Groen, *Xavier Herbert*, Chapter 6.
[23] De Groen, *Xavier Herbert*, pp. 118-21.
[24] Xavier Herbert, *Poor Fellow My Country*, Chapter 20, pp. 1027-1087.
[25] Clyne transcripts, pp. 1390-94; Muirden, *Puzzled Patriots*, p. 121.
[26] *CPD*, Vol. 179: Harrison, 19 July 1944, p. 224: On 14 March 1946, Page named the sum as £5,000. *CPD* Vol. 186: 14 March 1946, p. 329.
[27] Muirden, *Puzzled Patriots*, p. 121.
[28] Bath, *Injustice Within the Law.*
[29] *CPD*, Vol. 186: Fadden, 14 March 1946, p. 349.
[30] In equivalent 2004 values, that would have been close to $2,500,000.
[31] Bath, *Injustice Within the Law.*
[32] AWM68: 3DRL 3670/3: Hasluck Collection. Bath died about 1967.
[33] Clyne transcripts, p. 1191.
[34] Reg Bartram, letter, 25 March 1999.
[35] A472: W8518: AFM Objections.
[36] *CPD*, Vol. 201: Evatt and Lang, 22 February 1949, p. 516; Holloway, 3 March 1949, p. 1013; *Sydney Morning Herald*, 23 February 1949, p. 4.
[37] A11022: 12: [Copy of CRS A6206. Exhibits H and J] [Formerly part of A6026:

Royal Commission on Espionage Exhibits].
[38] A472: W8518: Stephensen, Downe, Hooper & Crowley, objection against DETENTION.
[39] *CPD*, Vol. 186: J. P. Abbott, 14 March 1946, p. 345.
[40] Muirden, *Puzzled Patriots*, p. 177; 'Some Reminiscences of P. R. Stephensen at East Warburton, Bethanga, Sandringham, Victoria, Period 1945-1956', by Eric Stephensen, in P. R. Stephensen Papers, UQFL55/3; NSW Supreme Court, Probate Index. Moir and Percy Stephensen also became friends, and Eric Stephensen joined the Bread and Cheese Club. (UQFL55/3, pp. 12, 30.).
[41] Reg Bartram, 10 May 1999.
[42] Muirden, *Puzzled Patriots*, p. 174; and see note above re Stephensen.
[43] *Age*, 8 September 1976, p. 8.
[44] A373: 4120: Edwin Arnold & Reference to others.
[45] A472: W8518: AFM Objections. Hattam Report, 15 August 1944.
[46] A367: C69193: William Bullock. ('Clem' to Watchtower Society, Strathfield, 11 April 1944.).
[47] A367: C73002: Krakouer, Nancy Rachel (Report by Captain Blackett, 5 March 1945).
[48] A367: C69207: BULLOCK, Lawrence Frederick.
[49] A367: C73002: Krakouer: Blackett Report.
[50] A367: C73002: Krakouer, Blackett Report.
[51] A367: C73002: Krakouer, Blackett Report.
[52] D1901: M2469: Alexander Mortimer.
[53] A472: W5932: Thomas P. Graham.
[54] Stephensen papers, UQFL 55/8/8 (Stephensen to Mills, 14 October 1953).
[55] David Harcourt, *Everybody wants to be Fuehrer*.
[56] Dr Drew Cottle, examined this topic in a Ph. D. thesis, The Brisbane Line: A Reappraisal, Chapter 2. Macquarie University, 1991.
[57] Stephensen's understanding of practical finance was minimal. Herbert has 'the young Economist' (Masey?) say, concerning 'the Bloke' (Stephensen), '[When] he's the Great Dictator, gnomes will mint money for him in the basement.' [Xavier Herbert, *Poor Fellow my Country*, p. 1032].

Index to Appendices

Appendix I

THE COMING LARGER MONTHLY. AUSTRALIA FIRST.

THE INDEPENDENT SYDNEY SECULARIST.

No. 12. JUNE, 1936. Price, 1d.

THE COMING LARGER MONTHLY.

The "Australia First" Group, which may develop into an "Australia First" League before Australia's sesqui-centenary on 26th January, 1938, expects to issue a larger monthly than this "Secularist" in July (next month), named the "Publicist", and to make it true to name in strict "Australia First" interests. Although it will be much larger than this "Secularist", the "Australia First" Group will use it all for their particular propaganda.

The "Secularist", however, will be maintained by the writer, who expects never to lose his belief that religion is the chief cause of human behaviour being as bad as it is. Religion appears to him to spring from or base on superstition, and to be maintained by ignorance on the one hand and by hypocrisy on the other.

The writer's plan for the "Secularist", after this month, is to make it more or less similar to the "Literary Guide", the "Freethinker" and the "Rationalist", all known to Australian Secularists, so far as space will permit.

The "Secularist" will be kept almost quite Australian articles by Australians and Australian secularist news.

No doubt many Rationalists (or Freethinkers, or Secularists) have been out of sympathy with this "Secularist" on its political side, because it has been advocating a distinctly pro-Australian policy for Australians—by its "Australia First" propaganda. (This world is a "queer" world, and Australia the not least queer part of it.)

On the other side, many who are favourable to "Australia First" in a secular sense, claim "Heaven First" in a religious or superstitious sense, and so many are hurt by the complete secularity of the "Secularist". So from next month the "Secularist" will be restricted to rationalist propaganda, and the "Publicist" to "Australia First" propaganda.

However, so far as political propaganda was possible through the "Secularist", this little paper, or large leaflet, has served its purpose better than was expected. We were pointed out the "badness" of the name for political purposes by many who are interested in the "Australia First" idea, which was not unreasonable in view of the relatively few Australians free from religious superstition; but it has been a real satisfaction to us that although many Secularists have been unsympathetic, even hostile, towards our particular politics, not one has objected to the use of the name "Secularist". This, we think, shows at least some strength among Secularists.

We could not, no matter how greatly we might have felt tempted, accept the advice to change the name to Sensualist or Sexualist!—we are not publishing the "Secularist" for money-making reasons, and so are not asking for advertisements, nor are we needful of a large circulation.

Next month, then, we shall render unto Secularists that which is secular, and unto Bone-o Publico that which is publicist.

A.K.

"THE PUBLICIST".

Now is the last opportunity I shall have of writing for the "Secularist". This is the twelfth issue, and the success of the leaflet, with its two particular propagandas, has been greater than expected.

Its small area was a serious limitation, and sometimes the secular propaganda was almost excluded. However, after this, the new editor will have all the space for secular propaganda—unless he is so kind as to give the "Publicist" a little free advertisement.

It is intended that the "Publicist" will confine itself directly and indirectly to the political propaganda now becoming widely known as "Australia First".

As that subject includes full empire and national and racial ranges it can be claimed as a universal provider of political issues, theories and philosophies, and it is intended to treat of all the chief points, with which Australia is particularly concerned, more or less fully. We shall aim to make the paper's circulation Empire-wide. We hope to smash many political, social and economic shibboleths—including, perhaps, some in the sciences and the arts.

We are convinced that Australia needs greatly to defend herself, and think that her best defence *may* be in strongest attack—we shall be guided empirically—her enemies will have a lot to say.

Mr. P. R. Stephensen will be our Chief Knight—Knight of the Inky Lance—and in him we have great confidence. His "Foundations of Culture" are our "Foundations of Existence", for the "Publicist" got its life from his book. Mr. Stephensen's tilting—or gassing—will be something new. He is a fighting man well worth watching in his verbal battles. We challenge, between us, all weights—we are an all-round fighting combination. All stars!—we shall make our opponents see.

Australia First? Of course! What Australian should place her second? Whom should he place first?

What are Australians waiting for? For the painter to break or be cut? Why wait till Britain calls, "The painter has broke, save yourselves!"?

Why should Australians rely on the British? Four times have Australians helped the British, and the British have helped Australians never! Australians should culti-

B1. The Ten-Point Policy of the *Publicist*, 1 July 1937, p. 20.

"THE PUBLICIST" ADVOCATES:

1. DEVELOPMENT OF AUSTRALIAN CULTURE
2. AUSTRALIAN SELF-DEPENDENCE
3. AUSTRALIAN SELF-DEFENCE
4. NATIONAL, NOT COLONIAL, IDEAS.
5. WORLD TRADE, NOT "EMPIRE TRADE"
6. FREE OCEANS, NOT DOMINATED OCEANS
7. A DISTINCTIVE AUSTRALIAN POLICY IN FOREIGN AFFAIRS
8. NO CONSCRIPTION FOR SERVICE ABROAD
9. A NEW AUSTRALIA *IN* AUSTRALIA
10. AUSTRALIA FOR THE AUSTRALIANS

B2. The Stationery of the Australia-First Movement with the logo designed by Eric Stephensen.

10 MAR 1942

A Non-Party, Non-Sectional Organisation, pledged to uphold Australia First

ROOM FORTY-FIVE, FOURTH FLOOR . 26 O'CONNELL STREET . SYDNEY
TELEPHONE B 3668 ● SUBSCRIPTION: TEN SHILLINGS PER YEAR

THE AUSTRALIA-FIRST MOVEMENT

CIRCULAR to MEMBERS of THE COMMONWEALTH and N.S.W. PARLIAMENTS

The Publicist

THE PAPER LOYAL TO AUSTRALIA FIRST

No. 48. SYDNEY 1st JUNE, 1940. MONTHLY, 6d.

PRINCIPAL CONTENTS

Principles, Not Planks

This 48th number of THE PUBLICIST completes its fourth year of publication. From its first number, of July, 1936, till now, its influence has been steadily increasing. From now on, because of Australians' growing realization that their community prospects are, *at best, not good*, THE PUBLICIST expects its influence to increase rapidly. THE PUBLICIST is as a forerunner showing the way that Australians should take.

When, in February, 1936, it was decided to issue THE PUBLICIST, in the then-coming July, it was realized by its intending publishers as very likely to be a more or less premature venture: it was soon found to be less premature than more.

Between that February and July — on the 20th of May, 1936 — our Commonwealth Government made its historic decision to deliberately limit trade between Australia and Japan, and the effects in Australia of that historic decision — particularly upon the wool-growers of Australia — was of help to THE PUBLICIST. Its view *was*, simply, that any trade restriction against Australia's chief primary product was certain to result more or less badly for Australians. Our view is that the decision was a very bad blunder, and that its inherent evil continues in operation against our Australian interests.

Were that the only bad blunder we Australians have made it might be easily retrieved, but our total of bad blunders is more than seven millions, and we are all stewing together in our own-made socio-political pot, unprincipled and unpolicied, nationally aimless — a stew of muttonheads.

So THE PUBLICIST last month offered its readers "50 Points of Policy for an 'Australia First' Party after the War", which we now reprint below as a preliminary set of principles, not planks, from which a progressive political policy for a nationalist party could be derived.

We are well aware, however, that our fellow-Australians are politically apathetic, and so are politically ignorant, and therefore need to be shaken or blasted out of their ridiculous complacency to make them seek political education for our community survival-needs. We are not now stewing for our own benefit but for the ultimate benefit of others.

Most Australians make the blunder of thinking they know enough for their own future needs, largely because most of them think that pensions are permanent and sure to grow greater as Australian progress proceeds. Of course our Kookaburras laugh: no humans are vainer or more ignorant than most Australians.

Australians think that the only true function of cleverness is to "have it both ways"; so they think themselves clever in thinking that a monarchical form of government is a democracy and that a democratic form of government is a monarchy; and that, therefore, they have both either way, which is the same as having either both ways; and that as such perfection has been reached it will be permanent, unless such perfection can be more perfect, in which case it will duly grow so. Most Australians are quite unconscious of illusion: we think them on the eve of disillusionment: hence these 50 Points are here reprinted.

1. For "Australia First"; against secondariness.
2. For Australian culture; against imitativeness.
3. For self-dependence; against colonial status.
4. For nationalism; against "inter-nationalism".
5. For equality and alliance; against imperial federation.
6. For national socialism; against international communism.
7. For forthright diplomacy; against "moralising".
8. For national self-protection; against pacifism.
9. For conscription for defence; against conscription for abroad.
10. For territorial integrity; against cession.
11. For autonomy in foreign affairs; against interference.
12. For autonomy in military affairs; against interference.
13. For peace in the Pacific; against war-seeking.
14. For higher birth-rate; against immigration.
15. For "White" Australia; against heterogeneity.
16. For Aryanism; against Semitism.
17. For government; against anarchy.
18. For monarchism; against republicanism.
19. For authority; against dictatorship.
20. For resolute government; against vacillation.
21. For statesmanship; against parliamentary careerism.
22. For leadership; against demagogocracy.
23. For personal responsibility; against government paternalism.
24. For long-range policy; against short-term expediency.
25. For political principle; against unpolicied opportunism.
26. For national unity; against sectional disunity.
27. For mutuality; against individualism.
28. For political partisanship; against class sectionalism.
29. For "Rightism"; against "Leftism".
30. For civil service; against bureaucracy.
31. For the right to vote; against compulsory polling.
32. For legitimate speech; against "free" speech.
33. For responsible journalism; against "freedom of the press".
34. For political education; against political apathy.
35. For women in the home; against women in industry.
36. For babies; against birth-restriction.
37. For Australian schooling; against imported pedagogy.
38. For discipline; against casualness.
39. For loyalty; against subversiveness.
40. For the police; against criminals.
41. For economy; against extravagance.
42. For saving; against waste.
43. For work; against doling.
44. For industrial development; against speculation.
45. For competition; against monopoly.
46. For private ownership; against government encroachment.
47. For conservative banking practice; against inflation.
48. For less taxation; against greater taxation.
49. For reduction of debt; against increase of debt.
50. For world trade; against restricted trade.

JOHN BENAUSTER.

THE AUSTRALIA-FIRST MOVEMENT

(Established 20th October, 1941)

ANNUAL SUBSCRIPTION, TEN SHILLINGS

EXECUTIVE COMMITTEE

P. R. Stephensen (Chairman), W. F. Tinker (Treasurer), L. K. Cahill and Adela Pankhurst Walsh (Organisers), Vera Parkinson, Marjorie Corby, Elaine Pope, G. T. Rice, Ian Mudie, Sheila Rice (Secretary).

PUBLIC MEETINGS

will be held in

THE AUSTRALIAN HALL,

(Ground Floor), 148 Elizabeth Street, Sydney,

EVERY WEDNESDAY, AT 8 P.M.,

From 5th November to 17th December, 1941.

Manifesto of the Australia-First Movement

1.—In view of the extreme gravity of the military situation abroad, and of the political situation at home, an AUSTRALIA-FIRST MOVEMENT has been founded in Sydney, to arouse public opinion to the need of protecting Australia's vital interests during the coming post-war period.

2.—Affirming loyalty to the King, and upholding established authority, law, and order, the Australia-First Movement calls upon all Australians to work for UNITY in "internal" policies, and for AUSTRALIAN INDEPENDENCE in "external" affairs.

3.—The Australia-First Movement is OPPOSED TO SECTIONAL POLITICAL PARTIES AND FACTIONS, and urges the subordination of sectional and factional interests to the welfare of Australia First.

4.—The Australia-First Movement will work to cultivate A DISTINCTIVELY AUSTRALIAN NATIONAL SENTIMENT, and to encourage an Australian National Culture through educational mediums, including universities, schools, newspapers, cinemas, theatres, and broadcasting stations.

5.—The Australia-First Movement advocates AUSTRALIAN SELF-RELIANCE IN MILITARY, NAVAL, AND AIR DEFENCE; and in particular the complete Australian control of all Australia's Armed Forces.

6.—The Australia-First Movement OPPOSES THE SURRENDER OF ANY OF AUSTRALIA'S SOVEREIGN RIGHTS OF SELF-GOVERNMENT to any "international" body, union, federation or league dominated by non-Australian nations.

7.—The Australia-First Movement will advocate, after the present War ends, an INDEPENDENT FOREIGN POLICY FOR AUSTRALIA, including the unrestricted right of the Australian Government to make war or peace at its own choice, to enter separately into agreements or treaties with any foreign powers, and to appoint Australian Diplomatic Representatives to any foreign countries.

8.—The Australia-First Movement upholds AUSTRALIA'S RIGHT TO CONTROL IMMIGRATION; and will oppose any attempts which may be made by non-Australian powers to dictate to Australia regarding the numbers or quality of immigrants to be admitted to Australia.

9.—The Australia-First Movement desires removal of THE HINDRANCES WHICH HAVE BEEN PLACED ON AUSTRALIA'S OVERSEAS TRADE by preferential tariffs, exchange control, boycotts, peace-time blockades, and political restrictions.

10.—The Australia-First Movement opposes any ATTEMPTS BY OVERSEAS MONOPOLIES, COMBINES AND POLITICAL POWERS to control, regulate, or restrict Australia's primary and secondary industrial development.

ADVANCE AUSTRALIA FIRST!

Address Communications to the Secretary, Australia-First Movement, Room 45, Fourth Floor, 26 O'Connell Street, Sydney.

Stafford Printery, Chippendale, N.S.W.

Australia First!

The Australia-First Movement, a non-Party, non-sectional organisation of Australian patriots, supports the Australian Government in all actions taken for the defence of Australia, and urges the following **Two Points of Australian National Defence:**

1—Recall to Australia of all Australian Armed Forces:

In the present time of danger, Australia cannot afford, financially or physically, to maintain expeditionary armed forces, with men and equipment, in any non-Australian war zone. Our allies—including China, Russia, the U.S.A., and Britain, with their immense populations and resources—should not now expect aid in manpower and munitions to be shipped away from Australia, at a time when Australia itself requires maximum defence. It is the privilege of Australians to defend Australia first.

2—National Independence for Australia:

The safety of Australia can best be secured if Australia acts as an independent power, not accepting an inferior status as a dependency at the disposal of other powers. Alliance should not imply subordination. The Australian Government, representing only the Australian people, has the responsibility of upholding Australia's Independent Status in all inter-national discussions and negotiations, for both war and peace. No Government, except the Australian Government, would ever be likely to consider the interests and welfare of Australia first. In the making of war, and in the eventual making of peace, Australia's statesmen should permanently be guided, not by European or American interests and desires, but by the interests and desires of Australia first.

Recall Australia's Armed Forces to Australia!

Uphold Australia's Independence!

Advance Australia First!

Issued by THE AUSTRALIA-FIRST MOVEMENT, Room 45, Fourth Floor, 28 O'Connell St., Sydney, 29th January, 1942

[illegible]

APPENDIX "B".

AUSTRALIA FIRST MOVEMENT.

PROCLAMATION.

An Armistice has been arranged with the Japanese Military Command; the terms of the armistice will be discussed and decided upon by an armistice commission. The names of this commission will be announced later. The Australian Military Forces are now ordered to cease fire and lay down their arms. The civilian population is ordered to resume their normal way of living in so far as it is possible at the moment. The government will endeavour to bring sympathy and succour to the people as rapidly as humanly possible. Any national disobeying the governments decisions and found, or suspected of engaging in sabotaging the peoples' NEW ORDER will be summarily shot.

MEN and WOMEN of Australia, the Curtin Democratic Government and those persons comprising the opposition in the democratic Jewish parliament are traitors and warrant the contumely of a free peoples. You are therefore warned that any act, word or deed committed by you and which is calculated to assist them to avoid the penalty they so rightly deserve for plunging this country into torture and misery will bring upon yourselves the death penalty without trial.

Today Australia and Australians witness the greatest and proudest moment of their brief-history. Today sees this nation reach adult stature and independence; the era of British and American Judaism with its vile extortion and exploitation of our national resources; the recurring murders and physical distortion of our young man and womanhood is now at an end. Australia must and will play its part with the Japanese Empire in building and maintaining the Pacific for the Pacific nations.

Today we set our hands to the task of building a physically fit and moral and industrious nation. No one will be allowed to lead an idle and useless life. Your government will give to its people proper homes, the best education, sufficient food, proper leisure. The people will then decide for themselves to what extent they need spiritual assistance. Priests and parsons alike will labour physically in the interests of the nation.

This ends the proclamation of the Australia First National Socialist government. I * (Laurence Frederick Bullock) * of the A.F. Party, have taken governmental power and authority in the name of the Australian people. The armed forces of the Commonwealth are now under the orders of my Minister for the Army, and the war in the interests of Capitalism and Communism has finished. Resistance by anyone will bring instant death.

ADVANCE AUSTRALIA.

Signatories to this proclamation ....Leader

Party Secretary.
" Organiser.
" Members.

* In the original document this name was typed in and then crossed out, but it was still legible.

PA:

EXHIBIT "J"

THE PROCLAMATION OF THE AUSTRALIA FIRST GOVERNMENT WHOSE POLITICAL SYSTEM IS FOUNDED IN SOCIALISM WITHIN OUR NATIONAL BORDERS AND ABSOLUTE SOVERIGNTY OF THE COMMONWEALTH OF AUSTRALIA.

MEN and WOMEN of AUSTRALIA
Today a new government assumes control of your destines, your government brings with it an entirely new system, this system is based upon a negotiated peace with JAPAN, and guarantees p eace and economic security to our Nation and People.

Henceforth the destiny of Australia will be guided by the single dominating thought and slogan of "Australia First", which is the name of the political organisation introducing the new system to our country, the nation is now governed by decree, xxx parliamentary democracy, xxx party organisations,and all democratic associations and institutions are now abolished.

This government expresses on behalf of the Australian Nation a tribute to the valiant efforts of the Japaneese who have so successfully fought for the liberation of our peoples from Jewish domination and the danger of communism. We welcome to our country as our friends and liberators the Japaneese military leaders and army, who have , and are assisting the true patriots of this country to smash forever the British stranglehold over our people.

The australian people must now be made fully alive to the fact that with the passing of the old Democratic system, lying, deception , insecurity of the masses, prostitution and exploitation of the people for the benefit of the few has now gone forever. In its place socialism within our national borders will give to our people Peace and Economic security, it will prove to the people the real aims of Jewish capitalism which is control the British Empire and impose communism and financial slavery upon the peoples of the world, to this end your government has unsheathed a sword on your behalf and will fight Jewish controlled Democracy in the defence of xxx a free and enlightened people.

The principles laid down by your government are based upon personal responsibility, Ministers of State will have complete and absolute control of their respective departments, decisions regarding departments of State will be made by Ministers based upon expert technical advice from the best practical and teoretical intellects available whatsoever their station in life maybe.

PRESS. All broadcasting facilities will be directed by the dept of information. The excisting press will continue publication, The State will institute its own newspress.

The policy of your government is as follows,

1. A friendly foreign policy towards all anti-Jewish xxx anti-communistic, and anti-democratic powers.
2. The abolition of the system of production for profit instead of for use.
3. The abolition of the "White Australia Policy".
4. Absolute soverignty for the Australian Nation.
5. The use of the national credit of our nation based upon raw material and the physical ability of our people.
6. The abolition of the system of interest and the repudiation of the illegally accumulated and unjust debts.
7. The commonwealth bank to be the only bank of issue in Australia, all excisting private trading banks will henceforth be merely administrative and working under the control of the central bank of Australia (namely) the Commonwealth Bank. The assests of private trading banks will be assessed soley on the original capital introduced into the business by the owners of the banks, and they will be compensated accordingly.
8. Interest will be charged on governmental loans only to the extent neccessary to cover handling charges.
9. Private insurance companies and socities are no longer recognised as legal, all monies and properties etc to be confiscated forthwith, monies contributed by the public will be credited to the

Exhibit "J" (Contd.) 2.

individuals concerned under a new government Insurance scheme.

10. Farmers are given sole ownership of that proportion of their properties that they are able to bring and maintain to maximum seasonal production. Agricultural interest and mortgage interest is now abolished.

11. Literature, arts and the professions are open to all, entrance to which shall in future be governed by ability only, and not as in the past by wealth, influence or the Old School Tie.

12. Marriage loans, £100 to be loaned to couples on marriage, at birth of first child debt to be reduced by 25/% and similar reduction for subsequent children untill the debt is abolished.

13. All persons contemplating marriage must submit themselves to the recognised medical authorities for examination including blood tests for racial purity.

14. Euthanasia to be the governmental policy in regard to hopelessly crippled,&insane,persons, also habitual drunkards and drug addicts.

15. Removal of jews from all governmental positions or any place of authority confiscation of all their monies, proporties, or investments, liquidation of all jewish organisations, synagogues, and their monies and investments, Sterilisation of all practising jews internment of other religious practising jews according to determination by a department set up for this control

16. Religion will be bought within the jurisdiction of the government the heirachy of all denominations will be dispossessed of the power and prestige of their positions, complete freedom of worship for the people.

17. Absolute equality of the sexes.

18. Complete exploitation and development of the countrys natural wealth conservation of exhaustible natural resources.

19. Rehabilitation of returned soldiers in whatever final form it may take will be based on the fundamental principle of economic security justice and peace.

20. The laws regarding divorce will be amended for the purpose of easier divorce with the object of eradicating many forced immoralities under the crude and inhuman jewish democratic system.

21.

Appendix II

The programmes of the *Publicist* and the Australia-First Movement were constantly being changed, because there was in fact very little on which there was a fair degree of consensus. This is a further selection of the various programmes.

The ADVANCE AUSTRALIA LEAGUE (Miles, ca 1916):

1. To Resist any Reduction of Australian Autonomy.
2. To Maintain a 'White Australia.'
3. To Foster Australian National Sentiment.
4. To Urge Australians to Make Most of their Country's Resources.

THE TEN POINTS (for the Australia First League):
(Suggested in a letter from Valentine Crowley to W. J. Miles, 17 June 1936. Copy in C421: 30: Sydney Benjamin Hooper.)
I believe:

(1) That this Continent is destined to be the Home of at least 20 million white inhabitants by year 2000.

(2) That Australia should leave the British Empire.

(3) That the Republican form of Government is the logical one for Australia.

(4) That the post of State Governor is not necessary and must be abolished.

(5) That while the existing system lasts the Governors-General be appointed by the Commonwealth Government from the ranks of Australian citizens.

(6) That the Australian National Flag be as at present without the English Flag in corner.

(7) That it is an insult to every Australian for anyone to fly any flag above the Australian Flag in this country.

(8) That all statues of English Kings and Queens by removed from pedestals.

(9) That no further Government Loans be floated overseas.

(10) That the existing Overseas Debts be paid off at the rate of twenty million pounds yearly: The Trade Balance to be adjusted to ensure this.

E. C. Quicke's political agenda, 1941, as set out in a statement of 20 September 1943: [A373: 3750: Australia First Movement and the internment of E. C. Quicke]

1. A one-party government involving the abolition of all other parties during the successful party's term of office. (This would involve the abolition of the Opposition).
2. The abolition of the Senate and all State parliaments.
3. A system of marriage loans to encourage the birth rate.
4. Socialisation of essential produces and services.

5. Confiscation by the Commonwealth of land not being put to any use.
6. The fixing of all interest rates at not more than 1%.
7. Australian independence of Great Britain.

THE TWELVE POINTS:
(Leaflet, October 1938; printed in the *Publicist*, November 1938)

Point 1. – THE PARTY SYSTEM.

'Having regard to the failure of the existing "democratic" institutions in Australia to provide for Australia's need of population and progress in the twentieth century, the Australia-First groups recommend intensive study of Australian conditions and need in totality, with a view to the ultimate formation of an "Australia-First" Party, to give effect to a policy of Australian self-dependence and self-defence.'

Point 2. – COMPULSORY POLLING.

'The Australia-First groups recommend a campaign for organised informal voting ("Non-Co-operation") as a first step in drawing public attention to the need for fundamental revision and modernisation of Australia's law-making apparatus.'

Point 3. – MONARCHISM.

'The Australia-First groups advocate, within the existing constitutions, the appointment of Australian-born Governors and Governor-General, the abolition of legal appeals by Australians to the judicial committee of the British House of Lords (Privy Council).'

Point 4. – CONSCRIPTION.

'The Australia-First groups endorse the policy of Conscription for military service, when used for the bona-fide defence of Australia, in the extreme case of invasion or threat of invasion, but oppose conscription for service abroad, and oppose any sending of Australian troops away from the immediate jurisdiction of the Australian Government and laws.'

Point 5. – MILITARY CONTROL.

'The Australia-First groups advocate that all Officers in the Australian armed forces shall be men of Australian birth or permanent domicile.'

Point 6. – DEFENCE POLICY.

'The Australia-First groups advocate that Australian Defence policy should be devised in terms of Australian territorial defence, and that aggressive war abroad, in any territory outside the Australian continent and its dependencies, should be entirely renounced as an instrument of Australian foreign policy.'

Point 7. – FINANCE.

'The Australia-First groups advocate a study of Australian finance directed towards Australian local control of the Australian system, both public and private. In particular it is affirmed that the burden of overseas public debt, both as to capital and interest, must be regulated within the limits of Australia's "capacity to pay", and alternatively that imports from Australia's creditor-countries should be drastically reduced.'

Point 8. – OVERSEAS TRADE.

'The Australia-First groups advocate that there should be no economic (trading) discrimination against non-British nations, in the application of tariffs, by Australian Governments, and that every effort should be made, by trading relations and otherwise, to operate a good will foreign policy, on the part of Australia, towards all overseas nations impartially.'

Point 9. – POPULATION.

'The Australia-First groups do not look to immigration as a solution of Australia's population problem, but recommend, instead, an intensive campaign for the encouragement of early marriage, endowment of motherhood, and child-welfare, combined with the statutory elimination of females of child-bearing age from industrial employment at wages lower than are paid to males.'

Point 10. – HOMOGENEITY.

'The Australia-First groups oppose formation of distinct exotic racial minorities, by immigrants to Australia. (As regards aborigines, who are indigenous, a raising of status, leading to ultimate absorption, is advocated.)'

Point 11. – PUBLIC WORKS.

'The Australia-First groups advocate compulsory labour-training of all youths between the ages of eighteen and twenty and employment of the trainees in public works under camp-community discipline. The youth so withdrawn from industry should be given education (technical and general), instruction in the use of arms, physical training, political training in ideals of civics, and an opportunity to develop stamina and physique by open air work in the service of the community. Food, clothing, shelter, medical services, supervised sports and entertainment, and a small pocket-money allowance should be sufficient recompense to the trainees for performing a service of national benefit.'

Point 12. – AUSTRALIAN CULTURE.

'The Australia-First groups pledge themselves to foster the growth of a specifically Australian culture, as a means of arousing Australian self-respect, and urge reform of the educational system, to include an effective study of Australian literature, art and history.'

COMMENT:
At first glance, these '12 Points' appear innocuous, and while some were controversial, more so then than now, they were hardly seditious or subversive, but some points should be noted.

Point 2: This was at the urging of W. J. Miles. As John Benauster, he wrote in the *Publicist*, December 1937, that he always voted informal, but he stopped short of urging others to do so. (* In law, to do so constituted a summary offence, not an indictable one.)

Points 4 and 6, regarding conscription and defence, were close to standard Labor Party policy. Point 7 was verging on Social Credit policy. Point 8 was one of the things the Japanese fervently desired: to undermine British trade relations with Australia as a preliminary to separating Australia politically from Britain.

Point 9 did not aim at obtaining equal pay for women, but at making it so difficult for women to obtain jobs that they would be forced to marry and breed. Point 10, regarding homogeneity, was aimed at the recent Jewish refugee migrants perhaps more than at the concentrations of other nationalities, such as Italians in the Queensland sugar districts.

Point 11 was a basic plan for a service similar to the German *Arbeitsdienst* (Labour Service); however, it is too simplistic to label something automatically as bad just because the Nazis also did it. Some of their ideas were very practicable and workable.

Point 12, concerning Australian culture, is probably the only point that Stephensen thoroughly endorsed, though he was held responsible for them all.

Appendix III

Genealogy of P. R. Stephensen

The ancestry of Percy Stephensen is not particularly relevant to the Australia-First Movement, but there are so many minor errors in published accounts that the facts need to be stated. According to the accepted story, Stephensen's father, Christian Julius, was born on 7 October 1878, at Tinana, son of Jens Christian Julius Stephensen and Christine née Hansen, but there is no such birth registration. He was probably registered as Christian Julius Hansen, son of Christine Hansen, born 7 October 1877.[1] Two Stephensen children were registered only as 'Hansen', several of the youngest only as 'Stephensen', and the middle ones were registered as 'Hansen' and altered to 'Stephensen'.

Percy's grandfather had arrived in Maryborough, aged 25, per *Alardus* on 13 June 1873, having left Hamburg on 11 November 1872. He was indentured to William Canny of Eaton Vale for six months. With him in *Alardus* were his wife, Elna not Christine, his daughter, his elder brother Anders Peter and his wife and child, with the name recorded as 'Steffensen'.[2] The family prided itself on its *Danish* heritage, but in the published record of the naturalisation of J. C. J. Stephensen his nationality was given as German. This was probably a clerical error, as it was not uncommon in Queensland at that time to refer to Danes as Germans.[3] The Family History Index shows the parents of Jens Christian and Anders Stephensen as Stephen Christensen and Johanne Marie Andersdotter, as does the Queensland death registration for Anders Peter. Jens Christian Julius Stephensen and Elna Andersdatter married at Sankt Paul's, Copenhagen, 2 July 1871, witness Anders Stephensen. No death has been found in Denmark, Queensland, Victoria, New South Wales or at sea for Elna Stephensen, nor a marriage of Jens Christian Julius Stephensen and Sidsel Christine (or Kirsten) Hansen (daughter of Hans Madsen), even allowing for spelling errors. J. C. Stephensen was christened at Jerslev near Hjørring, 24 December 1847.

Appendix IV

Summary of the analysis by *The Times* (London) of *The Protocols of the Meetings of the Learned Elders of Zion*

The Protocols of Zion appeared first in Russia in 1905, having been translated from French by Professor Sergei Nilus, whom *The Times* described as 'a learned, pious, credulous Conservative, who combined much theological and some historical erudition with a singular lack of knowledge of the world'.[4] In 1905, Nilus said they had been given to him by a woman who stole them in France from 'one of the most influential and most highly initiated leaders of Freemasonry'. In 1917 he said it was given to him by Alexis Nicolaievich Sukhotin, who became Vice-Governor of Stavropol. A commentary to the English version said it had been found in the safes of the Society of Zion in France, and comprised notes made by Theodor Hertzl at the first Zionist Congress in Basle, 1897. The material was translated back into French in 1917 and published in English in 1920. A second translation into English was made by Victor Marsden, former Russian correspondent of the London *Morning Post.*

In 1921, the Constantinople correspondent for *The Times* came across a copy of a fairly obscure French book by a Paris lawyer, Maurice Joly: *Dialogue aux Enfers entre Machiavel et Montesquieu, ou la Politique de Machiavel au XIX. Siècle,* published in Brussels in 1865. Recognised by French authorities as a thinly disguised attack on Napoleon III, it earned the author 18 months in prison. On 17 August 1921, *The Times* began to run a paragraph-by-paragraph comparison between this book and the *Protocols.* Allowing for variations from the original in the process of translating it from French to Russian, thence to English, the origin was irrefutable. General opinion is that the Tsarist secret police, the *Okhrana,* had taken advantage of the unworldly naiveté of a respected priest to fabricate evidence against the Jews, possibly as psychological preparation for a pogrom.

The *Protocols* set out how to subvert, weaken and destroy a society by encouraging self-indulgence, debt and vice, while discouraging thrift, diligence and self-reliance. Commentators traced the origins of the plot beyond the alleged scope of the *Protocols* themselves, back to the time of King Solomon,[5] blaming the French Revolution, the Reign of Terror, and World War I on 'Jewish malevolence'.[6] A commentary to the German edition, shortly after the war, said that only physical extermination could stop the Jews.[7] Fascist movements around the world sponsored the publication and distribution of the *Protocols*, and still do so.

Stephensen believed in the authenticity of the *Protocols*, but attributed them to Russian Jews.[8] Miles wrote that he did not know if they were authentic or not, but they revealed 'the methods by which the Jews exercise an influence among Gentiles far in excess of *what could be expected from their numbers*'.[9] In fact, the outlined methods of destroying the financial, psychological and physical well-being of a nation are very effective, and they have been and are being used for this purpose, by both corrupt governments and well-meaning ones, governments that have no connection with Jews or Zionism.

Notes

[1] Queensland Genealogical Index Master Report: All Indexes Consolidated. 1829-1889.
[2] Some accounts say he arrived with *two* brothers, but Danish records in the Family History Index of the Church of Jesus Christ of Latter Day Saints show that Niels Carl Steffensen, entered on the same passenger list, could not have been a brother. Confirmed by E. D. Stephensen, 8 March 1999.
[3] Naturalisations 1851-1905: State Library film no. 0381.
[4] *The Times*, 18 August 1921, p. 9.
[5] Richard Griffiths, *Fellow Travellers of the Right. British Enthusiasts for Nazi Germany*, p. 60.
[6] Introduction to New Zealand edition of the *Protocols*, by A. N. Field.
[7] John J. Stephan: *The Russian Fascists: tragedy and farce in exile, 1925-1945*, p. 22.
[8] P. R. Stephensen Papers, UQFL MSS55/8/12. (Stephensen to Mills, 1 July 1954, p. 3).
[9] *Publicist*, 1 May 1940, Benauster, 'Australia and the Jews', p. 1. Emphasis is in the original.

Appendix V

Odinism in the Philosophy of A. R. Mills

In some aspects of his attacks on Judaeo-Christianity, Mills is factually correct. The date of Christmas has nothing to do with the birth of Christ, but is the Nordic festival of Yule or Jul. The name 'Easter' had nothing to do with the Passover or the crucifixion, but was derived from the name of the goddess Eostre (or Astarte). Christianity is indeed based on Judaism, mixed ritually with Nordic and Mediterranean paganism. Religion is a matter of faith, not of fact. Mills's Odinism cannot be judged by appealing to scripture, only by considering whether it was reasonable and consistent.

Mills claimed that Odinism was the true religion of the Britons. That is untrue; the religion of the original Celtic inhabitants of Britain was Druidism. Odinism was imported with Anglo-Saxon and Danish invaders. Stonehenge dates from 2,000 to 1,500BC. If Mills wanted to return to the 'original' British religion, he might have been worshipping oak trees and mistletoe and painting himself blue. Christianity, which Mills condemned as alien, reached Britain before the Angles, the Danes, the Eddas or Odinism. Christianity was introduced into Britain by the Romans, although it did not take firm hold at that time. Mills's heroes, Hengist and Horsa, were Angles who invaded Kent about 443 AD. The Danes arrived in the late 9th century, and were firmly settled in 'Danelaw', mainly in the north-east of England, by the 11th century. The Edda sagas followed them to Britain.

Mills's other hero was Beowulf, an 'Old English' epic, but also based on a Scandinavian saga. Mills has woven these stories together to form a peculiar body of 'faith'. Odinism as portrayed in the Eddas was a myth of things past and a vision of the future, rather than a system of spiritual beliefs. Apart from his use of names from the Eddas, Mills's Odinism bore so little resemblance to the original form that it appears as simply an illogical means to attack Christianity and Judaism. Nevertheless, on some points his criticisms of both, and of democracy, were accurate enough to be seductive. While Odinism served its natural milieu of time and place well enough, its modern adherents, who mix Odinism with White Supremacy and the Ku Klux Klan, tend to come from unstable and violent fringes of society.

Appendix VI

Membership of the Australia-First Movement

The nominal list, stolen by communists during the meeting on 19 February 1942 and passed to Security, is not complete, as a few others joined between then and 9 March (e.g. Keith Bath, who paid his subscription on 17 February). Spelling has been corrected, and additional information added. The list gives an idea of the range of ages and social status of members.

20 October 1941:
01 Percy Reginald STEPHENSEN, Box 1924, KK, GPO Sydney. (Address, March 1942: 847 New South Head Road, Rose Bay.) Born Maryborough, Qld, 20 November 1901; died 28 May 1965; married Melbourne, 7 November 1947, to Winifred Sarah Venus née Lockyer. Publisher, editor, author; former communist. Interned 10/3/42 - 17/8/45.

02 Walter Frederick TINKER-GILES, 147 Woolooware Road, Cronulla. Born Camperdown, 24 March 1906. Married 1930 to Gertrud(e) Elizabeth Clinton. Shoe store proprietor. Treasurer of AFM. Interned 10/3/42 - 22/8/42

03 Leslie Kevin CAHILL, c/o 209a Elizabeth Street, Sydney. (Address at internment given as Fairfield.) Born Sydney, 1 October 1904 (as Norman Patrick Gunderson); died 1955. Ex-communist. Organiser of AFM. Rejected for AIF, January 1942, joined AMF. Interned 10/3/42 - 6/2/44.

04 Mrs Vera Dorothea PARKINSON née Bone, 373 Alfred Street, North Sydney. Born 1891; married 1915, Allan C. Parkinson. Associate of Adela Walsh in Women's Guild of Empire; fund-raiser. Two sons in AIF overseas.

05 Mrs Adela Pankhurst WALSH, 21 St. Giles Avenue, Greenwich. Editor. Born 19 June 1885, Manchester, UK; married Melbourne 30 September 1917 to Thomas Walsh; died 23 May 1961. Suffragette;

former communist; Women's Guild of Empire, People's Guild. Interned 19/3/42 - 13/10/42

06 Mrs Marjorie CORBY, 21 Reed Street, Cremorne. Widow. Women's Guild of Empire; associate of Adela Walsh.

07 Miss Elaine Elizabeth POPE, 'The Octagon', St. Marks Road, Edgecliff. Born Wahroonga, 25 August 1905. Her father, Parke W. Pope was managing director, Farmer & Co.; mother was an associate of Adela Walsh.

08 Mrs (Catherine) Sheila RICE, née Rahaley, Flat 2, 19 Collins Street, Annandale. Born 5 May 1905, Victoria. Wife of G. T. Rice, No. 10. Secretary of AFM.

09 Ian Mayleston MUDIE, 16 Shell Cove Road, Neutral Bay. Born 1 March 1911, South Australia; died in Britain, 23 October 1976. Married 1935 to Renee Doble. Journalist, author. Maternal grandmother of German descent (Gertrude Wurm).

10 Gordon Thomas RICE, Flat 2, 19 Collins Street, Annandale. Born Ascot Vale, 19 June 1906; married 1938 to Catherine Sheila Rahaley. Motor driver, printer. Interned 10/3/42 - 19/10/42.

30 October 1941:
11 Malcolm Carlyle SMITH, 6 Balmoral Avenue, Balmoral. Born Kew, Victoria, 1895. Accountant with Flack & Flack. From 1936, 'Public Officer' for Dychem, Australian agents for IG Farben. Served in 1914-18 war, corporal, 5th Field Artillery Brigade.

12 Mrs N. SMITH, 6 Balmoral Avenue, Balmoral. Wife of No. 11, M. C. Smith.

6 November 1941:
13 Cecil Walter SALIER, 33 Parkes Road, Artarmon. Born Petersham, 27 October 1880; died 5 December 1949. Married 1916, Ella M. Carter. Insurance agent; associated with Australian Institute of Political Science. Interned 10/3/42 - 22/8/42

14 John William Venus LOCKYER, 57 Cross Street, Double Bay. Born USA, 1 February 1913. Stepson of P. R. Stephensen. Enlisted in 18th Army Field Company, R.A.E., N217613, and was serving at Narellan, NSW, early in 1942.

15 Prosper Cologne LANG, 84 Beach Street, Coogee. Born Casino, NSW, 1897. Accountant. Vice chairman, ANA luncheon club.

16 Giles Eyre BLAKE, No. 1, Osborne Road, Manly. Born Deniliquin, NSW, 1889. Stock and station agent. Friend of Miles and Hooper.

17 Sydney Benjamin HOOPER, 78 Bayswater Road, Sydney. Born Melbourne, 12 February 1869; died 20 August 1959; married (1) at Deniliquin in 1899 to Alexandra E. Watson; (2) at Sydney in 1909 to Ida Margherita Fiorelli, d. 1941. Retired bank manager. Interned 10/3/42 - 12/9/42. Rationalist; associated with 'Australia First' since 1916.

18 Clarence CROWLEY, 8 Dumaresq Road, Rose Bay. Born Mornington, Vic., 1 April 1889; died February 1972; married 1927, to Eileen M. Egan. Brother of V. Crowley, No. 26. Retired grazier. Air Raid Warden. Interned 10/3/42 - 22/8/42.

19 Eric Dudley STEPHENSEN, c/o Box 1924 KK, GPO Sydney. Born Maryborough, 16 March 1914. Art student. Brother of P. R. Stephensen. Interned 10/3/42 - 12/9/42. Served in Ambulance Corps.

20 Mrs Renee MUDIE, 16 Shell Cove Road, Neutral Bay. Wife of No. 9, Ian Mudie.

21 James Francis TIMMONY, 12 Richmond Avenue, Cremorne. Clerk. Attended Yabber Club. (Appears in reports of Agent 222 under various spellings, including Timmerly.)

22 A. McDONNELL, 34 Hunter Street, Sydney. Not on electoral roll for this address. Attended Eureka commemoration evening, 6 December 1941.

23 John Charles HOGER, 103 Silver Street, St. Peters. Born 1915, St Peters; married 1937 to Florence Maud(e) Orford. Labourer. (Electoral roll 1941: given as varnish maker, 79 Park Road, Tempe)

24 Florence Maude HOGER, 103 Silver Street, St. Peters. Wife of No. 23.

25 Clive Kirkwood DOWNE, 48 Matthews Street, Punchbowl. Born Waverley, NSW, 30 October 1911; married 1943. Clerk with Marcus Clark Co. Interned 10/3/42 - 12/9/42.

26 Valentine CROWLEY, 18 Clanalpine Street, Mosman. Born Victoria, 18 October 1884; died 21 August 1954, Avalon Beach; married 1917. Insurance agent; retired electrical engineer. Air Raid Warden. Interned 10/3/42 - 19/10/42

27 (Valentine) Ford CROWLEY, 18 Clanalpine Street, Mosman. Son of Valentine Crowley. Joined AMF, artillery, June 1940; transferred to AIF February 1943.

28 John Balfour MILES, 16 Khartoum Avenue, Gordon. Son of W. J. Miles. Born 1901; married 1924.

29 Mrs Mary Josephine HEINEKEN, née Mitchell, 44 George Street, Rose Bay, North. Born Ulladulla, NSW, 22 April 1876. Pianist, music teacher. Widow of Eduard Heineken, manager of German-Australian Chamber of Commerce, 1937-38. Associate of Adela Walsh.

30 Edward Cory de la Roche MASEY, 3 Maitland Street, Killara. Born Summerhill, 6 January 1906. Violet Masey, given in his dossier as his wife, was his mother; she was an old friend of W. J. Miles. Sales manager, Johnson & Johnson. Interned 10/3/42 - 19/10/42

31 Kenneth BOCKMASTER, 62 Sir John Young's Crescent, East Sydney. Born in New Zealand. Former sergeant with 58th Battalion.

13 November 1941:
32 Alexander Rud MILLS, Queen Street, Melbourne, C1. Private address: Canterbury Mansions, Canterbury. Born 15 July 1885, Forth, Tasmania; died 8 April 1964. Solicitor, admitted to bar in 1917. Air Raid Warden. Interned 7/5/42 - 17/12/42.

33 Mrs. Winifred STEPHENSEN, c/o Box 1924 KK, GPO, Sydney. Born in England, September 1886. Wife of P. R. Stephensen.

34 Richard Egon LUDOWICI, Warrangi Street, Turramurra. Company director, leather goods factory. Born Chatswood, NSW, 1910; married 1935. Director of family-owned a leather goods manufacturing company.

35 Mrs Pauline BUDGE, 24 Agnes Street, Strathfield. Home duties. Associated with Adela Walsh in the Women's Guild of Empire.

36 Mrs Lilian May MONTGOMERIE née Jacobs, 54a Darling Point Rd, Darling Point. Home duties. Associated with Guild of Empire. Married 1919, William G. Montgomerie.

37 Archibald Leslie WRIGHT, Grangeview, Dartford Road, Normanhurst. Died 17 August 1953, Penrith; married 1922. Freeholder.

38 Mrs Mary Elizabeth COLLINGRIDGE, née Heydon, 58 Mary St., Hunter's Hill. Home duties. Married 1911, to William E. Collingridge.

39 Ronald Arthur MOORE, 43 Wellington Street, Waterloo. Labourer. Imprisoned for evading military service.

40 Robert Rudolf Richard von Broock RHIEN, P.O. Captain's Flat. Married 1944. Engine driver. Naturalised 27 July 1938. Prior to that, member of NSDAP, No. 3,708,992; joined 1 April 1936.

41 Miss Phyllis May WALTON, 23 Elizabeth Bay Road, Elizabeth

Bay. Married 1944 to Arthur Williams. Associate of Adela Walsh in Women's Guild of Empire; teacher.

42 Miss Beatrice MILES, 69 Roslyn Gardens, Elizabeth Bay. Daughter of W. J. Miles.

20 November 1941:
43 Edwin John ARNOLD, Flat 2, 110 Victoria Street, Potts Point. Born Richmond, NSW, 10 December 1904. Railway porter, clerk, painter and docker. Theosophist, supporter of Aryan supremacy. Interned 10/3/42 - 19/10/42

44 Arthur Herbert BORDER, 2 Fuller Avenue, Hornsby. Labourer. Born 1913; married 1945.

45 L. FLETCHER, 22 Challis Avenue, Dulwich Hill. Not traced; not on electoral roll at this address.

46 Harold Roy MURRAY, 227 Parramatta Road, Annandale. Chemist.

27 November 1941:
47 Thomas Potts GRAHAM, c/- 30 Holdsworth Avenue, North Woolstonecraft. Not on electoral roll for this address. Born Newcastle on Tyne, 17 October 1906. Author of anti-Semitic and racist pamphlets. Imprisoned February 1942; interned 11/7/42 - 11/1/44.

11 December 1941:
48 Alexander Leo FINN, 'Lisieux', 149 Dover Rd., Dover Heights. Born Randwick, NSW, 1897; married. Director.

49 John ISACKSON, c/- Repatriation Department, Chalmers Street, Sydney. Not traced.

50 Mrs Betty Mary CUMMINS, 17 The Avenue, Strathfield. Home duties. (Wife of No. 56)

51 R. G. COSTIN, c/- Rev. Leslie Richards, Rectory, Guildford. Not on electoral roll for this address. Not traced. Possibly the Robert Gordon Costin mentioned in C421: 55.

52 John RAMSAY, 24 Handley Avenue, Thornley. Salesman.

53 John PHILLIPS, 52 Dutruc St, Randwick. Not on electoral roll for this address. Not traced.

54 George HUNT, Captain's Flat, NSW. Plumber. Not traced.

55 Mr. G. D. MURRAY, 19 Ocean Street, Edgecliff. Not on electoral roll for this address. Possibly Gerald Douglas Murray, dental surgeon, 12 Macleay St.

12 December 1941:
56 William Alfred CUMMINS, 17 The Avenue, Strathfield. Married 1937 to Betty Mary Hair. Printer. Mentioned by Bruce Muirden in *The Puzzled Patriots*.

18 December 1941:
57 John Kendall PURCELL, 124 Alison Road, Randwick. Born Ashfield, 1918. Sales assistant.

58 Joseph John HURNEY, 13 Alexander Street, Concord. Engine driver. Not traced.

8 January 1942:
59 Reginald (Rex) INGAMELLS, 3 Harcourt Road, Rugby, SA. Born Orroroo, SA, 7 January 1913; killed in car accident, 30 December 1955; married 1938 to Eileen Eva Spensley. Editor, author and publisher.

22 January 1942:
60 George Herbert DONSWORTH, 75 Chester Street, Epping. Born 1908, married 1932. Electrician.

29 January 1942:
61 A. HACKMANN, Tennant Creek, Northern Territory. Not traced.

62 E. M. McMAHON, c/o Mrs. Macarthur, Vale SS, Cooma. Not traced.

12 February 1942:
63 Frank CUSACK, mechanic; 24 Russell Street, Bendigo, Victoria. At the time of applying, he was with the 6th Infantry Brigade.

64 Ernest F. McLEAN, 4 51 Warrangi St, Turramurra. Not on electoral roll at this address.

65 John R. St L. GWILT, 'The Turrets,' (23 Flat) Royston Square, King's Cross. Married 1933. Not on electoral roll at this address.

Index

[Owing to the frequency of occurrence, references to Percy Stephensen and W. J. Miles have not been indexed.]

Bibliography

Primary Sources:

Archival Documents:

(Series numbers only are cited. Individual files are given in the Endnotes.)

Canberra:

A367: Correspondence files, single number series with year prefix, 1916 - 1927, and 'C' prefix, 1927–1953.

A368: Name Index Cards to CRS A367, A369, A1533, A7919, and CP573/2. 1 Jan 1916 - 31 Dec 1955.

A373: Correspondence Files, Single Number Series: 1 Jan 1941 - 31 Dec 1949: members of the "Australia First" Movement Group: 1 Sept 1945 - 31 Dec 1945.

A467: Special files, SF single number series: 16 Jul 1952 - : CA 5: Attorney-General's Department, Central Office. [Contents date from 1905]

A472: Correspondence files, single number series with 'W' [War] prefix: 01 Sep 1939 - 31 Dec 1949: CA 5: Attorney-General's Department, Central Office.

A981: Correspondence files, alphabetical series. 1 Jan 1927 - 31 Dec 1942.

A1107: Transcript of Evidence: 3 Jun 1944 - 17 May 1945.

A1606: Correspondence files, two-numbered system with letter prefix, secret and confidential series (Third system) 1 Jan 1926 - 31 Dec 1939.

A1838: Correspondence files, multiple number series. 01 Jan 1948 - 31 Dec 1989.

A5954: The Shedden Collection [Records collected by Sir Frederick Shedden during his career with the Department of Defence and in researching the history of Australian Defence Policy]. 1 Jan 1937 - 8 Jul 1971.

A6119: Personal files, alpha numeric series.

A6122: Subject files, multiple number series: 16 Mar 1949 - :

A6126: ?01 Jan 1960 - : Microfilm copies of personal and subject files:

A8911: Correspondence files of the Commonwealth Investigation Service: 14 Jan 1916 - 21 Apr 1960.

A9108: 'HQ Miscellaneous Files' [Headquarters microfilm of Investigation Branch, Commonwealth Investigation Service and ASIO files]: c01 Jan 1968 - 06 Mar 1968:

A11022: 12: [Copy of CRS A6206 Exhibits H and J] 1954. (Formerly part of A6202: Royal Commission on Espionage Exhibits, single letter series, 1954.)

C443: Consular investigation files, alpha-numeric series: 01 Jan 1946 - 31 Dec 1946: [Material seized from German and Japanese consulates; contents date from 1897.] [German material with G prefix]

Sydney:

C123: Dossiers concerning internees, single number series: 1 Jul 1940 - 15 Dec 1945.

C320: Investigation files (Persons and Organisations), single number with alphabetical prefix: 1 Jan 1942 - 31 Dec 1946: [Contents date from 1921.]

C329: Transcripts of internees' appeals before the Aliens Control Tribunals and Advisory Committees: 3 Oct 1939 - 1 Aug 1945.

C418: Transcripts of the Australia First Inquiry: 19 Jun 1944 - 17 May 1945.

C419: General Summary of the Australia First Inquiry: ?01 Jan 1944 - 31 Dec 1944: CA 946: Security Service, New South Wales.

C421: Correspondence concerning the Australia First Inquiry: 1 Jan 1944 - 31 Dec 1945:

C443: Consular investigation files, alpha-numeric series: 1 Jan 1946 - 31 Dec 1946: [Material seized from German and Japanese consulates; contents date from 1897.] [Japanese material with J prefix]

C447: Miscellaneous correspondence relating to Japanese and German Consulate records: 1 Jan 1946 – 31 Dec 1947.

SP109/3: General correspondence, Dewey decimal system: series 1 Jan 1945 - 31 December 1946.

SP822/57: Whole of Series: Minutes of director's meeting of the Dychem Trading Company Pty. Ltd. 1939–1939.

SP1714/1: Investigation files, single number series with 'N' [New South Wales] prefix. 1 Jan 1920 – 31 Dec 1957

ST1233/1: Investigation files, single number series with 'N' [New South Wales] prefix: 1 Jan 1914 - 31 Dec 1946: CA 904: Investigation Branch, New South Wales.

Melbourne:

B741: Correspondence files, single number series with "V" (Victoria) prefix. 12 Feb 1924 – 21 Dec 1962.

B3720: Nominal index cards to registers and dossiers for enemy prisoners of war and internees. 1939-1947. Whole of Series.

MP508/1: General correspondence. 1 Jan 1939 – 31 Dec 1942.

MP529/3: Transcripts of evidence. 22 Jan 1941 – 20 Aug 1942.

MP729/6: Defence Army Series (401) 1 Jan 1936 – 31 Dec 1945.

MP742/1: General correspondence 1 Jan 1943 – 31 Dec 1951.

MP1103/1: Registers containing 'Service and Casualty' forms (Form A112) of enemy prisoners of war and internees held in camps in Australia: 1 Sept 1939 - 31 Dec 1947:

MP1103/2: Dossiers containing reports on Internees and Prisoners of War held in Australian camps, single number series with alphabetical prefix: 1 Aug 1939 - 24 Dec 1945: CA 3055: Prisoners of War Information Bureau. [Form A111: basic details and property statement]

MP1582/6: Australia Station Intelligence Reports. 01 Jan 1927- 31 Dec 1939.

Brisbane:

BP242/1: Correspondence files, single number series with Q (Queensland) prefix. 1 Jan 1924 - 17 Mar 1942:

Adelaide:

D1901: Loveday Internment Camp internees files, single number series with variable alpha prefix. 1 Jan 1939 - 31 Dec 1947.

D1915: Investigation case files, single number series with 'SA' (South Australia) prefix. 1 Jan 1917 - 31 Dec 1969.

Perth:

PP14/1: Intelligence reports of internments, repatriations, affiliations and general investigations, multiple number series. 1 May 1915 - 27 Jan 1920.

PP14/2: Reports and personal files, single number series. 27 Nov 1914 - 18 Feb 1920.

Australian War Memorial:

AWM27: Records arranged according to AWM Library subject classification. Circa 1 Jan 1927 - circa 31 Dec 1970.

AWM68: Official History, 1939 - 45 War, Series 4 (Civil) Volumes I & II: Records of Paul Hasluck: 1 Jan 1947 - 31 Dec 1969.

3DRL 3670/3: [Official History, 1939-45 War: Records of Paul Hasluck:] Australia First Movement. 1939–1962.

3DRL 8052/101: [Official History, 1939-45 War: Records of Paul Hasluck:] Volume II, Appendix 5. Research notes on the Australia First Movement. 1941–1963.

University Of Queensland Archives:

UQA S154: Senior Public Examination Results Registers, 1910-1972.

UQA S130: Subject files, Awards, Rhodes Scholarship - Stephensen, P. R., 1924.

Government Publications:

Commonwealth of Australia: Parliamentary Papers: General and Finance: Session 1945-46: Vol. IV: (pp. 941–960):

Inquiry into Matters Relating to the Detention of Certain Members of the "Australia First Movement" Group. Report of Commissioner (His Honour Mr. Justice Clyne).

Commonwealth of Australia: Commonwealth Parliamentary Debates (Hansard). Volumes as cited.

Western Australian Law Reports, Volume 38, 1936.

Manuscript Collections:

Xavier Herbert papers, National Library of Australia, Canberra: MS 758 and MS 2106.

Walsh papers, National Library of Australia, Canberra, Petherick Reading Room:

M.H.E.8:8 (*Japan as viewed by foreigners*) and M.H.E.14:7 (*The New Order in Asia*).

Percy Reginald Stephensen papers, Mitchell Library, Sydney: MSS 1284.

Fotheringham Papers, University of Queensland, Fryer Library: UQFL46.

P. R. Stephensen Papers, University of Queensland, Fryer Library: UQFL55.

Sadie and Xavier Herbert Papers, University of Queensland, Fryer Library: UQFL83.

Lockyer Papers: Papers relating to P. R. Stephensen, University of Queensland, Fryer Library: UQFL247.

Ian Mudie papers: Mortlock Library, Adelaide: PRG 27.

Australian Joint Copying Project, 'M' Series.

SECONDARY SOURCES:

Published Works:

Books:

Ball, Desmond, and Horner, David. *Breaking the Codes: Australia's KGB network*. St Leonards NSW: Allen & Unwin, 1998.

Bath, Keith P. *Injustice Within the Law (With no Apologies to H. V. Evatt)*. Sydney: K. P. Bath, 1948.

Black, David and Bolton, Geoffrey. *Biographical Register of the Members of the Parliament of Western Australia, Volume 1; 1870–1930*. Perth, WA: Western Australian Parliamentary History Project, 1998.

Brown, Douglas. *Criminal Law*; Western Australia. Sydney: Butterworths, 1990.

Campbell, Eric. *The New Road*. Sydney: Britons Publications Co., 1934.

— — *The Rallying Point: My Story of the New Guard*. Carlton, Vic.: Melbourne University Press, 1965.

Coleman, Verna. *Adela Pankhurst: The Wayward Suffragette*. 1885-1961. Carlton, Vic.: Melbourne University Press, 1996.

Dalziel, Allan. *Evatt the Enigma*. Melbourne: Lansdowne Press, 1967.

De Groen, Frances. *Xavier Herbert*. St Lucia, Qld: Queensland University Press, 1998.

Domvile, Admiral Sir Barry. *From Admiral to Cabin Boy*. London: Boswell, 1947.

Field, A. N. (ed.): *Protocols of the Meetings of the Learned Elders of Zion*. Nelson, New Zealand: Field, 1934 (translated by Victor E. Marsden).

Fox, L. P. *Australia and the Jews*. Melbourne: International Bookshop, 1939. (1943 edition cited).

Frei, Henry. *Japan's Southward Advance and Australia: from the sixteenth century to World War II*. Carlton, Vic.: Melbourne University Press, 1991.

Grenville, Kate. *Lilian's Story*. Sydney; London; Boston: George Allen and Unwin, 1985.

Griffiths, Richard. *Fellow Travellers of the Right.:British Enthusiasts for Nazi Germany, 1933-39*. London: Constable, 1980.

Hall, Richard. *The Secret State. Australia's Spy Industry*. North Melbourne: Cassell Australia, 1978.

Harcourt, David. *Everybody wants to be Fuehrer.* Sydney, Angus & Robertson, 1972.

Hasluck, Paul. *The Government and the People, Volume I.* Canberra: Australian War Memorial, 1952.

— — *The Government and the People, Volume II.* Canberra: Australian War Memorial, 1970.

Herbert, Xavier. *Poor Fellow My Country.* Sydney: Collins Fontana, 1977 edition.

Johst, Hanns. *Schlageter: Schauspiel.* München: Albert Langen/Georg Müller, 1934.

Laurie, A. P. *The Case for Germany.* Berlin: Internationaler Verlag, 1939.

Lockwood, Rupert. *War on the Waterfront: Menzies, Japan and the pig-iron Dispute.* Sydney: Hale & Iremonger, c1987.

McKnight, David. *Australia's Spies and their Secrets.* St Leonards, NSW: Allen & Unwin, 1994.

McMullin, Ross. *The Light on the Hill: the Australian Labor Party.* Melbourne: Oxford University Press Australia, 1991.

Malloch, H. W. *Fellows All: The Chronicles of the Bread and Cheese Club.* Melbourne: Bread and Cheese Club, 1943.

Mills, Alexander Rud. *And Fear Shall be in the Way.* (written as Tasman Forth) London: Watson & Co., 1933.

— — *Hael, Odin!* (written as Tasman Forth) St Kilda, Vic.: A. R. Mills, 1934.

— — *First Guide Book to the Anglecyn Church of Odin.* Sydney: A. R. Mills, 1936.

— — *The Odinist Religion overcoming Jewish Christianity.* Melbourne: A. R. Mills, 1939.

Muirden, Bruce. *The Puzzled Patriots: The Story of the Australia First Movement.* Carlton, Vic.: Melbourne University Press, 1968.

Munro, Craig. *Wild Man of Letters: The story of P. R. Stephensen.* Carlton, Vic.: Melbourne University Press, 1984.

Reimann, Guenter. *The Vampire Economy: Doing business under Fascism.* New York: Vanguard Press, 1939.

Roberts, Morley. *Bio-Politics: an essay in the physiology, pathology and politics of the social & somatic organism.* London: Dent, 1938.

Roberts, Stephen Henry. *The House the Hitler Built.* London: Methuen, 1937.

Skidelsky; Robert. *Oswald Mosley.* London: Macmillan, 1975.

Stephensen, P. R. *The Foundations of Culture in Australia: An Essay towards National Self-Respect.* Gordon, N.S.W.: W. J. Miles, 1936.

Walsh, Tom. *The Sino-Japanese Conflict.* Sydney: Angus & Robertson, 1939?.

— — *Japan as Viewed by Foreigners.* Tokyo: Japan Foreign Trade Federation, 1940? The New Order in Asia, Sydney: Robert Day, Son & Co. 1939?1940

Watts, D. (Dora). *The Dangerous Myth of Racial Equality: Genocide for the White Races?* Melbourne: New Times, 1962.

Newspapers:

Advocate (Melbourne)

Australian Quarterly (Sydney)

Beckett's Budget (Sydney)

Die Brücke (Sydney)

Daily Telegraph (Sydney)

Design: A Critical Review of Australian Thought (Melbourne)

Labor Daily (Sydney)

New Times (Melbourne)

New York Times (New York)

Publicist (Sydney)

Smith's Weekly (Sydney)

Sydney Morning Herald (Sydney)

Tribune (Sydney)

West Australian (Perth)

Workers' Weekly (Sydney)

Articles:

P. R. Stephensen. 'Culture and Politics', *Design: A Critical Review of Australian Thought*, January 1940, pp. 9-15. Hawthorn Press.

P. R. Stephensen. 'The Reasoned Case Against Anti-Semitism', *Australian Quarterly*, Vol. XII, No. 10, March 1940, pp. 52-62. Australian Institute of Political Science.

Theses:

Cottle, A. R.: The Brisbane Line: A Reappraisal, Ph. D. thesis, Macquarie University, 1991. (Chapter 2)

Fox, Charles: The Relief and Sustenance Workers' Union 1933-1934. An anti-Labor political and industrial organisation, BA Hons thesis, University of Western Australia.

Fotheringham, Richard: A biographical study of Percy Reginald Stephensen, born on the 20th November, 1901 at Maryborough, Qld, and died in Sydney on the 28th May 1965. THE5426, Fryer Library, University of Queensland.

Correspondence:

R. F. Bartram: especially 25 February 1999.

J. W. V. Lockyer: 5 November 1998.

E. D. Stephensen: 8 March 1999.

Interview:

Dr Craig Munro: 15 October 1998.

www.ingramcontent.com/pod-product-compliance
Lightning Source LLC
Chambersburg PA
CBHW020605270326
41927CB00005B/181

* 9 7 8 1 8 7 6 8 1 9 9 1 0 *